ELIZABETHAN TASTE

Also by John Buxton

SIR PHILIP SIDNEY AND THE
ENGLISH RENAISSANCE

The Phoenix Jewel, *c.* 1574, by Nicholas Hilliard
(see p. 11)

ELIZABETHAN TASTE

BY

JOHN BUXTON

MACMILLAN
London · Melbourne · Toronto

ST MARTIN'S PRESS
New York
1965

First Edition 1963
Reprinted with minor alterations 1965

MACMILLAN AND COMPANY LIMITED
Little Essex Street London WC2
also Bombay Calcutta Madras Melbourne

THE MACMILLAN COMPANY OF CANADA LIMITED
70 Bond Street Toronto 2

ST MARTIN'S PRESS INC
175 Fifth Avenue New York NY 10010

PRINTED IN GREAT BRITAIN

PREFACE

FOUR centuries have passed since the first Elizabeth came to the throne, yet we live still among things which her subjects made. The houses they built are to be found in every county of England, and many are open to those who wish to see them. In their chambers and galleries hang contemporary portraits of the men and women who lived there when the houses were new, and of their friends who visited them ; in many are contemporary tapestries and needlework and furniture and panelling and plaster ceilings. Here and there even the lay-out of the Elizabethan garden is discernible. In the Cathedrals, in College chapels, in many a village church are the gaudy, self-confident monuments of these Elizabethans, with inscriptions, often in verse, that here seem to us quaintly antique or here ring with the phrasing of Shakespeare's day. In the Cathedrals and Colleges again, the music is often the music of Elizabethan composers; and the liturgy and the Bible preserve the cadences of sixteenth-century prose. The Church of England of the Elizabethan Settlement, with its incomparable traditions of word and music, is to some the greatest of all the creations of that time; to others, who lack their faith, the drama of the age of Shakespeare is yet greater. Wherever we look, the imaginative power of those who were proud to be subjects of Queen Elizabeth I impresses and delights us still.

My purpose in this book has been to discover what they thought of all these things : why they built, painted, carved, composed, wrote as they did, and how the generation for whom these artists worked responded at the time, when the work was new. Our responses, inevitably, are different : we cannot divest ourselves of these four centuries of experience. But we ought to hesitate a little longer than we sometimes do before questioning the taste in buildings, or pictures, or monuments of those for whom Byrd and Shakespeare wrote. Certainly their finest achievements were in music and literature, in their opinion the two greatest of the arts ; but the same principles which informed their taste for these guided their judgment of the others.

I have confined myself to the fine arts, both because the domestic arts of silver, glass, furniture, textiles, gardening are subsidiary, and because it is less easy for us to study these things. The best collection of Elizabethan silver is in the Kremlin ; not much glass has survived ; furniture and costume and embroidery, though more widely accessible in country houses, are yet scarce compared to the number of pictures and tombs that remain. The gardens retain only a few architectural features, and are now far richer in variety of plants.

So far as possible I have chosen to describe only those houses, pictures, and monuments which I myself have seen: since I have seen them, anyone who reads this book can see them too. I wish I could have seen every house, every picture, every monument that survives. I should like to hear every lute-song and every piece of music for the virginals, though not, I think, to see every play that they produced. I ought, perhaps, to have read every letter and diary of the time that survives, but so many of these are concerned with the ephemera of the law or politics — it is such letters that men carefully preserve, for practical reasons. But the fact is that there is such a huge mass of evidence on Elizabethan Taste still available that I could not do other than select. At least I can claim to have selected without prejudice, with the aim, not of declaring my own preferences but of understanding theirs.

In the last section of the book I have not attempted to treat of Elizabethan Literature generally, but instead have discussed a few works which were greatly admired at the time and which still retain, if not their original popularity, at least something of their fame. There are other works which were popular then but are now almost forgotten, and a few whose present reputation would have seemed excessive to an Elizabethan reader. In addition, I have briefly examined their appreciation of Chaucer, for what they thought of the Middle Ages was as important in the development of literature as of architecture or of sepulchral monuments. Throughout the book I hope the reader may be reminded of the unity of their experience in this way, and that the comments which they made on a poem or a piece of music may recall other comments on a building or a picture — their comments, not mine: for

> A perfect judge will read each work of wit
> With the same spirit that its author writ.

Counsel of perfection, no doubt, but then the Elizabethans, as well as Pope, thought that perfection was within man's reach. If we do not, that is our misfortune, but surely it could be exciting, for a brief time, to suspend our doubt and to try to look again through their eyes at the works these Elizabethans so plentifully left us.

To the greatest single monument of Elizabethan taste, *The Faerie Queene*, I have often referred, without attempting to confine it within a single chapter. Some day I hope to write at more length on Spenser, and do not therefore wish now to offer a preliminary sketch : a lover of Spenser may learn from him to wait until he is ready to publish. Not that I wish to suggest that another ten years, or twenty-five, might not increase my knowledge of the kind of evidence of that taste here presented: I hope they may. But I hope also that by now I have seen, or heard, or read enough to be able to act as a guide to the principles upon which it was founded, so that unobtrusively (for that is the most necessary quality in any guide) I may persuade those who are ready to applaud *Hamlet* or to admire

Longleat, to delight in a motet by Byrd or a madrigal by Wilbye, also to be willing to appreciate *The Countess of Pembroke's Arcadia* or Wollaton Hall, or the tomb of Lord Burghley at Stamford or of the Queen herself in Westminster Abbey.

J. B.

ACKNOWLEDGMENTS

In the course of writing this book I have become indebted to many people, the owners of houses and of pictures, the incumbents or vergers of churches where Elizabethan tombs remain, the singers and performers of Elizabethan music, whom I cannot thank by name. Many friends have helped me by telling me of, or taking me to see, houses or monuments near where they live. My pupils, by a decent scepticism, have made me strive to substantiate my opinions. To all I am humbly grateful.

The staffs of the Bodleian Library, the Ashmolean Museum, the British Museum, the Courtauld Institute, the National Buildings Record, and the London Library have invariably been patient and helpful. At the Victoria and Albert Museum I was given every assistance to discover in which department the Hill Hall frescoes are preserved from sight, and was provided with photographs. I am most grateful to the Wardens of the Goldsmiths' Company for allowing me to see their plate, and to reproduce a photograph of the Gibbon Salt, and to their Librarian, Miss Susan Hare, for showing it to me; to Mr O. R. Bagot and to Col. Nigel Stopford Sackville for allowing me to reproduce photographs of their property. Mrs Geoffrey Williams kindly took photographs for me in various parts of the country, and Mr A. R. G. Heward helped me to obtain two of the illustrations.

I wish to thank especially the Earl and Countess of Radnor who not only showed me Longford Castle and its contents but lent me the Rev. H. Pelate's manuscript History (1678); and Mr and Mrs O. R. Bagot, for their gay and instructive hospitality at Levens on many occasions. Most of all am I obliged to those friends and colleagues who read and criticized parts of the book in typescript or in proof: Mrs J. S. Bromley (Miss Jean Robertson), Dr H. K. Andrews, Mr John Bayley, Mr H. E. Bell, and Mr David Piper. Mr D. G. Neill read the proofs with meticulous care, which has saved me from a variety of disasters ranging from damaged letters to improbable consanguinities.

I wish also to thank Mr A. L. Rowse, who allowed me to read two chapters of *Ralegh and the Throckmortons* before publication; Professor E. K. Waterhouse, who answered an enquiry about one reference; and Mr E. C. Yorke, who helped me to track down another. Miss June Waymark kindly typed out part of the book at an early stage. My wife has helped me throughout by her encouragement, and by practical assistance in making notes for me on monuments, copying inscriptions, typing and retyping, reading proofs and (least rewarding of connubial tasks) making the indexes.

J. B.

CONTENTS

ILLUSTRATIONS

I

INTRODUCTORY

I. INTRODUCTORY

ELIZABETHAN gentlemen never complimented one another on the excellence of their taste. There was no such phrase, for good taste was too vague and subjective, too unreasonable a concept, implying as it does that a man may be naturally endowed with aesthetic discrimination as with good eyesight, and not need to build upon a foundation of sense, or to train his judgment through years of experience and study. But in the sixteenth century to acquire this discrimination, by practice as well as by observation, was a part of the education of the complete man. The power of reason distinguished man from all other creatures: in the universe of God's creation he alone had the gift of detached comprehension, and could stand aside to appreciate the Art of God. The world which he inhabited was a rationally ordered world to which his aesthetic response must also be rational. The artist therefore did not impose a human order on experience, but revealed the divine order on which it was framed; his imagination presented this in forms which would give pleasure in themselves, and his skill elicited admiration of the learning by which it had been acquired.

So Castiglione advised the courtier to write both verse and prose, not in any expectation that he would become an eminent writer, but because 'at the least wise he shall receive so much profit, that by that exercise he shall be able to give his judgment upon other men's doings'. He must be skilled in the art of painting for 'beside it is a help to him to judge of the excellency of images both old and new . . . it maketh him also understand the beauty of lively bodies'. Again, a knowledge of music was desirable, for few would care to risk the humiliation of Morley's Philomathes who, having to confess his inability to sing his part in a song after dinner, overheard some of his fellow-guests who 'whispered to others demanding how I was brought up'. We may believe too that every Elizabethan gentleman who watched the walls of his new country house rising in token of his favour at Court would have considered himself capable of directing and advising the builder.

In Italy all the arts flourished at the Renaissance: poetry and music, architecture, painting, and sculpture. Our recently acquired ignorance of Italian literature should not lead us to assume that the work of Ariosto and Tasso, of Politian and Bembo, fell as far below that of Raphael and Titian, of Donatello and Michelangelo, as in England the painters and sculptors who were contemporary with Spenser and Shakespeare, Byrd and Dowland, failed to match their genius. There was no such disparity. But only Nicholas Hilliard among English painters and Epiphanius Evesham among English sculptors deserve to be added to the long roll of poets and musicians who distinguished the reign of Queen Elizabeth. Why this was so is by no means clear. The Reformation with its iconoclasm brought to an end, it is said, the work of a native school of sculptors who adorned the canopied niches of church tower and cathedral front with statues of saints and martyrs. Stained-glass windows were broken; paintings of superstitious images were destroyed; but the secularization of arts whose patrons had previously been found in the Church is not tantamount to cessation. Heraldic glass may provide less opportunity for a master of the craft than the representation of human (though saintly) forms; but to carve an effigy of the recently dead, or to paint the portrait of the living have been customary tasks of sculptor and painter throughout the history of these arts. And the musicians, more seriously interrupted in their principal task of composing church music by the extinction of the Latin rite except in a few privileged places, accepted the challenge of the times, so that for a generation English composers, like English poets, had no equals in all Europe. The Reformation then can no more justly be blamed for the scarcity of good English painters and sculptors than praised for the abundance of good poets and musicians.

Another explanation is commonly offered : that music and poetry enjoyed a social prestige denied to painting and sculpture, and that therefore, in an aristocratic society, men of breeding would disdain to paint or to carve, themselves, or to take much interest in these arts. But this is not true. As early as 1531 Sir Thomas Elyot had had a chapter of *The Governour* devoted to the proposition 'that it is commendable in a gentleman to paint and carve exactly if nature thereto doth induce him' ; and the fact that Elyot derived his argument from Aristotle only made it the more acceptable. George Gower, grandson of Sir John Gower of Stettenham, Yorkshire, painted in 1579 a self-portrait with a device showing a pair of dividers in a balance against his coat of arms. Some crude verses claim that his skill as a painter, far from disgracing the arms which his father bore 'by just renown', maintained the praise of his family : there was nothing unseemly in a gentleman born becoming a painter. In 1581 Gower was appointed Serjeant-Painter and in that year (significantly perhaps) by a charter granted to the company of Painter-Stainers gentlemen were excepted from the requirement of apprenticeship if they painted 'for recreation or private pleasure'. Yet the Serjeant-Painter was by no means concerned only with what we might regard as the more dignified commissions of his art : Gower himself on one occasion received £40 for 'drawing and painting of 347 branches of diverse kinds of flowers' upon the white satin hangings of a bed. Jacques le Moyne des Morgues in dedicating *La Clef des Champs* to Mme de Sidney suggested that learning to draw was suitable for the young of noble families 'pour leur préparer en l'Art de Peinture ou Graveure'. Twenty years later Henry Peacham wrote *The Art of Drawing* 'for the behoof of all young Gentlemen', and said that he had always regarded drawing as one of the accomplishments required in a scholar and a gentleman. Peacham considered that one of these, Sir Nathaniel Bacon, who was younger son to the Lord Keeper, Sir Nicholas, was 'not inferior to the skilfullest masters'. He had studied painting in Italy and his few known paintings are among the best English work of the time. Others of good birth were known as painters, among them Sir William Segar, Garter King-at-Arms, and his brother Francis; and even one lady, 'Margaret, daughter of Sir John King . . . now wife of Sir Gerard Lowther, Chief Justice of the Common Pleas in Ireland, whose excellent skill is such . . . that she can draw any proportion to the life, either of personage, landscape, or story, or any other thing'. But the most striking proof of the prestige which painting enjoyed in the sixteenth century comes from Nicholas Hilliard himself, the son of a sheriff of Exeter, who wished 'that none should meddle with limning but gentlemen alone'.

In sculpture gentlemen would be less likely to engage. Leonardo da Vinci had considered painting a more respectable occupation because it demanded less manual labour, though Castiglione preferred painting for aesthetic, not social reasons. Yet the most distinguished of English sculptors, like the finest of English painters Hilliard, was of gentle birth. Epiphanius Evesham was the son of William Evesham of Burghope, and of his wife Jane: both his father's family and his mother's were of the Herefordshire gentry, but they seem to have had no objection to their son studying under the Flemish sculptor Richard Stevens at Southwark. There was no social degradation in being a sculptor, any more than in being a painter, or musician, or poet.

Gentlemen who could best acquire an understanding of the arts by experiment, might thereby discover a natural talent and become artists. Conversely, artists could aspire to be accepted as gentlemen. The leading musicians of the day became 'Gentlemen of the Chapel Royal' whatever their birth, and were so regarded. Spenser asserted his kinship with the Spencers of Althorp, who did not deny it ; Michael Drayton was proud to be called Esquire on his title-pages after he had attended Sir Walter Aston when he was made Knight, and the coat of arms to which he was thenceforth entitled is shown in a seventeenth-century manuscript side by side with that granted to Shakespeare.

This view of the artist as gentleman derived from Italy no less than did the ideal of the Courtier. The courtier must learn to do whatever he did with a grace ; it was 'a sauce to everything, without the which all his other properties and good conditions were little worth'. This is the quality of the amateur, of the man who does all he attempts without the appearance of strain or excessive preparation, who realizes that however important to himself is the task on which he is engaged it may not seem so to others. His manner must suggest an elegant disdain, *sprezzatura*, and therewith imply that he will neither overestimate his present performance nor allow it to appear his principal concern. So Philip Sidney, who is the epitome of grace, begins his *Apology for Poetry* with a disarming request that the reader will not think him as absurdly devoted to poetry as his riding-master at Vienna had been to equitation. Queen Elizabeth would admire the dancing of a courtier, but not of a professional dancing-master : 'I will not see your man,' she once told Leicester, 'it is his trade.' The artist, working for an aristocratic taste, must therefore have the art to conceal art, and must, like Hilliard, be willing to set his work aside at a moment's notice : 'moreover it is secret, a man may use it and scarcely be perceived of his own folk'. This most gifted and fastidious artist, working in a medium which requires extreme concentration, accepted the importance of grace like any courtier whose portrait he painted.

The whole of human experience might be investigated by human intelligence, and it was the duty of the courtier, the man who would serve and advise his prince, to comprehend it. Specialization was banausic, out of date, mediaeval, a subject for mockery. Castiglione tells of someone — he will not name him — who refused the various entertainments offered him by a worthy gentlewoman in a noble assembly, on the grounds that music and dancing and so forth were not his profession. '"What is then your profession?" she asked. He answered, with a frowning look, "To fight." Then said the Gentle-woman: "seeing you are not now at the war nor in place to fight, I would think it best for you to be well besmeared and set up in an armoury, lest you wax more rustier than you are."' But Chaucer's Knight would have made the same reply, and would not have been laughed at.

Chaucer, who may have met Petrarch, and who knew Boccaccio's writings, contrasts with the Knight the elegant representative of the younger generation, his son. For of the Squire we are told,

> He coude songes make and wel endyte,
> Iuste and eek daunce, and wel purtreye and wryte,

as every sixteenth-century courtier strove to do. But a century and a half of dynastic war and religious contest delayed the final return of Chaucer's squire to England until the reign of Queen Elizabeth. Then, heralded by Sir Thomas Hoby's translation of Castiglione's delightful book, he enters once more, in the person of a Philip Sidney, or of a Hamlet, to sum up the civilization of that golden age.

For not only to the eighteenth century, or to the nineteenth, did the reign of the first Queen Elizabeth seem a golden age: it seemed so then. Neither was this an empty phrase of commendation, as it was to become, but it contained a precise and well understood reference to the four ages described by Ovid in the first book of the *Metamorphoses*:

> The Golden Age was first; which uncompelled,
> And without rule, in faith and truth excelled.

Peace was universal under the reign of Saturn; there were no armies, and, since everyone was naturally virtuous, no laws.

As yet there were no seasons, but it was always spring, and men needed no labour to produce their food. There was neither master nor servant, rich nor poor, but the bliss of the golden age was compared to the primal innocence in Eden. After the turmoil of the century and a half since Chaucer wrote, Englishmen hoped for a return to peace and justice, and the accession of a Virgin Queen gave especial promise that this would be so. Therefore, early in her reign, 'one upon happy hope conceived, made an half of the zodiac, with Virgo rising, adding *Jam redit et virgo*'. This allusion to Virgil's famous fourth eclogue would have escaped no one, for there the greatest poet of the world (as he seemed to them) had looked forward with similar hope to a new golden age under Augustus :

Jam redit et virgo, redeunt Saturnia regna.

The Augustan age was recognized as the time when Roman civilization had reached its full perfection, not only in political power but, especially, in the arts of poetry and architecture. Later, the Emperor Constantine had adapted Virgil's poem to refer to the establishment of Christianity throughout the Empire, and the end of persecutions. The virgin Astraea, who had been the last of the immortals to abandon the blood-soaked world of the iron age, was re-interpreted as the Virgin Mary. Foxe in his so-called *Book of Martyrs*, the most universally popular work of his time, took up this point, and compared the ending of the Marian persecutions on Elizabeth's accession to Constantine's achievement.

To them the golden age which Elizabeth had restored was distinguished by its peacefulness and good order, with the opportunities which these gave at last for the development of a civilized life, and for the flourishing of the arts. We may not think of the reign as a very peaceful one, for the battles which they fought were heroic and memorable, so that we forget how few they were. But of persons of fame, in those forty-five years, only Sir Philip Sidney, Sir Richard Grenville and Sir John Wingfield were killed in action, and the Elizabethans themselves were for ever contrasting the quiet which they enjoyed with the unrest which had gone before, or which even then was distracting the Netherlands and France. Into the religious life of England also Elizabeth had brought peace, by a practical preference for a middle way; and if many of her subjects were unable to share her disinclination for asking awkward questions, at least they did not slaughter one another for the answers, as they would all too soon. The Reformation meant, to them, literally the re-formation of the original Church of Christ, the restoration of another golden age of pure religion, unsullied by long centuries of corrupt human tradition.

This idea of a return to an earlier and better state pervaded all their thinking, and was justified by their belief in the perfection of the world which God had created in the beginning. From that perfection it had continually declined since the Fall, owing to man's wickedness, but now with the restoration of true religion and the recovery of ancient learning man might make a new start. Of this rebirth the Queen's virginity was a most potent symbol: she was Astraea, to whom Justice was attributed, and her return to rule was associated in men's minds with the imperial rule of Augustus, so that she was an 'imperial votaress',

> A fair vestal, throned by the West.

Sir John Davies, in the first of his *Hymns of Astraea*, gaily celebrates the maid who, descended from heaven,

> Hath brought again the golden days,
> And all the world amended.

And he was writing not in happy hope at the outset of the reign, but in proud acknowledgment towards its close.

The Queen herself, needless to say, was well aware of all this. She was as learned as any of her subjects, and more astute ; she delighted, as they all did, in the ingenious elaboration of symbol and allegory. One of her favourite devices was the Phoenix — Constantine also had used it, though that she may not have known — and to this belongs her motto of *Semper eadem*. There is a splendid jewel in the British Museum showing on one side a bust of the Queen surrounded by a wreath of roses in enamel and gold, and on the other the Phoenix in its nest of flames, with the royal cipher and crown.[1] There are silver badges related to this jewel which perhaps the Queen presented to some of her courtiers. She is shown wearing another enamelled jewel of a Phoenix in a painting in the National Portrait Gallery. There is also an enamel of the Phoenix in the pendant which she gave to Sir Francis Drake after his voyage of circumnavigation, perhaps intended to imply that her favour to him would remain constant. These jewels and badges belong to the first half of her reign, and no doubt conveyed the idea of England reborn under the rule of the Queen. There is a wooden statue in St Mary Redcliffe, Bristol, perhaps made by a local carver of ships' figure-heads to commemorate her visit to the city in 1574, where she is shown standing upon the Phoenix ; and even after her death Nicholas Stone portrayed her so, in a statue made for the Royal Exchange.

To this theme must be related the Tudor interest in King Arthur ; for who better than princes of Welsh origin could hope to revive the glories of a legendary Britain ? So Henry VII called his eldest son Arthur, and though the young prince died, the selection of this name for the heir to the throne was significant. Spenser's choice of Prince Arthur as the hero of his great patriotic poem was in part determined by a wish to associate his name with the court of Gloriana, though neither poet nor Queen took the Matter of Britain as serious history. That was not necessary, though many less sceptical persons did so ; myth no less than history can powerfully move men's

[1] Frontispiece.

minds. Golden ages might be perceived in the beginning of things in Britain as in the early Church, the age of Augustus, or the garden of Eden ; and where it was customary to look back towards an ideal world, men's gaze might travel far along the horizons of history and legend without too sharp a discrimination between them.

They were conscious of much that was new in their experience of their own time, and they sought the assurance of ancient tradition recovered from beneath the debris of the Middle Ages. They were for ever talking of the new, and the modern, but were not content simply to draw the contrast with what of the recent past had been abandoned. The long custom of authority compelled them to quote the support of Plato and Aristotle, of Homer and Virgil, of Vitruvius and Phidias and Apelles, of Cicero and Pliny and Seneca. 'The combustions and tumults of the middle age had uncivilized' good literature, and good architecture, as well as good religion. In order to restore them again men turned to the civilizations of Greece and of Rome, and especially of Rome because Italy was more accessible than Greece, and Latin better understood than Greek. Often the classicism is scarcely distinguishable after travelling through fifteen centuries and from the Mediterranean to the shores of the North Sea. An Ionic column may be stuck on to ornament a house by a mason who displays his ignorance by spelling it 'Yonk' ; the gaiety of Ovid may still have to suffer the hesitations of a Northern morality ; and in a wood near Athens the story of Pyramus and Thisbe may be presented with less than classical elegance. But the Elizabethans were not attempting to copy the ancients, rather to learn from them the means of creating something new. Longleat and Moreton Corbet and Hardwick Hall are not in the least like any building that was ever erected or imagined by Vitruvius and his contemporaries ; but they would not be as they are had his work not been most attentively studied in sixteenth-century England. *The Faerie Queene* is so unlike the

Aeneid that it would never occur to us to classify the two poems together ; but to Spenser, and to his contemporaries, who proudly claimed him as the English Virgil, both were heroic poems, designed to frame the reader's mind to virtue, and with a patriotic element in that design. At the end of the century Francis Meres concocted a series of comparisons between English poets, painters and musicians and those of Greece and Rome. The resulting catalogue is tedious and absurd, but the motive which led to its making derived from a dim comprehension of what the artists of the time were attempting.

Now and again we come across protests against an excessive deference to the classics, especially in literature. 'But why not all in English ?' asked Richard Mulcaster, 'It is our accident which restrains our tongue, and not the tongue itself, which will strain with the strongest, and stretch to the furthest . . . not any whit behind either the subtle Greek for couching close, or the stately Latin for spreading fair.' And, twenty years later, Samuel Daniel proclaimed, in the noble phrasing of which he was master, a like faith : 'Me thinks we should not so soon yield our consents captive to the authority of Antiquity, unless we saw more reason : all our understandings are not to be built by the square of Greece and Italy. We are the children of nature as well as they.' Francis Bacon, by an ingenious paradox, claimed that your moderns are your true ancients : 'As for antiquity, the opinion touching it which men entertain is quite a negligent one, and scarcely consonant with the word itself. For the old age of the world is to be accounted the true antiquity ; and this is the attribute of our own times, not of that earlier age of the world in which the ancients lived ; and which, though in respect of us it was the elder, yet in respect of the world it was the younger.' Thus the Elizabethans assert their independence at the same time as they acknowledge the influence of Greece and Rome ; they adhere to the great European tradition, as they had received it direct from Italy, through France or the Netherlands, but they make out of it something essentially English. Hardwick Hall and *The Faerie Queene* (to return by no means for the last time to these examples) are not only unlike the inventions of imperial Rome, they are also very unlike the creations of modern Italy, or modern France ; are, in fact, self-confidently English.

In the seventeenth century this confidence in the native tradition began to fade, and a purer classicism replaced the mixture of mediaeval English with modern Italian which characterizes the art of the Elizabethan age. The exquisite limnings of Hilliard, which derive from mediaeval illumination, no longer suit the fashion, and Oliver, whose paintings are indebted especially to Parmigianino and not at all to the illuminators, takes his place. Inigo Jones, who so sumptuously staged the masques of the neo-classic Jonson, could never have cooperated successfully with Shakespeare ; and his buildings owe everything to the inspiration of Palladio, nothing to English Perpendicular from whose lofty windows the glittering fronts of many an Elizabethan mansion take their origin. Most of all we observe this contrast in the literature : between Spenser, who discovered in Chaucer a well from which to draw huge, spilling draughts of the dazzling language which Mulcaster taught him to love, and Milton, who, ambitious to leave to after times work so written that they should not willingly let it die, based his style more securely (he supposed) in Virgil. For by then the glory of Chaucer's numbers was lost, and those who wrote English were aware of the impermanence of their work, compared to the poetry of Greece or Rome :

> We write in sand, our language grows
> And like the tide our work o'erflows.

So Waller ; and it was precisely to avoid this disaster of obsolescence that Milton wrote as he did. But fear of this danger had never occurred to Spenser or to Shakespeare, who knew that their verse would eternize their mistress' virtues or beauty. They believed, with Mulcaster, that 'whatsoever shall become of the English state, the English tongue cannot prove fairer than it is at this day'. Or what contemporary of Milton would have repeated that astonishing prophecy of Samuel Daniel's that English would become the language of the New World where

> This gain of our best glory shall be sent
> To enrich unknowing nations with our stores ?

Yet when Daniel wrote there was no permanent English settlement in that New World : when Milton wrote there were thousands of Englishmen from Barbados to Newfoundland, and even a university in New England.

I cannot here discuss the reasons for this sudden lack of confidence in the native tradition which afflicted the seventeenth century, for I am concerned with the time of confidence. The Elizabethans were so sure that what they were doing was new that they did not hesitate to accept whatever they might require from an earlier generation of Englishmen. The present-day fashion for alleging mediaeval survivals in the life or work of the Elizabethans would have seemed very ridiculous to them : whatever survived, in the worship of God, in the conduct of political life, in the arts, did so not by some undetected persistence, but through their own deliberate choice. They sang *Te Deum* and *Magnificat* not because they were incapable of divesting themselves of mediaeval liturgy, but because parts of it still acceptably expressed the praise they too wished to offer to God : yet now they sang them in English. Very typically, on hearing news of the deaths of Mary and Cardinal Pole, on that first day of the new reign, they 'sang and said *Te Deum laudamus* in every church in London'. Visitors from the Continent record in their diaries surprise that Anglican services so much resemble Popish ones, failing to understand that the Church of England is a catholic church, though not Roman Catholic. No doubt they expected that the revolution which had happened here would have been more thorough and violent, and could not recognize the characteristic English qualities of compromise and conservatism—a disinclination ever wholly to reject what was old, or wholly to accept what was new, a preference for making something generally acceptable out of both. The Elizabethan prayer book takes the words of administration of the sacrament from both of Edward VI's prayer books: from 1549 words that assert the Real Presence, 'The Body of our Lord Jesus Christ, which was given for thee, preserve thy body and soul unto everlasting life', and from 1552 the emphatically Protestant words, 'Take and eat this in remembrance that Christ died for thee, and feed on him in thy heart by faith with thanksgiving'. The Queen herself (or so it was said) spoke for her rationally minded subjects in quoting four brief lines:

> Christ was the word that spake it,
> He took the bread and brake it;
> And what his words did make it,
> That I believe, and take it.

We should ponder long before calling them either cynical or reverent, and remember that compromise may sometimes abjure clarity of definition.

'Judicious' is the epithet traditionally associated with the name of the great apologist of the Anglican Church, Richard Hooker [1]: hardly a stock epithet attached to the names of all such persons. But Hooker, above all else, is reasonable, and assumes that his opponents in controversy must be so too, because they are men. The Law of Reason, he says, 'is such that being proposed no man can reject it as unreasonable and unjust. Again, there is nothing in it but any man (having natural perfection of wit and ripeness of judgment) may by labour and travail find out. And to conclude, the general principles thereof are such, as it is not easy to find men ignorant of them. . . . This Law, I say, comprehendeth all those things which men by the light of their natural understanding

[1] It appears on his monument at Bishopsbourne, Kent.

evidently know, or at leastwise may know, to be beseeming or unbeseeming, virtuous or vicious, good or evil for them to do.' Hooker owed his education at Oxford to John Jewel, Bishop of Salisbury, who, at the beginning of the reign, had been a vigorous apologist of the Anglican Church, and whose chief opponents then had been the Papists. By the end of the reign, when Hooker wrote, the principal challenge came no longer from them, but from the Puritans, whose rejection of tradition seemed to him as unreasonable as their distrust of reason itself. He defends the retention of ceremonies used in the Church of Rome on rational grounds, and with an understanding of the value of ceremony characteristic of a generation that was always conscious of human dignity.

This native good sense the seventeenth century lost for a time, deviating into an alien violence of opinion and expression. Even then, in the midst of civil war, there were Englishmen on both sides civilized enough to believe that 'the cause was too good to have been fought for'. The words are Marvell's : they might as easily have been Lord Falkland's. But they and their like were all too few. No one has ever called Laud or King Charles judicious ; and though Milton the poet makes his appeal always to reason, Milton the apologist for the Commonwealth does not, for he will not concede the reasonableness of his opponents. There is the difference between the generation of Spenser and of Milton, of Hooker and of Laud : between the courteous reasonableness of the man who sincerely believes that his opponents are open to rational argument, and the scurrilous rant of the man who swears that they are not ; between the moderate man and the fanatic ; between the man who, confident in the rationality of his opinions, can state them quietly, and the man who, lacking that confidence, must shout. These differences pervade the whole life of English society in these two generations, and the taste of the Elizabethan age must be discussed as the taste of men who, for all the passionate intensity of their imaginations, could, and habitually did, stand aside to take a detached critical view ; who expressed their judgment in terms which, being rational, they would expect to command assent.

The Elizabethan courtier, who modelled his life on the pattern of Castiglione's, and for whom Spenser wrote, was more aloof in his aristocratic assurance than the seventeenth-century citizen of London whom Henry Peacham or John Milton addressed. Peacham's Compleat Gentleman is one who apes his betters : the courtly ideal has been diluted for the refreshment of a generation which could admire but not accept the stimulants of a Sidney, an Essex, or a Ralegh. Spenser, who knew personally all three, had written his heroic poem 'to fashion a gentleman or noble person in virtuous and gentle discipline'. Milton wished his poem to be 'doctrinal and exemplary to a nation', and concentrated all his powers on the virtuous discipline, not on the gentle : he does not stoop to commend the accomplishments of a courtier. The audience has widened, and the ideal has shrunk. The turmoils of the seventeenth century led Englishmen to spend more time in London and less in the country houses than they had done in Elizabeth's time, and King James's speech in the Star Chamber in 1616 or King Charles's proclamation of 1630 commanding the gentry to reside upon their estates in the country can have had but a temporary effect. The process culminated in the Restoration when, in emulation of Paris and Augustan Rome, England achieved a metropolitan culture unique in her history. The country houses with their long galleries hung with full-length portraits, with their formal gardens and topiary, were neglected or transformed. Royal progresses no longer demanded the lavish and spectacular entertainment with which her courtiers had welcomed the Virgin Queen : Kenilworth was in ruins ; Holdenby and Theobalds were destroyed ; Nonsuch was granted by Charles II to one of his mistresses, who frivolously demolished it. But in Elizabeth's time these and other great houses had been the resort of poets and musicians and painters, who adorned and celebrated the stately and ceremonious life which they so fittingly sheltered.

This matter of ceremony is pertinent. In defending religious ceremonies against the attacks of the Puritans Hooker argues that they reinforce and make more memorable the effect of words; also, that it is presumptuous to object to ceremonies simply because they are traditional. 'The things which so long experience of all ages hath confirmed and made profitable, let not us presume to condemn as follies and toys, because we sometimes know not the cause and reason of them.' We must assume that those who established these ancient ceremonies were themselves reasonable men, who understood what they were about. But by ceremony they meant something more than the ritual of Church or Court; not only what might serve to impress upon men's minds the glory of God, or the majesty of the Queen, but what would more generally assert the dignity of man.

So Chapman, in his continuation of *Hero and Leander* almost immediately introduces the goddess Ceremony who reproves Leander for his

> bluntness in his violent love

and compares his seduction of Hero to various forms of uncivilized behaviour,

> Not being with civil forms confirmed and bounded,
> For human dignities and comforts founded.

The satisfaction of sexual desire, unless accompanied by ceremony, by imaginative adornment, is mere animality; it must, like the satisfaction of hunger, be made worthy of human dignity. Nebuchadnezzar's consumption of grass symbolized his loss of humanity: sane and civilized persons satisfy their hunger with well-prepared dishes at elegantly dressed tables. The goddess departs leaving Leander suitably chastened not because of the immorality of his behaviour, but because of its indecency, its inadequacy to the human context.

Musidorus in the *Arcadia* allows himself to envy the uninhibited desires of beasts whose 'minds grudge not their bodies' comfort, nor their senses are letted from enjoying their objects', whereas 'we have the impediments of honour, and the torments of conscience'. This hankering after a primal innocence is not inconsistent, but is part of that vision of the golden world, of which we were deprived by Adam's fault, which they celebrate in countless pastorals. But if literature may properly be concerned with the world as it might be, even with the world as once it was created by God before man corrupted it, yet it must also be concerned with human life as we know it. 'Ay, now am I in Arden,' says Touchstone, 'the more fool I. When I was at home I was in a better place.' For however regretfully they may look back to the golden age when the world was young, they also look very steadily and objectively at the world they inhabit, after Spenser has shown the way in the first of the New Poetry, his pastoral *Shepheardes Calender*. They too lived in a golden age, not of innocence and natural virtue, but of justice restored and peace achieved, a richer and nobler world than the first had been ; as for Milton Adam redeemed would know a far happier paradise than Adam unfallen. The world the poets presented was enriched in its idealism by contrast with the brazen world of nature, and they imagined the human condition as something more exalted than the loves of Daphnis and Chloe.

The English, foreign travellers remarked, were lovers of show : great state was kept about the Queen whether at Court or on progress ; the ritual of the Church remained elaborate ; the impersonality of the Law was made visible by stately robes and processions ; the ceremonies of the Order of the Garter were a famous sight to see. In the portraits which they had painted to hang in their houses, in the effigies which they ordered for their tombs, they were shown with as much state and magnificence as painter or sculptor could devise. The entrances to their houses were ceremonious: designed not functionally with regard only to convenient access to the rooms within, but (as it were) heraldically, to announce to all who visited the house what was the quality of its master. So in the literature: Spenser writing a Christian heroic poem, uses ceremonious language in keeping with the dignity of his theme, and employs every device of rhetoric and metre to give stateliness to the movement of his verse. The sonneteers similarly deck out an often tenuous passion with sumptuous and elegant ornaments filched from Italy and France.

This love of the ceremonious is consistent with the principle of decorum which governed their taste: man, who was made in God's image, must never forget the dignity of his condition, must act the part cast for him; and where he found that he shared the destiny of other animals, in love, in hunger, in death, all the more must he distinguish the unique quality of his humanity. No Elizabethan had cause to observe, as had an eighteenth-century wit, that the art of love had been reduced to the simple phrase, 'Lie down'. The *fête champêtre* and the picnic are Romantic forms of self-abnegation. And death was not a tiresome and sordid irrelevance, to be evaded at the last under an anaesthetic, but a challenge to be accepted in the high heroic manner, on the scaffold, on the battlefield, or at home, with family and friends at hand to record those carefully rehearsed last words:

> For 'tis the evening crowns the day.
> This action of our death especially
> Shows all a man.

Such was their creed, but how superbly, when their time came, could they live up to it. 'We are as near to heaven by sea as by land.' 'Thy necessity is yet greater than mine.' 'What dost thou fear? Strike, man, strike.'

And when they had time, as Ralegh had, as Mary Queen of Scots had, with what a detached sense of the dramatic would they prepare the scene! So Mary, dressed in black, walked firmly down the great hall at Fotheringay, holding the crucifix high before her, towards the place where she could see the block already prepared. She read her Latin prayers, her voice rising above the voice of the Dean of Peterborough at his English prayer-book; then in English she prayed for the soul of her cousin Elizabeth. She stood alone now on the black-draped scaffold, and the two executioners approached to help her disrobe. 'I was not wont to have my clothes plucked off by such grooms,' she said, and smiled; and suddenly her black gown was off, to disclose the Queen, clad from head to foot in crimson silk, the colour of her Church's martyrs. Some sixty years later her grandson, a martyr (as some would have it) for another Church, a martyr for the people, as he himself said, met his death on the scaffold in Whitehall with equal courage and with equal dignity.

Kings and Queens, it may be said, can hardly fail to see themselves dramatically in any age: they are symbolic personages surrounded by state and ritual which is intended to emphasize the part they have to play and to conceal their personal qualities. But in the Elizabethan time others had this same dramatic awareness of their role in the society of which they were members, as courtiers or soldiers, prelates or adventurers. Society was hierarchical, that is to say, they imagined it as a vertical scale or ladder with the Queen, God's vice-gerent, at the top, and below her the nobility, the knights, esquires, gentlemen and so on down to the lowest peasant. It was possible to ascend the scale, as many did by ability or thrift, and by the patronage of those above them. The Queen alone could grant a patent of nobility (and did so very rarely), but the noble could confer knighthood, as Essex did to excess; the knight could summon a friend of lower rank to be his esquire. Of these different ranks different behaviour was expected, and when courtesy was the moral virtue by which men could know how

> to beare themselves aright
> To all of each degree, as doth behove,

decorum was the corresponding aesthetic principle.

Jonson accused Sidney of failing to keep decorum in the *Arcadia* by making everyone speak as well as himself—an absurd charge, but one which shows how much importance they attached to the principle. The dramatists all respect decorum, and thereby make their persons speak in character (as we should say) : clearly this is an ability which Shakespeare most of all discloses.[1] But he possesses it, not through a mysterious power of untutored genius, but because he accepted a principle which every man of his time accepted as reasonable, and because the range of his imagination enabled him to apply it more widely than any other. He could imagine how men and women of every rank in society would speak and act : he took little trouble over historical accuracy, to distinguish between early British and mediaeval, between Roman and modern Italian. 'His story requires Romans,' said Dr Johnson, 'but he thinks only on men.' That was enough, for him and for his audiences ; but if they were indifferent to period, they were insistent upon rank, and decorum referred to the one but not to the other. The same principle is observed by the Italian painters of the Renaissance : they make no attempt to reconstruct the architecture of Bethlehem, or the costume of the Jews in a *Nativity* ; they do not hesitate to include self-portraits in an *Adoration of the Magi* ; but they distinguish the pomp of the Orient Kings from the poverty of the Holy Family, and a Medici shown among the attendant crowd is still a Medici. The scholarship of a Mantegna who, in the *Triumph of Caesar* at Hampton Court, thought on Romans,

[1] 'Had all the speeches been printed without the very names of the persons, I believe,' said Pope, 'one might have applied them certainly to every speaker.'

and displayed his knowledge of Roman arms and costume, was exceptional, and no more relevant than historical accuracy in *Antony and Cleopatra*, or *Henry IV*. Besides, Mantegna himself Romanizes Christian subjects so that, as Berenson observes, 'the *Crucifixion* of the Louvre is, in the first place, a study of the Roman soldier. The *Ascension* in the Uffizi is the apotheosis of a Roman athlete. The *Circumcision* on the companion panel represents the interior of a Roman temple.' This is true. Mantegna's imagination had been led captive in a Roman triumph; Shakespeare's had not. Mantegna thinks of men as Romans; Shakespeare, of Romans as men.

To these men of the Renaissance rank was more significant than nationality, for degree was part of the order of the world as God created it, whereas nationality and the divergence of tongues were not. Even colour differentiated men less than rank: *Othello* shows that well enough. We find in the literature of the times no impassioned tirade against, no lofty apology for, the negro. Othello, the noble Moor who is the general of Venice, is of royal descent, and not even Brabantio suggests that Desdemona by her marriage has lowered herself in rank. But all would have applauded Ulysses' outburst against social upheaval.

> O, when degree is shaked,
> Which is the ladder of all high designs,
> The enterprise is sick! How could communities,
> Degrees in schools, and brotherhoods in cities,
> Peaceful commerce from dividable shores,
> The primogenitive and due of birth,
> Prerogative of age, crowns, sceptres, laurels,
> But by degree, stand in authentic place?
> Take but degree away, untune that string,
> And hark what discord follows!

The principle of decorum governs man's aesthetic response to this orderly world of God's creation, to divine reasonableness. It is therefore itself reasonable, and judgments founded upon it will command the assent of all reasonable men. It is objective, and excludes the uncertainties of subjective Romantic taste. And it is an intellectual principle, so that aesthetic judgment must involve not only the sensibility which is moved by a work of art, but also the sense which can form a detached judgment of the technique by means of which the artist contrives to move men. To an Elizabethan our responses would have seemed naïve and uneducated, nowhere more so than in the drama which, at present, we incline to praise beyond all their other achievements and to think we best appreciate. Our most admired actors are those who most resemble Hamlet's description: they 'tear a passion to tatters, to very rags, to split the ears of the groundlings, who for the most part are capable of nothing but inexplicable dumb-shows and noise'. And if they no longer seek to disguise the fact that Shakespeare and his contemporaries often wrote in verse, they effectively conceal the poetry. By his contemporaries Shakespeare was praised especially for his 'fine-filed phrase', for the elaborate skill with which he would use the figures of rhetoric and other technical devices of the poet's learned art. He was blamed for a certain carelessness in revision, for not blotting his lines. The range of his sympathetic understanding of human nature would be worthless (because undiscovered) if it were not matched by technical ability of the same extraordinary power. By it he can persuade us that we are listening to Mark Antony, or Romeo, to Hamlet, or Benedick, to Cleopatra, Juliet, Beatrice, Rosalind, to Falstaff or Mistress Quickly, to Emilia or Dogberry, because he can use language to express their thoughts and feelings in a manner appropriate both to their rank and to their personality. No lovers have ever made love with such exquisite persuasion as do Romeo and Juliet. No Prince of Denmark was ever capable of the infinitely varied eloquence of Hamlet. No village constable ever had quite the self-revealing limitations of Dogberry's vocabulary. But we ought to be persuaded by all these, and at the same time to observe how Shakespeare (not Romeo or Hamlet) is persuading us. In the drama of the time, as James Shirley, who was brought up in the tradition, puts it, 'You may find passions raised to that excellent pitch and by such insinuating degrees that you shall not choose but consent, and go along with them, finding yourself at last grown insensibly the very same person you read', — he is addressing the Reader of Beaumont and Fletcher's folio — 'and then', he says, 'and then stand admiring the subtle tracks of your engagement'. But this detached, intellectual appreciation of the technique by which the poet had persuaded us to be Arbaces or Amintor or Evadne, Hamlet or Romeo or Cleopatra, is what we, producers, actors and (therefore) spectators ignore. The tracks of our engagement are too subtle for our untrained perception.

Now there is some excuse for us, partly because the study of rhetoric, which is the means of persuasion, is no longer included in our normal education, and partly because 'in the art of persuasion, one of the most fundamental precepts is the concealment of art'. The rhetoric is seldom so obvious as in Antony's reiteration that Brutus and those who conspired against Caesar were 'honourable men', for the art to conceal art was also among Shakespeare's powers. Where the rhetoric is obvious, as in puns, we resist it, because for us puns are only a feeble kind of humour. We do not see that, for the Elizabethans, this elaborate playing on words was comparable to the ingenious decoration they devised in their architecture and their music, and that it seemed fitting then to match a moment of high drama or to pay a courtly compliment with a display of virtuosity in the use of words. 'I'll gild the faces of the grooms withal, for it must seem their guilt', is not intended to make us laugh, or to cringe at the sinister chance of homophony. Shakespeare is driving home the horror of Lady Macbeth's proposal by the verbal decoration, just as a musician may use *coloratura* to decorate and to emphasize a tense moment in the drama. If our attention is distracted by such devices that is our misfortune : it should have been concentrated.

To be acceptable this ingenuity in which they took such pleasure must be apposite. There was ancient precedent for shaping poems like altars, crosses, wings and so forth in the *Technopaegnia* of the Alexandrians, but the shape of the poem on the page must have some relevance to its content, as in George Herbert's *The Altar* and *Easter Wings*. Sir John Davies' *Hymns of Astraea* are bound to the acrostic ELISABETHA REGINA, but then the poems are in praise of the Queen. Spenser organizes his *Epithalamion* about the twenty-four hours of his wedding day : an introductory stanza is followed by ten where he describes the gathering of the procession which is to lead his bride to church, and its passage there ; two central stanzas describe the marriage ; ten more describe the bringing home and bedding of the bride, and a final brief *commiato* rounds off the whole. There are other devices, related to this : the word 'day' recurs seventeen times in the first part of the poem, and twice in the last ; 'night', five times in the first and ten times in the last part. Such ingenious care in this most impassioned of all love-poems must neither be ignored as irrelevant — Spenser wrote it — nor allowed to detract from the sincerity of the poem — it is one of the few Elizabethan poems in which we know that personal feeling was involved. But for Spenser, composing a song to deck his bride on her wedding day, intensity of feeling must call forth the utmost of which his art was capable. The Romantic heresy that powerful feeling has only to overflow spontaneously in order to produce a work of art had not yet been invented. How could it have been by men who believed not that 'reason is, and ought only to be, the slave of the passions', but that reason is the law by which men know what is beseeming or unbeseeming for them to do ?

Art of this elaboration is not confined to poetry and music. In architecture they will display a similar ingenuity, as in Sir

Thomas Tresham's Triangular Lodge at Rushton (pl. 5), a mathematical fantasy of bewildering complication, fashioned of variations on the figure 3. But all these are relevant to the worship of the Trinity, to which Tresham (having the same number concealed in his own name) was born a devotee; and therefore decorum is still kept. So it must be in the design of fountains, a favourite Renaissance diversion, in which it was an established principle that when statues were used the water must flow only from those parts of the creature's anatomy, whether man or beast or bird, from which it might properly be supposed to flow. We have a succession of lions and birds and dolphins spouting water from mouth or beak; a goddess may spill bright water from her breasts; at Hawsted in Suffolk 'was a stone figure of Hercules, holding in one hand a club across his shoulders, the other resting on one hip, discharging a perennial stream of water, by the urinary passage, into a carved stone basin'. This fountain was erected in 1578 for the Queen's visit, and it was the first object to be seen on looking into the garden: an unexpected but (in the sixteenth-century sense) decent gesture of welcome to the Virgin Queen. As Sir Henry Wotton relates, Michelangelo himself contrived a fountain 'in the figure of a sturdy woman, washing and winding of linen clothes — in which act she wrings out the water that made the fountain; which was a graceful and natural conceit in the artificer, implying this rule, that all designs of this kind should be proper'.

This propriety is not functional. The way in which they approached problems of design in such things is shown by a note which Inigo Jones jotted down in his sketchbook. 'In all inventions of capricious ornaments one must first design the ground, or the thing plain, as it is for use, and on that vary it, adorn it. Compose it with decorum according to the use and the order it is of.' First of all the use must be considered: a fountain must be capable of throwing a spray or releasing a fall of water. But since a fountain is something different from a stand-pipe, and is intended not for use but to entertain the eye and to refresh the air, the designer is at liberty to introduce all sorts of fanciful variants, provided that these enhance, or at least do not impede, its primary purpose. Fountains were commonly used by the Elizabethans. There are drawings of many in the Lumley Inventories, though none survive ; some of these had probably been at Nonsuch, where in 1599 Thomas Platter noted an elaborate fountain, in the form of 'a rock out of which natural water springs into a basin, and on this was portrayed with great art and life-like execution the story of how the three goddesses took their bath naked and sprayed Actaeon with water, causing antlers to grow upon his head, and of how his own hounds afterwards tore him to pieces'. Presumably this was a carving in relief at the back of a basin, such as may still be seen in many an Italian or Portuguese garden. Their love of ingenuity also could find opportunity in the design of fountains, as in the one which Sir John Harington had made at Kelston, 'a fountain standing on pillars, like that in Ariosto, under which you may dine and sup', and under which in 1592 he entertained Queen Elizabeth. In his translation of the *Orlando Furioso*, published the previous year, Harington somewhat altered Ariosto's description, presumably to conform more closely to the fountain he had actually built. The pillars were statues of 'eight chaste and sober dames that now do live', who rested their feet on statues of poets who

> their worthy fames,
> In time to come, should praise with learned pen ;

and with their left hands these eight female statues held up

> a brazen trestle
> On which there stood a large white marble vessel.

From this (apparently) water spilled in a curtain outside the table at which the guests were seated. Sir John must have had (as indeed he usually seems to have had) great confidence in his plumbing, to risk inviting the Queen to dine under this fountain. She would probably not have been amused by a wetting at the hands of her witty godson. But in the gardens of Hampton Court there was 'an excellent water work with which one may easily spray any ladies or others standing round, and wet them all', which suggests that the Royal sense of humour has happily not much changed over the centuries.

Besides fountains, they ornamented their gardens with pillars and pyramids of stone, with painted wooden railings and trellises, with statues of gods and goddesses and also, at least at Nonsuch, with statues of animals such as dogs and hares 'all overgrown with plants, most artfully set out, so that from a distance, one would take them for real ones.' Topiary was much admired and the clipped shapes, geometrical very often, but also representing birds and animals, centaurs and sirens, and serving-maids with baskets, gave great pleasure, and added to the gay frivolity which they sought in their gardens.

For they were gay, as we may still discover in their music and literature, even sometimes in their architecture. The little banqueting-houses that survive on the roof of Longleat are comparable to the gay arbours that once adorned their gardens. There is gaiety in their compliment, and in their wit ; in the entertainments which they contrived for the Queen's progresses; in the comedies which Shakespeare wrote ; in their singing and dancing. They were so certain of themselves that they might be light-hearted without incurring a charge of folly ; frivolous now and then without being thought incapable of ever being serious. And characteristically they use the mediaeval to display this side of their nature. They convert the curtain walls of a grim mediaeval castle into garden walls where flowers may shelter, and the bastions into summer houses from which to see them ; or they imitate a castle in timber and canvas, and mount upon the turrets guns that fire scented water upon those who attack them with balls of flowers. The tilting armour is mediaeval, but with a difference. Sir

Henry Lee, the Queen's Champion, had two suits of white armour, one of them decorated with bands of engraving in black and gilt, the other with bands of multicoloured enamel; one with a device of a bird flying towards the sun on the shoulder-pieces, the other with Anne Vavasour's monogram many times repeated. The Earl of Cumberland, whose suit of armour (which, like some of Lee's, survives) is shown in Hilliard's miniature (pl. 14), was no less resplendent and fantastic a Champion. These holders of a mediaeval office properly appeared in mediaeval fancy dress in order to take part in mock encounters founded on mediaeval warfare. Oberon and Puck, Ariel and Pigwiggen are creatures who have been uncovered from mediaeval fogs by the shining imagination of Renaissance poets: not survivors, rescued and stared at, but treasure-trove new-minted to gaiety.

They could not take the Middle Ages seriously. They lumped those several centuries together; saw no difference between, say, Early English and Perpendicular; cared very little for the splendours of stained glass or sculpture or wall-painting — were not these full of saints and Popish idolatry? — preserved St George as the patron of England, though Edward VI had abolished him; attributed the Tower of London to Julius Caesar. And when they were forced to acknowledge an achievement such as Chaucer's they were patronizingly surprised that one living in that misty time (at the court of Richard II!) could see so clearly. Neither was this condescending ignorance due entirely to religious prejudice, nor even, though this was more important, to their preoccupation with what was new. But the Middle Ages seemed to them disorderly and chaotic and irrational, given over to mysticism and superstition, and were unenlightened by the rediscovery of Greek learning and the new understanding of the Roman world which had accompanied it. 'In those days', the Queen herself said, 'force and arms did prevail; but now the wit of the fox is everywhere on foot.' She and her subjects preferred wit to force, and were more willing to concede victory to intelligent argument than to dogma. And because they could not respect the Middle Ages, the architecture, the stories, even at times the chivalry provided them with a playground, a means towards not taking themselves seriously either, a source of fun. They liked to relax, to imagine that for an hour or two they might 'live like the old Robin Hood of England . . . and fleet the time carelessly as they did in the golden world'. Oberon could not have been a Greek god,[1] nor Falstaff a Roman soldier, yet Spenser could without offence use Pan to represent both Henry VIII and Christ. Those ancient civilizations were too rational and orderly to be treated with levity. In Sidney's eyes the *Aethiopica* of Heliodorus was 'an absolute heroical poem', but *Amadis de Gaule* 'wanteth much of a perfect poesy'. He must apologize for his own barbarousness in being moved by the ballad of *Percy and Douglas* 'evil apparelled in the dust and cobwebs of that uncivil age', — a mediaeval poem which no cultivated gentleman of the Renaissance could enjoy unashamed. But the courtiers vied with one another in acknowledging unattested debts to Homer and Virgil, Pindar and Horace, and ambitious young gentlemen made a habit of dedicating to privy councillors their youthful translations from the classics. Most famous of these was Sir Thomas North's version of Plutarch's *Lives of the Noble Grecians and Romans*, a book which more influenced men's conduct in sixteenth-century Europe than any other except, perhaps, Castiglione's *Courtier*. Plutarch's *Lives* replaced the *Lives of the Saints*. Similarly, Bess of Hardwick cut the saints' heads out of the copes from Lilleshall Abbey which she acquired for hangings at Chatsworth, replaced them with classical heads, and, to prevent any confusion, identified them by their names embroidered above. It was less important that these noble Greeks and Romans had all been pagans than that

[1] Actually, he was the son of Julius Caesar by the grandmother of Alexander the Great.

they had all been men of action. By reading Plutarch the Queen's subjects would be animated to the better service of her Majesty, as North suggested ; there is no reason to think he was merely puffing his own work, for no one would have disputed this. Besides, men were more likely to try to emulate a historical hero than a legendary or fictitious one : what men had once achieved they might achieve again.

This ambition to rival the Greeks and Romans inspired the Renaissance courtier and the Renaissance artist alike. And just as the courtiers studied Plutarch, the artists studied other ancient authority, Plato and Aristotle, Cicero and Vitruvius and whoever else had discussed the arts in Greece or Rome. Their passion for rationality had made them erect into rigid rules that must be obeyed observations which the ancient authors had never so intended. The three unities which bedevilled dramatic writing (but in France and Italy rather than in England) were unfairly fathered on Aristotle. 'Vitruvian man', developed from a casual aside in a work on architecture, became 'the foundation of a whole philosophy' and for a time prevented painters and sculptors from truly observing the human body. John Shute followed precedent in relating the proportions of classical pillars to the human form. Theories such as these had a specious look of reasonableness, which, above all else, was being sought.

Man was the measure of all things, for God had created man in his own image, and endowed him with the power of reason whereby to understand the divine order of creation. 'The world,' says Thomas Campion, who was doctor, poet, and musician, 'the world is made by symmetry and proportion, and is in that respect compared to music, and music to poetry.' Sir Henry Wotton, who was diplomat, poet, and connoisseur, extends the comparison (on the authority of L. B. Alberti) to architecture, by transporting the proportions of fifth and octave from audible to visible objects, confident that 'there will indubitably result from either a graceful and harmonious contentment to the eye'. Others would have further extended the comparison to painting and sculpture; indeed to all human experience. For a reasonable world must also be a unified world, and (to quote Sir Henry again) 'All art was then in truest perfection, when it might be reduced to some natural principle', that is, to a rational principle, for it was the nature of man to be reasonable. Pope's advice,

> First follow Nature, and your judgment frame
> By her just standard which is still the same,

would have been acceptable to Wotton and Campion and their contemporaries, as to the Augustans, since by Nature they all intended rational Human Nature, not the Romantic chaos of rocks, and stones, and trees. Such things were not for aesthetic contemplation in the raw, but for use: man could build houses out of them, or carve them into statues, and contemplate these. A perfect garden should be so designed that 'you may have in small compass a model of universal nature made private'. So the voyagers to the New World do not pause to admire the scenery, they find out what trees provide good timber, what rocks are loaded with valuable ore, confident that all has been designed by God for the use of man, if once he can discover what that use may be. Even geography must be rational: hence the indefatigable search for the North-West Passage which, in a world as reasonably ordered as they supposed, would not have been choked with ice. That it was so was indecent, improper, unbeseeming — how difficult it is to find a word that they would have used and which we can understand simply, as they understood it! They did not expect the laws of reason to fail them anywhere: divine order was universal. And if it seemed, sometimes, to be abrogated, this was due to human incompetence, not to divine negligence. If they could not find the North-West Passage this was not because there was none to find, it was because their navigating instruments were at fault perhaps, or

Montacute House, Somerset, Garden Architecture, *c.* 1600 (see p. 43)

3

The Gibbon Salt, 1576, a statue of Neptune enclosed within rock crystal pillar in centre (see p. 35)

because they had failed to see it in the fog. Not only did they know it must exist, they knew also that it must be potentially useful to man: 'there is no land unhabitable, nor sea innavigable'.

This confidence that inspired the courage of the discoverers also inspired the artists. For in a reasonable world, made by symmetry and proportion, the designs and compositions of painter and architect, poet and musician, must also be in keeping. The principle of decorum is that by which the critic judges, and it is therefore concerned especially with context. A fountain must spill water from the mouth of bird or dolphin, not from its tail. A vessel to hold salt may properly be supported by a figure of Neptune, which may as properly be enclosed in a column of rock crystal, to suggest that he is under water and offering its product to man's use above the salt sea waves (pl. 3). A musician must dispose his music according to the words of the poem which he is setting: 'You must therefore, if you have a grave matter, apply a grave kind of music to it; if a merry subject you must make your music also merry.' Chaucer keeps decorum in the *Miller's Tale* because the Miller is the sort of rough character who always does talk bawdy. The entrance to a house must respect both the proportions of the building and the dignity of its builder. A monument in a church must likewise reveal the rank of the man whose grave it covers, and defer to its sacred setting. Wherever possible, works of art should instruct as well as delight (though the artist must remember that only by delighting will he be able to instruct), they should, that is to say, be useful as well as reasonable. This a monument may be by reminding the beholder that he is mortal and ought to be pious; a painting may convey a moral by emblem or allegory; and the greatest poems will instruct by forming the mind to heroic virtue by example. Yet it is a sign of the emancipation of art from morality at this time that so much that was not didactic was produced. A sonnet cannot be of much use, unless (as Sidney gaily suggests) as an aid to seduction ; a madrigal still less. Even for Milton, in whom didacticism reached its zenith of power, the grand masterpiece to observe was still decorum, which is an aesthetic, not a moral principle.

There is no reason to suppose that Milton did not mean what he said. The objections which he and others raised to the dramatists' 'error of intermixing Comic stuff with Tragic sadness and gravity' were based upon this same principle, and on the lack of classical precedent for such a mixture. Elizabethan confidence had borne such objections aside in the vigorous rush of creativity, but even for them decorum was the surest guide to imitation of the ancients. The Greek and Latin poets had set a standard of perfection which the Middle Ages had lost, had 'uncivilized' (as they said), and which it was their task to recover. The study of rhetoric was a method of cataloguing the means used by the ancient writers for obtaining particular effects : the reader of Virgil or Cicero observed that this or that passage moved or persuaded him, paused to enquire how it had done so, and tabulated his answers under a series of learned terms. It was a way to attentive reading and therefore to good writing. But rhetoric was concerned with the parts, decorum with the whole. The differences may be fitly illustrated from the first work of the New Poetry, *The Shepheardes Calender*. In his glosses on the poem E. K. is constantly drawing the reader's attention to successful use of the rhetorical figures : 'a pretty Epanorthosis', 'a very poetical πάθος', 'an Ironical Sarcasmus' and so forth. In the prefatory letter he praises the unnamed New Poet for 'his due observing of decorum everywhere, in personages, in seasons, in matter, in speech, and generally in all seemly simplicity of handling his matter, and framing his words'.

Decorum was the principle by which the rational order of the world was represented in works of art of whatever kind, and which therefore governed the aesthetic judgment by which men appreciated them. Since the world was founded on reason, perfection was attainable, and had once been attained in the arts of Greece and Rome, which were therefore to be imitated. For 'always a man by sundry ways may climb to the top of all perfection'. Men of the sixteenth and seventeenth centuries were not so shy of using the word 'perfect' to describe human achievements as we have since become : but then we no longer believe that the world is made by symmetry and proportion. These are perfectible, as asymmetry and disproportion are not, and it would not offend or surprise us if some object (preferably mechanical) were described as 'perfectly symmetrical'. We restrict our belief in perfectibility, because we no longer believe in an all-pervasive reasonableness : for us, some seas are innavigable ; and chaos is come again.

But for the Elizabethans perfection was within man's reach : he was noble in reason, and infinite in faculty. It is beside the point to say that Hamlet's encomium is in the purest mediaeval tradition, and to find precedent in a fourth-century Syrian bishop, just as it is beside the point to discover that the Prince of Denmark was a Swedish king mentioned in *Beowulf.* Shakespeare and 'the wiser sort', to whom the play especially appealed, were not very likely to be thinking either of King Onela or of Bishop Nemesius : there is consequently not much reason why we should. What they were more likely to have in mind was a recollection of Castiglione's *Courtier*, of Plutarch's *Lives*, of Spenser's Sir Calidore, of Sir Philip Sidney, or of the Earl of Essex ; of that ideal man of the Renaissance, universally accomplished, and with a grace to conceal the severity of discipline he had undergone,

> The expectancy and rose of the fair state,
> The glass of fashion, and the mould of form,
> The observed of all observers.

This was, or they thought it was, something new, and yet something modelled on an idealized classical past. Periclean

Athens and Augustan Rome were very different, doubtless, from Elizabethan England ; very different, again, from what Elizabethan Englishmen imagined they were like. But men are moved less by history than by myth, less by what impeccable scholarship can prove than by what uncritical enthusiasm believes. Reprehensible this may be, but here is the source of Elizabethan art ; for nature's world is brazen, the poets only deliver a golden.

II

ARCHITECTURE

II. ARCHITECTURE

THE Elizabethans built houses, not castles or churches: their architecture was civilized, and secular. Appropriately, the most celebrated builder of the age was a woman, Bess of Hardwick, for now first a feminine concern with hospitality and comfort replaced in the design of the greater houses a masculine assertion of power and independence. The rooms where the owner entertained his friends were no longer forced to huddle under a curtain wall lest they should interfere with a field of fire or impede the urgencies of defence: they became the main rooms of the house. The hall of the mediaeval manor had served various purposes which in the sixteenth century were distributed through a series of rooms, but the way of life in an Elizabethan country house succeeded to the life of the manor rather than of the castle, just as new men from the lesser gentry often succeeded to the seats left vacant by mediaeval barons. They had also taken the place of the dispossessed abbots and priors, and the conversion of monasteries into country houses immediately followed the conversion of monastic lands into gentlemen's estates. Indeed this process, rather than the civilization of military fortresses, led to the erection of most of the great sixteenth-century houses which remain. When we think of these houses we think first of Longleat and Lacock, of Burghley and Montacute, of Welbeck and Buckland and Newstead, not of Kenilworth and Ludlow, Rockingham, Raglan, or Wardour.

This may be in part because, in the conversion of a castle, the Elizabethan owner would preserve more of the mediaeval structure than in the conversion of an abbey; for the church walls, often lately broken for their immense Perpendicular windows, were more easily destroyed than were the solid walls of keep and bastion, and it was only rarely that the new owner inserted floors and built rooms in the church itself, as did Sir Richard Grenville at Buckland. Also, these defensible mediaeval remnants were more likely to invite the suspicion, if not the hostility, of the Parliamentary forces a generation or two later, so that the slighted castles are ruinous now, but the abbey houses still stand inhabited or at least habitable. Of these also some suffered in the Civil War : Reading Abbey, which Henry VIII had converted into a palace, was destroyed in the construction of defences against the Parliamentarians ; Lilleshall Abbey in Shropshire was garrisoned and reduced to ruin ; the Grey Friars at Gloucester was damaged by Royalist gunfire when Sir William Massey made it the Governor's quarters. But captured castles must be made permanently indefensible by mines, whereas the abbey houses, once captured, could be allowed to stand. Consequently, in the converted castles the strong mediaeval walls remain but the flimsier furnishings of Renaissance rooms have vanished, and only an oriel or a pillared doorway, a classical frieze or a fire-place flanked by grotesque caryatids, still suggest that once the place was lived in by men and women who need not constantly be alert to civil war. The structure and plan remain mediaeval, so that when we visit these places we think of them first as castles, not as houses ; as buildings defensible against enemies rather than welcoming to friends. In the houses built on monastic sites conversion was easier and therefore normally more drastic ; the mediaeval origins are no longer dominant as in the castles.

Many of the old castles were occupied until the Civil War, though extensive conversions were carried out at only a few. They might provide excellent background for an entertainment to the Queen on progress, as at Kenilworth, but they were obsolete and, to an Elizabethan eye, barbaric as much in their lack of symmetry as in their perpetual reminder of war. For the mediaeval castle was functional in design, the site chosen for its defensive possibilities, the towers placed to give the best field of fire against attackers. Only very late in their history, and in special circumstances, would the builder of a castle be prepared, as at Bodiam or Herstmonceux, to risk defence for the sake of symmetry. Even here the domestic parts of the castle faced inward on to a courtyard, and conformed to the overriding needs of defence. If the space between two bastions cramped the hall more than was desirable, cramped the hall must be : the placing of the bastions was determined by necessity. The outer walls of the castle were narrowly pierced for the projection of missiles, not for the contemplation of a view, and were topped by a walk for sentinels, not by a balustrade formed of the letters of a pious quotation or of the initials of the builder. Turrets there might be, to shelter a watching soldier against the rigours of the weather : on an Elizabethan roof these would become airy banqueting houses where on a summer evening a lady and gentleman might remove to take their banquet (that is, their dessert) privately together while they enjoyed the prospect over the park. A moat, once devised to prevent the stealthy approach of men in armour, might now provide the means of staging a delightful water-pageant where classical nymphs and tritons would disport themselves before the visiting Queen and her courtiers. William Lawson in *A New Orchard and Garden* advised the digging of a moat about the house : it 'will afford you fish, fence and moisture to your trees, and pleasure also, if they be so great and deep you may have swans and other water-birds, good for devouring of vermin, and a boat for many good uses'. Thus even the very pattern of mediaeval fortification might be converted to the adornment of a garden, or as at Montacute, where 'the gatehouse has become a gateway, the curtain walls open balustrading, the bastions toy temples, the corner towers bower-like pavilions' (pl. 2), and all in the elaborate symmetry which delighted the Elizabethan eye but which was unthought of by the builder of an early castle. All here, as is very suitable to a garden, is turned to favour and to prettiness, and wall and temple and pavilion are related to the more imposing symmetry of the house whose great windows allow a view down over this charming pattern. To such civilized frivolity did the Elizabethan architect convert the grim military necessities of his ancestors.

Often the old castles, damaged perhaps in the Wars of the Roses, would be allowed to fall down. Richmond Castle had begun to fall by 1538. Castle Ashby had fallen, or perhaps had been demolished, when Leland was there about the same time. Sudeley Castle he says, 'goeth to ruin, more pity', but was soon to be restored by Thomas Seymour to whom it was granted by King Edward. Warwick Castle was in decay until it was granted by King James to Fulke Greville. Peak Castle was ruinous and was never restored. The owner might or might not wish to build a new house on the same site: Richmond was abandoned; at Castle Ashby the new house was begun by 1574, at Moreton Corbet five years later. There and elsewhere the old buildings could be retained so long as they did not interfere with the gay and elegant ease of social life. If for some reason the owner decided to build his new house on the old site, he might prefer that it should turn its back on the ruined castle. When Sir Andrew Corbet built his sumptuous classical range to the south of the thirteenth-century keep at Moreton Corbet (pl. 4), he altered the gate-house, which was still of use, so that it might conform a little; but the keep itself he left unaltered, either because it was too refractory to the new classicism, or because its contrasting uncouthness amused him. He was not put to the expense, which an eighteenth-century gentleman would readily incur, of building a Gothick folly, but he probably regarded the old keep in much the same way. That very unsentimental man Francis Bacon could confess to a romantic feeling for the antique: 'it is a reverend thing to see an ancient castle or building not in decay'.

Not far away from Sir Andrew Corbet, and a year or two later, his friend Sir Henry Sidney faced the more formidable problem of civilizing Ludlow Castle, where he found that he could do no more than fit a Renaissance house into a corner of the great fortress. He lacked the wealth of his brother-in-law, the Earl of Leicester, who had been modernizing Kenilworth Castle a few years before, or of the Earl of Worcester, whose new building and conversions about the Pitched Stone Court at Raglan Castle still give a vivid impression of what could be done. Here Lord Worcester provided himself with a grand Elizabethan mansion, complete with its Long Gallery (one hundred and twenty-six feet long), 'having many fair windows, but most pleasant was the window at the furthermost end', a great bow window made as if in an ancient bastion, with stone mullions and transoms framing a view of the mountains of Breconshire. 'That part of the castle, standing out like a tower, being about sixty feet high, was most pleasant for aspect.' On the north side was a broad fire-place, where, in the stone surround, two standing figures remain high in the wall from which floor and ceiling have long since gone. Lord Worcester raised the height of his hall, gave it a lofty oriel to light the dais, and a porch of three storeys at the entrance from the court. It had 'a rare geometrical roof built of Irish oak, with a large cupola on the top for light', which 'remained whole above twenty years after the siege' of 1646. The treatment is conservative, with such details as cusped window-heads ; as if Lord Worcester had chosen to make his new building respect the ancient architecture which was its context. But he had not hesitated to throw down the old north wall of the castle in order to accommodate the offices and kitchens of his new house, and such drastic rejection of the old was much more common, in this self-confident age, than any hint of respect. At Oxford, a generation later, John Chamberlain noticed a similar consideration of the architectural context in Sir Thomas Bodley's addition to the library, which he found 'suitable on the outside to the Divinity schools'. But the assertive frontispiece of the five orders in the Schools Quadrangle was much more characteristic.

Lord Worcester's son, who succeeded him as fourth Earl in 1589, continued to beautify Raglan Castle. Probably he built the brick gazebos outside the old walls, and converted the walk about the moat which surrounds the Keep to the fashionable classicism : 'a pleasant walk set forth with several figures of the Roman Emperors in arches of divers varieties of shell works'. These arches are niches with rounded tops, made of brick ; they were lined with cockle-shells arranged in geometrical patterns in the plaster that covered the brick. Here again, as at Moreton Corbet, the contrast of styles must have been most inspiriting. As Lord Worcester and his guests walked by the moat, on the one hand they would see towering above them powerful fifteenth-century fortifications, built to withstand siege and assault ; on the other, statues of heroes of an age on which they sought to base their lives, standing beside the walk in their classical niches : others than Shakespeare could find inspiration both in the history of Henry V and in Plutarch's *Lives*. The statues are all now gone ; the shell-work in the niches is battered into triviality ; and the mighty tower, wrecked though it may be, has the site to itself.

In the fifteenth century the castle was built by Sir William ap Thomas and his descendants, Welsh soldiers who took the name of Herbert and fought with distinction, though not always with success, in the Wars of the Roses. Their brave acts and their women's beauty several Welsh poets of the time celebrated, Dafydd Llwyd, Lewis Glyn Cothi, and Guto'r Glyn among them. Their successor at Raglan in Queen Elizabeth's time, the fourth Earl of Worcester, in spite of being (as the Queen said) 'a stiff Papist' was her Master of the Horse ; and he showed his taste not only in the improvements which he made at Raglan, but also in his patronage of William Byrd, who had rooms in the Earl's London house, and of Edmund Spenser, who wrote the *Prothalamion* for the betrothal of his two daughters. The Earl of Worcester's men, who included Edward Alleyn, showed the family's interest also in the theatre. Thus with means to command the best in architecture, in music, and in poetry, succeeding generations at Raglan had the wit to discover it.

Of all the ancient castles converted by their Elizabethan owners for the luxurious and civilized pleasures which they enjoyed, the most famous is surely Kenilworth. This the Queen granted to Lord Robert Dudley in 1563, the year before she created him Earl of Leicester, and there she first visited him in 1565. Leicester had not yet begun the extensive alterations which she was to see when in 1575 she spent seventeen days there as his guest, but he had the familiar example of his father's conversion of Dudley Castle to inspire him, with its Italianate work of the Ionic order, with its elegant doors and windows. John Shute, whom the Duke sent to Italy in 1550 'to confer with the doings of the skilful masters in architecture, and also to view such ancient monuments hereof as are yet extant' may have influenced these. Kenilworth Castle had indeed been granted to the Duke of Northumberland a few months before his execution in 1553, and he had intended to continue the conversion begun forty years earlier by Henry VIII. The King had erected a new wing on the east side of the inner court, a timber-framed building, of which nothing now remains; but the extension of this range towards the south, built in stone in the 1570s, still stands to a considerable height. The walls are pierced with tall windows of which mullions and transoms survive, and the whole projects beyond the original curtain wall of the castle, in that deliberate disregard of old fortifications which Sir Henry Sidney's work at Ludlow and Lord Worcester's at Raglan reveal. Robert Laneham, who saw it when it was new in 1575, was carried away by its rare beauty, 'all of the hard quarry stone; every room so spacious, so well belighted, and so high roofed within;

so seemly to sight by due proportion without ; a-day time, on every side so glittering by glass ; a-nights, by continual brightness of candle, fire, and torch-light, transparent through the lightsome windows, as it were the Egyptian Pharos relucent unto all the Alexandrian coast'. Of the ancient buildings he remarks only the strong and large Keep, 'that is called Caesar's Tower, rather . . . for that it is square and high formed after the manner of Caesar's forts than that ever he built it'. There is no doubt of his preference for what was new. Leicester also built the gatehouse, (which is still inhabited,) to the north-east of the castle, a rectangular building where the four corner towers imply some wish to conform to the older manner : a Renaissance version of the Keep. Within the castle Leicester even attempted the difficult task of modernizing the Keep itself. He pierced the fifteen-foot thick walls to insert large windows with mullions and transoms ; excavated the solid base of the south-western tower in order to provide rooms there ; and reconstructed the fore-building on this side to give a view over the new pleasure gardens which he laid out. The arches of this building are thought to have enclosed a small open court, which would have completed the architectural transition between mediaeval Keep and formal Renaissance garden. Of this Laneham gives another enthusiastic description, too long to quote here. There was a terrace along the castle wall, formal paths and arbours, 'obelisks, spheres, and white bears all of stone' : the white bears of Leicester's heraldry. Especially was he delighted, perhaps because he was a musician, by the aviary on the north side of this garden, with its holly trees for perching and preening, its nesting holes, its windows covered with wire mesh, and its collection of birds from as far afield as Canary and Africa with their gay plumage, 'delightsome in change of tunes, and harmony to the ear'. In the outer court Leicester built a platform of stone and rubble to provide a view over the Mere, which formerly protected the castle to south and west, and on which some of the shows for the Queen's entertainment were produced. He had built a long wooden bridge across the north end of the mere, with rails on either side, to give access to the Chase where the Queen went hunting : Laneham says it was fourteen feet wide and six hundred feet long. When the Queen arrived within the castle she was greeted with Arthurian compliment suited to a Welsh Princess by the Lady of the Lake who, with two attendant nymphs, floated ashore upon an artificial island, 'being so conveyed that it seemed she had gone upon the water'. Leicester, like other courtiers, thought of his house as a place fit for the Queen to visit, and devised pageants to show her as Arthur's heir, the Princess destined to revive the legendary glories of England. The great castle which she had given him, where Roger Mortimer had once presided over a tournament at which King Arthur and his Knights of the Round Table had been honoured, where King Henry V had built his Pleasaunce en Mareys beside the Mere, was best suited of any site in her realm for these lavish and romantic Princely Pleasures. Leicester, of all her subjects, was least likely to miss the opportunity of dramatizing his Queen on such a stage.

He was not alone in thinking of his house as a place where he might entertain the Queen, or in sparing no expense for this purpose. For her, Lord Burghley wrote to Sir Christopher Hatton, 'we both meant to exceed our purses in these' their houses of Theobalds and Holdenby. And he wrote also of the 'consecration' of Holdenby to her Majesty, an extravagance of phrase echoed by Hatton himself when, in a letter to Sir Thomas Heneage about a visit to another of his houses, Kirby Hall, he confessed that he was leaving his 'other shrine, I mean Holdenby, still unseen until that holy saint may sit in it, to whom it is dedicated'. So they thought of the Queen, in terms of worship which repel us by an almost blasphemous adulation ; they would even leave their houses unvisited, uncontaminated by their own gaze, until the Virgin Queen could be installed there, as a holy saint in a dedicated shrine. So we see her in the famous picture being carried to Blackfriars like the Virgin Mary in a religious procession: a comparison which her subjects did not hesitate to draw. She was, besides, the fair vestal whom her poets proclaimed, and if we can accept Shakespeare's or Spenser's words without cavil, we must also accept Hatton's. For to all of them this poetic vision of the court of Gloriana, of the Fairy Queen, was genuine. Burghley and Hatton and Leicester and Spenser all knew, at first hand, the hard, practical, dominating woman who was their Queen. But she was their Queen, and Queen of England. Or, as she put it herself with characteristic vigour, 'I know I have the body of a weak, feeble woman, but I have the heart and stomach of a King — and of a King of England too.'

Her subjects did not have to make a dishonest compromise with their understanding in order to worship her as they did. They did not talk of her as 'a symbolic personage' nor make a conscious imaginative effort towards poetic description of her political significance. These things were secondary. Their minds were accustomed to allegory, and Mr. Forster's scathing comment on the 'public virgin' reveals a lack of comprehension which is almost total: for where he is attempting wit, her subjects would have discovered only a platitude. She and Burghley and Hatton knew very exactly what political advantages and disadvantages were involved in her remaining unmarried, with no acknowledged heir; but they also and simultaneously understood that her virginity had almost religious implications. The worship of the Virgin Mary had been especially popular in England in the fifteenth century, and the transference of this devotion to a Virgin Queen was a natural response to the Reformation. It happened also to be politically convenient. The Perpendicular Lady Chapels which their grandfathers had built on to the east end of English churches were now replaced by these secular shrines for their devotion to the Queen. The Queen's grandfather had begun, the Queen's father had completed, the most magnificent of all these chapels, at Westminster Abbey. When, in due time, her body was laid to rest there an engraving was published with this inscription : 'This Maiden Queen Elizabeth came into this world the Eve of the Nativity of the blessed Virgin Mary ; and died on the Eve of the Annunciation of the Virgin Mary.'[1] To an Elizabethan such things were not fortuitous, not by chance. But now, while she was living among them, her principal courtiers would consecrate to the Virgin Queen the noblest houses yet built in England.

These houses are not acceptable to modern taste : we should not expect them to be so, since we do not share the Elizabethan adulation of the Queen for whom they were built. Of them all Wollaton Hall (pl. 6) has been the most severely criticized, for its ostentatious vulgarity, for its mixture of styles — Gothic and Renaissance, Flemish and Italian — for its sheer arrogance. It is a coal magnate's assertion of his right, as Sheriff of Nottinghamshire, to entertain the Queen, and suggests similar châteaux of the *nouveaux riches* Victorians. Now all this is plausible, for Sir Francis Willoughby was a coal magnate, with, so far as we know, much less interest in poetry and music and the other arts than Leicester or Worcester, Sidney or Hatton.[2] He was not a member of the cultivated Court circle ; he was a rich provincial. But we must look beneath the surface if we are to appreciate his fantastic palace.

In the church at Wollaton is a monument to the memory of Robert Smythson 'architector and surveyor unto the most worthy house of Wollaton with divers others of great account'. Thus, most exceptionally, we know the name of the architect

[1] Cf. Thomas Dekker : *The Wonderful Year*, 1603. 'She came in with the fall of the leaf, and went away in the Spring : her life (which was dedicated to Virginity) both beginning and closing up a miraculous maiden circle ; for she was born upon a Lady Eve, and died upon a Lady Eve'.

[2] But the Earl of Worcester's men performed at Wollaton on 31st December 1572 and again in January 1574, at Sir Francis Willoughby's (earlier) house ; and he often employed musicians to sing and play there. He commissioned George Gower to paint portraits of himself and of Lady Willoughby.

who designed this house for Sir Francis Willoughby. We also know that he had previously worked at Longleat, a house of which the classical symmetry and elegant ornament are as universally praised as Wollaton is condemned. Willoughby probably heard of him from Sir Matthew Arundell, his brother-in-law, who seems to have employed Smythson in civilizing Wardour Castle. Wollaton, begun in 1580 and finished in 1588, is then a work of the maturity of one of the greatest of English architects, who seems later to have worked at Hardwick Hall and Worksop Manor, which again were not extravaganzas. If Wollaton seems to be such, then it was so intended. It is not designed as another Longleat, but both in plan and in detail is exuberant and romantic — in the old sense of being the sort of thing one would expect to find in a romance. It owes more to the tradition of chivalry and the tournament than to the rediscovered dignity of Rome ; and the huge central block containing the hall (a room fifty feet high) with the Prospect Chamber over, soars above the surrounding walls of the house as a mediaeval keep soars above the curtain walls and bastions. To site such buildings on top of a rise in order to give them a prospect over the countryside, had now become both easier, because of improved means of raising water from the valleys, and desirable, because the landscape could now be enjoyed, instead of being anxiously scanned for enemies. The suggestion of Gothic tracery, of a Venetian kind, in the uppermost windows of the central block is a piece of archaism such as Spenser affected in order to give a sense of mediaeval chivalry to his Renaissance poem. As at Montacute the plan of a mediaeval castle was to be converted to the decoration of a garden, here at Wollaton a mediaeval castle is interpreted in terms of Elizabethan chivalry, for the entertainment of the Queen. It is the sort of house which Bacon sourly observes should be left to the poets 'who build them with small cost'. But Sir Francis Willoughby wished to make an extravagant gesture, the more extravagant the better, of his devotion to the Queen. (The cloak which Sir Walter Ralegh laid on the muddy earth for her to step on may have been fictitious ; it was not a cheap reach-me-down.) To this end Sir Francis invited the greatest architect of his time to build a gorgeous palace in stone. He set it high on the top of a hill, and his purpose was display : a mediaeval castle with keep and curtain walls, with towers at the outer four corners, with round turrets at the corners of the 'keep', but all made light with a multitude of high windows, and richly ornamented with exquisite carving ; the corner towers topped with pierced gables adorned with strap-work, and balancing statues on their tops, with obelisks at the angles, and decorated with busts of gods and heroes in roundels framed by elaborate cartouches. The whole effect is theatrical, as of a castle whose artillery would fire scented water, and whose besiegers would assault its glittering walls with flowers and such fancies.

To appreciate Wollaton therefore it is necessary to forget Longleat with its classical dignity, and to think rather of the tournament with its sham mediaevalism — no Elizabethan ever supposed it was not sham — with its colour and fantasy, its ceremonious worship of the Queen, its gallantry and courtesy and pride. Wollaton, even if it derives from Serlio's version of the Poggio Reale at Naples, with decoration suggested by de Vries, and with some hints taken from Venice, is not a serious building, any more than Inigo Jones's stage sets for his masques, in which Palladio's Teatro Olimpico at Vicenza jostles with drawings by travellers to the Indies, were serious architecture. It was then permissible to be gay and frivolous. So Wollaton is a stately palace

> Of pompous show . . .
> With many towres, and tarras mounted hye,

built, this once, not of wood and painted canvas, to be thrown aside after a Queen's holiday, but in the more lasting splendour of brittle glass and of stone carved to seeming fragility ; a palace fit for Gloriana, worthy to welcome the Fairy Queen.

The monumental gaiety of Wollaton survives (even though it is inhabited now by stuffed animals), but of other houses built to entertain the Queen, Theobalds and Holdenby were destroyed in the next century. These two, the most sumptuous private houses in England, must have been much alike. In a letter to Burghley of 9th August 1579 Hatton invites his criticism of Holdenby: 'for as the same is done hitherto in direct observation of your house and plots of Theobalds, so I earnestly pray your Lordship that by your good corrections at this time, it may appear as like to the same as it hath ever been meant to be'. Hatton's other mansion, Kirby Hall, which was modernized by Inigo Jones in the seventeenth century, was fast going to ruin and decay by the beginning of the nineteenth. It is a long, low house of unusual elegance, built about a large courtyard, with twin bays carried the full three storeys, to gather, with exceptional daring, the suspect southern airs and sun. The ruins of Kirby Hall,[1] cared for now with scholarly understanding, alone remain to illustrate Lord Chancellor Hatton's delight in the new architecture; but Burghley House and Longleat still stand in the possession of the families that built them.

Both houses were long in building, and their history reveals much of the development of architectural taste. Both were on monastic sites, though nothing of the mediaeval buildings remains. At Longleat Sir John Thynne bought the derelict buildings of a long-decayed Canonry in 1541, and a few years later began to convert them into a dwelling-house in preparation for his marriage, which took place in January 1548. He had already been concerned in the building of Somerset House in the Strand, in which certain Renaissance features such as pilastered windows were for the first time seen in England.

[1] Sir John Summerson has shown that the ornament on Kirby Hall derives from Serlio, from Hans Blum's *Quinque Columnarum exacta descriptio atque delineatio* (Zürich, 1550), and from the title-page of John Shute's *Chief Grounds of Architecture*, 1563: the eclecticism is as English as the result.

But at Longleat he, like Sir William Sharington at the not far distant Lacock, began by making use of the conventual buildings. He was in a hurry to get his house ready, and was constantly urging his agent, Dodd, to hasten the work. Dodd seems to have shared his employer's modern tastes, for when the building was almost finished he warned Sir John that 'the chapel window which you appointed to stand will do very ill and much disfigure your building', presumably by the contrast between the barbarous Gothic arch and the fenestration of the new work. Of this building nothing now survives, and chapel and cloister, which were retained in 1547, were soon swept away.

When Protector Somerset, in whose service Thynne had first made his name, fell from power in October 1549 both Thynne and Sharington were arrested and imprisoned. No doubt they had already conversed about their master passion for building, and certainly they did so after their release. Sharington seems then to have supervised the work at Dudley Castle for the Duke of Northumberland, whose interest in the new classical style of architecture had prompted him to send John Shute to Italy. Thynne himself had been described as 'an ingenious man and a traveller' before his introduction at Court. We may assume that he had visited France, and perhaps Italy, and had studied the new buildings there : in general the models of his buildings are French rather than Italian.

During the 1550s Thynne began rebuilding Longleat, and probably the last of the old monastic buildings were destroyed at this time. His new house was burnt in 1567, but work was resumed at once, and though Longleat still retains many of the features of the house that was damaged its general character is very different. Certainly the hall was of the same size, and similarly raised above ground level (a feature which Sir Henry Wotton admired in Italian houses), but the old house had battlemented towers and a long array of gables. In the first rebuilding after the fire Longleat still had gables and domed turrets, and the delightful fancy of constructing 'banqueting-houses' on the roof in the domed pavilions at the tops of four of the turreted staircases was proposed as early as 1569. In 1572 the classical façades which we see today were at last erected, with Doric and Ionic orders in the pilasters of the great bays, with lion masks on the pedestals of the Ionic order, and with roundels containing Roman busts between them. These details are evidence of classical taste as it was then accepted. So too are the acanthus leaves on the corbels, and the Corinthian columns in the timbers of the hammer-beam roof of the hall, and the chimneys designed as Doric columns. The third storey, with its Corinthian pilasters in the bays, if a little later than the rest, continues the same classical design which the original builder had established. So, after a period of nearly thirty years, this house which, like Lacock, began as a conversion of a mediaeval monastery with classical ornament tentatively applied here and there, now declared to all who visited it a restrained and confident classicism of design. To Camden it was 'a very fair, neat, and elegant house', epithets which we would not dispute. It looks outward to every side, proclaiming that here is no compromise with mediaeval obscurity and barbarism, but full acceptance and understanding of the new classical taste that had at last reached England.

Many of Thynne's contemporaries were interested in his work. Even from the beginning some were pleased, and some, we are told, were grieved, as must always happen when new things are attempted. Those who mattered were pleased. The Queen, for whom Sir John had acted as Comptroller many years before, was for ever eager to see Longleat, but its owner properly made excuses until it was ready for her reception in 1574. Lord Burghley was sent plans of the house, which are still preserved at Hatfield. Sir William Cavendish wrote to ask for the loan of a plasterer to work at Chatsworth. Edmund Plowden asked for Sir John's head carpenter to work on the roof of the hall of the Middle Temple ; he wrote on the Queen's behalf, and could not be refused. Robert Smythson, who came to work at Longleat after the fire, when he was still quite young, carried much of what he learnt there to the other great houses on which he worked, including Wollaton.

At the outset of his career William Cecil, like Sharington and Thynne and Sir Thomas Smith, the builder of Hill Hall in Essex, had been in the service of Protector Somerset ; and though, so far as is known, he was not personally concerned with the building of Somerset House, as was Thynne, he was observant and intelligent enough to learn of the new architecture there. He continued to take a learned interest in building, sending to Smith, who was English Ambassador in Paris, for a copy of Philibert de l'Orme's *Nouvelles Inventions pour bien bastir* ; making use of du Cerceau's *Livre d'Architecture* ; corresponding with other ambitious builders such as Thynne and Hatton. He ordered chimney-pieces to be shipped whole from Antwerp, and he sent there for skilled craftsmen. He visited his friends' new houses to learn what he could from them. He seems to have supervised the design of his house, as did Sharington and Thynne and Smith, but as the less learned Sir Francis Willoughby probably did not. The result of his interest, as we see it at Burghley House (for his other buildings have gone) may well seem to a modern critic unsatisfactory, since the mixture of French classicism and Flemish ornament cannot disguise a remnant of the mediaeval hankering after soaring vertical lines. Theobalds was more in the latest fashion, and was much larger, than Burghley House ; but it was built in a few years, whereas Burghley House was long a-building.

The property at Stamford Baron had been acquired by Richard Cecil at the time of the Dissolution of the Monasteries, for this too was a monastic site. William Cecil began his house there, like Sharington at Lacock and Thynne at Longleat and many another, by building on to and making use of the monastic remains. The first house, begun in 1552, Sir Ralph Sadler visited on his way to Scotland in August 1559, and he wrote to Cecil: 'I like what is done, and the order of the rest as your man showed it cannot but be fair. God send you money enough to end it with; other lack I see none.' Money enough was sent even for two rebuildings: one of them was completed in 1574, by which time the last monastic remains had been destroyed, and the final rebuilding was finished by 1587. Cecil did not escape criticism for his extravagance in building. Spenser boldly accused him of peculation for this purpose:

> But his owne treasure he encreased more
> And lifted up his loftie towres thereby,
> That they began to threat the neighbour sky.

And the poet contrasted Burghley with those peers of more distinguished ancestry who

> for povertie
> Were forst their auncient houses to let lie,
> And their olde Castles to the ground to fall.

Burghley House owes something to the plan of a castle, as Wollaton does to the elevation: it is built about a courtyard and has corner towers and a gatehouse in one side with flanking turrets rising to five storeys. Wollaton Hall looks only outward; Burghley House looks both inward and outward, and so combines a sense of privacy with the display of its façades. Within, the courtyard is dominated by a loggia decorated with the three orders, and with classical busts in roundels, the whole surmounted by an achievement of arms with free-standing lion supporters above which is a stone obelisk two storeys high. Obelisks were very much in fashion, yet it is undeniably odd to see one rising, as here, from the paws of heraldic beasts. The fenestration has something of the elegance of Longleat, though at Burghley there is more stone and less glass. String-courses and balustrade emphasize the horizontal lines at both houses, but at Burghley the corner towers, the capped turrets of the gatehouse, the great obelisk and the forest of chimneys in the form of Tuscan columns suggest that the new fashion had not wholly suppressed an older impetus towards height. Lord Burghley was more eclectic, perhaps more conservative in his tastes, than Sir John Thynne; less romantic and less pretentious than Sir Francis Willoughby. But then he was building for different reasons. Sir John Thynne was a purist, intent to show the perfection of the new architecture in an English country house: he kept the Queen from visiting him until he could show her a finished work of art. Sir Francis Willoughby built a palace for the Queen's pleasure, and but for the romantic chivalry with which her subjects regarded her would never have built Wollaton. Lord Burghley built a house to mark the new position in the nation's affairs which, through him, his family had attained; built it (as a contemporary said) 'for the mansion of his barony'. The Queen would visit her Lord Treasurer there certainly, and the house must be worthy to receive her; but we can imagine her discussing affairs of state with her host in the privacy of Burghley House, as we cannot amid the holiday splendour of Wollaton.

In a few buildings the Elizabethan love of symbolism and of ingenuity predominates. Most remarkable of these is Sir Thomas Tresham's Triangular Lodge (pl. 5) which he built in the grounds of his noble Rushton Hall in Northamptonshire. Sir Thomas was a papist with a special devotion to the worship of the Trinity, which was proper to one whose family name contained the number 3, *tres*, and whose emblem was the trefoil. This emblematic building was begun in 1593 and completed three years later: it has three sides, each with three gables; three storeys, with three windows in each on each side; the windows are composed of groups of three units, triangles in threes within trefoil frames, or trefoils alone; the central chimney is three-sided. The frieze of the entablature is thirty-three feet long, and the inscriptions on each side contain thirty-three letters.[1] In the trefoil over the door (which necessarily interrupts the symmetry of the building) is the motto *Tres testimonium dant*, from the first Epistle of St John, 'There are three that bear witness'.

Trinitarian fantasy is to be found also in Longford Castle in Wiltshire. This is not a pious 'folly' but a large mansion begun in 1580 by Sir Thomas Gorges, to replace the old manor-house by the Avon. Sir Thomas had married the widow of the Marquess of Northampton, a Swedish lady named Helena Snakenborg, and her influence may be seen in the castle, which was modelled upon Tycho Brahe's castle of Uranienborg. Longford was a triangular building, with round towers at each of the three corners, to represent the three persons of the Trinity, joined by the three main ranges. John Thorpe drew the plan of this house, and recognized its affinity to the mediaeval symbol of the Trinity. The house was too heavy for its site close to the river, and Sir Thomas would have been ruined by the provision of piles and woolpacks, had not his wife 'begged the wreck of a Spanish galleon that was cast away about Hurst Castle', of which Sir Thomas was Governor, 'and in that hull (as 'tis reported) there were silver bars as well as iron ones and such a vast (though concealed) treasure as served to complete their pile at Longford'. This house did not replace an ancient castle, but seems from the first to have been called Longford Castle.

Where an Elizabethan owner converted a mediaeval castle he would retain the name, Kenilworth Castle, Raglan Castle, Castle Ashby, Wardour Castle; but where he converted monastic buildings to his domestic use, he would never call his house Abbey or Priory. That was a romantic affectation of the Gothic revival. The Elizabethans rejected an association of names which was too recent for comfort, and were too much concerned with the modern to be often sentimental about the

[1] Aperiatur terra & germinet salvatorem (Isaiah xlv. 8).
Quis separabit nos a charitate Christi (Rom. viii. 35).
Consideravi opera tua domine et expavi.

antique. Besides, they were confident that the country houses which they were building would rival the abandoned monasteries, which no longer had any part to play in the life of the countryside : the new houses were replacing them not only in the fields and valleys where they were set, but in the society which moved about them ; and the patrons of new learning, of new poetry, and music, and painting, and sculpture, were not men in religious orders dedicated to the service of God, but courtiers devoted to the service of the Queen. It has always been characteristic of England that those who have prospered in the cities, whether in government, in the law, or in trade, should buy estates and build themselves houses in the country, where so many of the old castles and monasteries were to be found. A property qualification for service in parliament may have helped to perpetuate an old habit : it cannot have been its origin. Our tradition in this contrasts with those of France and Italy where the 'nobility live commonly close together in their cities, and ours for the most part scattered in their country houses'. Tudor governments tried, from time to time, to discourage this tendency, but with no success : the tradition is intrinsic in the English character.

Many of these country houses therefore survive. But the town-houses, and especially the palaces of the nobility in London which excited the admiration of every sixteenth-century visitor, and prompted comparison with Venice (for the still silver-streaming Thames was the main highway for traffic) have all perished. Those that were not burnt in the Fire were pulled down to make way for later mansions in the eighteenth century, or the nineteenth. The provincial towns, Shrewsbury and Chester most notable of them, which preserve town-houses of this time can show only lesser houses, timber-framed and gabled, and deriving from a mediaeval tradition, rather than from the Renaissance. The merchants who built them were unaware of the new movement in architectural design, and if we find Renaissance ornament carved somewhere in the timber jetties or gables this is all the evidence there is likely to be that the builder had seen some modern pattern-book, Italian or French or, more probably, Flemish. So it had been early in the century with houses of more importance: the first sign of the new age had been in the conversion of the classical orders to decorative pilasters, or to chimneys, or in the demotion of column, entablature, and pediment to frame a door where (like imperious Caesar) they might keep the wind away.

The 'new fashion' — John Shute called it so in the 1560s, as twenty years later men were to write of the 'new poetry' which Spenser introduced — was inevitably the fashion of the courtiers, and especially of that group who had first seen its introduction into England at Somerset House. They followed it, in their individual ways, in the country houses which they built, and no doubt in their town-houses also. And it would be followed in the few public buildings of the time, of which Sir Thomas Gresham's Royal Exchange was the most celebrated. This was built about a courtyard, with an arcade all round of arches on slender Doric columns: above these were Ionic pilasters framing niches with statues of the Kings of England. The Exchange was wholly Flemish in design and even in workmanship, since much of the stone was brought ready cut from the Netherlands. The Queen opened it in 1571, and it was burnt down in the Fire of London.

The buildings which those who were not courtiers erected show, by their surviving mediaevalism, to how small a group the new architecture appealed. About the same time when Longleat was rebuilding, or the Royal Exchange, some of the Inns of Court rebuilt their halls, but though Sir John Thynne's master carpenter came to work on the roof of the Middle Temple Hall, it is only in detail that this shows anything of the new fashion. The London lawyers were conservative in their tastes: perhaps the construction of a large hall necessitated this, or perhaps it is a perpetual characteristic of persons whose profession is to uphold established order. At Cambridge Ralph Simons continued the Gothic tradition in an attenuated form, as if he accepted the belief (proclaimed in the twentieth century on many an American campus) that in Gothic gloom the torch of learning will more brightly shine. In Emmanuel College, the first buildings of which he adapted from the Black Friars, his portrait informs us that Simons was *architectus sua aetate peritissimus*: a compliment which the fellows of the college would have assumed that they had an especial right to confer.

Cambridge can boast of better things. At the college which he refounded Dr Caius, who had studied medicine at the University of Padua (where for a time he shared rooms with Vesalius), had visited Rome, Florence, and Bologna, and had observed, if not very accurately, the buildings which he saw all about him in these cities. The ranges of rooms in his new court are still mediaeval, as if tradition was too strong for him to allow modern illumination to their inmates. But he broke away from this in his invention of a series of three gates to symbolize the passage of the undergraduate through his college. He would enter by the Gate of Humility; he would then follow a straight path to the Gate of Virtue; from this he would emerge in Wisdom, and finally he would pass through the Gate of Honour to the old Schools for his degree. The significance of the three gates was decorously shown in their architecture. The Gate of Humility has fluted pilasters on either side of the arch, and above it scrolls instead of a classical pediment, but is little more than a simple doorway in a wall. The Gate of Virtue is of three storeys with three orders of pilasters, and is surmounted by a pediment; in the spandrels on either side of the archway are reliefs of Victories extending laurel wreaths towards those who pass below. On the east side (that is, on entering this gate) is the inscription *Virtutis*, on the west side, *Io Caius Posui Sapientiae 1567*: the undergraduate's acquisition of Virtue must precede (however briefly) his acquisition of Wisdom. So is he prepared to enter the Gate of Honour, which is very ambitious, but also, unfortunately, very small. The two lower storeys are adorned with Ionic columns and pediments, with roundels and obelisks and niches ; but the top storey is a most unclassical hexagon ending in a dome. Dr Caius's classicism was not of the purest (he was, after all, a scientist), but at least he was bold enough to introduce into Cambridge architectural features which, whatever else they were, were not Gothic. His series of symbolic gates was appropriate to a college in an age when sermons might be found in stones, and anticipated the architectural symbolism of Sir Thomas Tresham and Sir Thomas Gorges. The improperly diminutive scale of the Gate of Honour cannot be blamed on Dr Caius, who died before it was built. The fellows of his college would no doubt have been divided between those who, out of piety to their late Master, were eager to carry out his known wishes, and those who, conscientiously believing that his money might be better spent, were not : the Gate of Honour is a symbol of compromise. Dr Caius's monument in the College chapel, which is in a similar style to the Gate of Honour, was perhaps made in his lifetime : its scale is appropriate and its present absurd position is due to the impiety of a later generation.

The conservatism of merchants, and lawyers, and dons, most of whom would not have had Dr Caius's experience of travel, sometimes appears even in the courtiers' work, though they strove to be in the latest fashion in architecture as in dress. In the greatest houses built on monastic sites the old buildings would gradually be removed until nothing was left, as at Longleat and Burghley. Elsewhere some parts, retained originally for economy's sake, may still survive, as at Lacock, Flaxley, Forde, Haughmond, Michelham, even at Petworth where a thirteenth-century chapel lurks behind the sumptuous magnificence of the long Augustan façade. A wall might be re-used ; a refectory, too strongly built for destruction to be easy, could be converted to a hall ; an undercroft would make a convenient cellar, where its old-fashioned arches and vaulting would not obtrude upon the fastidious gaze of the owner and his friends. There might even here and there be an owner with some taste for the antique : Sir William Sharington is portrayed in a picture at Lacock leaning against a wall of mediaeval masonry, and his earliest work there was still in the Gothic tradition. Very occasionally, as at Lacock, a cloister might be preserved as a covered walk about an inner courtyard, perhaps because its symmetry pleased more than the antique Gothic detail offended ; and the Italian liking for open arcades was often imitated, as at Burghley, or Longford, or Ingatestone, or Condover, until a less hardy generation, preferring warmth and comfort to fashionable elegance, walled them in. More often, as at Leez and Titchfield, the foundations of the cloister would merely determine the area of a new courtyard, but the central courtyard of many an Elizabethan house may owe as much to monastic cloister as to castle bailey. Sometimes a chapel would be retained for the use of the house, for the new Elizabethan settlement inclined men to adapt rather than to make new, in church buildings as in liturgy, as we may learn from the absence of an Elizabethan parish church throughout all England.

Often the old buildings were regarded simply as so much stone, as a quarry conveniently close to the building site ; and the sculptured detail of arch or niche or boss was waste, to be thrown aside when the squared wall-stones were removed. (That is why, on these sites, such carved stones are disproportionately common : they were no use.) To Longleat Sir John Thynne brought stone from Farleigh Hungerford Castle, and lead from the roof of Amesbury Priory, with a characteristically impartial disrespect for the obsolete, whether secular or religious. This lack of interest in the preservation of mediaeval buildings by those who built the great new houses may seem to us brutal, unsqueamish, even vulgar ; but we preserve the old because we lack their confidence in the new, because we fear, with some reason, that any replacement is likely to be inferior to what has been destroyed. Or else, which is worse, we contrive some academic hybrid of styles which insults the old and apologizes for the new. This the Elizabethans never did. Where they preserved some part of an old castle or abbey they made very little attempt at conformity — as little as Chapman attempted when he completed Marlowe's *Hero and Leander*. What was new was not ashamed of its newness, but

New light gives new directions ;

and the Elizabethan additions would assert their Renaissance quality as candidly as the builder could.

This readiness to make use of existing buildings was in keeping with the normal Elizabethan attitude to such matters, which was practical. 'Houses are built to live in, and not to look on ; therefore let use be preferred before uniformity, except where both may be had.' So Francis Bacon, whose father's new house at Gorhambury was built about a courtyard, and had tall octagonal towers at either end of the main front. But while he stresses the practical, he also reveals the aesthetic principle which underlies their best architecture, uniformity (as he calls it), symmetry, a harmonious balancing of parts. The lack of such qualities in mediaeval buildings made the Elizabethans indifferent to them, and if they had recognized the functionalism to which they owed their design, they would not have been moved to any greater respect, for the function, whether of defence or of dedicated celibacy, was obsolete. The Elizabethans had no museums, and were not interested in historical relics, or in the preservation of dodos. They would have despised the warped and twisted timber frames of inns and tea shoppes which nowadays pass for Elizabethan ; and whatever remnants of appreciation they retained for a mediaeval manor-house would have been dissipated by the merely capricious irregularity of Gothick imitations. There were many more mediaeval houses still inhabited in their day than now survive, for, besides the defensible houses that were slighted in the Civil War, others were pulled down or allowed to decay when eighteenth-century architects introduced new standards of comfort and elegance. With those improvements they would have been in sympathy.

Where good stone was accessible the Elizabethans preferred it : stone accepted the carving with which they delighted to adorn doorway, window, and cornice, and seemed more suited to the new classical forms. Brick had been used with extraordinary skill in the fifteenth century, especially in the stoneless eastern counties : Tattershall Castle in Lincolnshire had proved that brick might serve even military needs, and houses such as Oxburgh Hall in Norfolk and Helmingham Hall in Suffolk had shown how delightful it could be for domestic building. In Cambridge the principal court of Queens' College had been faced with brick when it was built, and early in the sixteenth century brick was used even in a church building, for the piers and arches of the parish church of St Osyth in Essex. Cardinal Wolsey seems to have had a liking for brick : he used it in his Cardinal College at Ipswich as well as at Hampton Court, though for his college of Christ Church, in a country where excellent stone was available, he preferred to use this. In East Anglia brick remained in fashion, for practical reasons, throughout the sixteenth century : at Layer Marney in Essex Lord Marney built his two extravagantly lofty towers in brick ; the gatehouses of Trinity and St John's Colleges in Cambridge show a similar display in brick ; and so do the gatehouses of the royal palaces of St James's and Hampton Court. All these were buildings of Henry VIII's time : later in the century brick was used more modestly, for Eastbury Manor in Essex, for Queen Hoo Hall in Hertfordshire, even, sometimes, for smaller houses in stone counties such as North Wiltshire or Somerset. A few larger houses were built in brick in the eastern counties: Sir William Petre's Ingatestone Hall in Essex, which dates from the 1540s, a courtyard house of the older fashion, disdaining symmetry; Sir William Cordell's Melford Hall in Suffolk, also originally built about a courtyard but altered later to the E-plan by the removal of one side; and Sir Thomas Smith's Hill Hall at Theydon Mount. Smith had travelled on the Continent in his youth, was a graduate of Padua as well as of Cambridge, and was one of Protector Somerset's young men, by whom the architecture of the Renaissance was first understood in England. Hill Hall has been much altered, but some classical features survive in the fenestration in the courtyard, where Tuscan and Ionic columns separate the windows, and a classical frieze runs between the two storeys. These brick houses were necessarily more austere than the stone houses, and such ornament as they have is confined to the stone surrounds of windows, to the finials of gables, or to a projecting stone porch as at Melford Hall. Three classical pilasters flank the doorway and the window above, which has a triangular pediment; and the whole porch is surmounted by a shell-topped niche. For the rest Melford Hall has an almost neo-classical lack of adornment.

The bricklayers had decorated their walls with a diaper in blue headers, but even this frivolity went out of fashion, and only in the patterning of their lofty chimney-stacks did they allow themselves much liberty. Here, as if suddenly released from the strong necessities of wall-building, they would delight to show the plasticity of their material: their chimneys, round or square, polygonal, star-shaped, singly or in groups, writhe and twist and spiral towards the sky. There they mock the solemn classical forms from which they have emerged, as the bosses, high in a Cathedral roof, irreverently leer and grimace at those who move sedately unseeing below. These fantastic chimneys are, surely, no part of the master's or architect's design: they are the product of craftsmen intent on exercising their ingenuity and skill.

Brick chimneys are to be seen in other parts of the country where timber was the principal building material, contrasting in shape and colour with the black and white of many a house from Cheshire to Herefordshire. Most of these half-timbered houses retain an older fashion of building than brick or stone: often, as at Bramhall or Adlington in Cheshire, the Elizabethan work is only an addition or alteration to something much older. Or if, as at Little Moreton Hall, the building is all of the Elizabethan age, this is not evident in the appearance of the house, which has no concern with symmetry or classicism or any such newfangledness. Pitchford Hall in Shropshire is respectful of symmetry, most exceptionally for a timber building: it is E-shaped, and even the brick chimneys, for once, are all to the same pattern, of a star. Perhaps this was a local conceit: star-shaped brick chimneys rise from the stone of Condover and even of Ludlow Castle. Timber could be carved, usually to grotesques as in the Rows in Chester, or it could be arranged in simple geometrical patterns of lozenges, circles, quatrefoils, or 'herring-bone'. But these houses, in town and country, along the Welsh border are not in the new fashion: they show (what no one ever doubted) that in Elizabeth's England many continued to build with traditional materials in a traditional manner. They show also that timber-framing was not so readily adaptable to the architecture of the Renaissance as was stone, or even brick: it imposed its own limitations on builder and architect, and though a timber-framed building might be as symmetrical as any other, this was about the only way in which it could conform to fashion. Sir Henry Sidney at Ludlow, and Sir Andrew Corbet at Moreton Corbet must have thought the timber houses in Ludlow and Shrewsbury and about the county very old-fashioned; and, since the cult of the picturesque was still two centuries away, they were probably contemptuous of such mediaeval barbarousness.

Some mediaeval houses were retained and improved by

their Elizabethan owners, most famous of all, Sir Henry Sidney's own house in Kent, Penshurst Place. The old house, built about 1340 by a rich wool merchant, Sir John de Pulteney, was granted by Edward VI to Sir William Sidney whose son, Sir Henry, added ranges to north and west, thereby making two open courts. The house thus became more or less H-shaped, a plan that is often found in Elizabethan and Jacobean houses, but it remains irregular, since Sir Henry Sidney did not demolish the fourteenth-century house or its fifteenth-century additions. Ben Jonson's poem implies that Penshurst was not in the fashionable taste of the time. (Ben Jonson worked for a time as a bricklayer, and must have had some appreciation of the technique of building.)

> Thou art not, Penshurst, built to envious show,
> Of touch, or marble ; nor canst boast a row
> Of polish'd pillars, or a roof of gold :
> Thou hast no lantern, whereof tales are told ;
> Or stair, or courts ; but stand'st an ancient pile,
> And these grudg'd at, art reverenc'd the while.

He goes on to praise the situation of the house, the orchards and park, and above all the hospitality which it provides to all who visit it. So he turns a compliment to Robert Sidney and his wife in spite of the antique lack of fashion of their house, very much in agreement with Bacon's opinion that houses are built to live in :

> Now, Penshurst, they that will proportion thee
> With other edifices, when they see
> Those proud, ambitious heaps, and nothing else,
> May say, their lords have built, but thy lord dwells.

Bacon, in that austere essay of his, advised his reader to 'leave the goodly fabrics of houses, for beauty only, to the enchanted palaces of the poets' : no doubt he was thinking of the prodigy houses, as they have been called, palaces for the entertainment of the Queen and her Court, Wollaton,

Burghley, Holdenby, Theobalds. Yet these houses, for all their extravagance, conformed to the principles which he, like the rest of his contemporaries, acknowledged in architecture as in the other arts: symmetry, proportion, decorum. He may have scorned the excessive concern for beauty that Lord Burghley and Sir Christopher Hatton showed in building their houses; he would have approved their comments on that beauty. In August 1578 Burghley visited the still unfinished Holdenby House, and wrote to tell Hatton of his pleasure in seeing the new mansion. 'Approaching to the house,' he says, 'being led by a large, long, straight, fair way, I found a great magnificence in the front or front pieces of the house, and so every part answerable to other, to allure liking.' The magnificence and the symmetry are the two qualities of the exterior which he commends. It was a house for show, to be admired on the approach as a palace fit to welcome the Queen. Hatton himself, we are told, visited it but once in two years, yet 'many gentlemen and strangers that come but to see the house are there daily welcomed, feasted, and well lodged'. Within doors Burghley was no less enthusiastic. 'I found no one thing of greater grace than your stately ascent from your hall to your great chamber; and your chambers answerable with largeness and lightsomeness, that truly a Momus could find no fault.' Burghley's approval of a noble staircase, and of the lightsomeness (that is, the well-lit character) of the rooms, are both very characteristic of the age. Before Elizabeth's time a grand staircase was almost unknown, for the Hall, on the ground floor, had not yet given pride of place to the Long Gallery and Great Chamber, on the first floor, and a narrow spiral stair in a turret, or in the thickness of a wall, normally gave access to the upper floors. In his own Burghley House there still survives the 'Roman' staircase, with stone barrel-vault of French antecedents, which is unique in England: with it he had set the pattern for a stately ascent some years before. The staircase at Holdenby House was more probably of wood, with the wide, shallow steps and elaborately carved balusters that are still to be seen in many houses of the time. The tall windows with mullions and transoms which give so much of their special character to Elizabethan houses carried on the English love for filling their buildings with light, which the architects of the fifteenth century had shown in their Perpendicular churches. Leland had used the same word, lightsome, to praise Glastonbury Abbey: it is a favourite word in these years, when men were at last secure enough to be able to open the walls of their houses to the light and the scene, without fearing an enemy. Laneham used the word of Leicester's new building at Kenilworth, no doubt contrasting the windows there with those that remained in the old castle. Bacon seems even to echo Burghley's comments: 'Lucullus answered Pompey well; who, when he saw his stately galleries and rooms so large and lightsome in one of his houses, said: "Surely an excellent place for summer, but how do you in winter?"' 'Stately', 'large', 'lightsome' — the epithets are repeated, not because Bacon had read his uncle's letter, but because these were the qualities which an Elizabethan sought.

These huge windows were not needed, would indeed be a source of discomfort, in countries where the light was more brilliant, the sun more scorching, than in England. The houses and churches of the Mediterranean shores are places in which to seek shade, and to keep cool; needs that are seldom insistent in England. Thus, as Sir Henry Wotton says, 'a good parlour in Egypt would perchance make a good cellar in England'. Bacon, always inclined to disparage contemporary fashion, criticized the excessive use of glass: 'You shall have sometimes fair houses so full of glass, that one cannot tell where to become to be out of the sun or cold.' This is the point of his story of Pompey and Lucullus. But he approved the introduction of bay windows, 'for they be pretty retiring places for conference; and besides, they keep both the wind and sun off, for that which would strike almost through the room, doth scarce pass the window', a practical criticism in accordance with his precepts.

Sir Henry Wotton, who was a friend of Bacon, spent many years of his life in Italy, and especially in Venice where he was three times English Ambassador. In his *Elements of Architecture*, published a few months before Bacon's essay, he shows a much more elegant taste than the older man. Both devote their attention exclusively to the ideal country house : to an Elizabethan gentleman 'to build' implied 'to build a country house', and not anything else ; architecture was concerned with this, not with the construction of public buildings, religious or secular. But whereas Bacon insisted upon use and comfort, Wotton believed that the architect's 'truest ambition should be to make the form, which is the nobler part, as it were triumph over the matter'. The antithesis is not exactly balanced, for by 'matter' Wotton meant the stone or brick and mortar and timber of which the house was built ; but it is clear that he regarded elegance and proportion, which he had learned to appreciate in Italy, as the principal concern of the architect, the end towards which a true ambition would lead him. He had no liking for Gothic architecture, in spite of his years in Venice, but considered that these pointed arches 'both for the natural imbecility of the sharp angle itself, and likewise for their very uncomeliness, ought to be exiled from judicious eyes, and left to their first inventors, the Goths or Lombards, amongst other relics of that barbarous age'. What would Ruskin have made of such taste ?

Wotton had nothing to say of the Doge's Palace, of St Mark's, of the Ca' d' Oro. Instead, he admired the modern work of Palladio and of Jacopo Barozzi of Vignola, the great church of S. Giustina in Padua whose rebuilding to the designs of Andrea Briosco had been completed only a few years before he saw it, and the Villa which Palladio had built at Maser for Daniele Barbaro. This famous house, than which Wotton knew none 'more artificial and delicious' is still considered one of Palladio's masterpieces, though nowadays we would choose other epithets than Wotton's. To describe a work of art as artificial was almost tautologous: Wotton meant that Palladio had designed the house with the concentration of a great artist learned in his art. By 'delicious' he implied, perhaps, a certain luxurious delicacy in the ornamentation of the house, though he made no reference to the incomparable frescoes with which Paul Veronese decorated the interior. Thomas Morley's comment on the madrigal comes to mind: it is, he says, 'next unto the motet, the most artificial and, to men of understanding, most delightful'. The difference between 'delightful' and 'delicious' is a difference of austerity. Morley was emphasizing the intellectual appeal 'to men of understanding' of his music; Wotton, the more sensuous appeal of floral swag and figured pediment.

We can very easily pass over the choice of epithets in such a phrase as Wotton used, interpreting them carelessly as denoting praise, without attending to the quality of the praise. But to understand the taste of Wotton and his contemporaries we must discover precisely what he meant, for his words carried precise meaning. We are much more likely to be imprecise in our praise, to call the Villa Barbaro one of the most beautiful of Palladio's buildings, or to use such words as 'splendid' or 'magnificent' which indicate nothing but an exclamation of pleasure. Wotton is less subjective, though well aware that there is something subjective in all criticism. He ends his essay with a 'methodical direction how to censure fabrics' which, since it is very rare to find any such method of proceeding clearly stated, it will be well to examine.

First, he acknowledges that it may be more difficult to be a good critic of architecture than to be a good architect, 'because the working part may be helped with deliberation, but the judging must flow from an extemporal habit'. Hence the need of a well-trained, experienced mind in any intending critic, so that his judgment will not be too prompt and unconsidered. At the same time the critic must have an open mind, and Wotton roundly condemns that Arnoldian exclusiveness which has constricted much that has recently passed for criticism. 'I could wish him that cometh to examine any nobler work, first of all to examine himself, whether perchance the sight of many brave things before (which remain like impressed forms) have not made him apt to think nothing good but that which is the best; for this humour were too sour.' He goes on to insist on the importance of a historical approach: the critic must 'seek to inform himself precisely, of the age of the work upon which he must pass his doom'. Having thus divested himself of the prejudices which may arise from too much haste, or from a failure to look at a building for what it is (condemning a manor-house for not being modern), the critic will now be prepared to look at the building dispassionately. But here again Wotton offers a warning, against being seduced by the beauty of the ornaments 'which first allure the eye'; for the critic must begin by paying attention to the more essential elements of design. When the first suggestions of the Renaissance appeared in English buildings they were in ornament, not in design: travellers returning from Italy or France remembered the surface, not the organization, of the buildings they had seen, and imitated detail, not the whole. Wotton advises the critic against this superficiality: he must observe the whole building, 'till at last he be able to form this conclusion, that the work is commodious, firm, and delightful; which . . . are the three capital conditions required in good buildings'. So it is under these three heads that the critic must order his judgment: the house must be suited to the use for which it is intended; it must be well built and not in need of constant repair; it must be pleasing to the eye. Who would dispute Wotton's claim that this is 'the most scientifical way of censuring'?

Sir Thomas Heneage, writing many years before of Hatton's new Holdenby House, had also made a triple division in the grounds of judgment. 'If the praise of a house consist in the seat, beauty and use, both within and without . . . Holdenby shall hold the preeminence of all the modern houses I have known or heard of in England.' His division differs from Wotton's in that he omits the firmness and includes the site; but the difference is only apparent, for Wotton has already had much to say upon the site, and we may reasonably suppose that Heneage considered it important to the use of a house that it should not fall down. The house which he built in the 1560s, Copped Hall in Essex, survived until the eighteenth century when it was demolished to make way for a Georgian house.

After preparing his critic's mind in this way, so that he can properly approach the difficult task of judging the merits of a building, Wotton takes from Vitruvius, the standard authority for all Renaissance writers on architecture,[1] 'four heads which every man should run over, before he pass any determinate censure upon the works that he shall view'. Vitruvius' terms are *Eurythmia*, *Symmetria*, *Decor*, and *Distributio*, on each of which Wotton has his own comments. These show the expected balance between sense and sensibility which makes him so helpful a critic.

Eurythmia 'is that agreeable harmony between the breadth, length and height of all the rooms of the fabric, which suddenly, where it is, taketh every beholder by the secret power of proportion'. This is very well said. Wotton recognized the immediate effect of a well-proportioned room on anyone who enters it, an effect which may or may not be capable of rational analysis. In the Renaissance men were disposed to think that such analysis was possible, that the proportions which satisfy the eye are mathematically determined. Hence Inigo Jones's double cube room in Wilton House, and many another designed in accordance with a mathematical theory, which please us still, though not necessarily (we suppose)

[1] Sir Thomas Smith had six editions of Vitruvius in 1566.

because the theory is correct. Wotton had earlier referred to Alberti's establishing a rule of proportion on the basis of musical intervals, 'reducing symmetry to symphony, and the harmony of sound to a kind of harmony in sight'. This idea of harmony pervades all their thinking, not only on aesthetics.

> From Harmony, from heav'nly Harmony
> This universal Frame began.

The idea is as old as Pythagoras, who discovered the numerical ratios that determine the principal intervals of the musical scale, and from that brilliant insight developed his theory of the numerical basis of universal order. To men of the Renaissance this theory had a special attraction, as a proof of the inherent rationality of the universe, of its divine orderliness. Since mathematical relationships underlay musical harmony, it was reasonable to suppose that they also provided the harmony of sight by which Wotton defines *Eurythmia*. (Besides, the poets, from Virgil to Shakespeare, distinguished their verse from the other harmony of prose by referring to their lines as 'numbers'.) Elizabethan architects therefore took these opinions into account, and designed for the taste of men who accepted them also, and who believed that aesthetic judgment must be based upon rational principles. Good taste was thus objective and reasonable, not a matter of subjective, and therefore irreconcilable, judgments. If the proportion 2 : 3 was pleasing to the ear, it must also be pleasing to the sight, and a window or door whose proportion of breadth to height was such must please not merely some of those who saw it, but all, since it is the nature of man to be rational. This it would do in spite of the fact that the power of proportion is secret ; that is, the eye does not see, and the ear does not hear a mathematical relationship. The symmetry even of the façades of Longleat is apparent only, and cannot be precisely analysed. But 'the two principal consonances, that most ravish the ear, are by consent of all Nature, the fifth and the octave ; whereof the first riseth radically from the proportion between two and three ; the other from the double interval, between one and two, or between two and four etc. Now if we shall transport these proportions from audible to visible objects ; and apply them as they shall fall fittest (the nature of the place considered) namely in some windows and doors, the symmetry of two to three in their breadth and length ; in others, the double as aforesaid ; there will indubitably result from either a graceful and harmonious contentment to the eye.' It is a most satisfactory doctrine to those who believe in a world created by a divine intelligence, whose ways are mysterious only to those who are unwilling or unable to use their reason for its critical examination.

Symmetria Wotton defines as something more than mere symmetry, the correspondence of either side, as in the human body. It is 'the convenience that runneth between the parts and the whole'. This does not mean a functional coherence between the internal arrangement of rooms and the façade, but the suiting of parts, such as windows, doors, chimneys, and roof to the over-all design. By 'convenience' he means nothing practical — the word had as yet scarcely acquired this connotation — but rather an aesthetic congruity of proportion.

Decor is the principal element in all critical judgment at the Renaissance, and discloses a sensible recognition that most works of art, not only buildings, were made for the use or delight of somebody. All buildings must be made to order : self-expression never yet laid a foundation-stone. Therefore the taste and (at least in earlier times) the social position of the owner of the house are to be considered. *Decor* 'is the keeping of a due respect between the inhabitant and the habitation'. King James's cynical observation that Audley End was too large for a king though it might serve for a Lord Treasurer, derives its point from an acceptance of this principle. Decorum implies always consideration of the context : in architecture the relation of the building to its site, of the parts to the whole, of ornament to design, of habitation to inhabitant. Wotton adds to his definition a rule of his admired master, Palladio, that 'the principal entrance was never to be regulated by any certain dimensions, but by the dignity of the master', a rule which dissolves the rigidity of mathematical proportion and gives individuality to a house. Palladio also allows that the entrance should err on the side of flattery rather than otherwise, for this 'is a mark of generosity, and may always be excused with some noble emblem or inscription, as that of the Conte di Bevillacqua over his large gate at Verona, where perchance had been committed a little disproportion :

Patet janua, cor magis'.

How admirable all this is, the quiet and reasonable argument which will appeal to any man of understanding, the humorous acceptance of personal vanity, the charming wit to excuse it ! For Wotton and his friends discussion of matters of taste lacked the personal scorn and acrimony which degrade it nowadays. They began from rational principles, and while they did not exclude the subjective, the 'extemporal habit', the immediate response of a sensitive and instructed mind to good design, they insisted on a detached judgment based on learning and experience. They therefore expected agreement, since reasonable men agree on reasonable propositions. If it can be shown that the proportion 2 : 3 is pleasing, then the good design of a window can be demonstrated with a foot rule. But then they believed that to be reasonable was included in the definition of being human.

The last of the four Vitruvian categories under which the critic of architecture is to consider the building which he is examining is *Distributio*, 'that useful casting of all rooms for office, entertainment, or pleasure', the more practical aspect of decorum, which needs little comment. For as the entrance must suit the dignity of the owner, so must great chamber and long gallery, hall and parlour, kitchen and buttery be suited to their different uses, both in their position in the house, and in their intrinsic proportions. Thus the kitchen must be placed near the dining-room 'or else perhaps some of the dishes may straggle by the way', as the owners of later mansions have sometimes discovered too late to keep the roast hot. Generally, the entertaining rooms should appear 'fit for the welcome of cheerful guests'. Of these rooms the largest, the Long Gallery, was peculiar to England. The first was the Queen's Gallery at Hampton Court Palace, but the fashion soon became general not only in the largest houses, but even in houses of the modest size of Little Moreton Hall in Cheshire. The English climate, which invited large windows to make the most of the weak northern sun, also suggested a long indoor room where gentle exercise might be taken on cold days. The Gallery was usually on the first floor, and sometimes there would be an open loggia beneath it, where the master of the house and his friends might stroll up and down in warmer weather. The Long Gallery was soon discovered to be the ideal place for hanging portraits of the family and their friends, and must have helped to determine that other English fashion for full-length portraits, which would be more in keeping with the scale of the room, and with the dignified parade before them. So Lord Howard of Bindon wrote to Lord Salisbury to ask for his portrait in his Garter Robes, 'to be placed in the gallery I lately made for the pictures of sundry of my honourable friends, whose presentation thereby to behold will greatly delight me to walk often in that place where I may see so comfortable a sight'. In less chaotic prose Lord Herbert of Cherbury records an occasion when the Earl of Dorset 'invited me to Dorset House, where bringing me into his gallery, and showing me many pictures, he at last brought me to a frame covered with green taffeta, and asked me who I thought was there; and therewithal presently drawing the curtain, showed me my own picture'. The two men were not previously acquainted, but Lord Dorset, hearing of Lord Herbert's prowess, had got a copy of his portrait to hang in the gallery of Dorset House.

The houses which Wotton admired were hospitable places, where a man might talk with his friends, apart in a bay window, or less privately as they walked together in the Long Gallery to admire the portraits hung there. The ceilings and windows were high so that the rooms (to quote Burghley, Bacon, and Wotton) were large and lightsome, airy and spiritous. The grand staircase too must be well-lit, to prevent stumbling; well ventilated, 'because a man doth spend much breath in mounting'; broad and stately to look well, and to make it possible for two persons to pass. These houses were built not for defence, but for the conduct of civilized life in which ladies and gentlemen shared alike. Lady Anne Clifford, when she was Dowager Countess of Dorset, Pembroke, and Montgomery, might complain that 'the marble pillars of Knole in Kent and Wilton in Wiltshire were to me oftentimes but the gay arbours of anguish', but she implies, as who could doubt, that these houses were designed for gaiety and pleasant company. Lady Anne herself preferred to these elegant southern houses of her two husbands the three ancient houses of her own heritage, Appleby Castle and Brougham Castle in Westmorland, and Skipton Castle in Craven where, she admitted, 'I do more and more fall in love with the contentments of a country life'. But the improvements which she made to her castles had to wait until the second of her husbands died in 1649: only then could she come into her own.

In Elizabeth's time another termagant Countess, Bess of Hardwick, Countess of Shrewsbury, had a like passion for building, but whereas Lady Anne Clifford, proud of her ancient inheritance, preferred to restore the houses which came to her as of right, Elizabeth Hardwick built new. When she was the wife of Sir William Cavendish she began the first great house at Chatsworth in 1552. Three years later the building had so far progressed that Sir William asked Sir John Thynne for the 'cunning plasterer' whom he employed at

Longleat where (so Sir William had heard) he had 'made divers pendants and other pretty things'. Sir John seems to have been unwilling to lend this craftsman, for in April 1560, after her husband's death, Bess herself wrote again to ask him to spare her 'your plasterer that flowereth your hall'.

The elaborate plaster ceilings and friezes of Elizabethan houses seem heavy and oppressive in the electric lighting of the twentieth century, but they were designed for candlelight, when ribs and medallions and pendants would be alive with the constantly moving shadows, and their three dimensions would not be flattened out of recognition. Sir Richard Grenville's warriors resting with their discarded arms piled beneath branching trees, in the hall at Buckland ; the lively animals in the hall frieze at Levens ; all the menagerie of birds and bats, elephants and tortoises, butterflies, dragonflies, fish, flesh and fowl that inhabit the compartments of these ceilings were intended to be seen in the incessant flicker of candlelight, animated by it, and worth watching. Our lighting has slaughtered them all, so that they seem stuffed. Our flat ceilings are intended to reflect light, and have no interest in themselves ; when illumination was by candles ceilings had other purposes, to interrupt and diversify the varying light, to use, not to eliminate, shadows, and therefore they were to be looked at and enjoyed.

So it was also with the panelling : the flickering light of candles gave greater interest to the simple chamfer or moulding of the divisions, and to the geometrical shapes of square, lozenge, oval, or round with which the small early panels were decorated. At first panelling was treated much as we treat wallpaper, with the pattern repeated as often as the surface to be covered might require, but by the end of the sixteenth century a more sophisticated taste demanded some architectural relevance, and introduced classical pilasters and masks and roundels, or the 'antique' work which, in Elizabethan eyes, was also suggestive of ancient Rome. These features appear first in the surround of fire-place or door, the parts of a room which, more obviously than the walls, need architectural treatment. Often the fire-place was in stone, and column, entablature and pediment, used by the mason on the outside of the house, would here be repeated, with little or no influence on the panelling of the walls. In the drawing-room of Lyme Park paired Ionic columns in stone flank the fire-place, above which are the Queen's arms in plaster between pairs of grotesque terms. The panelling is in three bands, of which the lower and the upper repeat a geometrical design, but the central band carries an arcaded design, where fluted pilasters and grotesque masks and a suggestion of brickwork in the spandrels recall a distant classical heritage. This room, which astonishingly was allowed to survive within Leoni's severely Palladian mansion on the Cheshire hills, was built about 1580. Farther north, and fifteen years later, the drawing-room at Levens was panelled (pl. 7), and here the carpenter had learnt the classical manner. Fire-place and overmantel are in wood, with the three orders correctly used in the frame-work, and with the Queen's arms and those of the Bellingham family in panels over the fire. The doors of the room are flanked by 'antique' grotesques, and surmounted by heraldry, and there are classical pilasters in the angles of the room. But the walls are still covered with lozenges in square panels, upon which the design of fire-place and doorway is imposed without any attempt at conformity. The next stage, of which the corner pilasters give promise, was to promote classical ornament to design throughout the room, and to use pilasters to divide panel from panel, as in the Great Chamber at Chastleton House in Oxfordshire. With this development there went an increase in the size of the panels, and also a division between the main area of panelling and the lowest band, as if the pilasters stood upon a deep base. Thus the classical influence which had at first, as usual, appeared only in applied ornament came to dominate design throughout the room.

Bess of Hardwick's Chatsworth was completed early in Elizabeth's reign, and it stood until late in Charles II's time, the first of the Wonders of the Peak in the poem which Thomas Hobbes dedicated to its owner, the Earl of Devonshire. This house, of which a needlework picture is preserved at Chatsworth, was built about a courtyard, which was entered through a high archway flanked by triangular turrets five storeys high. At either end of the front were rectangular turrets of four storeys, and next to these, on the top floor of the main block, were large windows with triangular pediments. There were coats of arms and roundels, perhaps with classical busts, above the entrance. Charles Cotton, who had known both houses, preferred the new :

> Yet Chatsworth, though thy pristine lineaments
> Were beautiful, and great to all intents :
> I needs must say, for I have seen both faces,
> Thou'rt much more lovely in the modern graces.

His poem was published only three years after Hobbes's, and it is perhaps a little surprising to find one who aptly described himself as 'an old-fashioned country squire' so much approving a very modern building. Cotton gave some of his reasons. Especially he praised the new fenestration, with sashes giving still more light to the rooms than had the mullioned windows of the old house.

> The glaziers work before substantial was
> I must confess, thrice as much lead as glass,
> Which in the sun's meridian cast a light
> As it had been within an hour of night.
> The windows now look like so many suns
> Illustrating the noble room at once :
> The primitive casements modell'd were, no doubt,
> By that through which the pigeon was thrust out,
> Where now whole shashes are but one great eye
> T'examine and admire thy beauties by.

The Elizabethan delight in well-lit rooms continued, and though Bess of Hardwick's Chatsworth had some large windows, her later houses at Hardwick had still larger windows throughout. The forty years that had passed since work was begun at Chatsworth had made the old house, with its courtyard and entrance turrets and battlements, look old-fashioned; in nothing more, perhaps, than in its fenestration. Hardwick Hall is, as the old rhyme has it, more glass than wall: this is the first and most striking impression it makes upon its visitors (pl. 8). In this, but in little else, Hardwick resembles Wollaton, where the Dowager Countess of Shrewsbury visited Sir Francis Willoughby on her way home from London in the late summer of 1592. On the same journey she had called at Holdenby, where she was welcomed by Sir William Newport, the nephew and heir of Sir Christopher Hatton. From him she bought the famous Gideon tapestries to furnish the Long Gallery of the new house she was building at Hardwick. (She paid £326 : 15 : 9 for them, and characteristically insisted on a rebate of £5 to cover the cost of replacing the arms of Hatton with those of Hardwick: Hatton's golden hind was easily converted to a stag by the addition of antlers, and the Hardwick arms, painted on cloth, were sewn over those of Hatton.) She bought other tapestries and pictures for her new house while she was away from home: clearly it occupied most of her thoughts, and we can imagine her noting this at Holdenby and that at Wollaton, comparing, modifying, improving for her last and best house.

Hardwick Hall, like Holdenby House, was built to glorify its owner's family home. Sir Christopher Hatton was the son of William Hatton of Holdenby, Elizabeth Hardwick was the daughter of John Hardwick of Hardwick; both had risen to the summit of power and affluence in the mobile society of their time, and both would have agreed with Bacon's aphorism, 'when men sought to cure mortality by fame, that buildings was the only way'. Thus Camden records a saying of Hatton, that he built Holdenby House 'for the greatest and last monument of his youth'. Hatton had died in 1591 at the age of fifty-one ; Bess of Hardwick was twenty years his senior, and it was time therefore to seek a lasting cure for mortality. The motive was very typical of the Renaissance, as was the wish to make the place of birth memorable. So Aeneas Sylvius, on becoming Pope, rebuilt his native village of Corsignano in the noblest fifteenth-century manner. A village it yet remains, but the most magnificent village in the world, in his honour renamed Pienza, with its one street, remote above the Tuscan countryside, matching the sumptuous frescoes in the Cathedral of Siena in which Pintoricchio narrates the story of the life of the poet, scholar, and humanist who became Pope Pius II.

There is no reason to believe that the Countess of Shrewsbury ever expected, as did Sir Christopher Hatton and Sir Francis Willoughby, to entertain the Queen in her new house, though her granddaughter, Lady Arabella Stuart, had a serious claim to succeed to the English throne. Above all, Hardwick is a house to be lived in, and since it has preserved more of its Elizabethan furnishings than any other house, and has suffered very little alteration or restoration, it is the most complete of all surviving Elizabethan houses. There is here no grand ceremonial entrance, for the pillared portico keeps the doorway always in the shade, and prevents any of that elaborate upward extension such as there is at Burghley House, or Kirby Hall, or Montacute, and which developed eventually to such Jacobean extravagances as the entrance to Hatfield House or (most pedantic and fantastical of all) the tower of the five orders at the Bodleian Library. The entrance to Hardwick is at ground level, not raised and approached by a flight of steps as at Longleat or Wollaton : thus it has a modesty which is not indicative of Lady Shrewsbury's character, but when the eye travels, as it is compelled to do, up those flanking towers, it discovers in the balustrades at the top, framed by strapwork scrolls, and beneath a coronet, the reassuring initials ES, Elizabeth Shrewsbury.

This cresting on the towers and the simple balustrade

between them is all the ornament that Hardwick Hall offers. For the rest the house depends on the pattern of the windows, highest in the second storey, which is the top storey of the central block, but with the third storey windows of the six towers higher than the windows of the first floor. The effect is not so much classical, for the pilasters and busts of Longleat and Wollaton are disdained here, as anti-Gothic, and English. Here is no reminiscence of the Middle Ages, for chivalrous gaiety or for heraldic grandeur ; no suggestion that the builder had jotted down a sketch of a Venetian palazzo, or of a French château, or that he had Serlio's book, or Philibert de l'Orme's, open before him while he drew his elevations. The experience that the Countess of Shrewsbury could use, after a long life spent in studying and making houses, is all refined in this, her last, house to a perfected simplicity of symmetrical design which must have satisfied her, as it still satisfies. In the truest sense, this house is in the classical taste with every part contributing to the whole, with nothing stuck on or irrelevant, not even an Ionic pilaster or a triangular pediment, but the whole glittering with glass so that whoever sees it knows that it must be filled with light and colour.

So indeed it is, though the glass of the windows may have dimmed, though the colours of tapestry and embroidery have faded in the years that have passed since the old Countess ordered an inventory to be made in 1601. On her visit to Sir Francis Willoughby she must have admired the marble fire-places in his new house at Wollaton, and she brought his mason, Thomas Accres, to work for her at Hardwick. The fire-place was still the focus of every room, the part most constantly looked at when the company sat together about the fire : it must therefore be worth looking at. Everywhere at Hardwick are these dignified fire-places in alabaster and coloured marbles, often with classical columns framing hearth or overmantel, with a shelf corbelled out to support a pediment, or with an allegorical figure, or a group of statuary in alabaster above. In the High Great Chamber (pl. 9) the Queen's coat of arms is blazoned above the blue and grey, white and black marble. In the Long Gallery are two fire-places with coupled pilasters, white banded with blue below, and above coupled columns of touch, carrying a frieze of touch and alabaster. Between these columns is an alabaster oval with an alabaster figure, in the one of *Justice*, in the other of *Mercy*, in high relief against the black marble. Best of all these sculptures is the alabaster relief of *Apollo and the Muses* in the bedroom next to the High Great Chamber : Lady Shrewsbury brought it here from Chatsworth, but where she originally obtained it, and who carved it, no one can say. Even where there is no sculptured figure to contemplate, the eye travels with pleasurable ease over these varied shapes and surfaces, stone and marble and alabaster, classical column and pediment, geometric patterns of round and square, oval and lozenge, strapwork scroll, cartouche and obelisk. All this variety of design is matched by a variety of colour, but, most important of all, the polished, shining surfaces and the effect of relief everywhere obtained, contrast with the light-absorbing, infinitely broken texture of the tapestries which clothe the walls. Such an effect must have been normal in any Elizabethan mansion : here only is it still wholly preserved. The stone staircase, of extreme simplicity, without handrail or guard, but of great breadth and of easy ascent, passes from shadow where there is no direct light from outside up into a brilliantly lit space before the High Great Chamber is reached. This dramatic lighting announces the main rooms of the house as they are approached : no doubt it was so intended. To that effect its austerity contributes : on other staircases carving, heraldic beasts or classical deities, coffered or plastered ceilings, pleasantly delay and distract us as we climb. Here at Hardwick the staircase is a means of ascent from the lesser rooms to the greater, and is designed to emphasize this and this alone.

There are other contrasts too, in the woodwork of doors

and panelling, in the plaster ceilings, and in Abraham Smith's coloured plaster frieze that runs round the High Great Chamber. Sacheverell Sitwell has called this room 'the most beautiful room not in England alone but in the whole of Europe', praise of the sort that inevitably provokes dissent. Indeed these scenes of the forest and hunting, of ordinary persons cheek by jowl with Diana and Venus and an allegory of Summer, are crude and provincial compared with the tapestries illustrating the Odyssey which have hung below since the room was made; as crude and provincial as Shakespeare's telling of the story of Venus and Adonis compared with Titian's painting of it. That is not to deny to Abraham Smith, or to William Shakespeare, a delightful vigour, and a freshness of vision. But an Italian or a Frenchman brought into this room when it was new would have been in familiar surroundings so long as he looked at the tapestries: when he raised his eyes to the frieze he would have suddenly remembered that he was in the barbarous North.

This English eclecticism characterizes Elizabethan taste in all they did. Hardwick Hall is the consummation of the native tradition in architecture: it is mere English, and could not have been built in any other country, or at any other time. It is as English as Shakespeare. Later, when more Englishmen travelled on the Continent they became more self-conscious, more anxious to avoid any charge of being provincial. The neo-classicism of the seventeenth century may be purer, more correct; it is also less confident and vigorous. No one would accuse Milton or Dryden or Wren of timidity or diffidence; yet their work is not so essentially English as Spenser's or Shakespeare's or Bess of Hardwick's. Milton takes Virgil, not Chaucer, for his master. Dryden is very much aware of French theories and French practice. St Paul's Cathedral would not look out of place in an Italian city. But it would be very odd indeed, among the ilexes on a hilltop in the Veneto or in Tuscany, to come upon Hardwick Hall.

III

PAINTING

III. PAINTING

THE walls of the rooms in the country houses were hung with tapestries, which served both to adorn them and to keep them warm. Sometimes, as at Hardwick, a room might be designed for a famous set which the owner already possessed, but more often they were bought to furnish an existing room. In the most luxurious houses they would be changed from time to time, but in few, we may suppose, so often as once a week, as were the hangings in Cardinal Wolsey's rooms at Hampton Court. Mural paintings were rare, perhaps because of a preference for the warmth of tapestry and the cheaper painted cloths, but also because, as Sir Henry Wotton observes, our climate is too moist for frescoes to last. Also, no doubt, there were no painters in the country capable of working on this scale, though if they had been needed they would have been found, and we should have had mural paintings of those biblical and classical stories which form the subject of most of the tapestries.

History-painting, as this type of work was called, was considered to be the parallel of heroic poetry, and therefore the greatest kind : its general absence must be due to a practical rather than an aesthetic preference for cloth hangings and panelling in this northern climate. Occasionally remnants of history-paintings survive. At Hill Hall in Essex were murals [1] of scenes from the story of Cupid and Psyche after designs by Raphael (pl. 11) ; each subject in the sequence is framed with a rich border of fruit, foliage, flowers, and birds. These paintings probably date from shortly after 1580, for the house, which was begun by Sir Thomas Smith, was unfinished at his death in that year. At Queen Hoo Hall in Hertfordshire

[1] Now in the Victoria and Albert Museum.

survive paintings of King Solomon worshipping false gods, and also a frieze of horsemen and riders. At Harvington Hall in Worcestershire are the faint remains, drawn in black upon the plaster, of battle scenes from the Old Testament. Such paintings would normally be the work of English artists, working perhaps, as at Hill Hall and Queen Hoo, from engraved designs by Continental masters ; they imitate tapestry, and show the same taste for the heroic as do the tapestries, for

> Oft cruel fights well pictured forth do please.

But the surviving remnants are few, and much must have been covered over or destroyed in the centuries since they were made.

Elsewhere the classical taste is shown in the simpler decoration found in lesser houses and in inns, where the upright timbers of the walls were treated as classical columns, and base, arch, and capital were painted in black on the plaster filling between the uprights. Often this classical ornament became very fanciful and elaborate, but its fashionable origins still appeared. In more important houses, such as Eastbury Manor House at Barking, or Rothamsted House in Hertfordshire, a more carefully designed classical arcade was painted in *trompe-l'œil* manner, with columns supporting an entablature, and with the intervening spaces treated as niches in which naturalistic seascapes or figures of men and animals were painted. The columns may be Corinthian or Salomonic ; the heads of the niches may be simple or scalloped ; but the effect is still a Renaissance version of the classical.

Even the humbler decorations show the same taste. The Elizabethans gave the name Antique (*antico*) to the fantastic kind of ornament, using animal and vegetable forms linked with lines and curves, or coalescing grotesquely together : 'an unnatural or unorderly composition for delight sake, of men, beasts, birds, fishes, flowers etc. without rhyme or reason', as Peacham describes it. This did derive from archaeological discoveries in Rome, but the favourite strapwork ornamentation, which may have had Saracenic origins before it passed through Italy and the Netherlands to England, was also regarded in the sixteenth century as of classical derivation. We may know that it had no counterpart in the decoration of Roman houses ; but if in the sixteenth century men believed that it had, that is what matters, for men are influenced, not by what later scholarship proves, but by what they believe to be the truth. We no longer believe that these intricate designs were used in Rome, any more than we believe that Homer's principal intention was 'the moral of preventing discord amongst confederate princes'. But the Elizabethans did.

On walls hung with huge tapestry pictures of scenes from the life of Ulysses, or from the story of Gideon, it would be absurd to impose framed pictures which would interrupt the design, and, especially if these were 'histories' also, would distract attention. Sir Henry Wotton, familiar as he was with Venetian painting of the age of Titian, Veronese, and Tintoretto, gave admirable advice about the hanging of pictures. He was very insistent upon this, and even suggested to those to whom he gave or bequeathed pictures where they should hang them. The Provost of King's was invited to hang in 'a luminous parlour, which I have good cause to remember' the portrait which Wotton sent him of Paolo Sarpi. An anonymous friend was given 'a piping shepherd done by Cavalier Bassano, and so well as may merit some place in your chamber, which I hear is the centre of good music'. In his will Wotton asked Sir Francis Windebank to arrange for *The Four Seasons* by old Bassano, which he left him, 'to hang near the eye in his parlour (being in little form)'. He pleaded for restraint, so that no room should have many pictures, except the Long Gallery, that peculiarly English room which, among its various uses, might serve for the display of pictures. His advice seems to have been in accordance with the best practice of the time :

at Lambeth, when Archbishop Parker died in 1575, all his pictures hung in the Gallery, though a few of his maps were in other rooms; at Leicester House, when the Earl of Leicester died in 1588, twenty-eight pictures were in the great Gallery, and no other room seems to have had more than one or two; at Hardwick Hall in 1601 nearly half the pictures in the house were hanging in the Long Gallery. But Albius, in Jonson's *Poetaster* of the following year, seems to have been exaggerating when he advised his wife, 'hang no pictures in the hall, nor in the dining-chamber, in any case, but in the gallery only, for 'tis not courtly else'. Wotton further suggested that the pictures be hung where there were fewest lights, for 'no painting can be seen in full perfection, but (as all nature is illuminated) by a single light'. The owner must also study his pictures, to find 'how the painter did stand in the working, which an intelligent eye will easily discover', that is to say, how the subject was illuminated while it was being painted. 'Italian pieces will appear best in a room where windows are high, because they are commonly made to a descending light, which of all other doth set off mens' faces in their truest spirit.'

In that last comment Wotton showed that when he thought of paintings he thought first of portraits. In 1575 Archbishop Parker had owned forty-five portraits, thirty-eight maps, and only four other pictures, an allegory of Death, and three religious pictures — a *Solomon*, a *Hester*, and an *Adoration of the Magi*. In 1601 the Countess of Shrewsbury had at Hardwick about seventy portraits, but less than ten other pictures, one of them of *Ulysses and Penelope*. The famous inventory made for Lord Lumley in 1590 shows again a predominance of portraits, but it also shows that a considerable number of paintings of religious subjects remained in a collection which in part he had inherited from his father-in-law, the last Fitz Alan Earl of Arundel. Among these was a painting 'of an Italian gentlewoman drawn by herself and presented to the old Earl of Arundel in Italy', and another 'brought into England from Rome by Cardinal Pole'. There were paintings of mythological subjects, a *Rape of Helen*, a *Venus and Adonis*, an *Anchises and Aeneas*; and there were allegories of *The Fickleness of Fortune*, of 'an old man fancying a young woman', of 'a young man fancying the rich old woman'. There were also some Dutch genre pictures, 'a Dutch woman selling of fruit', and 'a huge table of the manner of banqueting in Flanders', presumably a painting of some domestic feast. 'A table of cookery' was perhaps a still life painting of a kind familiar in the following century; 'a counterfeit of an old book' was probably a *trompe-l'œil* painting.

In the Lumley collection were certainly some very fine paintings: Holbein's *Duchess of Milan*, now in the National Gallery; his cartoons of Henry VII and Henry VIII, recently acquired from Chatsworth by the National Portrait Gallery; the famous book of portrait drawings, now at Windsor Castle. Dürer's water-colour portrait of Lord Morley, now in the British Museum, was then in Lord Lumley's collection; Eworth's vigorous portrait of Thomas Wyndham, which Pennant admired at Lumley Castle in the eighteenth century, is now at Longford Castle; Antonis Mor's portrait of the Duke of Alva, which is now in New York, was a distinguished work. 'A table on the cunning perspective of death and a woman' if really 'done by Hilliard' as the inventory states would have been one of the now unknown pictures in large done by the great miniaturist. It might even have provided the type for the painting now at Corsham Court, where the skeletal figure of Death lurks behind the bowed figure of the old Queen.

Most of the painters named (and the great majority of the pictures are unattributed in the inventory) were minor Flemish artists and their English followers. Jacques de Poindre of Malines, Jan Scorel of Utrecht, Cornelis and Hans van Cleef are at least still known. The German painter Gerlach

Flicke (improbably concealed as 'Garlicke') had some reputation in his own day. The name of Frans Floris (de Vriendt)

> whom the Flemings greatly praise,

was inserted by Sir John Harington in Ariosto's list of famous painters in the 33rd canto of *Orlando Furioso*, alongside Leonardo da Vinci, Giovanni Bellini, Michelangelo, Raphael, and Titian — company of a distinction which de Vriendt has scarcely kept since. 'The famous painter Steven' was probably Flemish, but is famous no longer. Vincent of Macklen, who painted 'a large table of Charity', Lucio, who painted the portrait of Ariosto, and Hubbert, to whom four portraits of English courtiers were attributed, are unknown. Hubbert, at least, must have had some contemporary reputation, for he is the only painter named in the inventory of paintings at Kenilworth Castle in 1588, and Leicester had employed him four years before to paint a portrait of the Countess and her son.

The Lumley collection, the largest in England apart from the Royal collection, was made for the interest of the subjects of the pictures, whether portraits or history-paintings (including those on religious themes), not because those who formed it had much critical discrimination in the art of painting. Its basis was thus very different from that of the collection of Lord Lumley's great-nephew, Thomas Howard, Earl of Arundel, into which some of the Lumley pictures (including Holbein's book of portrait drawings) eventually, though not by bequest, found their way. It was the collection of a family with an interest in possessing portraits of the family itself, of friends, and of the great, whether of the present or of the past. In this century most of these would be represented by signed photographs in Court dress, standing, silver-framed, on sofa-table or writing-desk. Exceptionally, in the Lumley collection, some religious pictures survived because the family was still of the old religion, and did not scorn such super-

4

Moreton Corbet, Salop, 1579 (see p. 44)

5

Triangular Lodge, Rushton, Northamptonshire, by Sir Thomas Tresham, 1593–95
(see pp. 28, 59)

stitious stuff. The mythological pieces, like the portraits of Chaucer, Dante, Boccaccio, Petrarch, and Ariosto, were evidence of a taste for literature rather than for painting. Perhaps we may also see in this a hint of that antiquarianism which led Lord Lumley, a few years after the inventory was taken, to erect the series of effigies of his mediaeval ancestors in the church at Chester-le-Street. The presence therefore in such a collection of work by artists of the distinction of Holbein, Dürer, and Antonis Mor was, if not fortuitous, at least due rather to Lord Lumley's, or Lord Arundel's, wish to have portraits of certain persons, than to a wish to possess paintings by these artists. Those who owned so many portraits would learn to prefer a portrait of a friend or of a famous man done by a good painter to one done by a journeyman: but they remained interested in recognizable representation, not in great painting. There is little evidence yet of any attempt to collect the work of certain painters in preference to others, and the prevalence of German and Flemish work only confirms what was obvious before, that portraits of Englishmen in the sixteenth century were more likely to be painted by these Protestant Northerners than by Italians even when commissioned by a Roman Catholic. The preservation of working drawings, such as the cartoon of Henry VII and Henry VIII and the Windsor portraits, suggests that the old Lord Arundel had some true appreciation of Holbein's genius as a draughtsman; beyond these only that Dutch flower-seller and three or four other pictures seem to have been acquired, or perhaps presented, by someone with a detached interest in the art of painting.

The Earl of Leicester who, in his country houses of Kenilworth and Wanstead, had collections mainly of portraits, displayed a very different collection on the walls of Leicester House in London. There he had about fifty portraits, but he also had a number of history paintings of mythological subjects which may have been Italian, or copies of Italian pictures, some Dutch pictures which he may have recently brought back from the Low Countries, and, very unexpectedly for the leader of the Puritan party, several religious pictures. These included a *Nativity* ('Christ how he was born in an ox-stall'), *St John the Baptist preaching in the Wilderness*, a *Persecution of Saul*, a *Mary Magdalene*, and also Old Testament history paintings of *Elijah taken up in the fiery Chariot*, of *Susanna and the Elders*, of *Noah and the Flood*. There was also a painting listed by the maker of the inventory (a servant who was not very good at iconography) as 'Christ calling Peter out of the Custom House'. Could this be the Flemish painting of the *Calling of St Matthew*, now at Hampton Court? Traditionally, this painting is supposed to have been taken by the Earl of Essex in the plunder of Cadiz, though it seems odd that it should have had much appeal to him; but he might well have received it from his mother after the death of the Earl of Leicester, who was his stepfather. At Kenilworth Leicester had only one religious picture, a *St Jerome*; at Wanstead he had a *Deposition*, a *St John the Baptist* 'beheaded', and another picture of *Susanna and the Elders*. Why did Leicester have most of his religious pictures in his town house? Why did he have them at all? And where did he collect them? A letter to him from Philip Sidney, dated 18th March 1573 from Frankfurt, may refer to the sending of pictures to him from Germany: 'this bearer having showed me the works he doth carry into England . . . hath promised me to let no man see that which he carrieth until he have showed them unto your Lordship'. Sidney apologizes for his own want of judgment (he was eighteen at the time) if the works, whatever they were, and 'works' could then as now mean 'works of art', seemed unworthy. His letter is written in a cryptic manner so that it should not give away anything to any inquisitive person who might open it before it reached his uncle: it therefore keeps its secret also from us. But it seems most probable that the works which Leicester was to receive from Germany were paintings. He must at this time have been busy with plans for the conversion of Kenilworth Castle, and there would be nothing unusual in asking his gifted nephew to look out for suitable pictures while he was on the Continent.

Leicester also possessed at least two Venetian paintings, a *Marriage in Venice*, which hung in Leicester House, and a *Lady of Venetia* which was at Wanstead. Perhaps these too were sent by Philip Sidney, while he was in Venice a year later. There were also several paintings of classical myths, which may have been Italian : we have no means of knowing. At Leicester House there were two of *Venus and Cupid*, and another (which was of the same subject) described as 'a naked Lady sleeping and Cupid menacing her with his dart', there were two of *Diana*, one of her bathing, the other of *Diana and Actaeon*. There were paintings of Petrarch, and of Laura, of Julius Caesar, of Penelope, of 'an old man looking on his book and a Lady by him enticing him from it', which may derive from an epigram by Marcus Argentarius in the Greek Anthology. At his two country houses Leicester had no such pictures: these modern paintings in the classical tradition were more appropriate to his town house.

In allegorical paintings Leicester seems to have had little interest : there was a picture of *Occasion and Repentance* at Kenilworth, 'a naked boy with a dead man's skull in his hand and an hour glass under his arm' at Leicester House, and paintings of *Faith* and of *Charity* ('a naked woman with three babes about her') also there. Both at Kenilworth and at Wanstead were paintings of 'the baker's daughter', which may have had some scurrilous reference to a mistress of Philip II of Spain, for the picture at Kenilworth in 1583 is listed next to a portrait of the King ; a painting of the Pope at Wanstead must surely also have been a caricature. The ten small pictures of Dutch women at Leicester House may have been recent acquisitions in the Low Countries.

In all Leicester owned at his death about two hundred and twenty pictures, including the maps and the planets. Of these about one hundred and thirty were portraits, a smaller proportion than in Lord Lumley's collection, which may suggest that Leicester's taste was less restricted. Unfortunately none of the paintings which he owned can now be identified (though surely some must have survived), and we cannot therefore know anything of their quality. But he certainly owned some Italian paintings, and he was painted by Zuccari on his brief visit to England. He had greater opportunities for collecting paintings from the Low Countries than any of his contemporaries, and as his patronage of poets and writers shows he was interested in the arts to an extent that his great opponent Burghley never was. It is more likely that some of his pictures were of high quality than that they were all second rate. Of this we cannot be certain, but we do know that Leicester collected a large variety of pictures, and that he thought religious pictures and history paintings of classical myths could be more suitably shown in London than in the country.

Lord Lumley, who had pictures in his house on Tower Hill as well as at Lumley Castle, may have made a similar division: the pictures which Lord Arundel acquired from his collection were from Lumley House. Lord Lumley may even have bought some of Leicester's pictures after his death; certainly many, in the brief entries in the two inventories, sound the same, though the evidence is inadequate for proof. Lumley's *Mary Magdalene* and *Noah* were by de Vriendt, his *Charity* by Vincent of Macklen; he owned a *Nativity*, a *St Jerome*, a *Conversion of St Paul* (which is presumably the same subject as Leicester's *Persecution of Saul*); a 'table of Cookery' — Leicester a 'history of Cookery'; a 'Dutch woman selling of fruit' — Leicester 'a froe selling fruitage'. We cannot know whether these were the same pictures or not, but in any event they show similar taste in the two collections.

The first of the English connoisseurs was Sir Henry Wotton. He had spent many years abroad in Italy and in the Low Countries, and thereby had had more opportunities for seeing great paintings, and conversing with those who appreciated them, than had most of his contemporaries. He was thus far in advance of them in his understanding of the art of painting, the precocious leader of that distinguished company of English connoisseurs of Venetian pictures. From his letters and from his will we know of some of the pictures which he at one time or another possessed : among them were portraits of the four Doges of Venice in whose time he had served there as English Ambassador, all painted by Odoardo Fialetti. These, together with a painting of 'the Venetian College, where Ambassadors had their audience', also by Fialetti, hung in his ordinary dining-room at Eton when he was Provost, and in the same room was the portrait of an earlier Doge 'done either by Titiano, or some other principal hand, long before my time'. All these he bequeathed to King Charles I, 'most humbly beseeching his Majesty that the said pieces may remain in some corner of any of his houses, for a poor memorial of his most humble vassal'. To Charles Prince of Wales he left a portrait by Gerard Honthorst of Elizabeth Queen of Bohemia,[1] to whom he had addressed his charming and elegant verses. He had also owned portraits of Paolo Sarpi, the admired friend whom he had once described, too sanguinely, as a Protestant, but who was at least the leader of the anti-Papal party in Venice.

Wotton sent portraits of Sarpi to King James, and to a few friends : it seems very likely that he sent Donne the portraits of Sarpi and of his biographer Fulgenzio which the Dean left by his will to Henry King. Donne specified a number of pictures in his will : an *Entombment*, a *Magdalene*, a *Virgin and Joseph*, an *Adam and Eve*, and a *Virgin Mary*, all of which he left to friends. This last was Titian's *Madonna and Child with Three Saints,* which the Earl of Carlisle gave to Charles I, and which is now in the Louvre. There were also four large pictures of the four great prophets, and a large picture of an ancient church

[1] Now at Hampton Court.

which he directed should remain in the hall and in the lobby leading to his chamber where, perhaps on Wotton's careful advice, he had placed them. He had, characteristically, a 'picture called the Skeleton', but he made no mention of any history-painting and we should hardly expect to find him in possession of mythological pictures. If he had other portraits than those of the two Venetian friars, he made no special bequest of them : presumably they would go to his family.

Long before, in 1608, Wotton had sent from Venice to Lord Salisbury, who confessed to a desire for 'ancient masterpieces of painting', a copy of some anti-Papal picture of a kind that was popular enough at the time, but which (whatever their vigour as propaganda) seldom attained much artistic quality. Perhaps this was the picture entitled, in a Hatfield House inventory of 1611, 'the Pope's pages'. In such pictures Queen Elizabeth sometimes figures, most remarkably perhaps in Pieter van der Heyden's engraving, where she is shown as Diana, naked and crowned, while the Pope (the Whore of Babylon) is represented as the unchaste nymph Callisto, wearing the tiara. Nudes, it may be noted in passing, were not much to the English taste : Mediterranean classicism had not yet divested our furred and farthingaled shapes, and the nude figures that we sometimes see carved by Elizabethan fire-places look as if they had gone there to keep warm. The cataloguer of Leicester's pictures inserts the word 'naked', as if in surprised comment, after a number of pictures : 'St Jerome naked', 'a naked woman with three babes about her', 'the Lord of Denbigh naked' and so on. We should not expect his taste to be as sophisticated as his master's. Even one of Lord Arundel's correspondents writing from Brussels in 1618, disparages nudes : an acquaintance of his has some 'fair pieces' which might be obtained, he says, 'but they are all of naked women'. To the Puritan inevitably nudes were suggestive : in the gallery at Whitehall the Duke of Stettin observed 'the portraits of two naked women whom Henry VIII had enticed from their husbands', and mannerist engravings were often not far removed from pornography.

Wotton possessed other allegorical pictures of a less crude type: one showed 'Heraclitus bewailing, and Democritus laughing at the world'; another portrayed Divine Love, and this at some time he presented to King Charles. He sent Lord Salisbury a map of Italy in 1608, no doubt intending that it should be framed and hung on a wall, as was the huge picture map of Venice by Fialetti which he presented in 1636 to Eton, where it still hangs in College Hall. He possessed genre pieces: the *Piping Shepherd* already mentioned, and another of a 'Messara playing on a Timbril' by Padovanino 'a rising Titian, as we esteem him'. This is revealing, both for the implied tribute to Titian, and for the exaggerated hopes of a painter who, when Wotton left Venice, was thirty-five years of age but may still have seemed something more than a mere imitator. Wotton's small painting of *The Four Seasons* was probably by Jacopo da Ponte; he also had a painting of *Prometheus devoured by the Eagle*, which he attributes to 'Giacopo Palma in concurrence with Titiano, which for the emulation between two painters (both of no small name)' he ventured to think might be worthy of a place at Hatfield. Lord Salisbury perhaps thought otherwise, for there is no such picture listed in the inventory taken at Hatfield on his death in 1611. The collection then included several religious paintings which may have been Italian, a *Crucifixion*, which hung in the Gallery, *Christ and the Virgin*, and a *St Lawrence* and a *Mary* (perhaps the *Magdalene*) both unframed. There was the usual preponderance of portraits in Lord Salisbury's collection, a few mythological and allegorical pieces, and also, more unexpectedly, two of the Royal Exchange, and a *Solemnity of a Marriage* which was presumably Hofnagel's *Marriage Fête at Horsleydown* which is still at Hatfield House.

Apart from Honthorst's portrait of the Winter Queen

there is nothing to suggest that Wotton, who had travelled widely in Europe, was interested in other than Italian, and indeed principally in Venetian painting. He did not, like most Elizabethans, accept the Mannerists as the purveyors of perfection. He was one of the first to collect Italian pictures, whether for himself or for Lord Salisbury or for the Duke of Buckingham, and his opinion was valued even by so great a connoisseur as King Charles who, in February 1631, sent for Wotton to give his judgment on four pictures which had just reached Whitehall.

But if Wotton is the first of a long line of English collectors of Italian painting, other English visitors to Italy before him had been alive to its splendours. In the Lumley inventory the one certainly Italian painting is the self-portrait of an unknown lady, though it seems likely that portraits of Raphael and of the Italian poets were also Italian. There is also the mysterious entry of 'a special picture of Christ cast in mould by Raphael de Urbino, brought into England from Rome by Cardinal Pole', whatever that may have been. At least Cardinal Pole and the old Earl of Arundel seem to have been aware of the excellence of Italian painting, and to have brought back a picture or two from their travels.

Philip Sidney was in Venice for a year, 1574–75, soon after going down from Oxford, and promised to send his portrait to Hubert Languet, the Huguenot diplomat who was his self-appointed mentor. Titian, who had painted Languet, was still alive, but for the nineteen-year-old Sidney the choice seemed to lie between Tintoretto and Veronese, 'who hold by far the highest place in the art'. Eventually he sat to Veronese, whose painting is no longer known.[1] Sidney's unexpected preference for Veronese, who painted few portraits, rather than for Tintoretto, who painted many, shows his discrimination, since his fair hair and youthful looks might

[1] Mr Bernard Berenson suggested to me that it might perhaps be the portrait of a young man now in the Getty collection.

be expected to suit Veronese the better of the two : probably he took the advice of Italian friends.

There are no other references to pictures in Sidney's letters, but in the *Arcadia* he shows something of his own understanding of the art and of his knowledge of actual pictures. When he describes Basilius 'holding up his hands as the old governess of Danae is painted, when she suddenly saw the golden shower', he must be referring to a picture which he and his friends knew. He is reminding them of a visual image, not inventing one of his own ; and he seems to suggest Titian's painting of the subject, of which there may have been a copy in England. Kalander had a room full of delightful pictures, some of which are described. 'There was Diana when Actaeon saw her bathing, in whose cheeks the painter had set such a colour, as was mixed between shame and disdain : and one of her foolish nymphs, who weeping, and withal lowring, one might see the workman meant to set forth tears of anger.' Sidney must have seen his uncle's picture of *Diana and Actaeon* at Leicester House : perhaps he was describing it here. There were other mythological pictures, of *Atalanta*, *Helen*, *Omphale*, and *Iole*. This may well be in the conventional style of pictorial description of the time, but there is another picture, more beautiful (Sidney says) than the rest, in which are portrayed 'a comely old man, with a lady of middle age, but of excellent beauty', and between them 'a young maid, whose wonderfulness took away all beauty from her, but that which it might seem she gave her back again by her very shadow'. And in addition to Philoclea — for this young maid was she — there should have been in this conversation piece her elder sister Pamela. We cannot say whether or not Sidney was thinking of a picture he had seen, but the kind is not very common and he may have had in mind those paintings of Henry VIII and his Queen Jane Seymour, with Prince Edward, in which the Princesses Mary and Elizabeth are also shown. However, the point is not whether Sidney was thinking of an actual picture which he had seen, but whether he was capable of describing a picture. There cannot be much doubt that the man who had been painted by Veronese, and who discussed perspective with Hilliard was interested in pictures. He understood the importance of shading for giving the effect of a third dimension, of solidity, for (as he put it) a picture 'receives greater life by the darkness of shadows than by more glittering colour'. So, when he describes Philoclea in prison, he tells us that Amphialus found her '(because her chamber was over-lightsome) sitting of that side of her bed which was from the window; which did cast such a shadow upon her, as a good painter would bestow upon Venus, when under the trees she bewailed the murder of Adonis'.[1] His elaborate description suggests a painting in a way that many do not: it is the sort of description of which a man who had never looked critically at a painting would be incapable.

The relation between the two arts of painting and poetry was a commonplace of aesthetic theory in the Renaissance, as it had already been when Plutarch wrote of poetry as a speaking picture, and of painting as mute poetry. Sidney twice uses Plutarch's phrase in the *Apology for Poetry*, but he is exceptional among Englishmen of his time in preferring mythological or historical paintings to portraits. He contrasts 'the meaner sort of painters (who counterfeit only such faces as are set before them) and the more excellent, who having no law but wit, bestow that in colours upon you which is fittest for the eye to see', and he instances a painting of *Lucretia* where the painter 'painted not Lucretia, whom he never saw, but painteth the outward beauty of such a virtue'. Whether or not he had ever seen a picture of *Lucretia*,[2] he seems to have had a liking for

[1] There is 'a table of Venus and Adonis' in the Lumley inventory of 1590, and Titian's *Venus and Adonis* had been seen in England. Another belonged to the Earl of Somerset.

[2] Paul Hentzner saw one of *Lucretia* 'a Grecian bride, in her nuptial habit', at Whitehall: in the Lumley inventory of 1590 is another, by Cornelis van Cleef; and there were others, at Hatfield House in 1611, and belonging to Sir George Herbert of Swansea.

this kind of subject, on the accepted Aristotelian principle that the arts are concerned not with what is, but with what might be, with the ideal, the golden world of poetry. In other words, to Sidney painting was a fine art; something more than a practical means of providing himself with remembrances of his friends.

Most of them, his fellow-courtiers, would have agreed with Sir John Harington that pictures are to be valued 'as pleasing ornaments of a house, and good remembrances of our friends', or so at least it seems. They seldom mention pictures in their letters or journals, and few of them at this time spent long in Italy, in spite of the fascination it exercised over their minds. It was too risky, except in Venice and Padua, for resolute Protestants, and many shared the prejudices of Lord Burghley or Ascham against a country where Ascham spent but nine days, 'and yet I saw in that little time, in one city, more liberty to sin, than ever I heard tell of in our noble city of London in nine years'. The principles of Englishmen impeded attention to Italian art, since so many of the paintings which they might see in Italy would be on religious, that is on Roman Catholic, subjects; and the proliferation of nudes in mythological paintings would be equally shocking to most of them. We cannot expect a detached, aesthetic appreciation of Titian's *Assumption* in the Frari, of Tintoretto's paintings in the Scuola di S. Rocco, of Veronese's *Lo sposalizio di S. Caterina*, from a Calvinist; and Raphael's paintings of *Parnassus*, of the *School of Athens*, of *Galatea*, or Michelangelo's paintings of Prophets and Sibyls, of the *Creation of Adam*, were inaccessible in Rome. English Catholics who visited Rome in the year of Jubilee, 1600, told William Burton (the antiquarian brother of the anatomist of Melancholy) something of the riches of Italian painting which they had seen there, in the Vatican and elsewhere; but this was perhaps many years later. Peacham may have derived his knowledge of painting in Italy from the same source. We must not blame them for making no comment on paintings which they could never have seen, or which (if they had seen) they could not on religious grounds approve. Lord Lumley (who was a Roman Catholic) had a number of religious paintings in his collection, inherited from his Roman Catholic father-in-law, but except for the 'special picture' attributed to Raphael, these were not Italian.

There cannot have been many Italian paintings in England. Castiglione had brought Raphael's *St George* [1] as a gift to Henry VII in 1506, and Henry VIII later owned a set of anti-Papal allegories by Girolamo da Treviso. Queen Elizabeth showed some knowledge of Italian painting in her much misquoted conversation with Hilliard, and was painted by Zuccari during his brief visit to England in 1575. Leicester, of whom Zuccari painted a companion portrait, owned two Venetian paintings, and may have had others by Italian artists. Richard Haydocke, in 1598, says that various noblemen and private gentlemen have 'their Galleries carefully furnished with the excellent monuments of sundry famous ancient Masters, both Italian and German', but he does not tell us who they were, or what pictures they possessed. There were no public collections or museums yet, and there is not enough evidence in inventories or elsewhere to allow us to know what pictures by these famous Masters an Englishman might hope to see in England. The absence of comment on works of art in letters of the time is inevitable : very few letters survive and those that do have been preserved mostly because of their political or legal content. Discussion of books or of paintings in a letter requires that the recipient as well as the writer should be interested in these things ; there can be no doubt that for the great majority painting meant, first and last, portraiture.

Even this interest was quite new. There were royal portraits from an early date, and series of imaginary portraits of the Kings were manufactured early in the sixteenth century, or before. One mural portrait of a fifteenth-century landowner, Thomas Tropenell, survives at Great Chalfield Manor

[1] Now in the National Gallery at Washington.

in Wiltshire. But it was not until Elizabeth came to the throne that it became fashionable for the heads of any but the noblest families to have their portraits painted, in order to remind posterity of ancestral greatness. The portraits therefore become ceremonious, to suit this purpose, as if, like the sepulchral effigies, they were intended to show to the sitter's descendants not what kind of man he had been, but what office he had held, what dignity he had achieved. The resulting full-length portraits of great personages in superb costume are uniquely English, remote from the more naturalistic portraits that were in fashion on the Continent ; and even the painters who came here from the Netherlands found it necessary to conform to the English taste, and, like Dick Tinto, 'to levy that tax upon the vanity of mankind which they could not extract from their taste and liberality'.

Thus Hans Eworth, whose portrait, at Longford Castle, of Thomas Wyndham has been called 'the first truly informal portrait in England . . . burly, untidied, almost sweaty', found no encouragement for such candour, and his later portraits, such as the pair of the Duke and Duchess of Norfolk,[1] are ceremonious rather than informative : portraits of public persons on state occasions, rather than of individuals relaxing naturally in their private houses. Similarly Cornelis Ketel, who could show Martin Frobisher in all his rough determination in the Bodleian portrait, for the most part conformed to the taste of the Court for decorative and formal design. These paintings were to hang in the Long Gallery, where the owner of the house and his guests would stroll up and down together, to admire their distinction, not to criticize their revelation of character. Hence Wotton's paradox that of the four qualities required in a painter, truth and grace in drawing, force and affection in colouring, only truth may be carried to excess.

[1] The portrait of the Duke belongs to Lord Rothschild ; the portrait of the Duchess is at Audley End. I am aware of the uncertainty into which attributions to Hans Eworth have recently been cast, but prefer to use his name in place of cumbersome circumlocution.

Dürer and Michelangelo are criticized on these grounds, because their 'severe observation of nature . . . must needs produce . . . a kind of rigidity and consequently more naturalness than gracefulness'.[1] The Elizabethan always insisted on grace whether of behaviour, as in a Sidney or an Essex, or of form corresponding to this. For the present, it is adequately defined by Wotton as 'a certain free disposition in the whole draught . . . which doth animate beauty where it is, and supply it where it is not'. To such a taste the puritanical insistence on warts and all would be offensively plebeian.

In drawing then grace took precedence over truth, a doctrine which L. B. Alberti had been one of the first to establish. Even that severe Calvinist Fulke Greville would have agreed, for all his insistence on a good likeness :

> For as of pictures, which should manifest
> The life, we say not that is fineliest wrought,
> Which fairest simply shows, but fair and like.

Truth was (as Wotton said) an essential quality, so was grace ; he never said grace alone was enough. Greville seems to be aware of a tendency to emphasize the fair, rather than the like, and is correcting this, but with no suggestion that the fair is dispensable.

The qualities in colouring which Wotton requires, force and affection, stand in need of some explanation, since these are not terms we should use in the criticism of painting. 'Force', he says, 'consisteth in the roundings and raisings of the work, according as the limbs do more or less require it ; so as the beholder shall spy no sharpness in the bordering lines ; . . . not any flatness within the body of the figure'. That is to say, force means the three-dimensional quality which a painter can give to the human figure so that (in Pliny's definition) 'it standeth off, as if it were carved', the quality in

[1] Cf. Bellori *ap*. Dryden : *A Parallel of Poetry and Painting* : 'In our times, Michael Angelo da Caravaggio was esteeemed too natural. He drew persons as they were.'

which Raphael and Michelangelo and Mantegna are supreme. It is a quality which we, at least, find somewhat lacking in many Elizabethan portraits, which often are rather flat, and with the outline too much accentuated. Venetian painting which became, and remained, so much admired in England, tended to have rather different qualities, to which Wotton alludes, in a letter of 4th April 1608, when he is sending Lord Salisbury from Venice, among other gifts, a portrait of the Doge Leonardo Donato 'done truly and naturally but roughly alla Venetiana, and therefore to be set at some good distance from the sight'.

By affection is meant 'the lively representment of any passion whatsoever, as if the figures stood not upon a cloth or board, but as if they were acting upon a stage'; not, it must be noted, as if they were taking part in ordinary, everyday life, but in a theatrical representation of it. This again is very indicative of the Elizabethan taste in pictures, of their insistence on the decorative, the formal, and the ceremonious. Our taste today may differ very much from theirs: we should have preferred more portraits from Eworth like his *Thomas Wyndham*, more from Ketel like his *Martin Frobisher*. But my purpose throughout is to show what the Elizabethans themselves liked, and why; also, where possible, to discover the comments they made on the pictures they commissioned, the houses they built, the poems they read.

For the taste of men and women for whom Spenser and Shakespeare wrote is revealed also in their houses, and in the pictures they hung on the walls. It would be rash to pretend to an understanding of the poetry and drama of the age, and at the same time to disparage contemporary painting, where men and women are portrayed 'as if they were acting upon a stage', or to condemn Wollaton Hall as 'the most notable monument to Elizabethan bad taste'. The great dramatic works of the time derive in part from the detached self-observation which is so characteristic of these Elizabethans, the power to see themselves playing a part which is evident throughout their lives, and especially perhaps in those great death-scenes which were carefully rehearsed, and publicly presented. Their taste in painting as in other things was for the dramatic, and ceremonious, or else for the severely practical. They hung maps — highly decorative, no doubt, with their nymphs of river and spring, and their ships and marine monsters, but still, maps — on their walls, not landscapes : the Earl of Leicester seems to have had an especial liking for these, for he had no less than twenty-three at Kenilworth in 1588. At Lambeth in 1575, when Archbishop Parker died, there were about thirty maps, of England and Europe and America, and of the Land of Promise. Leicester had also 'five of the planets painted in frames' which were presumably mythological paintings of Jupiter, Mars, Venus and the rest as in a series of tapestries at Hardwick Hall. They very sensibly sent competent draughtsmen with their expeditions, or, on their return, got them to provide sketches of what they had seen. So Sir Walter Ralegh had Jacques le Moyne des Morgues, who had been on Laudonnière's expedition to Florida in 1564, to draw in colours 'divers things of chiefest importance' in Florida for his own information and interest in colonial enterprise. Jacques le Moyne, who fled to England after the destruction of Charles Fort in 1565, made some drawings of fruit and flowers in water colour, perhaps, as in *La Clef des Champs*, to provide designs for goldsmiths, embroiderers, and others. These are exquisite, naturalistic drawings, with the flowers carefully arranged in a more or less symmetrical pattern ; but an artist of such accuracy could provide useful drawings for a colonial prospectus. Ralegh, stimulated perhaps by Le Moyne's drawing, sent out John White to Virginia in 1585, and he returned with the well-known water-colour drawings of Indians and American plants and animals which are now in the British Museum. John White amused himself (and Ralegh too) by making drawings of Ancient Britons, to compare with the

6

Wollaton Hall, Nottinghamshire, 1580–88, Robert Smythson, 'architector and surveyor' (see p. 51)

Levens Hall, Westmorland, The Drawing Room, 1595 (see p. 83)

American savages: and here, where factual drawings were not possible, his imagination showed the influence of the Flemish mannerists.

No doubt other Englishmen accompanied the voyagers as draughtsmen, though their work has not survived: it would have been strange indeed if Drake had not carried a draughtsman on his voyage of circumnavigation. On his return the famous botanist Charles de l'Ecluse came to discuss the botanical discoveries of that voyage with him, and it is more likely that Drake showed him drawings than specimens, which would not easily be preserved throughout the three years' voyage. Landscape was not yet imported into England: Haydocke seems to have introduced the word, in his translation of Lomazzo, but probably the first to be painted by an Englishman were on Inigo Jones's scenery for Jonson's Masques. Such were the distinguished beginnings of the kind of painting in which Englishmen have most excelled.

Even the portrait might serve a practical purpose, to disclose to a prince the features of the foreign princess proposed for his bride, or to establish a legend of majesty in a picture hung in an ambassador's house. In either, matter-of-fact realism would be stupidly out of place, and psychological insight impertinent. Imaginary historical portraits were also acceptable for similar reasons, as a focus of attention, as icons. Series of portraits of the kings had long been known, but towards the end of the century there are other series, of the Constables of Queenborough Castle, which Sir Edward Hoby commissioned in 1593, of the Founders of Oxford Colleges painted by Sampson Strong from 1589 until his death in 1611. There was no traditional likeness of most of the persons portrayed, but that was irrelevant. These pictures were intended to suggest the dignity and the achievements of these persons, not their features.

Of the Queen herself there are no portraits from the early years of her reign. This is probably not through the accidental loss of portraits painted in those years, though Sir Walter Ralegh tells us that by her command all 'pictures by unskilful and common painters were knocked in pieces and cast into the fire', but because of her refusal to sit until 'some cunning person meet therefore' might be found. The earliest portrayal of her as Queen is in Hans Eworth's mythological picture at Hampton Court, in which she is shown as a female Paris, holding not an apple but the orb, while the three discomfited goddesses, Juno, Pallas, and Venus shrink from her in dismay. The contemporary frame with its verses interprets the allegory, in case anyone might miss it, though this can hardly have been necessary when the Judgment of Paris was a favourite source of compliment. It was not until the 1570s that the large portraits, still so numerous, began to be painted, perhaps in connection with the proposals for her marriage to Alençon. Later, especially after the Armada, and in the exalted patriotism that followed that revelation of England's new greatness, came the more magnificent portraits, in which the Queen was shown almost as a mythical figure, as Gloriana. To Horace Walpole these portraits showed her as nothing more than 'a pale Roman nose, a head of hair loaded with crowns and powdered with diamonds, a vast ruff, a vaster farthingale, and a bushel of pearls'; but to the Elizabethans they disclosed a portrait of Majesty, to which they could pay their patriotic devotion. It would have been as inappropriate, an offence against decorum, for the woman who was Queen Elizabeth to have appeared in these portraits, as for her to have been realistically presented in *The Faerie Queene*. Her portraits proclaim not the features of an ageing woman, but the splendour of a youthful England.

In many of her portraits there are devices and emblems and mottoes which we can no longer fully interpret. In the famous portrait from Ditchley [1] she stands with her foot upon Ditchley in a map of England; above her right shoulder is a blue sky with white clouds; above her left shoulder lowers a

[1] In the National Portrait Gallery.

stormy sky. As Sir John Harington wrote in that most moving letter to Robert Markham : 'When she smiled, it was a pure sun-shine, that every one did choose to bask in, if they could ; but anon came a storm from a sudden gathering of clouds, and the thunder fell in wondrous manner on all alike'. Beneath the stormy sky is the motto *Potest nec ulciscitur*, which may have general reference to the Queen's merciful nature or (perhaps) some allusion to a forgotten act of forbearance. The sonnet in a cartouche at the edge of the picture is unfortunately no longer entirely legible, but after mention of the sun which is

> Of heaven the glory, and of earth the grace,

passes to the other side of the picture, where is

> Thunder the image of that power divine
> Which all to nothing with a word can bring.

And the sonnet ends

> Rivers of thanks still to that ocean flow
> Where grace is grace above, power power below.

The allusions in this portrait are not very obscure : they interpret in terms of policy what Harington observed as qualities of temperament. This was also the means which the painter used to interpret the Queen's character, rather than by some indecorous distortion of the features of Majesty. Spenser uses allegory and symbol to suggest human personality in *The Faerie Queene*, a method different from that of the dramatists but not less effective : in this he resembles the painters, and those who drew cartoons for the tapestries which he so much enjoyed describing. His portrayal of Queen Elizabeth as Gloriana or as Belphoebe is not dramatic, but pictorial. The portrait at Hatfield House in which the Queen holds a rainbow in her right hand, above which is the motto *Nec sine sole Iris*, no doubt has a very similar intention to the Ditchley portrait : the rainbow implies a storm, but it also implies the sunshine, and traditionally bears the promise of relenting power.

Elsewhere the symbolism is much less intelligible, though a thorough study of Elizabethan devices might well establish the identity of many an unknown sitter. In the Hatfield portrait, the spotted snake embroidered upon the Queen's left sleeve probably signified wisdom, and the cloak patterned with eyes and ears may refer to her ability to know everyone's part, as Harington puts it; or it may refer to individual courtiers, since if she nicknamed Leicester her Eyes and Hatton her Lids she may have nicknamed some other her Ears; or it may announce her Fame. The silkworms embroidered on her dress in the portrait at Parham Park may show her wish to encourage the production of silk in England, for which an Italian had introduced the insects in 1581. The sieve which the Queen holds in the portrait at Siena was (so Camden says) her favourite device. It was a symbol of virginity; by its means the Vestal Virgin Tuccia proved her chastity, carrying water in it without letting it through. The motto about it, *A terra il ben — mal dimora in sella*, is obvious enough in its reference to a sieve, however obscure in its reference to virginity. But what of the column on which is inscribed *Stanco riposo e riposato affanno*? or of the globe inscribed *Tutto vedo et molto* [*manca*]? On this column are set cameos, illustrating the *Aeneid*, with an imperial crown on the lowest one. Perhaps here, and in the globe with its motto, is some claim to imperial rivalry with Philip of Spain.

Many another portrait has some device of which the interpretation, if we knew it, would add to the significance of the picture, indicating what aspects of the Queen's Majesty the painter wished to emphasize, her power, her mercy, her imperial destiny. The portrait at Welbeck, in which she holds an olive branch, while a sheathed sword of state lies at her feet, indicates the peacefulness of her realm, which her subjects so often contrasted with the unquietness of France and the Netherlands, and the clemency, which Spenser celebrated in the person of Mercilla in *The Faerie Queene*. Her dress is embroidered again with snakes, and with a variety of flowers which, like Ophelia's, no doubt had some symbolic significance. Elizabeth is addressed as Flora in one of Sir John Davies' *Hymns of Astraea*; and to an Elizabethan flowers suggested the eternal spring of the golden age that had returned with Elizabeth. To Manilius a love of flowers and their scents symbolized a love of elegance and of the arts and graces of life:

> munditiae cordi cultusque artesques decorae
> et lenocinium vitae praesensque voluptas.

Sir Calidore has a vision of Gloriana amidst a hundred dancing maidens, who include the three graces:

> And ever, as the crew
> About her daunst, sweet flowres, that far did smell,
> And fragrant odours they uppon her threw.

At Hatfield House there is another portrait of the Queen with an ermine on her left wrist, an animal of royal and heraldic symbolism, which was reputed to be so dainty that it would not go near dirt for fear of spoiling its skin; it is therefore a symbol of chastity.

The magnificence of the Queen's dresses was proverbial, and it was matched by her jewellery. Among the jewels which she wears in her portraits it is scarcely possible to identify miniatures, but we know she possessed and made gifts of these. In 1564 the Ambassador of Mary Queen of Scots saw her unpacking a little cabinet in her bedchamber which was filled with small portraits. At Longford Castle is a small carved and gilded cabinet, which is traditionally said to have been given by Queen Elizabeth to Penelope Rich with the five miniatures which it contains, each in its contemporary ivory box. Probably the cabinet and portraits which Sir James Melville saw were similar to this. Later miniatures were jewels containing portraits, rather than portraits set in a jewelled case — 'jewels of gold, for the service of noble persons', Hilliard called them: that is to say, they were intended to be worn, not to be displayed, and the portrait was normally hidden in its case, to be looked at by the possessor in private. Lord Herbert of Cherbury describes this sentimental fashion in his *Autobiography*.

'There was a lady also, wife to Sir John Ayres, Knight, who, finding some means to get a copy of my picture from Larkin, gave it to Mr. Isaac [1] the painter in Blackfriars, and desired him to draw it in little after his manner ; which being done, she caused it to be set in gold and enamelled, and so wore it about her neck so low that she hid it under her breasts.' Her husband discovered this, and was not unnaturally jealous, though the infatuation was all on the lady's side, at least, so Lord Herbert says. He himself knew nothing of this at first, but 'coming one day into her chamber, I saw her through the curtains lying upon her bed with a wax candle in one hand, and the picture I formerly mentioned in the other. I coming thereupon somewhat boldly to her, she blew out the candle, and hid the picture from me ; myself thereupon being curious to know what that was she held in her hand, got the candle to be lighted again, by means whereof I found it was my picture she looked upon with more earnestness and passion than I could have easily believed.'

In this or a similar context we must consider the miniatures, which, in the work of Nicholas Hilliard and Isaac Oliver, far surpass in quality any of the contemporary painting on a larger scale. Most of them were set in pieces of jewellery to be worn about the neck, by men as well as by women, as mementoes of mistress or lover, to be adored in secret. The Queen had among her jewels 'one little flower of gold with a frog thereon, and therein Monsieur's physiognomy', no doubt given to her by her Frog, Alençon, at some moment when he would a-wooing go. Constable, in his sonnet to Hilliard 'upon occasion of a picture he made of my Lady Rich'

[1] Oliver. This was the same portrait that the Earl of Dorset had copied in large (see p. 80).

calls it 'the jewel which you paint', and refers to the representation in the miniature of diamonds, rubies, and pearls — gems which were sometimes actually used in the miniature itself. They are comparable to the sonnets, and are as highly wrought, as allusive, and as private. They were not meant, originally, for public exhibition, any more than the sonnet was intended for publication. We must think of them being looked at by candlelight in a curtained bed, or held in the hand in the window of a room, where they could quickly be hidden again in bodice or doublet. This is what they were for, not for exhibition in a glass case, with the two sides of the jewelled locket separated for display beside the painting. The jewelled case, like the conceits in the phrasing of a sonnet, was intended to conceal from public gaze a private message between two lovers.

Hence the incomprehensibility of some of Hilliard's most famous limnings. Who is the man portrayed in a miniature dated 1588, who clasps a hand that reaches to him from a cloud? Whose is the hand? And what does the motto *Attici amoris ergo* mean? Or this long-legged young man, who with his hand on his heart leans against a tree, and is embowered in white roses — can he be the Earl of Essex? And to what incident does the motto, *Dat poenas laudata fides*, refer? No doubt he is love-sick, for this was fashionable, but why does his praised fidelity bring punishment with it? Who again is the young man whose portrait, pasted on to the ace of hearts, shows him against a background of flames, and fingering a locket on his breast? But who is the dark lady, and who the fair youth of Shakespeare's sonnets?

This convention of wearing some favour of the mistress — a glove, a handkerchief, a sleeve, a ring, a bracelet of bright hair — is part of the elaborate code of sentiment, which is so characteristic of the Elizabethan Court. The Queen herself subscribed to it: she sent Mountjoy, after he had performed well in a tournament, a gold queen from a set of chessmen.

He bound it on his arm with a crimson ribbon, which provoked Essex to remark: 'Now I perceive every fool must have a favour'. Mountjoy challenged Essex, and disarmed him in the duel that followed. The Queen observed that it was fit that someone should take him down and teach him better manners. In the amorous code the lady was invariably cruel, and the lover was invariably love-sick, as the bower of white roses, or the background of flames suggest. Spenser, who addressed the most exalted love poems in the language to the lady whom he actually married (and is unique in this), mocked in *Colin Clouts Come Home Againe* at the fashionable sentimentality of the Court:

> For all the walls and windows there are writ,
> All full of love, and love, and love my deare,
> And all their talke and studie is of it.
> Ne any there doth brave or valiant seeme,
> Unlesse that some gay Mistresse badge he beares:
> Ne any one himselfe doth ought esteeme,
> Unlesse he swim in love up to the eares.

One can hear the ironic tone of Spenser's voice, where he mimics the affectation of the young man of fashion fatuously reiterating 'love, and love, and love my dear'. But it was for this fashionable world that Hilliard produced his incomparable miniatures. His is the one achievement in the plastic arts that is fit to stand beside the multitudinous achievements of the poets. He is, as it were, the sonneteer among painters, perfecting a work of art in a formally controlled pattern, in little, and in the tradition of compliment that Elizabethan lovers inherited from Petrarch. There was no Botticelli, no Raphael, no Titian in Elizabethan England partly because the religious sources of their painting were closed to Englishmen. But we have no Mantegna to record nobly imagined scenes of imperial Rome, no Veronese to decorate the new country houses with portrayals of the grand sumptuousness of courtly life, and that may be for some deeper and stranger reason, for our painters have never yet attained the continuing greatness of our poets.

There can be no doubt that Hilliard's painting exactly suited the taste of the Elizabethan age ; a large number of miniatures from his hand survives, and though many of the sitters are no longer identifiable, we know that he portrayed most of the leading men and women of the Court. But it is not enough to know that he was fashionable : we need to know what it was in his painting that especially appealed to the Elizabethans. Fortunately there is some evidence on this, in occasional comments made by those who knew his work, and in his own *Treatise on the Art of Limning* which he wrote at the request of Richard Haydocke. Haydocke, who was a Fellow of New College, published in 1598 a translation of Lomazzo's *Trattato dell' Arte della Pittura* which had originally been published in Italy in 1584. To Haydocke, as to Sir John Harington, limning was 'the perfection of painting', superior to large paintings in oils, though whether that was a widely accepted opinion we cannot know. It may well have been, for the miniatures derived, as they themselves recognized, from illuminations in manuscripts, and in this English artists had already in the fifteenth century developed a notable tradition of portraiture. Hilliard himself (as we might expect) thought that limning excelled all other painting ; but his reasons are pertinent. 'It is', he says, 'a thing apart from all other painting or drawing and tendeth not to common men's use, either for furnishing of houses, or any patterns for tapestries, or building, or any other work whatsoever'. In other words it is to be judged (like a sonnet) purely on aesthetic grounds, and has no practical application or purpose ; and it is essentially aristocratic, an art to please a courtier. Donne also, perhaps, shared this view when he wrote that

> a hand, or eye
> By Hilliard drawn, is worth an history
> By a worse painter made,

for by 'a history' he means a large 'historical' painting, or subject picture.[1] At least he was emphasizing the importance of the artist's skill in contrast with the subject of his painting, and he chose to mention not the face but the hand and the eye. I would not insist on any likelihood of Donne's deliberate and purposeful selection of these details, yet Hilliard has something to say in his *Treatise* on the drawing of both : 'Tell not a body when you draw the hands, but when you spy a good grace in their hand take it quickly, or pray them to stand but still, for commonly when they are told they give the hand the worse and more unnatural or affected grace'. And of the eye he says that it is to be 'perfect round for so much thereof as appeareth'; and the eye is 'the life of the picture'.

This interest in Hilliard's technique can be found elsewhere. Sir John Harington says that he himself had seen Hilliard 'in white and black, in four lines only, set down the feature of the Queen's Majesty's countenance, that it was ever thereby to be known ; and he is so perfect therein (as I have heard others tell) that he can set it down by the idea he hath, without any pattern'. To this comment Hilliard refers in his *Treatise*, and points out the importance of line, rather than of shadow 'for the line without shadow showeth all to a good judgment, but the shadow without line showeth nothing'. This emphasis on the line, which is so apparent in Hilliard's work, is in conformity with contemporary Italian theory, but that may well have been less important to him than the tradition of manuscript illumination in which he had been trained. Queen Elizabeth showed her own acute understanding of these technical problems in a conversation with Hilliard which he records.

The Queen told Hilliard she had noticed 'great difference of shadowing in the works and diversity of drawers of sundry nations, and that the Italians, who had the name to be cunningest and to draw best, shadowed not', and asked him the reason

[1] Cf. *Elegy V*. He was painted by Oliver, and the portrait of him as a young man may have been engraved after a miniature by Hilliard.

for this. The Queen here implies a knowledge of contemporary Italian painting which is surprising since, so far as is known, the only Italian mannerist to visit England was Federico Zuccari. However, he had made a drawing [1] of the Queen, and perhaps had discussed his views on line with her, and she was clearly interested in the subject.[2] Hilliard told the Queen that 'shadows in pictures were indeed caused by the shadow of the place' where the painter was working; and that some painters preferred a studio with light coming in only at some small or high window, since by this means they obtained 'a grosser line, and a more apparent line to be discerned', which would give the picture a good three-dimensional quality, such as Wotton desired, and would make it 'show very well afar off'. But to the miniature painter this was unnecessary, since his work was 'to be viewed in hand, near unto the eye'. The Queen recognized the validity of Hilliard's argument 'and therefore chose her place to sit in for that purpose in the open alley of a goodly garden, where no tree was near, nor any shadow at all, save that as the heaven is lighter than the earth, so must there be that little shadow that was from the earth'.

This famous conversation has often been misrepresented, as if the Queen were insisting on being painted without shadows in order to flatter her beauty, or to cancel the signs of age. It was no such matter. She knew something of modern Italian and Flemish painting, and sought the expert opinion of the most gifted English painter of the time in whose work, we may suppose, she, like her godson Sir John Harington, was capable of noticing the dominance of line. When Hilliard explained to her the cause and effects of shadowing, and distinguished between large paintings to be seen at a distance, and miniatures to be held in the hand, she at once understood, and chose to sit to him in a place that best suited his style.

[1] In the British Museum.

[2] But if we are to take Hilliard literally, this conversation with the Queen must have taken place about 1569, before Zuccari's visit.

Later, as Harington tells us, Hilliard was able to draw the Queen's portrait from memory, but by that time, some fifteen or twenty years after the conversation which had taken place 'when first I came in her Highness' presence to draw', his task was not so much to portray Queen Elizabeth as to produce a picture conforming to expectation of the Queen's Majesty. Realistic description or psychological insight were no more appropriate to these portraits than they would be to a royal portrait on a coin or a medal. Indeed these miniatures of the Queen to some extent took the place of medals. In 1584 Hilliard, with Derek Anthony, was commissioned to make the Second Great Seal for Queen Elizabeth, and in his traditional portrayal of the Queen enthroned, and holding orb and sceptre, Hilliard produced an image which was both majestic and impersonal. The Queen gave jewels containing her portrait to some of her favoured courtiers, or to mark distinguished service. She gave Sir Humphrey Gilbert 'an anchor guided by a lady', and asked for his picture in return. The Drake pendant she gave to Sir Francis Drake after his voyage of circumnavigation, and this contains her portrait by Hilliard, together with a cameo and an enamel of the Phoenix. The victory over the Armada was commemorated by the Armada Jewel which the Queen gave to Sir Thomas Heneage, who had played an important part in raising the army to resist the expected invasion. This too contains a miniature of the Queen, and also a gold profile of her. Besides this magnificent jewel two other medals were struck to commemorate the victory : the Dangers Averted Medal, and a related Badge, both in gold, and both bearing the Queen's bust in relief. Both have the same device on the reverse : an island in the sea, in which ships are sailing, with a green bay tree flourishing on the island, on whose shore is the motto *Non ipsa pericula tangunt*, for the bay tree was traditionally immune from storm and lightning.

For such purposes the representation of Elizabeth exactly as she appeared would have been irrelevant. She was the

Queen in whose service victory over Spain had been won, and who now rewarded those who had played the greatest part in it. Such she appeared on these medals, about her the proud motto, *Ditior in toto non alter circulus orbe*, to proclaim that her crown was the equal of Philip's for whom, once, *Non sufficit orbis*. (But Drake, a couple of years before at San Domingo, had given the lie to that pretension.) And this presentation of her Majesty was as proper to the medal, as was the device of the formal island with its bay tree, instead of a map of England.

In portraits other than those of the Queen, Hilliard had a different task. It was his conviction that in painting 'of all things the perfection is to imitate the face of mankind', which he also considered the most difficult. In his treatise he gives evidence of that refined sensibility which his miniatures show. He states a theory, in true Renaissance style, but then modifies it as necessary to accord with his own delicate observation of the men and women who sat to him. There are, he says, three elements in facial beauty ; complexion (which is the least important) ; favour, or good proportion, which we judge instinctively, not by Dürer's rules ; and 'grace in countenance', which is the most important. In his reliance on intuition for judging the proportions of a face, Hilliard is very English. Bacon, in his essay *Of Beauty*, criticizes Dürer on the same grounds as a 'trifler' who 'would make a personage by geometrical proportions', which he rightly supposes 'would please nobody but the painter who made' it, for 'there is no excellent beauty that hath not some strangeness in the proportion'. Wotton's insistence on a classical love of proportion contrasts with Bacon's acceptance of mannerist theory in painting as strongly as his views on architecture differ from Bacon's : generally Wotton keeps to the middle way between naturalism and mannerism. But Hilliard, who had painted Bacon as a young man when he was in Paris in 1578, would certainly have agreed with him, not with Dürer. Sir Christopher Hatton, he says, was 'a man generally known and respected of all men amongst the best favours, and to be one of the goodliest personages of England, yet had he a very low forehead, not answerable to that good proportion of a third part of his face'. The empirical Englishman already confronts the German theorist. And it is characteristic of the age that grace should be the chief element in a good face, and one which a gentleman is more likely to appreciate than any other. For it is that 'by which the affections appear', the revelation of character. Or, if this theory must occasionally be modified for Socrates' sake, yet as Philip Sidney wrote to his young brother Robert, advising him to have care of his diet and consequently of his complexion, 'Remember, *gratior est veniens in pulchro corpore virtus*', that when virtue appears in a man of handsome presence it is all the more acceptable, and full of grace.

Hilliard, most handsome and elegant himself, was very susceptible to physical beauty, and aware of the dangers that beset a painter. For how can the artist 'catch these lovely graces, witty smilings, and these stolen glances which suddenly like lightning pass and another countenance taketh place, except he behold, and very well note, and conceit to like? So that he can hardly take them truly, and express them well, without an affectionate good judgment, and without blasting his young and simple heart.' For these reasons, and because the portrait painter can hardly fail to be 'amorous', the art is fittest for gentlemen, who brought up in the ideal of self-control and courtesy, will know how to behave. Here again he suggests the sonneteer who was also tempted by his imagination to fall in love with the lady whose beauty he was celebrating. Henry Constable, who had known Hilliard, and who carried to King James in 1589 a miniature of Penelope Rich on which he wrote a sonnet, seems to have been so afflicted, for Lady Rich wrote that year in a letter to Jean Hotman that she sent her wishes 'à monsieur Constable, qu'il ne soit plus amoureux'. But then as Hilliard said, after commiserating

Dürer on never having had the good luck to see the beautiful Italian women (which he had), 'rare beauties are . . . more commonly found in this isle of England than elsewhere, such surely as art ever must give place unto.'

We may discount the patriotic enthusiasm here, though we should not forget that visiting foreigners from Erasmus to Giordano Bruno also remarked on the beauty of English women ; but we can hardly deny to most of those whom Hilliard painted the chief element in beauty, that facial expression of a courtly elegance of character. His sitters, we never doubt, are men and women of lively intelligence and courteous manners, self-confident (except when affecting love-sickness), and self-controlled. They have, as was said of Philip Sidney,

> A sweet attractive kind of grace,
> A full assurance given by looks ;

and if they were vain of their magnificent clothes and handsome faces, then surely vanity is pardonable to a generation whose beauty was celebrated in Hilliard's limning, and in Shakespeare's sonnets.

Isaac Oliver, the Frenchman, was almost exactly Shakespeare's contemporary. He came to England as a child, and was in some sense Hilliard's pupil. Contemporary reference usually couples his name with Hilliard's, and the style of the older artist had probably so dominated contemporary taste that the Elizabethans tended to see the resemblances between their work where we are more conscious of the differences. (In a similar way George Puttenham found little difference between the poetry of Wyatt and Surrey, which does not imply a lack of discrimination so much as an awareness of their superiority to all the other poets of their time, whom we no longer trouble to read.) Isaac Oliver's work is indeed very different from Hilliard's : he was not trained as a goldsmith (though his father was one), and he was not influenced by the tradition of the illuminators ; his paintings are reductions in scale from paintings in large — many were indeed copies of larger works, as was the miniature of Lord Herbert which Lady Ayres had made — whereas many large paintings of the time, especially of the Queen, suggest rather enlargements of Hilliard's miniatures. He consequently used shadow instead of line, because he did not conceive his paintings to be seen in the hand as Hilliard explained to the Queen. And he was realistic, especially in his later work, as Hilliard never was. Congruously with these qualities of a painter whose natural medium would be the full-scale oil painting, but who was working for the most part in miniature (perhaps because there was a better market for miniatures) Oliver painted 'histories', and religious pictures, as Hilliard never did. Probably he conceived this ambition during his visit to Venice in 1596 when, as Mr Reynolds has suggested, 'he must have found himself in the company of Rottenhammer, who with Brill and Elsheimer was creating the small German cabinet picture as it were by looking at paintings in the Venetian grand manner through the wrong end of the telescope'. There he also studied Italian masters, especially Parmigianino.

Hilliard survived Oliver by more than a year, and was described in a grant from James I in 1617 as 'our principal Drawer for the small Portraits and Embosser of our Medallions of gold', but Isaac Oliver's work had naturally enough tended to supersede Hilliard's in popularity. For it was much more akin to the large-scale painting which was sought by collectors such as Lord Salisbury, Lord Arundel, the Duke of Buckingham, Henry Prince of Wales and Prince Charles. It is hard to imagine Hilliard copying in miniature a large painting as Oliver often did. He had worked in the wholly different tradition of the illuminator and the goldsmith, and did not think of his limnings apart from their jewelled settings, or (occasionally) the ivory boxes in which they would be enclosed in an elaborately carved cabinet. They are unique, and the courtly taste for which they were created gave place to something cruder, less exquisite, with the new century.

Hilliard might go on painting miniatures, as Drayton might go on adding to his sonnets, but the craze for sonneteering hardly lasted beyond the death of the Queen, and Hilliard's best work ceased at the same time. For, as Drayton said, to the golden age of Elizabeth had succeeded an iron age ; the elegant manners of her English courtiers had been flung aside by the drunken debauchery of the King's Scotsmen and the Queen's Danes.

IV

SCULPTURE

IV. SCULPTURE

THE memorials which men erect over the bodies of their dead often reveal more of their taste than the houses which they build for the living to dwell in. Here is no practical purpose to be met, no use to be considered ; but something must be made, to match an impulse to mourn, and a wish to remember. The pyramids in Egypt, the famous sepulchre of Mausolus, a Greek stele on which a young woman in her chair selects a jewel from the box her maidservant offers, an English brass where a pet dog called Terri lies at his mistress' feet, the Sagrestia Nuova in Florence, the Albert Memorial — all these were designed for no other purpose than to commemorate the dead, and all clearly announce what those who set them up considered to be fitting and worthy memorials. There is, no doubt, a wide difference between the barbaric ponderosity of a pyramid and the civilized elegance of Hegeso's monument, as there was between an Egyptian king and an Athenian girl, or, for that matter, between an empty desert and a city's graveyard. And there is another difference, between the pagan Greek, whose vision of the other world was of a place of shadows, without the joy and light of this, and the Christian, for whom this world, with its temptations and tribulations, was but a preparation for the bliss of the other. The way in which men commemorate their dead must be influenced by their beliefs about what happens to the dead, no less than by their participation in the society of those who live.

For the Elizabethans the Christian hope of the Resurrection to eternal life was sure and certain, or, if it was ever questioned, this could be only in the privacy of conversation, not in the publicity of epitaph. A monument is a public object, to be placed where it will draw attention, in a church or a piazza; rhetorical more often than reticent; and for that reason the extravagance needed to catch the eye of a busy generation might have seemed vulgarly over-emphatic in a quieter time. Mediaeval tombs, for all their splendour, retain a certain humility in the face of death, and invite a prayer for the soul of the departed. By the Elizabethans the Romish doctrine concerning Purgatory was dismissed: 'a fond thing vainly invented, and grounded upon no warranty of Scripture, but rather repugnant to the Word of God'. To invite a prayer for the dead was superstitious, and there was a change therefore in the first words of the inscription from the mediaeval *Orate pro anima* . . . to *Memoriae sacrum*. . . . To recite the ancestry of the dead man in his epitaph, to proclaim it by an array of heraldry on tomb-chest or canopy, and to record his personal achievements had become appropriate. The spectator is invited, not to pray for the dead, but to remember him as he was in life, in tilting armour or Garter robes, and he is assisted by an effigy intended for a portrait. In all this we may detect the secular change towards recognition of the dignity of man as an individual which is so important a part of Renaissance thinking, and which may be found also in Italian and French monuments of the time; for the maintenance of the old religion did not always imply the survival of the old humility.

Portraits had been made in memorial effigies long before, as in the superb alabaster of King Edward II in Gloucester Cathedral, in Torel's bronze of Queen Eleanor in Westminster Abbey, and on other royal tombs. At the funerals of Kings it had early been the custom to expose the corpse to public view — they bore him barefaced on the bier, as Ophelia sings — but by the time of King Henry III it was found more seemly to substitute an effigy, dressed in royal dignity, and with face and hands in wood or wax, painted to the life. This effigy was carried on the coffin, and probably remained upon the grave for some time after the burial, until it could be replaced by a permanent effigy. The remnants of some of these funeral effigies are still preserved in Westminster Abbey, where the head of King Henry VII, carved in wood, perhaps by an Italian, is a vivid and austere portrait.

From these royal examples members of the nobility derived, in time, an interest in portraiture of themselves. Even for the unique bronze effigy of Richard Beauchamp, Earl of Warwick, in St Mary's Church, Warwick, William Austin, brass founder of London, undertook to provide nothing more personal than the 'image of a man armed', though he certainly achieved a portrait. So did the alabasterer who made the beautiful effigy of Chaucer's granddaughter, Alice, Duchess of Suffolk, at Ewelme in Oxfordshire; but for the most part the sculptors provided the figure of a knight, or a lady, or a bishop for these earlier monuments, with no more attempt at portraiture than in the angels carved on the sides of the tomb. But in the contract (dated 27th October 1582) for a tomb to be erected at Somerton, in Oxfordshire, to Thomas Fermor and his wife portraits are specified: there are to be 'a very fair, decent and well proportioned picture or portraiture of a gentleman, representing the said Thomas Fermor with furniture and ornaments in armour' and so forth, and 'a decent and perfect picture or portraiture of a fair gentlewoman with a French hood, edge and habiliment, with all other apparel, furniture, jewels, ornaments and things in all respects usual, decent, and seemly for a gentlewoman', that is, appropriate to her social rank. The tomb survives, somwhat damaged, but if it failed to portray Thomas and Bridget Fermor, it failed through incompetence, not indifference. The extension of portraiture to the effigies of these lesser persons, which is paralleled in the increase of painted portraits, was something new, and though in these sculptures as in the paintings the portrayal of a living individual often had difficulty in struggling through the formal definition of rank, the best of the sculptors were at least as good as the best of the painters, Hilliard always excepted, then working in England.

The London sculptors, who sent their work all over the country, would contract now to make 'the similitude' of the person to be commemorated, and here and there an inscription will claim that an effigy presents 'a true portraiture'. This was a new ambition, to suppose that posterity might care to see what anyone but a King or a Duchess once looked like, just as it was new to record at length their personal virtues and achievements. But portraiture requires that the sculptor should have at least a sketch to work from, and though he might make use of an existing portrait of the dead, very often he would make his own drawing from the life. For, like Browning's Bishop, many an Elizabethan ordered his own tomb and (to avoid that suspicion of his heir's parsimony which so plagued the Bishop) even set it up himself. 'If a man do not erect in this age his own tomb ere he dies,' says Benedick, 'he shall live no longer in monument than the bell rings and the widow weeps.' The Lumley inventories include drawings for the monuments which Lord Lumley designed in 1597 to be set up in Cheam church in Surrey to the memory of himself and his two wives. 'Robert Lord Spencer built this monument in his life A.D. 1599' is inscribed on his tomb at Great Brington, Northamptonshire. An inscription on a monument at Burford, Shropshire, informs the spectator that 'These statues represent now living the son of Sir Thomas Cornwayll knight and Anne his lady', who no doubt regularly worshipped in the church, to be compared by their more inattentive fellow-parishioners with the effigies on the wall above. Maximilian Colt's drawing for the magnificent tomb which Sir Christopher Hatton ordered still survives[1], though the tomb perished when old St Paul's was burnt ; and Robert Smythson submitted his drawing[2] for the tomb of the Countess of Shrewsbury, now in Derby Cathedral, for her approval,

[1] In the Bibliothèque Nationale, Paris. [2] In the R.I.B.A., London.

just as Maximilian Colt in November 1609 'brought my Lord Salisbury a model of his tomb'. Walton's story of Donne's arrangements for his monument, which survived the Great Fire and is still to be seen in St Paul's, shows the famous preacher's detached concern with theatrical effect even as he was dying. 'Dr Donne sent for a carver to make for him in wood the figure of an urn, giving him directions for the compass and height of it ; and to bring with it a board of the just height of his body. These being got, then without delay a choice painter was got to be in a readiness to draw his picture, which was taken as followeth. — Several charcoal fires being first made in his large study, he brought with him into that place his winding-sheet in his hand, and, having put off all his clothes, had this sheet put on him, and so tied with knots at his head and feet, and his hands so placed, as dead bodies are usually fitted to be shrouded and put into their coffin, or grave. Upon this urn he thus stood with his eyes shut, and with so much of the sheet turned aside as might shew his lean, pale and death-like face.' Not content with this macabre performance, Donne had the finished picture set up by his bedside 'where it continued, and became his hourly object till his death'.

Here, as so often, Donne was looking back towards mediaeval tradition, to the shrouded cadaver exposed beneath the effigy of a great churchman in his vestments such as Bishop Fleming in Lincoln Cathedral, or Bishop Bekynton at Wells. He who as poet had so much asserted his own individuality and pride, now as priest turned to the Catholic humility in which he had been brought up, and preferred that his monument should be a *memento mori*, rather than the testimony of a life lived to the full. This mediaevalism, which led the poet to regret the new philosophy that had cast all in doubt, led the preacher to proclaim, as it were from the edge of his own grave, to an audience as fashionable as fascinated, 'We have a winding-sheet in our mother's womb which grows with us from our conception, and we come into the world wound up in that winding-sheet, for we come to seek a grave'.

Donne was neither the first nor the last to be depicted in his shroud, though he may have been the first to insist on combining a portrait with the shrouded figure. Usually, if the body was shrouded it was completely shrouded, as in one of the Foljambe monuments at Chesterfield, where the effigy lies on a bier beneath three panels in high relief showing Childhood, Old Age, and Death, while below it, arranged in two decorative trophies, are the spades, hoes, and bones of the sexton's trade. Perhaps the strangest, to us, of all these shrouded effigies are those on a Beresford tomb, also in Derbyshire, at Fenny Bentley, where husband and wife lie side by side, and their children stand upright, in the old way, against the sides of the tomb-chest : the whole family are completely shrouded, with a tie at their heads and a neat bow over their ankles. Such obsession with mortality, even on a monument, is not much to the taste of our time, and was not prevalent then, though there is no reason to think that an Elizabethan would have found it anything more than a little old-fashioned. Certainly they would not have been perplexed almost to laughter, as we may be, by a monument such as that at Churchill, Somerset, where John Latch, booted and spurred, his sword on his hip, reclines on one elbow and dotes on Death (so the inscription informs us) as he contemplates the shrouded body of his wife Sarah lying below.

The cadavers which the fifteenth-century sculptors liked to show beneath the effigy of the living were sometimes shown in their shrouds, sometimes without ; both fashions are *de rigueur* in Elizabethan monuments. A shrouded cadaver lies in a lower cupboard beneath the remarkable painted triptych [1] with its classical frame, erected to three members of the Cornwall family at Burford, Shropshire. Another is carved among the six pillars that support the effigy of Francis Fitton as he was in life, at Gawsworth in Cheshire. A naked cadaver is un-

[1] Signed, Melchior Salaboss, 1588.

expectedly exposed on the very classical sarcophagus of the monument to Anthony Cave at Chicheley in Buckinghamshire. There are other methods of stating the obvious, of reminding those who look at a tomb that it was erected over a corpse. At Chiddingly in Sussex the monument to Margaret Jefferay, who died at the age of twenty-five in 1618, includes an urn with an opening to reveal a skull, about which is the punning inscription *Margarita fui*. (But urns were uncommon as yet.) There is an especially nasty reminder at Clifton, Nottinghamshire, where beneath a monument to the first three of Sir Gervase Clifton's seven wives we are shown a glimpse through a charnel window of tumbled skulls and hands, made all the more shocking by the elegantly draped curtain carved above the window — as if their boudoir had been transformed overnight into a charnel. With such devices did the sculptors, or those who commissioned their work, from time to time still seek to impress upon the living the old lesson of σῶμα σῆμα, of the trivial worthlessness of the human body in which the human soul is here briefly incarcerated.

Yet the men of the Renaissance preferred to think, with the Greeks and Romans, that a noble soul was likely to inhabit a beautiful body, and logically so,

> For soul is form and doth the body make.

They preferred therefore the portrait of the man in his robes of high office, of the lady in her matronly dignity ; to remember them as they had been in their prime not as they had now become ; eventually, as fashions changed, to portray them not recumbent, with hands folded, in death, but alive, kneeling in prayer, perhaps, or even sitting conversationally in their paired niches. The monuments were painted and lavishly gilded, again to make them more life-like. So, when Leontes is confronted (as he supposes) by the statue of Hermione, he exclaims 'Her natural posture !', and Perdita must be restrained by

Paulina from kissing the statue's hand; 'the statue is but newly fixed; the colour's not dry'. Whatever the method, the purpose in the great majority of these monuments was to recall the virtues and achievements of the living, not to make a warning of the dead. There was also very often an attempt, through inscription and heraldry, to emphasize rather than the mortality of an individual the continuity of a family.

A pride in the family, a respect for famous ancestry is characteristic of the Elizabethans. The country was governed largely by the new men who had come in with the new dynasty, not a few of them Welshmen, among whom relationship within the ninth degree was always worthy of testimony. Often these new families had achieved wealth, and the power that went with it, by a judicious purchase of monastic lands; but they were usually at pains to hide their upstart quality, and if possible to establish connections with the older families which they had replaced. Spenser claimed kinship with the Spencers of Althorp, and his claim was not rejected by that 'house of ancient fame' which, in its turn, asserted, on funeral monuments and elsewhere, a descent from the Despencers that was not denied only because there was none left to deny it. The Welsh family of Sitsyllt, on becoming English country gentlemen, anglicized their name to Cecil, not without hope of some association in men's minds with the great Roman family of the Caecilii; and though the foremost of them, Lord Burghley, in the precepts which he gave to his son Robert, sceptically dismissed gentility as 'nothing else but ancient riches', he took care to marry his daughter to the seventeenth Earl of Oxford, whose ancient lineage outweighed, in Burghley's eyes if not in his daughter's, a reprobate character. Thomas Writhe, on being appointed Garter King ot Arms, made a series of experiments with his surname before finally deciding that Wriothesley had the most suitable look for a man whose profession belonged to the age of chivalry. Caius was thought to have a more humanistic appearance than

Keys, and so to be more appropriate as the name of the doctor who refounded a Cambridge college. At Wollaton the family which for three centuries had there survived the unproductive name of Bugge now emerged into the winged splendour of Willoughby. The forgery of pedigrees, and the emblazoning of bogus coats of arms were also favourite pastimes of Elizabethan gentlemen: signs of a patriotism which led them to wish to claim for earlier generations of their families as large a share in the past as they themselves had in the present history of England.

This eagerness to assert distinguished ancestry is nowhere better represented than in the church of Hughenden in Buckinghamshire. Here is a thirteenth-century knight, cross-legged, and in chain mail, his left hand on his sword; and on the scabbard, and on his shield, and on his surcoat were imposed in the sixteenth-century coats of arms intended both to claim him as an ancestor of the Wellesbournes (who had more recently come here from Wellesbourne Mountford in Warwickshire) and to suggest kinship with Simon de Montfort. On the sill of the east window of the chapel in which this effigy lies is another, of the time of Edward III: this too has been appropriated to the Wellesbourne interest by some sixteenth-century heraldry. There are also in this same chapel three slabs with figures carved in low relief, all hopefully made to assert the descent of the Wellesbournes from Simon de Montfort: their crude anachronism illustrates the sixteenth century's judgment of what a mediaeval knight looked like — an oafish barbarian with a knobkerry was acceptable, even as an ancestor; he looked antique, and the Middle Ages were as indistinct and remote in the sixteenth century as the Bronze Age is now. The scholarly scepticism of the nineteenth century has here disclosed pretensions which in the sixteenth century may well have been accepted in the lord of the manor.

The most remarkable assertion of a claim to long descent made through funeral monuments in the Queen's reign is, however, genuine. In the church of Chester-le-Street in County Durham is a series of fourteen effigies placed there by the ninth Lord Lumley, the famous collector and antiquarian, in the 1590s, to commemorate his ancestors 'in a continued line of succession even from Liulph unto these our days'. These monuments, Camden goes on to tell us, Lord Lumley 'had either gotten together out of Monasteries that were subverted, or caused to be made anew'. In fact only three are mediaeval, being monuments of the early fourteenth century which Lord Lumley in 1594 obtained permission to remove from the graveyard of Durham Cathedral. The other eleven effigies were made new but in what Lord Lumley no doubt supposed to be the mediaeval style. The family pride which could lead a Wellesbourne to invent a pedigree here prompted a man 'most honourable for all the ornaments of true nobility' to devise the effigies of his known ancestors, and to set them up in rows in the church near his ancestral home. This same pride led him to commission an unknown artist to paint the picture of Richard II delivering the writ of summons to Parliament to the first Lord Lumley: the King's portrait is copied from the Westminster Abbey painting, and Lord Lumley (who was killed at the age of thirty-nine, fighting for his King) is shown as an elderly Elizabethan in parliamentary robes. The motive is similar to that which caused Oxford colleges about this time to employ a Flemish painter on portraits of their Founders.

At Chew Magna in Somerset there is a very unusual effigy of painted wood, called Sir John de Hauteville, which at first sight could be taken for another of these Elizabethan claims to long descent. The knight, whoever he was, reclines in a theatrically awkward pose on left hip and left elbow, his head propped on his left hand above his shield, his right leg bent up and crossed by his left, whose foot rests on the neck of a standing lion. He has a finely chiselled Roman nose, a thin black moustache, and (as well he might) an enigmatic smile. His armour is said to be of the fourteenth century, but his pose is of the late sixteenth. Perhaps this monument has no genealogical purpose, but is simply a restoration of a mediaeval tomb that had been destroyed by some Puritan enthusiast for no better reason than that its inscription 'began with an *Orate pro anima*, or concluded with *Cuius animae propitietur Deus*'. For such monuments, according to Weever, were especially liable to destruction.

In the second year of her reign, and again later, Queen Elizabeth issued a proclamation ordering restorations to be undertaken. She charged and commanded 'all manner of persons hereafter to forbear the breaking or defacing of any parcel of any monument, or tomb, or grave, or other inscription and memory of any person deceased'. Further 'for such as be already spoiled in any church, or chapel, now standing' she gave orders to the responsible authorities 'to employ . . . such sums (as any wise may be spared) upon the speedy repair or re-edification of such monuments so defaced or spoilt, as agreeable to the original, as the same conveniently may be'. Such an order must have resulted in the restoration by reluctant Protestant churchwardens of many a battered saint, and though Weever, who quotes the proclamation in full, thought it had done little good, it can hardly have been universally ignored. The Queen herself set the example in 1573 by replacing in Fotheringay church the monuments of the second and third Dukes of York. Sir John de Hauteville may then owe his rather eccentric appearance to Queen Elizabeth's order ; perhaps even to her visit to Bristol in 1574 when the wooden statue of her which stands in St Mary Redcliffe was probably made. Chew Magna is very near Bristol, and it is tempting to think that the man who carved the statue of the Queen was invited to re-edify Sir John. In many churches effigies have been repaired with heads that did not belong to them ; so the new head to the decapitated effigy for King Athelstan in Malmesbury Abbey may have been found lying about somewhere and restored in deference to the Queen's commands.

A literal defacing of effigies was the commonest form of mutilation, and restoration might not necessitate the carving of a new head: there were likely to be plenty among the statues thrown down in the churchyard. But so far no one has studied these Elizabethan restorations, and it is permissible therefore to do no more than suggest that Sir John de Hauteville's effigy may be one such. The monument to Roesia de Verdun, who founded Grace Dieu Priory about 1240, in Belton church, Leicestershire, may be another: the Tudor rose in one of the spandrels seems to be evidence of this. A third may be the slab to Madog ap Gruffydd, grandson of the founder of Valle Crucis Abbey, now preserved there in the chapter house. In the sixteenth century it did not appear inconsistent to ruin an abbey but to respect the memory of its founder.

Whether or not the Queen's proclamations were effective, the fact that they were made at all is to be remarked. To destroy a monastery, to break the figures of saints, to pull down the rood, to smash the windows, melt down the plate, and use the manuscripts for wrapping fish, called forth no official rebuke and little private regret. The chantry chapels also must be withdrawn from the superstitious ritual of prayers for the dead, and their endowments sequestered. Yet, when so much else was being destroyed, the destruction of monuments to the dead seemed 'the foulest and most inhuman action of those times', and therefore they were often preserved. Weever, we may suppose, expresses the common opinion of the time when he says 'we cannot but love the memory of such, who upon the dissolution, and final destruction of our religious structures, caused so many funeral monuments, with the bodies therein included, to be removed into other neighbouring churches', as Roesia de Verdun is said to have been moved from Grace Dieu, as 'Sir John de Hauteville' was moved from Norton Hauteville to Chew Magna, and as Henry VIII's bastard, the Duke of Richmond, was moved from Thetford Priory to Framlingham, where he lies in the oldest of that church's incomparable series of Renaissance tombs. Weever commends Bishop Fox of Winchester for collecting together the bones of princes and prelates who had been buried in the Cathedral, and enclosing them in chests on the top of the choir screens he had built.[1]

This respect for the monuments of the dead is part and parcel of that respect for ancestry which their own monuments reveal; also, perhaps, of a conservative love for tradition which all human societies accept when it comes to the disposal of the dead. And though beliefs about what happens to the dead underwent a profound change in sixteenth-century England, so that prayers for the souls of the departed came to be thought superstitious, yet the tombs which covered their bodies were still designed as altars at which such prayers might be offered. Torrigiani, in the two noble monuments that Henry VIII commissioned, had accepted this traditional form (then still relevant), although in the monument to Dr John Young in the Rolls Chapel, where presumably he had a freer hand, he placed his terra-cotta figure upon a sarcophagus of classical derivation supported on a panelled base, the whole within a round arch. This is purely Italian, and would not seem out of place in Santa Croce or in the Cathedral of Florence, but the tombs of Henry VII or of the Countess of Richmond and Derby would be very unexpected there. However, Torrigiani was free to display the new Italian taste in the garlands and pilasters with which he decorated the sides of these tombs, and in the amorini which at either end support shields of arms. It was appropriate then to require Torrigiani to provide 'a step of marble stone round about the same tomb to kneel upon', and that the tomb itself should resemble an altar, for the belief in Purgatory had not yet been derided. But it was not appropriate that such a

[1] It is an odd comment on the vagaries of taste in the early sixteenth century that these wooden reliquary chests derive their design from the Italian Renaissance, but that the chantry chapel for Bishop Fox himself, built some years later in the same Cathedral, is pure English Gothic.

design should persist for long after the Reformation ; that it did so is yet another example of traditional design outlasting the purpose for which it had been created. On the sides of such tombs canopied Gothic niches were converted to Renaissance forms, with classical pilaster and shell-topped recess, even before mediaeval weepers gave place to the children, mourning upon their knees. At Framlingham in Suffolk the figures of the Apostles stand in the classical niches of the third Duke of Norfolk's tomb ; at Cobham in Kent Lord Cobham's children, each identified by name, kneel in their similar niches, and so unconsciously assert the obsolescence of the design. But most of the tomb-makers would see in the churches which they might visit far more mediaeval than modern tombs, and would therefore be held in the old tradition of their craft without observing its discrepancy with the new religion. To call these 'tomb-chests' is a mere evasion, but the sculptors of the seventeenth century came to treat them simply as pedestals on which the effigy might rest, or, eventually, as beds on which the person to be commemorated might be shown in his last moments of pious submission to the will of God. The elegant perfection of this treatment may be seen in the church of Withyham in Sussex, where Cibber portrayed young Thomas Sackville reclining on his bed, his eyes fixed on heaven, a symbolic skull in his hand, while the bereaved parents kneel on the 'altar' steps at either side of him. In a number of monuments the altar with solid sides was replaced by a table, where the effigy was carried on a slab of stone or marble supported on arches or pillars ; and the hollow space beneath might be left empty, or used for a cadaver as at Gawsworth, or for another effigy. Among the splendid series of monuments at Tong in Shropshire, is one to Sir Thomas Stanley and his wife Margaret (Vernon) and their son Sir Edward.[1] (This

[1] Father of Venetia, Sir Kenelm Digby's wife, whose beauty was celebrated by Ben Jonson and other poets. Aubrey saw the bust from her tomb in St Paul's, some years after the Fire, standing in a brazier's shop : 'they melted it down'.

is the monument whose inscription, according to Dugdale, who ought to have known, was composed by Shakespeare.) The effigies of Sir Thomas and his wife lie on a slab supported by four arches which spring from eight elaborately enriched rectangular pillars, outside which are marble columns, black at the angles, red in the middle of the sides. Within the space provided by these arches, resting on a classical sarcophagus, lies the effigy of Sir Edward Stanley. The obelisks which now stand on top of the tomb, at the corners, were formerly on the ground there, and four allegorical figures (now decapitated and absurdly enskied in the Gothic niches of Sir Harry Vernon's tomb, which are far too big for them) originally stood where the obelisks now are. Probably these represented the four Cardinal Virtues, unless one of them was intended for the figure of Patience which also (as Shakespeare knew) might grace a monument, 'smiling at grief'.

The replacement of the altar on which lay the effigy of the dead by a sarcophagus supposed to contain the corpse was another invention of the Renaissance, prompted by a careful attention to Roman and Etruscan sarcophagi in Italy. Torrigiani when no longer under the restrictions of royal command had devised such a monument for Dr Young, and his fellow Italian, Benedetto da Rovezzano, designed for Cardinal Wolsey the grand and dignified sarcophagus of black marble which now commemorates Nelson in the crypt of St Paul's. But there were few native English monuments of this type for many years. Perhaps the first is the sarcophagus made in 1552 for the tomb of Sir Robert Dormer at Wing in Buckinghamshire, which is decorated with swags of flowers and bucrania, and enclosed by paired Corinthian columns on enriched bases with corresponding pilasters behind them which support a flat ceiler with strapwork on the underside. Dormer was connected by marriage with the Duke of Northumberland, and therefore with Protector Somerset's intellectual circle, whose advanced taste manifested itself elsewhere, in Somerset House, at Lacock, at Longleat. In another Buckinghamshire church, at Chicheley, is the monument to Anthony Cave which his widow erected in 1576. The enriched sarcophagus is enclosed by elongated caryatids standing against fluted pilasters, supporting an entablature with triglyphs, with rosettes in the metopes, and with a triangular pediment, in which is an achievement of the arms of Cave. Upon the sarcophagus, as if to withdraw from too arresting a classicism, lies a naked cadaver. In the recess above are reliefs of Anthony Cave and his wife and children, kneeling at either side of a prayer desk, the pattern of so many monuments of the next fifty years. This extraordinary monument is typically English in its eclecticism: the sarcophagus has come from ancient Rome through modern Italy, the caryatids from Athens by a more circuitous route through Italy and the Low Countries; metope, triglyph, and pediment again from Athens but this time more directly through Rome and Italy; the cadaver and the heraldry from the Middle Ages. To make the mixture complete the caryatids have a Gothic sinuosity of form, and the cadaver a classical face.

In the celebrated church of Long Melford in Suffolk the effigy of Sir William Cordell, who died in 1580, reclines in armour on an elaborate sarcophagus under two coffered arches, which are carried by black and red columns with Corinthian capitals (pl. 12). About him on three sides stand in their classical niches the female figures of the four Cardinal Virtues, Prudence, Justice, Temperance, and Fortitude, statues of as high a quality as any of their time in England. This monument is purely of the Renaissance, in striking contrast to the almost contemporary monument at Chicheley. The family of Sir William Cordell, who had been Speaker of the House of Commons and Master of the Rolls, and who set a fashion for lavish entertainment of the Queen in Melford Hall, could no doubt command finer work than Mrs Cave, and it has been suggested, somewhat unnecessarily, that his monument was of Italian design and making. For the present purpose of estimating the development of English taste, this is irrelevant : both monuments were placed in English country churches, and both show very clearly the influence of the Renaissance. But where the Cordell monument is bold and uncompromising in its classicism, the Cave monument is tentative, and will not wholly abandon the mediaeval tradition. It could be said that the one is provincial, the other not, but the difference between the two is not so much a difference in understanding motifs of design, as a difference in self-confidence.

Two of the most remarkable monuments of this time which make use of the sarcophagus face one another across the chancel of the village church of Bosbury in Herefordshire (pl. 13). They are of the local sandstone, but suggest that the maker had somewhere seen monuments in terra-cotta. On the south side, set into the wall, is the monument to John Harford who died in 1558 but which was erected, as a Latin inscription informs us, in 1573 by his son Richard. Another inscription reads, 'Iohn Guldo of Hereford made this tombe wt his owne hande Ano Dni 1573'. The effigy of John Harford, his hands folded in prayer, lies on a sarcophagus which rests on the backs of two snarling lions. This is enclosed by a round arch whose soffit is carved with Tudor roses, and a device of roses and leaves fills the spandrels outside this arch. On either side Corinthian columns support the entablature, above which a triangular pediment encloses a roundel between formal leaves, with the arms of a Bishop of Hereford within it. In the recess above the effigy are reliefs of three vases of flowers, roses in two, lilies in the third, to symbolize the Resurrection ; and above these are three more coats of arms. The lunette is filled with a shell pattern. The whole monument is Italian in manner, and arguments about its precise derivation in Pisa, or Ferrara, or Modena, may be left to the experts ; but there is no reason to think that John Guldo(n) or Gildon of Hereford was other than an Englishman.[1] On the north wall is the monument to Richard Harford himself from which the inscriptions have almost entirely vanished.[2] However it seems certain that John Gildon was responsible also for this, for the treatment of the carving, in spite of the extraordinary contrast in motif, is the same, and it is likely that two monuments of about the same date to members of the same family in the same church would be by the same sculptor. Richard Harford died in 1578 but may well have ordered his own monument at the same time as his father's, who had been dead fifteen years when it was set up. In any event there cannot be many years between the two. But this monument is Flemish, not Italian, in character, already on the way towards the baroque, as if Richard Harford had invited Gildon to contrast father and son by a contrast of styles ; or perhaps Gildon himself suggested the two designs in order to display his own virtuosity. Basically the design of both monuments is the same : a sarcophagus with recumbent effigy, supported by animal forms, enclosed by a round arch, with free-standing columns outside it which carry an entablature surmounted by a pediment. It is easy to imagine Gildon drawing out their basic elements for Richard Harford and then converting the one to Italian, the other to Flemish forms. For here in Richard Harford's own monument his effigy and his wife's lie on their right side, not on their backs ; their hands are not folded in prayer, but he supports his head with his right hand, and she holds a prayer-book open in hers. The sarcophagus, though similar to the other, has bulged out on the underside into sumptuous curves, and instead of the lions we have crocodiles, or some such unclassical monsters. The pillars of the arch are no longer plain, but carved with what

[1] His signature on the tomb of Richard Willison at Madley, Herefordshire, is Jhon Gildo ; on the tomb of Dr David Lewis at Abergavenny, Monmouthshire, Jhon Gildon ; on the tomb of Robert and Anne Blount at Astley, Worcestershire, Jhon Gildon.

[2] The word OF incised in the return of the band at the top of the left pilaster, exactly in the same position as the same word in the inscription on the other monument, alone remains. Presumably the rest was painted.

might be called a pruned vine pattern which continues round the face of the arch. The soffit is carved with a diminutive rose among eight leaves, and in the spandrels are huge grinning masks with leaves sprouting from the corners of their mouths. To either side the columns are converted to grotesque caryatids standing on bases carved with acanthus leaves, and with acanthus capitals supporting an entablature whose base is carved to represent brick. The pediment is curved and the space at either side of it filled to the ceiling with more acanthus leaves and scrolls. Within the pediment, in a roundel of the Garter, between more leaves and stalks, are the arms of the first Marquess of Winchester. In the recess above the effigies are three coats of arms, and more leaves, fruits, and scrolls. It would be difficult to achieve a more complete contrast in two monuments whose basic design is the same, and surely Richard Harford and John Gildon must have decided to illustrate the contrast in taste between father and son.

That an artist should be willing to work in two such different manners at the same period — and his other signed monuments are altar-tombs with recumbent effigies, in the older fashion — may surprise us, who are brought up in the romantic belief that such virtuosity is a denial of artistic integrity. We should rather imagine John Gildon turning over the pages first of an Italian then of a Flemish pattern-book, and inviting his employer's comments ; and we may think of Richard Harford choosing the more old-fashioned and sober Italian design to commemorate his father, but preferring the latest importation from the Low Countries for himself. To do so would be to accept the principle of decorum that dominated their taste, in choosing what seemed most fitting to the context of the two generations.

Wall-monuments, such as these Harford tombs, were becoming increasingly fashionable, instead of the old free-standing altar tombs. These occupied too much room and there was obviously a limit to the number that could be admitted in a small parish church. There must have been many who, like Weever, criticized these monuments that 'take up the Church, and hinder the people from divine service', though it would need courage in parson or churchwardens to suggest this to the lord of the manor. Besides, it was not always possible to set back a monument into the wall as was done at Bosbury, and Sir Christopher Hatton's magnificent tomb in St Paul's, which provoked the rhyme

> Philip and Francis have no tomb
> For great Christopher takes all the room [1]

was a wall-monument. But generally such tombs were not so depopulating (to use Fuller's epithet) as were the free-standing altars.

The placing of a tomb against a wall presented the designer with new problems and opportunities: it was to be seen from one side, not from all sides, and very often the effigies would be above, not at or below eye-level. If there were two effigies, as there usually were, then the one farther from the spectator must be raised a little to be visible, as John Gildon raised the effigy of Richard Harford's wife above his, or as the effigy of John Latch at Churchill is raised far above his shrouded wife's. There would be an advantage also in turning the effigy on to its side, so that the facial portrait could be seen: John Gildon has turned Richard Harford and his wife a little on to their sides, but John Latch's doleful bearded countenance fronts the spectator. This turning of the figure towards the visitor to the church, instead of the old recumbent position with hands folded in prayer and eyes fixed on heaven, was considered by some to be irreverent. Webster has some caustic lines about it in *The Duchess of Malfi*:

> Princes' images on their tombs
> Do not lie, as they were wont, seeming to pray
> Up to heaven, but with their hands under their cheeks
> As if they died of the toothache; they are not carved

[1] Sir Philip Sidney, and Sir Francis Walsingham.

> With their eyes fixed upon the stars, but as
> Their minds were wholly bent upon the world,
> The self-same way they seem to turn their faces.

But the reason for the change of position was due less to a lack of piety than to a lack of space.

Many others must have shared Webster's opinions, and perhaps for that reason the design showing husband and wife on their knees facing each other across a prayer-desk, with their sons and daughters trailing off behind or below them, became the most popular of all. This could not be thought irreverent ; it could be treated in relief, and therefore would project little into the church ; and it could be as easily seen above as at eye-level. The first of these monuments date from the time of Henry VII, but by the end of the century they are far the commonest. A charming, but secular, variant is to be seen in the 'conversation piece' of Sir Giles and Lady Mompesson where she sits in her chair, chin on hand, the folds of her long gown ruffled on the floor, and he sits opposite her, his helm at his feet, and an open book in his hands. She died before him, and therefore her left hand rests on a skull in her lap, but in spite of this the memory of the domestic life of husband and wife is very vivid, and the suggestion that it is now broken is but faint.

The wish to portray the dead as they were in life had to be reconciled, at least in the opinion of most, with the context of the monument : the portrait must be like, but it must also be suitable for exhibition in a church. Preferably, therefore, it should show the deceased in a reverent attitude, recumbent on his death-bed with hands folded in prayer, or kneeling at a desk as in life. The figures propped on one elbow, staring at the members of the congregation, were unsuitable ; and for much the same reason (we may suppose) busts were seldom used until later, when Augustan taste had begun to suppress the appetence for piety. Busts or similar figures had occasionally been used long before. The exquisite monument to Sir

Geoffrey and Lady Foljambe at Bakewell in Derbyshire is of the fourteenth century, and shows their half-length figures facing the front with folded hands, under an elaborate canopy with two shields of arms. The sculptor has simply used the normal design of recumbent effigies, cut off at the waist, and set it upright in miniature; but he had no imitators. The church at Tong among its many monuments has a fine portrait bust, probably of Arthur Vernon who died in 1517, set on a bracket under an elaborate canopy, seen as if he were preaching in the pulpit, with his right hand turning the pages of a book. But again no one followed an excellent model, which very well combined portraiture with respect for the church in which it was placed, until long afterwards. Then towards the end of the century a bust of the preacher, framed in a more or less classical surround and surmounted by an achievement of arms, became the standard method of commemorating a divine. The monument to John Stow, in St Andrew Undershaft, has the effect of a bust, for it shows him writing at his table, with the quill pen (which the Stationers' Company still renews every year) held in his hand, and his eyes concentrated on his book: a secular portrait which has no relevance to its site. The bust of William Camden in Westminster Abbey, which is presumably some years later (for he died in 1623 and Stow in 1606), is again frankly a portrait of the great antiquary, with his hand on his folio *Britannia*: it would look more appropriate in a library such as the Bodleian, where indeed there is a bust of Sir Thomas Bodley in classical surround of arch and pediment. But generally at this period the bust was used in memorials to divines rather than to laymen, probably because, whereas the bust of a layman was simply a portrait, a portrayal of the preacher in his pulpit showed him engaged in an activity appropriate to a church.

This insistence on decorum, in the consideration of the physical context of a monument, is shown also in another, social context. John Weever, in his learned *Discourse* states the principle: monuments, he says, 'should be made according to the quality and degree of the person deceased, that by the tomb every one might be discerned of what rank he was living'. How like this is to Palladio's advice on the entrances of houses, and how characteristic of the age! For decorum is the natural principle by whose observation art attains perfection, and is natural because it is in accordance with the laws of nature, established by a rational intelligence and to be rightly understood therefore by reason. A monument should be a portrait of an individual, to identify the person of the deceased; it should indicate his rank and carry the same dignity as a memorial as the man had attained in life; and it should, by showing him at prayer or in the pulpit, be suitable for erection in a church. Memorials to the dead were not yet erected in unconsecrated places, but only in church or churchyard: there are not yet therefore full-length standing figures, or equestrian monuments. These would come before long: the Golden Cavalier at Lydiard Tregoze who has obviously just dismounted in order to go into the church, but who should be standing in the forecourt of some country house; Le Sueur's statue of the third Earl of Pembroke which, once at Wilton, now stands in the Schools Quadrangle of the Bodleian; and his most famous work, the statue of King Charles I on horseback, intended for Lord Treasurer Weston's garden, but now at Charing Cross. An equestrian monument in an English church at this time would be very surprising; and yet there is such a monument to an Englishman, the condottiere Sir John Hawkwood,[1] two centuries earlier than Le Sueur's Charles I, in the Cathedral of Florence.

In the Elizabethan age, as in any other, the majority had no memorial. Those of noble or gentle birth, or of distinguished attainments, were buried within the church itself, and there commemorated. Others were buried in the churchyard,

[1] Paolo Uccello's painting, commissioned in 1436, represents a bronze monument.

where most would lie with no stone to mark the place. Very seldom a simple ledger stone with a brief inscription might show where the parson himself lay buried, but those of lower rank would almost never receive even so much honour. 'Persons of the meaner sort of gentry' who were not thought to merit, or whose heirs were unwilling to afford a monument might have their grave marked by a ledger stone in the floor, or by a brass there or set on the wall. In Tideswell church, in Derbyshire, is a fine brass to Robert Pursglove, Bishop of Hull, which, but for the long inscription describing his achievements in the crudest doggerel, might well be of a pre-Reformation priest. More often the brass plaque would contain only an inscription, perhaps in verse like the acrostic on the name of Mawd Parker Thomas, who died in 1584, on the wall of the south transept of Northleach church in Gloucestershire ; or there might be no more than the dates of birth and death. Sometimes a local worthy might find a memorial, in spite of his humble station : one of the most notable of these is in Peterborough Cathedral, where a picture of 'old Scarlett' hangs on the west wall of the nave with an inscription below, from which we learn that old Scarlett was the Cathedral sexton, and that he lived to be ninety-eight,

> but at length his own turn came ;
> What he for others did, for him the same
> Was done.

He was buried in the Cathedral in July 1594, and how should so celebrated a character not have his memorial ? James Gray, who was park-keeper at Hunsdon in Hertfordshire for thirty-nine years, and who died in 1591, was such another whose memory must not die for want of a memorial : his brass shows him shooting at a stag, while Death prepares to throw a dart at him, saying *Sic pergo*. No doubt his master, like many since, placed this in memory of a faithful servant. It is unlikely that Gray's family, or Scarlett's, even if they could have afforded it, would have thought it in keeping with their station in life to order brass or picture, or would have had the temerity to ask the parson and the churchwardens for permission to set them up.

Elizabethan monuments are almost all to the noble or gentle, to the rich and eminent. Like the paintings of the time, these sepulchral effigies show us the faces and the clothes of those who played the principal parts in the great theatre of English life, or at least in the local scene. They are shown formally, not intimately: as Weever puts it, 'delineated, carved, and embossed, at the full length and bigness, truly proportioned throughout, as near to the life, and with as much state and magnificence, as the skill of the artificer could possibly carve and form the same'. In these effigies, as in the portraits, the state and magnificence often obscure the nearness to life, so that we sometimes have the impression that we are contemplating costume, not human personality; and the absence of monuments to persons such as Scarlett or Gray, who were neither stately nor magnificent, intensifies this. It is (except at Peterborough) *Hamlet* without the grave-diggers. But at their best the sculptors, more often and more successfully than contemporary painters, could achieve both the degree and the person: Maximilian Colt designed a monument for a Queen, but for Queen Elizabeth.

For this Colt was paid £765, a very large sum but less perhaps than the amount that some of the Queen's courtiers had paid for theirs. Colt, who came from Arras, was by that time well established, and able to command high fees; earlier, he had been willing to make a monument with two pairs of kneeling figures under canopies for as little as £10. That was in Chester, and though most of Colt's later work was in or near London he continued to accept commissions from as far away as East Anglia. Well-known sculptors, by no means all of them with their yards in London, were likely to receive commissions from all over the country. Joseph Hollemans, a Dutch sculptor who settled at Burton-on-Trent, presumably because it was near to the alabaster quarries, executed a series of monuments for the Spencer family at Great Brington in Northamptonshire. In 1612 the Countess of Berkeley, who must have seen these tombs or heard of their unusual quality, wrote to ask Lord Spencer whom he had employed on them, since she wished to erect a monument to her husband at Berkeley. Hollemans did not, in the end, receive her commission, which she gave to a local sculptor from Stroud, but perhaps through a similar recommendation he was invited to make other monuments in Northamptonshire, Oxfordshire, Warwickshire, and Lincolnshire. Other sculptors came over from the Low Countries to escape religious persecution, or because they foresaw better employment here. Theodore Haveus, whose work on the Porta Honoris Dr Caius is known to have approved, designed his memorial in the College chapel with classical sarcophagus, acanthus leaves, and Corinthian columns. Richard Stevens, as the English called him, who made Sir Christopher Hatton's notorious monument to the design of Maximilian Colt, settled in London ; and so did Gerard Johnson, of Amsterdam, whose sons followed their father's profession, and one of whom made the stodgy memorial to Shakespeare at Stratford-on-Avon. The family of William Cure, also of Amsterdam, who had come to England long before in the time of Henry VIII, kept up the tradition of sculpture : his son and grandson both worked on the tomb of Mary Queen of Scots.

These foreign sculptors who settled in England (and whose families, born and brought up here, were regarded as English) by no means dominated the profession. There were native English sculptors who could rival these French and Dutch, and in the country we must suppose that most of the work was always done by local men. Much of this is of little merit, yet we may find a John Gildon, whose work is known only from within twenty or thirty miles of his native Hereford, well aware of current fashion, and able to do work of good quality in several styles. A far greater man, the best of the English sculptors of his day, Epiphanius Evesham, was also from Herefordshire, but achieved a reputation that carried his work into country churches from Lincolnshire to Kent, and even perhaps into that national gallery of monumental sculptors, Westminster Abbey.

Epiphanius Evesham, like Hilliard and Gower and Nathaniel Bacon and the Segars among the painters, was of gentle birth: perhaps for that reason he was primarily a sculptor, not (as were so many) a mason turned sculptor. He was careless — some might say, ignorant — of the accepted treatment of architectural forms, but his mastery is shown in the freedom with which he regarded the whole design of his monuments, and especially in the refined naturalism with which he portrayed the human figure. The rows of sons and daughters, who all too often look like caterpillars in some children's book, are entirely human in Evesham's handling: they do not line up in dutiful rows, graduated in size, as a testimony to their parents' fertility; they kneel or stand in natural groups, and mourn sincerely if, in our eyes, a little extravagantly. The sons do not all wear the same clothes and the same whiskers, and the daughters differ in hair style and in hats. Their parents, the spectator suddenly realizes, must have been able to remember their names, not merely to count them. We know something about Lord Teynham's family when we see Evesham's reliefs of them on the base of his monument at Lynsted in Kent, and of Lady Teynham too, who kneels in her widow's weeds at the side of her dead lord.

This interest in children is shown in other monuments, in the mourning family of Sir Thomas Hawkins at Boughton-under-Blean in Kent, or in the allegorical children who cling to the dress of Charity on Lord Rich's tomb at Felsted in Essex. There Evesham carved three groups in relief, showing Lord Rich in each of them accompanied by the Virtues, an original treatment of a theme which elsewhere[1] is confined to representing the Virtues as isolated allegorical figures. At the east end of the tomb the young Lord Rich is accompanied by Truth; below his reclining figure he is shown in one panel as Speaker of the House of Commons, flanked by Fortitude and Justice, and in a second as Lord Chancellor supported by Hope and Charity.

Evesham was exceptionally inventive in his designs, and had a liking for allegory and symbolism, as had others of his time. On Lord Rich's monument besides the Virtues there stands the winged nude figure of Fame, proclaiming by her gilded trumpet the achievements of Lord Rich. Weever did not approve of such things: 'they garnish their tombs, nowadays, with the pictures of naked men and women; raising out of the dust, and bringing into the church, the memories of the heathen gods and goddesses, with all their whirligigs'. For such fashions he blamed not those who ordered the monuments but those who made them. One of Evesham's boldest inventions is at Stansted Mountfitchet in Essex where, on the monument to Hester Salusbury, he carved an achievement of arms with helmed crest, mantling, and supporters, but in which the quarterings, instead of being heraldic, are the traditional Emblems of Christ's Passion; the helm bears the crown of thorns, the supporters are cherubs, and a pair of hands extended in blessing protrudes above the shield. This heraldic conceit on a tomb is probably unique, but elsewhere, as on Edward West's tomb at Marsworth in Buckinghamshire, Evesham again shows his liking for these emblematic motifs: there are shields with a skull and cross-bones, and with ears of wheat or twigs of laurel, in token of the Resurrection, sprouting from the skull, and incised figures of Death with his scythe, of the Risen Christ, and of mourners. On Lord Rich's tomb are two incised black marble panels, in the same technique, showing Lord Rich in his hour of splendour, arriving at West-

[1] As on the Stanley monument at Tong, the Cordell monument at Long Melford, and the Earl of Salisbury's monument at Hatfield.

minster Hall as Lord Chancellor, and in death, with hooded figures mourning at his hearse. Not content with displaying his skill in relief and engraving on stone, at Marsworth Evesham also had a brass plate (which he signed) showing West with his wife and family at his bedside, while Death approaches from behind a curtain. Evesham was an artist of notable originality, as well as being a versatile craftsman. He does not seem to owe so much as did lesser men to foreign models and influences, just as Shakespeare is more independently English in plays and sonnets alike than any of his contemporaries. In his use of emblems Evesham was of his own day, though he was capable of adding to the stock patterns, but in his tender portrayal of children he seems to anticipate the poets of a later time, Herrick, Marvell, Vaughan, and Traherne. If his work were not by a necessity of its nature scattered about many churches in many counties, but could be gathered together fort exhibition, he would be recognized as one of the greates of English artists.

He founded no school, left no successors ; and until Mrs Esdaile's rediscovery of him, even his name, though George Vertue had recognized in him a 'most exquisite artist', was unknown. For it has been only through her pioneer researches that the work of these English sculptors of the Renaissance has begun to be appreciated ; and it is still very little regarded. This is not at all surprising, when the work is dispersed in thousands of churches all over the country, so that a day's journey may well separate two monuments by the same hand, especially of a sculptor with a contemporary reputation such as Evesham must have enjoyed. The local men more often than not would be at best competent craftsmen. Occasionally one of them, such as John Gildon, would show ability out of the ordinary, and yet achieve no reputation beyond his own district. The tombs are seldom signed at this date : Gildon and Evesham are exceptional in this too, perhaps because they knew that their work had an individual stamp to it which was worth identifying, though the artists of the time, in whatever medium they worked, had no Romantic dread of anonymity: they and their patrons thought about the finished work, not about the artists' *œuvre*. Richard Haydocke was another who chose to sign his work, the engraved brass plaques with emblematic and allegorical designs which may be seen in several cathedrals, as well as in college chapels and country churches. But Haydocke was an amateur, with varied connections with the artistic world of his time: as a Fellow of New College, he dedicated to Thomas Bodley his translation of Lomazzo's *Trattato dell' Arte della Pittura*; he knew Nicholas Hilliard well enough to persuade him to write his *Treatise on the Art of Limning*; and when later he settled in Salisbury as a physician he must have kept in touch with the scholars whose memorials he designed and for whom he might also write the verse epitaph.

The great majority of monuments are not attributable. Local sculptors would make use of published pattern-books just as architects and masons would, and might be fortunate enough to learn their craft in the yard of a mason of more than ordinary talent. It seems likely that Evesham was for a time a pupil of Gildon. They would have few opportunities besides of studying good modern work, unless there happened to be some in a neighbouring church, or unless they went to London and visited Westminster Abbey. One of the sights of London was already the monuments in the Abbey. Foreign tourists included it in their itinerary as insistently as modern Americans do Stratford-on-Avon and Stoke Poges, and they were promptly seized upon by

> the man that keeps the Abbey tombs
> And for his price doth with whoever comes
> Of all our Harrys and our Edwards talk.

Philip Gawdy, seeking to distract a seventeen-year-old nephew, who had been sent up to London by his parents in order to break off some unsuitable attachment to a Mistress Havers in

Norfolk, took him to see the lions in the Tower and the tombs at Westminster. Lady Margaret Hoby records in her arid diary one of her few moments of relaxation when, on 1st December 1600, she 'went to the minster to see the monements'. (She would spell it that way, to emphasize their monitory aspect: she could hardly take pleasure in anything more frivolous than a *memento mori.*) Fynes Moryson considered that among all the sepulchres which he had seen in his years of travel, none surpassed that of Henry VII. And John Weever, in the first book on English church monuments, remarks on the 'concourse of people who come daily to view the lively Statues and stately Monuments in Westminster Abbey . . . a sight (he says) which brings delight and admiration, and strikes a religious apprehension into the minds of the beholders'. A monument must offer both detached aesthetic pleasure and a warning of mortality.

Yet though many must have agreed with Moryson in admiring Torrigiani's noble monument, with its compromise between Italian taste and English tradition, the influence of the great Italian is negligible. Here and there, on Lord Marney's tomb at Layer Marney in Essex, on Prior Thomas Vyvyan's at Bodmin in Cornwall, on Sir Anthony Browne's at Battle in Sussex, Torrigiani's design of roundels separated by classic pilasters may be seen on the sides of the traditional altar-tomb. But after the break with Rome Italian artists were no longer invited to England, and the refugees from the Low Countries brought other designs which were less suspect in English eyes as inclining to Popery. A very notable copy of a Dutch tomb may be seen in the Abbey in the monument to Sir Francis Vere. The original, the monument to Count Engelbert of Nassau at Breda was, it is true, designed by an Italian, Tommaso Vincidor of Bologna, but there was nothing Popish in a monument where the four kneeling figures which supported the memorial slab represented Philip of Macedon and Alexander the Great, Julius Caesar and Regulus: Plutarch rather than any Christian apologist was the inspiration here. On Sir Francis Vere's monument, the four heroes at the corners represent the dead man's sons : they are dressed in armour, but bare-headed, and kneel upon one knee while supporting a marble slab on their shoulders. Upon this is shown Sir Francis's armour, and in the space below is his recumbent effigy on a half rolled-up mat. Maximilian Colt may have been responsible for this monument : certainly he contrived the very odd variant of it which commemorates the first Earl of Salisbury at Hatfield. Here the kneeling figures represent the four Cardinal Virtues : one of them (so far towards the Greek model had English taste now progressed) has her breasts bare. Upon the black marble slab lies the effigy of the Earl in his robes of state ; but below him, behind the backs of the kneeling figures, as if to remind the spectator that their exquisite refinement is but a passing fashion, lies a skeleton on a straw mat. Perhaps Colt had seen monuments such as Francis Fitton's at Gawsworth, where the effigy of the living was carried on pillars above a cadaver. Even from the great statesman for whom Sir Henry Wotton collected modern Venetian paintings the Middle Ages were not far removed ; and he himself had ordered his own tomb.

Maximilian Colt, the Frenchman from Arras, designing a tomb for an English patron on the model of an Italian working for a Dutchman, well represents the eclecticism of English taste at the time. The incongruity between the mediaeval cadaver and the Renaissance figures of the Virtues was surely not unintended : it was a deliberate discord, an untuning of the string on which the harmony of human life could be heard. Colt, like Evesham, like any artist of his age, was prepared to carry out his employer's wishes : to design a grandiose wall-monument with sarcophagus and canopy and free-standing pyramids for Sir Christopher Hatton ; an altar-tomb with canopy borne on black marble pillars to commemorate Queen Elizabeth ; a hearse with baroque baldacchino and coloured marble curtains looped about its black supporting columns for the Countess of Derby ; or the strange mixture ordered by Lord Salisbury. The universal principle of decorum allowed, at least to a skilful and imaginative artist, ample scope for variation ; but it did compel him to design a monument suited to a church. One man might wish that those who saw his tomb should be reminded of the transience of earthly glory ; another might choose to impress upon them the new splendour of an ancient family ; another, to suggest ancient splendour for a new family ; here a widow might wish to record her own sorrow, and her children's ; here, a great lady might pathetically hope to perpetuate in marble and a gilded monument beauty that the poets had more lastingly celebrated. All would have thought it right that they should be portrayed in an attitude of prayer, giving thanks to God for the glory of the bodily life which they had left, and submitting into His compassionate hands their immortal souls.

V

MUSIC

V. MUSIC

Of all the arts music is the least confined by national boundaries. In the time of Queen Elizabeth the English language, which has since (as Daniel foresaw) become the language of most of the New World, was restricted to a small population on an island far removed from the Mediterranean origins of the Renaissance, and scarcely any Italian or Spaniard or Frenchman would have deigned to learn it. Most would have thought, as Guarini told Daniel, that English was a barbarous tongue unsuited to poetry, and it was not until the eighteenth century that English began to be recognized abroad as one of the chief literary languages of the world.

But the English achievement in music, sacred and secular, vocal and instrumental, was immediately saluted on the Continent. The madrigalist Filippo di Monte in 1583 sent William Byrd a setting for eight voices of the opening verses of the 137th Psalm, *Super flumina*, and in the following year Byrd replied with his own setting of *Quomodo cantabimus* from the same psalm. Some of Thomas Morley's work was published in Germany not long after it was published in England. John Dowland was highly praised by Luca Marenzio ; received a pavan from the Landgrave of Hessen who was himself a skilled musician ; and was for several years lutenist to King Christian IV of Denmark. Compositions by him were published in France, Germany, and the Netherlands. John Bull, celebrated as virtuoso and composer, was much in demand on the Continent, and was ordered home in 1601 by the Queen who was afraid that some foreign court might engage him ; but he spent his last years as organist in Antwerp. Richard Dering, a convert to the Roman faith, lived much of his life abroad as organist to the English nuns in Brussels, but on Queen Henrietta Maria's marriage received an appointment at the English Court. Peter Philips, who became a Roman Catholic priest, spent all his life abroad, and both his and Dering's compositions were published on the Continent, but not in England. There is no need to multiply examples, but while the Italians and the French supposed that English poetry could not exist, they knew that English music might equal or surpass their own.

This was no new discovery. In the first half of the fifteenth century English musicians, of whom the greatest was John Dunstable, had had much influence on the Flemish composers, and the theorist of that school, Joannes de Tinctoris, regarded England as the principal source of the art of music. Martin le Franc, about 1440, also paid tribute to Dunstable and his English contemporaries. The two English universities instituted degrees in music in the fifteenth century, long before any Continental university, which was proof of an early interest in music as a serious branch of learning ; and most of the Elizabethan composers were proud to describe themselves on their title-pages as Bachelor or Doctor of Music.

Queen Elizabeth, like her father Henry VIII and her sister Mary, was herself an accomplished musician. Tallis and Byrd, in dedicating to her in 1575 their *Cantiones Sacrae*, praised her for the elegance of her voice and the dexterity of her fingers. Richard Mulcaster in some Latin elegiacs in praise of their music which he contributed to the book paid a compliment to the Queen which, however confidently it was to be expected, need not therefore be discounted :

> The Queen, the glory of our age and isle
> With royal favour bids this science smile ;
> Nor hears she only others' labour'd lays,
> But, artist-like, herself both sings and plays.

In her youth she 'composed ballets and music, and played and danced them' but she also kept up with the new fashions in music, would sing ayres and accompany her singing on the lute ; and she played the virginals. Once Sir James Melville, the Queen of Scots' ambassador, was taken by Lord Hunsdon secretly up to a quiet gallery, where he heard Queen Elizabeth playing the virginals 'excellently well. But she left off immediately as soon as she turned her about and saw me. She appeared to be surprized to see me, and came forward, seeming to strike me with her hand ; alleging she used not to play before men, but when she was solitary, to shun melancholy.'

The Queen's love of music was intelligent and instructed by more than usual ability ; and there can be little doubt that in her judgment the music which was composed for her Chapel Royal or for private enjoyment was a greater glory to her realm than the poetry written for her Court, or the plays written for the London theatres. There is no need here to enter into an argument which admits of no decision : whether Byrd was a greater artist than Spenser, or Shakespeare than either ; whether Morley's setting of *It was a lover and his lass* falls short of, or surpasses, the words of Shakespeare's song. Time has brought changes which no one could have foretold, and which no one can measure : the language of four million islanders has been enfranchised of undiscovered continents ; but the delicate music of lute and virginals, known then in the houses of educated men throughout Europe, is now the rare pleasure of an erudite few. Dowland and Bull, Sidney and Donne might as readily have imagined the pianoforte as Australia, but they wrote for neither.

The Queen was proud to have at least sixty musicians in her service. These included both the singers of the Chapel Royal and the instrumentalists of the Queen's Musick. Various lists of the musicians, and of the instruments which they played, survive, from which it is possible to follow certain changes of fashion during the Queen's reign. In 1558 she had forty-one musicians of whom half were foreigners, most of these North Italians from Venice, Cremona, Milan, and elsewhere, and among them were five members of the Bassano family which provided many musicians in the royal service from 1538 to the time of the Civil War. A rebec was listed for the last time in 1558: it was already being ousted by the newly invented violin. This year also, bagpipes were included for the last time: the player, an Englishman, died the same year and was not replaced. In 1570 the preponderance of foreign musicians was more marked: there were now seven members of the Bassano family, and the first of the Ferrabosco and Lanier families appeared. The Laniers were of French origin, perhaps from Rouen, and, as in 1558, there were a few Flemings. In 1603 the Queen employed thirty-eight musicians, among them six Bassanos, Alfonso Ferrabosco the younger (to whom the Queen had refused permission to leave England when his father absconded in 1578), and six Laniers. There was again a harpist, an Irishman, Gormock McDermott, who was apparently the first since the death of old blind William More in 1565. In 1558 and again in 1570 there had been a player of the virginals: his name is given in various forms, most of which suggest that he was French. After 1580 his name disappears, and no virginalist is named in 1590 or in 1603, but in 1597 the French Ambassador de Maisse noted in his journal that the Queen was having the virginals played to her in her chamber.

These musicians would play for the Queen's private pleasure, or would provide music at the tournament or at masques. Elizabethan masques were simple compared with the extravagant shows staged by Inigo Jones in the time of King James and King Charles, and the music required was also much simpler. At the masque written by Philip Sidney for the Queen's visit to Wanstead in 1578, the only music was of recorders and cornets; but for the masque Campion wrote for Lord Hay's wedding in 1607, which was presented before the King in Whitehall, he used almost the whole of the resources of the King's Musick. Campion arranged the musicians with great care in several groups: 'on the right hand were consorted ten musicians, with bass and mean lutes, a bandora, a double sackbut, and an harpsichord, with two treble violins ; on the other side . . . were placed nine violins and three lutes ; and to answer both the consorts (as it were in a triangle) six cornets and six chapel voices were seated almost right against them, in a place higher in respect of the piercing sound of those instruments'.

The chapel voices would be from the Chapel Royal, a much more important institution, which had been in existence at least as early as 1135, and to which the tradition of English music owed much of its splendour. In the fifteenth century Joannes de Tinctoris had observed that the greatest encouragement to the art of music in England came from the Chapel Royal, and this continued to be so throughout the sixteenth and early seventeenth centuries, when among the gentlemen of the Chapel Royal were such distinguished musicians as Tallis, Tye, Mundy, Byrd, Morley, Bull, Tomkins, and Orlando Gibbons. The Chapel Royal was an institution, not a building, and its members would accompany the Queen on progress, as they accompanied her father to the Field of the Cloth of Gold, as they would accompany King James to Scotland and King Charles to Canterbury when he went to welcome his Queen. By the time Queen Elizabeth came to the throne it had thirty-two members, of whom twelve were boys. The post of organist was not established until Thomas Tallis's day : previously various gentlemen must have been expected to act as occasion served. The position of Gentleman of the Chapel Royal carried much prestige : it was worthy of mention on a title-page together with a degree from either university. The gentlemen were quite well paid, and had the advantage of being in daily contact with the Court, with all the possibilities of aristocratic patronage which this gave them. The Queen herself especially favoured some of the gentlemen, granting to Tallis and Byrd, and afterwards to Morley, the monopoly of printing music, and ensuring that Dr John Bull should be appointed to the new music professorship at Gresham

College, in spite of the founder's requirement, which he was unable to fulfil, that he should lecture in Latin. (The lectures were to be given twice a week, each of an hour divided between theory and practice 'by concert of voice or instruments'.) And no doubt it was through her wish to have the best music she could for divine service that the papist Byrd became a gentleman of the Chapel Royal in 1570 and later organist. For some reason now unknown she refused to take Dowland into her service in 1594 on the grounds of his religion — he had not then renounced Popery — but Byrd, who never changed his faith, kept his position in the Chapel Royal throughout her reign. Perhaps her Master of Horse the Earl of Worcester, who was Byrd's patron, and also a Roman Catholic, persuaded the Queen that Byrd's loyalty was no less than his own.

Henry VIII had seen to it that Thomas Tallis, who had been organist at Waltham Abbey (which the King himself had often visited) should be taken into the Chapel Royal on the dissolution of the Abbey in 1540. The King also recognized the musical ability of Christopher Tye, who became a member of the Chapel Royal, and of whom the King is supposed to have remarked

> England one God, one truth, one Doctor hath
> For Music's Art, and that is Doctor Tye.

His reputation as one who did much to continue the tradition of English music through the turmoil of the Reformation continued till long after: 'Music', said Thomas Fuller, 'which received a grievous wound in England at the dissolution of Abbeys, was much beholding to Tye for her recovery; such his excellent skill and piety, that he kept it up in credit at Court and in all Cathedrals during his life'. Tye was choirmaster at Ely Cathedral from the founding of the new bishopric until 1561, and must have had an excellent opportunity for maintaining the choral services as he wished. Fuller's compliment to him is not exclusive, and our present inclination to regard Tallis as the Father of English Cathedral Music should not lead us to reject it. Tallis was the greater and more prolific composer, and at Court his influence must have exceeded Tye's, but Tye may well have done much for English Cathedral Music. That he was a man of bold and candid views Anthony Wood's story proves. The Queen, he says, 'would send the verger to tell Dr Tye that he played out of tune ; whereupon he sent word that her ears were out of tune'. Such a man is not likely to have lacked influence over his fellows.

The Reformation created two problems for those who were concerned with Church music. The dissolution of the monasteries brought to an end many choirs with a long tradition of sacred music. The consequent dispersal of a large number of trained musicians may have had a good effect on musical education, and no doubt the ablest of them, like Tallis, were soon employed again in their profession. But certainly the number of places where they sang must have been sharply reduced. The abolition of the Latin rite, except in a few places such as the colleges of Oxford and Cambridge and the schools of Eton and Winchester where Latin could be readily understood, and the substitution of the English service of the Book of Common Prayer in 1549, were much more serious matters, for the old music was immediately made obsolete. English musicians, who even before this had written church music to the English text, accepted the challenge, and in the choral services and anthems which they wrote provided a unique possession of the Anglican Church, and one of the noblest achievements of the Renaissance in England. The secular character of the age failed to inhibit the English composers in the provision of music that should enhance the worship of God ; and though Elizabethan poets produced no divine poetry to match this sacred music, Cranmer's litany, the Books of Common Prayer, the translations of the Psalms and of the Bible, and Richard Hooker's *Laws of Ecclesiastical Polity* form a literary monument not unworthy of the music of Byrd, Morley, Tomkins, Weelkes, and Gibbons. The love of God could inspire men to the tasks of providing for the English church translations of the Scriptures, a liturgy, and a wealth of music which no other Reformed church can equal ; and the cool elegance of Hooker's prose was more suited to rational controversy than the impassioned rhetoric of poetry. In time these would be combined by the genius of Milton. In *The Faerie Queene*, which Milton so deeply admired, controversy was not evaded, but rather demoted to the political world, so that in the figure of Duessa we are made aware not of the doctrinal basis but of the political consequences of Pope Pius V's impertinent and futile deposition of the Queen of England. Besides, Spenser, writing the Christian heroic poem, preferred, with that daring independence which characterized all he did, to set up Love, not Wrath, as its principal theme ; for the greatest of Christian virtues is Charity. To Spenser, to them all, every question of human concern was ultimately a question of man's relationship to God ; and the Anglican Church, the Elizabethan creation of means to worship God in their own tongue and with their own music surely was, as they intended that it should be, the greatest of all their achievements.

The older music for the church, both in England and on the Continent, had become ridiculous by its contrapuntal extravagance, with phrases of a dozen or fifteen bars to carry but one syllable. The demand for simpler settings, so that the words might be understood, was not confined to the Reformers. The Council of Trent abolished all but four of the sequences from the Roman liturgy, preferring comprehensible words to musical display, but even before this the composers themselves, Josquin, Clemens non Papa, and others, had turned away from the over-florid polyphony.

In the 1540s Archbishop Cranmer, in a letter to the King, had described his attempts to translate into English certain processions to be used on festival days, and (with reference to these) he had given his opinion that 'the song that shall be made thereunto would not be full of notes, but as near as may

8

Hardwick Hall, Derbyshire, West Front, 1590–97 (see p. 85)

9

Hardwick Hall, Derbyshire, High Great Chamber, 1594–97 : Fireplace by Thomas Accres ; Plasterwork by Abraham Smith (see p. 88)

be, for every syllable a note, so that it may be sung distinctly and devoutly'. A Royal Injunction to the same effect was given to the Dean and Chapter of Lincoln Minster in April 1548: they were to sing anthems in English 'setting thereunto a plain and distinct note, for every syllable one'. The demand of the Reformers that the Scriptures should be read in the vernacular, and that the liturgy also should be in English so that it might be understood of the people, thus found its complement in an insistence that musical settings should not obscure the text: it would indeed have been most ridiculous to translate the psalms and canticles into English, and then sing them so that the congregation could not tell whether they were in English or Latin.

This sacred music would not be heard in every parish church, where the liturgy and the Scriptures would accustom the people to the cadence of English prose: the parish church choir was an over-ambitious invention of the Oxford Movement. Psalm-singing was very popular, so much so that it became a Homeric epithet of the Puritan, who disapproved of the more elaborate forms of church music; but it was not heard within the walls of the parish church. In 1560 Bishop Jewel told Peter Martyr that 'sometimes at Paul's Cross there will be six thousand people singing together', which suggests that 'terrible singing' whereby on 14th August 1431 the Hussites also had routed their Popish enemies. There were no hymns, except *Te Deum*, other than the psalms which, in the angular paraphrase of Sternhold and Hopkins, provided the one crude pleasure of congregational singing throughout this time. The more extreme Puritans expressed their disapproval of Cathedral music with characteristic uncouthness: 'during the singing service they would stand without, dancing and sporting themselves until the sermons and lectures did begin'. Even to the singing of psalms some objected, 'displeased they are', said Hooker, 'at the artificial music which we add unto psalms of this kind'. And with a patient sigh he proceeds to justify the practice: 'but our desire is to content them if it may be, and to yield them a just reason even of the least things wherein undeservedly they have but as much as dreamed or suspected that we do amiss'.

The music of the great composers, their services and anthems, were performed by the Chapel Royal or by the choirs of Cathedrals and some Colleges: to these, and to these alone, was the tradition entrusted. The Queen's own liking for ceremonial in the church, for such things as Cross and candlesticks on the altar (which were christened or anathematized as the Offendicle) and her appreciation of good music were distrusted and criticized by the more extreme among the Reformers; but she had a short way with Puritans, and soon suspended her Archbishop Grindal from his functions for too much favouring them. In the creation of the Anglican choral service and anthems the Queen's personal taste was therefore of the first importance.

By the new Act of Uniformity the revised Prayer Book came into general use on the Feast of St John the Baptist, 1559. In one of a series of Injunctions for the guidance of the Church, the Queen, who was again its Supreme Governor, ordered that in those churches where there were endowments for choirs 'by means whereof the laudable science of music has been had in estimation, and preserved in knowledge', no alteration should be made. Further, 'for the comforting of such that delight in music it may be permitted, that in the beginning or in the end of common prayers, either at morning or evening there may be sung an hymn, or suchlike song to the praise of Almighty God in the best sort of melody and music that may be conveniently devised, having respect that the sentence of the hymn may be understanded and perceived' — almost the very words of Pope Marcellus, though it would have been tactless to point this out in 1559. From this injunction comes the provision of the anthem (hymn) which has ever since been so notable a part of the music of the English church.

To the task which the Queen had set her musicians, of writing music worthy of the Church which she had at last settled and guided, they eagerly responded. The greatest of them, William Byrd, who was only fifteen years old when she came to the throne, though remaining loyal to his Roman Catholic faith throughout his long life, wrote impartially for either rite, and magnificently for both. Tallis and others who were composing early in the Queen's reign, wrote more for the Latin than for the English text: John Shepherd, organist of Magdalen College, Robert White, organist of Westminster Abbey, which the Queen refounded as a Royal Peculiar, and William Mundy of the Chapel Royal, worked where the Latin rite was still permitted. Even Thomas Morley, who was no papist, composed Latin motets, but he also composed settings for the English services and — this writer of the gayest of madrigals — was one of the first to set to music the service at the Burial of the Dead.

In Queen Elizabeth's time, in spite of a preference for the 'Short' Service, in which the music must subserve the text as the taste of the time required, the 'Great' Service, with its contrapuntal elaboration, was also permitted, and Byrd's Great Service is nowadays considered 'the finest unaccompanied setting in the repertory of the English Church'. The Elizabethans are likely to have preferred the Short Services, though not necessarily for aesthetic reasons. Hooker sums up the reasonable man's attitude to sacred music better than any other: 'the force and equity of the thing itself, when it drowneth not utterly but fitly suiteth with matter altogether sounding to the praise of God, is in truth most admirable, and doth much edify if not the understanding because it teacheth not, yet surely the affection, because therein it worketh much'.

Such then were the principles which guided their taste in church music: it must be fitting to the worship of God, and must enhance the effect of the words of the liturgy by its power to move men's souls. Thomas Morley, who wrote more about his art than any of his contemporaries, expressed views very similar to Hooker's. Of all kinds of music which are written as a setting of words the motet, he says, 'requireth most art, and moveth and causeth most strange effects in the hearer, being aptly framed for the ditty and well expressed by the singer, for it will draw the auditor (and specially the skilful auditor) into a devout and reverent kind of consideration of him for whose praise it was made'. Morley had no doubt that the motet was the highest kind of music, and no one at that time would have disagreed with him. Campion, in the preface to his first *Book of Ayres*, compares sacred music to the heroic poem : 'as in Poesy we give the pre-eminence to the Heroical Poem, so in Music we yield the chief place to the grave and well-invented Motet'. How could it be otherwise, for the purpose of the heroic poem was to set forth the pattern of the Christian hero, and so to impel the reader towards the life of Christian virtue ; and music written for divine service, while it could not instruct, could move man's affections and so make his noblest duty, the service and worship of God, the more acceptable. 'The better the voice is', Byrd said, 'the meeter it is to honour and serve God therewith ; and the voice of man is chiefly to be employed to that end.'

Of the Elizabethan composers Byrd in his own day received the highest praise : to his younger contemporaries he was the Father of English Music, one 'never without reverence to be named of the musicians', the man who held the chief place in his art as Spenser, author of the Christian heroic poem, England's Arch-poet, the English Virgil, did among poets. Both delighted to use an old but vigorous native tradition, but both were ready to learn from Continental, and especially (as always in England) from Italian masters of their art. Both, in adapting foreign forms, made them thoroughly English ; were bold in experiment and pioneered new kinds of music and poetry ; were extraordinarily gifted, yet had the diligence to develop their technique with the utmost refinement ;

were more versatile, and more prolific, than any other composer or poet of their day. And perhaps it is not fanciful to compare Byrd's mastery of polyphonic music with Spenser's intricate interweaving of complementary or contrasted episode in *The Faerie Queene*.

Next to Byrd in contemporary judgment was his pupil Thomas Morley, who 'did shine as the Sun in the Firmament of our Art'. Beyond these two there is no need here to seek preferences, for when so many were composing such a variety of excellent music the rivalry between them was still friendly, as when Byrd and the elder Ferrabosco had 'a virtuous contention in love made upon the plain-song of Miserere'. John Farmer in 1591 published forty accompaniments in canon to this plain-song ; but these contests were easily won by George Waterhouse who, with tireless if tiresome ingenuity, wrote one thousand one hundred and sixty-three more. These canons satisfied a taste for academic ingenuity such as is to be found in the other arts, in Tresham's Triangular Lodge (pl. 5), in the poets' love of anagram and acrostic and reporting sonnet, and they have no more value.

The Queen's example must have encouraged her courtiers towards accomplishment in music — to be 'skilful auditors' — and to the patronage of musicians : both accepted as necessary to the ideal of the complete man. Scholarly scepticism of recent years has a little damaged the older picture of the Renaissance gentleman being able to sing a part at sight, or to accompany a song of his own on the lute ; but perhaps it is time to effect some restoration. Morley's famous dialogue, where Philomathes is put to shame for his inability to sing his part, is discounted : Morley's enthusiasm is supposed to have run away with him. But Morley was saying very much what Thomas Whythorne had observed in Italy forty years before : 'I perceived that among such as were of any account, they were esteemed to be but rudely and basely brought up who had no knowledge in music, or at the least able to play or sound on some musical instrument or else to sing pricksong, in such sort as they were able to sing a part when they were in company of such who were willing to sing songs of 2, 3, 4 parts etc.' And Henry Peacham's requirement of his complete gentleman — 'I desire no more in you than to sing your part sure, and at the first sight, withal to play the same upon your viol, or the exercise of the lute privately to yourself' — is watered down by modern commentators who cannot believe in such a high level not merely of performance, but of aptitude. Now, no one would wish to argue that musical aptitude was any more widespread then than at any other time ; but it was more esteemed then, and therefore more likely to be discovered and developed. Byrd himself made this point : the gift of a good voice 'is so rare as there is not one among a thousand that hath it' ; everyone therefore should learn to sing, lest a good voice be lost. Philomathes was not exceptional either in his ignorance of music or in his eagerness to replace it with knowledge. And there is plenty of evidence that gentlemen of the time could and did enjoy singing and playing.

When the first Earl of Essex lay dying in Dublin in 1576 'he called William Hewes, which was his musician, to play upon the virginal and to sing. "Play", said he, "my song, Will Hewes, and I will sing it myself." So he did it most joyfully.' By a happy chance the song which he sang, 'O heavenly God, O Father dear, cast down thy tender eye', is still preserved. It was probably still unusual to accompany a song on the virginals, but Thomas Whythorne tells us that he would sing his own songs 'sometime to the lute and sometimes the virginals' about 1550. In 1586 when Sir Philip Sidney lay mortally wounded at Arnhem, he too called for music, 'especially that song which himself had entitled *La cuisse rompue*'. In his father's household accounts there are various records of payments for singing lessons for Robert Sidney, as well as for a lute for his sister Mary. To her, who as Countess of Pembroke became so celebrated a patron of poets, Thomas Morley in 1593 dedicated his *Canzonets for three voices.* Sir Philip, in a well-known letter, advised his brother to 'take a delight to keep and increase his music', and Robert seems to have acted upon it. He became a patron of John Dowland, and on such friendly terms with him that he consented to act as godfather to his son Robert, who in 1610 dedicated to him *A Musical Banquet.*

Of Sir Philip's own musical education there is no evidence in his father's accounts, because these do not begin until Philip was away at school at Shrewsbury. Whatever his ability as a performer, there can be no doubt of his interest in music: in the *Arcadia* he not only included a madrigal of his own writing (the first in English) but frequently indicated the musical accompaniment intended for his songs. He wrote lyrics to Italian, Spanish, and Flemish tunes: one of these, *Basciami mia vita*, was included in *Il Secundo Libro delle Villotte alla Napoletana* which had been printed in Venice in 1571, a few years before his stay there. Another poem was to the tune which has since become the Dutch National Anthem, *Wilhelmus van Nassouwe*, a song of French Huguenot origin to which Sidney's friend, the Dutch leader Philips van Marnix, wrote the Dutch words. In Vienna he must have met Filippo di Monte, most prolific of all madrigalists, for di Monte was then living near Charles de l'Ecluse, with whom both he and Sidney were on terms of intimate friendship. We have one glimpse of Sidney arranging for music to entertain the company in his sister's house at Wilton in March 1584, when Sir Arthur Basset recommended to him one Thomas Richards 'chiefly for the rareness of his instrument with wires'; and several years before he had written from Wilton to his uncle the Earl of Sussex to ask him to assist an unnamed foreign musician.

To Sidney, his family and friends, music was a necessary pleasure: we must assume that they enjoyed music unless we can prove that they did not. Spenser's assertion that Astrophel 'could pipe and daunce, and caroll sweet' is in the convention of pastoral elegy ; all Arcadian shepherds could do the same — but so could most of Elizabeth's courtiers. In *Astrophel and Stella* Sidney tells us that Stella sings his songs, and we have in a sonnet by Henry Constable other evidence that Lady Rich could sing and play on the lute. Perhaps the setting by Charles Tessier of the eighth song in *Astrophel and Stella* was already written in Sidney's day for Lady Rich to sing, although it was not published till long afterwards in Robert Dowland's *A Musical Banquet*. In 1597 Tessier dedicated to Lady Rich his *Premier Livre de Chansons*, and said that he wrote the songs in England and that he now published them at the request of his friends here. Byrd, who set the sixth and tenth of the songs in *Astrophel and Stella*, mentions Lady Rich in his *Songs of Sundry Natures*, 1589 : these two settings may well have been written several years before, and it is charming to think that before he left England to meet his death in the Netherlands Philip Sidney may have heard his exquisite songs sung to Byrd's music by Penelope. Byrd concluded his *Psalms, Sonnets, and Songs* of 1588 with two funeral songs in Sidney's memory ; and when Penelope's second husband died in 1606 John Coprario joined the poets in mourning him with a collection entitled *Funeral Tears for the Death of the Earl of Devonshire*. John Mundy's dedication to her brother, the second Earl of Essex, of *Songs and Psalms* in 1594, which he intended 'for the use of all such as either love or learn Music', must include the Earl himself among their number.

We should expect in that most alert and elegant company about Sidney and Essex, the two most admired courtiers of the age, that music would be honoured and practised ; but there were many other families whose enjoyment was no less sincere, and of whose skill we have some record. George Whetstone in *A Remembrance of the Precious Virtues of Sir James Dier*, 1582, included a love of music as proof of the eminent lawyer's sound conscience. Behind the name Ferdinando Richardson, composer of a number of pieces in the *Fitzwilliam Virginal Book* and of a poem in commendation of Tallis and Byrd's *Cantiones Sacrae*, 1575, stands lightly concealed Ferdinando Heybourne, Groom of the Privy Chamber. (Heybourne and the elder John Harington had both been Tallis's pupils, as had Byrd.) Even the haughty Earl of Oxford, seventeenth of his line at a time when few peers of the realm were more than the second or third of theirs, did not disdain to develop a natural gift: in John Farmer's opinion, 'using this science as a re-creation, your Lordship has overgone most of them that make it a profession'. Such praise, from a professional, need not be entirely dismissed as flattery, for other composers did not hesitate to insist, in their dedications to aristocratic patrons, on the necessity of a high standard of performance.

Most of these men learnt their music at home rather than at school, where there was seldom time for such studies. At Ingatestone Hall in Essex the accounts of the Petre family show expenditure on music and musicians from 1548 onwards, and though Sir William Petre may not himself have been a skilled musician, his son John, who became the first Lord Petre, was so. In 1559, when he was nine years of age, he had his own virginals, and two years later a Cologne lute was bought for him. While he was a student at the Middle Temple he bought music for his lute, and eventually paid an Italian named Pietro fifty shillings for a new instrument. (His first lute had cost thirteen shillings.) Later John Petre got to know William Byrd, who visited him in the country, and who spent the twelve days of Christmas 1589 with him at Ingatestone. This same Christmas five musicians came down from London to play the violins, and John Petre bought a new pair of virginals for the very large sum of £50: it was placed upon iron brackets in the Great Chamber. A few years later Byrd came to live at Stondon Place, little more than an hour's ride from either of Petre's houses. Two manuscript song-books which belonged to Petre have survived, one of them with motets by

Byrd and other English composers, the other with music of foreign composers. For weddings in the family musicians were brought down from London, and for the wedding of his son William to Lady Katherine Somerset in 1596 John Petre or Lady Katherine's father, the Earl of Worcester, may have invited Byrd to compose some suitable music. Both knew Byrd well and admired his work, and for a marriage for which Spenser was invited to write his *Prothalamion* it seems very likely that music would also be commissioned.

Two of the most celebrated madrigalists of the age lived in East Anglian households where we may believe that they helped to instruct the younger members of the families, and probably wrote madrigals for special occasions. John Wilbye, whose father was a tanner of Diss in Norfolk with a taste for music — he bequeathed a lute to his famous son — was discovered by Sir Thomas Cornwallis of Brome Hall, near Diss; in 1593, at the age of nineteen, he went to live with the Kytsons at Hengrave Hall, where he remained until the death of Lady Kytson, who was Sir Thomas Cornwallis's daughter, in 1628. For the remaining ten years of his life he lived in Lady Rivers' 'great brick house' in Colchester. She was a daughter of Lady Kytson, and no doubt had been taught by Wilbye. Sir Robert Jermyn also lived near Bury St Edmunds at Rushbrooke Hall, and employed George Kirbye to teach music to his daughters. We do not know for how many years he remained with Sir Robert, but he lived in or near Bury St Edmunds until his death in 1634. Neither composer was known as a virtuoso performer, such as were Byrd, Bull, Dowland, and Gibbons, and the Kytsons' patronage of John Wilbye, and Sir Robert Jermyn's of George Kirbye seem both to have been as disinterested as they were perspicacious.

Philip Gawdy was the son of another gentleman of East Anglia who early learnt to play the lute, and whose letters show his continuing interest in music. In 1581 he wrote to his father: 'as for the lute, I will not say what liking I had of it because nobody shall hereafter say that I was somewhat newfangled of the same. But otherwise surely it is like enough I would have praised it somewhat more than I mean to do at this time.' He was afraid that his father might think excessive praise of the lute, which he was then learning to play, silly and affected. Many years later he was to send his sister-in-law in Norfolk two songs for the viol, 'that were given me from a very worthy musician at Court' — the kind of thing that must often have happened.

Edward Herbert, poet, philosopher, and diplomat, who became Lord Herbert of Cherbury, and who was one of Donne's friends, tells us in his *Autobiography* that while he was at Oxford in the 1590s, he 'attained also to sing his part at first sight in music, and to play on the lute, with very little or almost no teaching', just as Morley or Peacham thought a gentleman should do. 'And', he continues, 'my learning of music was for this end, that I might entertain myself at home, and together refresh my mind after my studies.' His younger brother George was also a musician, and when he was Rector of Bemerton used to walk into Salisbury to play music with his friends : no doubt he too learnt in childhood.

In spite of Lord Herbert of Cherbury's characteristic boast — he was a very vain man — that he needed little instruction, it is obvious that some provision was made for teaching the children of the house to play or sing at an early age. Often the task would be given to one or other of the servants : Sir William Petre gave his housekeeper, Mary Percy, extra money for teaching his daughters to play the virginals ; the Kytsons of Hengrave Hall employed a man named Cosen to teach their children the virginals ; in 1558 the Earl of Rutland paid a lutenist named Weston ten shillings for teaching his page to play on the lute. In 1586 Roger Manners wrote to the then Earl of Rutland to assure him that his daughter's music was not being neglected : 'I have not forgotten the Lady Elizabeth, but have a servant to play the virginals with her when Symons is away'. Symons, presumably, was her regular teacher and in the Earl's employ ; probably the Earl had taken him with him to London. A year later Edward Paston was writing to the Earl to recommend an organist from Norwich to teach his daughter the virginals. Thomas Banes, who taught singing to Sir William Cavendish's children, was not included among the servants receiving wages and livery : probably he was employed solely as a music master. Music was written specially for teaching : so Richard Alison framed some of the compositions in *An Hour's Recreation in Music* 'with two trebles, necessary for such as teach in private families'. Thus the teacher might be a servant or might be a professional musician brought into the household for a time, as Thomas Whythorne was variously employed in the household of the Earl of Warwick and of other but unidentifiable people. Most fortunate of all these aristocratic children was the daughter of the Earl of Northumberland whose tutor in 1579 was none other than William Byrd.

Inevitably some of these children would, through lack of aptitude, abandon the attempt to play or sing when they grew up ; but the general respect for musical accomplishment, and the expectation that a person of any account would be able to play and sing, must have ensured that the majority kept up their music. John Petre at the Inns of Court, Edward Herbert at the University were still enjoying their singing to the lute. The young Arthur Throckmorton, travelling in Italy in 1581, was astute enough while he was in Florence to have lessons on the lute from no less a man than Vincenzo Galilei, the lutenist and composer, whose dialogue *Fronimo*, first published in 1568, gave instruction in lute tablature and tuning, and who was a member of the famous Camerata. Throckmorton is not likely to have been the only Englishman to include music among his studies while on the Grand Tour, though few can have had the privilege of so distinguished a teacher.

In few schools which the sons of gentlemen attended was

music taught. But in the Choir Schools, such as Magdalen College School, where Thomas Whythorne was educated, or New College School, where John Case was a chorister before going as a scholar to St John's, very many of the professional musicians had their first training. At Merchant Taylors' the greatest headmaster of the age, Richard Mulcaster, insisted on both instrumental music and singing as part of the curriculum. The reasons which he gives are as severely practical as Byrd's reasons to persuade everyone to sing. 'Music by the instrument, besides the skill which must still increase, in form of exercise to get the use of our small joints before they be knit, to have them the nimbler, and to put musicians in mind that they be no brawlers, lest by some swash of a sword they chance to lose a joint, an irrecoverable jewel unadvisedly cast away. Music by the voice, besides her cunning also, by the way of physic, to spread the voice instruments within the body, while they be yet young. As both the kinds of music for much profit, and more pleasure,' which last clause eventually gets us away from mere hygiene. Surprisingly Mulcaster's most distinguished pupil, Edmund Spenser, does not show in his poetry any very great interest in music : perhaps Mulcaster's recommendation of it as good for the fingers and diaphragm did not much move Spenser, or perhaps the elaborate music which he himself made out of the English language satisfied him. But he provides music for the betrothal of Una and the Maske of Cupid in *The Faerie Queene*, and in the *Epithalamion* he imagines the music of choir and organs at his own marriage to Elizabeth Boyle. He also regards it as a normal accomplishment of the courtier :

> Thus when this Courtly Gentleman with toyle
> Himselfe hath wearied, he doth recoyle
> Unto his rest, and there with sweete delight
> Of Musicks skill revives his toyled spright.

But the best passages in which he describes music are those where he writes of the song of birds, the innocent wild music which has delighted man from the beginning of time. Another of Mulcaster's pupils, Sir James Whitlocke, remembered with gratitude Mulcaster's care for his musical education, 'in which I was brought up by daily exercise in it, as in singing and playing upon instruments'. Mulcaster also made his pupils write exercises in counterpoint and in composition, in order to develop their powers of appreciation, just as Castiglione had recommended that the courtier should attempt to write poetry and to paint so that his criticism of these arts would be more informed and intelligent.

In a time when music carried so much social prestige it is not to be wondered at that amateur composers sometimes showed remarkable gifts. This was especially true of Italy, where the Camerata included men of leading Florentine families, and where Gesualdo, Prince of Venosa, devoted his life to the composition of madrigals of startling originality and to acquiring the reputation of a virtuoso lutenist. Here in England King Henry VIII composed masses and motets, and the excellence of his compositions has been attested in this century when such praise may be less uncritically given than while his daughter was on the throne. Ferdinando Heybourne was one of her courtiers with a talent for writing music; but the most gifted of all was Michael Cavendish, of the elder branch of the famous family, who in 1598 published his lute songs — the very kind which we should most expect a Renaissance courtier to compose — only a year after Dowland had set the fashion with his *First Book of Ayres*. He dedicated the book to his second cousin, Lady Arabella Stuart, whose claims to the succession Queen Elizabeth had once favoured but had brusquely dismissed in the previous year. Many of Cavendish's family, besides Lady Arabella, took a lively interest in music and employed, or at least offered their patronage to, professional musicians. Cavendish subscribed his dedication from Cavendish Manor in Suffolk, his grandfather's house and the original home of the family. His grandfather's younger brother had in 1547 married, as his third wife, Bess of Hardwick, and though there is little to show that either of them had much love of music — in 1601 the only musical instrument listed at Hardwick Hall was a pair of virginals in the Long Gallery — their children certainly had. The splendid walnut table, which still stands in the High Great Chamber at Hardwick, made for the marriage of their eldest son Henry in 1568, is inlaid with representations, among much else, of lute, viol, and gittern. The accounts of the second son, William (who was created Earl of Devonshire in 1618), which remain at Chatsworth, contain many references to music : in 1599 Sir William (as he then was) bought a number of music books while on a visit to London, including *Melodia Olympica* by the Roman Catholic expatriate Peter Philips, and madrigals by Orazio Vecchi. In the same year he was paying for singing lessons for his son and daughter ; he also employed a French lutenist named Lambert. In January 1600 he bought his kinsman Michael's book of songs (which cost four shillings and eight pence) for his nine-year-old son, Master William. The third of the brothers, Charles, married Elizabeth Kytson of Hengrave Hall, daughter of a family which has been justly celebrated for their patronage of John Wilbye. Of Bess of Hardwick's daughters the eldest, Frances, married Sir Henry Pierrepoint of Holme Pierrepoint in Nottinghamshire to whom in 1604 Thomas Greaves dedicated his *Songs of Sundry Kinds*, describing himself as 'lutenist to Sir Henry' ; and Elizabeth, Countess of Lennox, was the mother of Lady Arabella, in whose service some years later Thomas Cutting was lutenist. There is no reason to suppose that such a record was exceptional : what is exceptional is the preservation of the evidence.

A family tradition of music of this kind, rather than the presence in the family of a composer of genius, can persuade us of the prestige which music had in Elizabethan society, for gifts such as Michael Cavendish's occur unpredictably, but so widespread a love of music comes of deliberate choice. There was a universal acceptance of music as one of the civilized pleasures, so that anyone who aspired towards the ideal of the courtier must be able to make music in company with his friends, or for his private recreation. It was the custom, Morley says, to bring out the music books when supper was ended: he does not say, this is what I wish people would do, but, this is what most of them already do.

During the troubled years in the middle of the century, as in the time of the Wars of the Roses, music and poetry had been at a discount. George Puttenham, writing in the 1560s, could complain that 'it is hard to find in these days of noblemen or gentlemen any excellent musician', but the new revival, in musical taste as in literary, began in the 1570s. By 1576, when Thomas Whythorne was writing his autobiography, the gentlemen had begun to follow the advice of Castiglione and others: 'the nobility and the worshipful . . . have schoolmasters in their houses to teach their children both to sing pricksong, and also to play on musical instruments'. Whythorne himself had been employed in several households, including that of Lord Ambrose Dudley, Leicester's elder brother. When in 1575 the Earl of Leicester received the Queen at Kenilworth music formed part of the entertainment. Robert Laneham, whose naïvely enthusiastic account is our most vivid record of the festivities, was himself a musician: 'And when I see company according, then can I be as lively too. Sometimes I foot it with dancing; now with my gittern, and else with my cittern, then at the virginals: you know nothing comes amiss to me. Then carol I up a song withal, that by and by they come flocking about me like bees to honey; and ever they cry "Another, good Laneham, another!"' Harry Goldingham, the singer, took part in the Princely Pleasures, figuring reluctantly, and briefly, as Arion. Edward Johnson, who enjoyed the patronage of the Kytsons, also waited on the Earl of Leicester on this occasion. In 1591 he composed some music for the Queen's visit to Lord Hertford

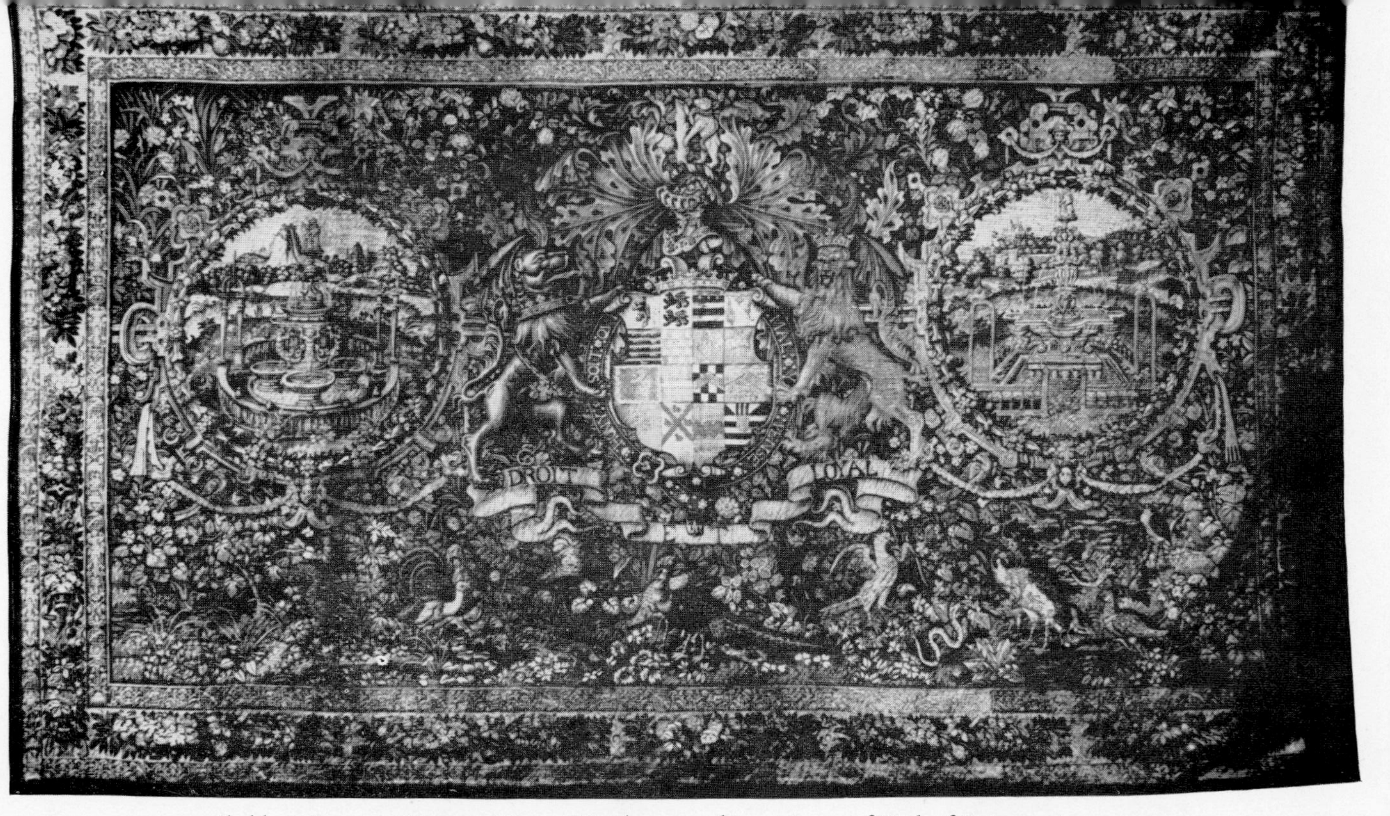

Sheldon Tapestry, Drayton House, Northamptonshire; Arms of Earl of Leicester in centre, fountains in roundels on either side (? 1575 for the visit of the Queen to Kenilworth Castle)

Mural Painting from Hill Hall, Essex, *c.* 1580, after design by the Master of the Die (see p. 93)

at Elvetham, and he may have done the same for her visit to Kenilworth.

The year after these famous Pleasures Sir Christopher Hatton entertained at Eltham the Sieur de Champagny, who had come as an envoy from the Spanish viceroy in the Netherlands. The ambassador wrote that one of the three things which had most impressed him on his visit, so that 'in all my travel of France, Italy, and Spain, I never heard the like', was 'a concert of music, so excellent and sweet as cannot be expressed'. On another occasion Hatton similarly entertained some ambassadors at his house with solemn music, while their underlings were gambling. Hatton may have had an especially important part in the revival of music in England, for his notorious love of dancing, which has been insisted on as if he had no other merits, was probably only the most conspicuous part of his love of music, or the part which his enemies could most easily attack as frivolous and unseemly. In 1588 Byrd dedicated to him his *Psalms, Sonnets and Songs of Sadness and Piety*, and in the following year he claimed that 'since the publishing in print of my last labours in music, divers persons of great honour and worship have more esteemed and delighted in the exercise of that art than before'. Byrd was in a position to know, but a dozen years before Hatton had thought of music as suitable entertainment for visiting ambassadors, and had been able to provide music of the finest quality. Byrd's dedication to him of his first collection of secular music may well have been due to his recognition that the Lord Chancellor was one of the first of Elizabeth's courtiers to acknowledge the dignity and charm of music. Byrd probably met Hatton many years before, when in 1567 *Tancred and Gismunda* was acted at the Inner Temple, for Hatton wrote the fourth act of the play, and Byrd composed for it the song *Come tread the path* ; but whether they kept in touch through the intervening twenty years we cannot know. Hatton died in 1591, unmarried, and his estates passed to a nephew and eventually, within a few years, to a cousin's son, another Christopher Hatton. He continued the Lord Chancellor's tradition, and in 1612 accepted the dedication of Orlando Gibbons' *Madrigals and Motets of Five Parts*. 'They were most of them', said Gibbons, 'composed in your own house, and do therefore properly belong unto you, as Lord of the Soil ; the language they speak you provided them', by selecting, with excellent judgment, poems by Spenser, Ralegh, Donne, Sylvester, and others. This set includes what is perhaps the best loved of all English madrigals, *The Silver Swan*, and the whole collection shows that the younger Sir Christopher shared to the full his more famous kinsman's taste for solemn music and good poetry.

In *Psalms, Sonnets and Songs* Byrd lists his eight reasons to persuade everyone to sing : of these, six are practical (it is easily taught and learnt ; it is good for health ; it cures stammering and procures a perfect pronunciation ; it is the only way of discovering a good voice) ; one is pious ; and only one aesthetic — the superiority of vocal over instrumental music. Yet it may not be too charitable to suppose that by this time many of Byrd's readers could be persuaded not because, as he assured them, 'it doth strengthen all parts of the breast and doth open the pipes', but because they enjoyed it. Byrd, as a Roman Catholic, and as a composer of Church music, would have been well aware of those Puritan suspicions of music which were frequently asserted in his younger days. He may have known, and must have heard of, John Marbeck, at one time organist of St George's Chapel, whose *Book of Common Prayer Noted* of 1550 is the earliest setting of the Anglican Service. Marbeck afterwards bitterly repented that he had 'consumed vainly the greater part of his life in the study of music and the playing of organs', and a conscience dominated by Calvin assured him that the laborious construction of the first Concordance to the English Bible was a task more acceptable to God.

Roger Ascham in *Toxophilus* regarded instrumental music

as effeminate, but agreed that the young ought to learn to sing (though shooting was better) for practical reasons such as Byrd endorsed. Twenty years later, when he was writing *The Schoolmaster*, Ascham had become more liberal, and was prepared to admit that 'to sing, and play of instruments cunningly' was 'not only comely and decent, but also very necessary for a courtly gentleman to use'. He had been reading Castiglione, whose Count Lewis insisted on the courtier being able to read a part in a song and to play various instruments. Since Ascham wrote times had changed, and by 1586 John Case in *The Praise of Music*, which is a defence against the Puritan disparagers, could boldly assert, 'The chief end of music is to delight'. Case refers the reader 'for the decent use hereof in gentlemen' to the eighth book of Aristotle's *Politics*, and to the seventh chapter of Sir Thomas Elyot's *The Governour*. There Elyot had been a little sceptical of the value of music to a gentleman, though he was willing to allow him to play in private for his own recreation, and also to learn enough to be able to judge the quality of music heard ; Case was prepared to go further, and to claim that music could be 'publicly commodious in matters both civil and ecclesiastical'. Byrd was delighted with Case's defence, and wrote a madrigal entitled *A Gratification unto Master John Case for his learned book lately made in the Praise of Music* to words by Thomas Watson :

> Let others praise what seems them best,
> I like his lines above the rest
> Whose pen hath painted Music's praise,
> By Nature's law, by Wisdom's rule,
> He soundly blames the senseless fool
> And barbarous Scythian of our days.

This was printed as a broadside soon after the publication of Case's book.

A little later in the same year in which Byrd published *Psalms, Sonnets and Songs* Nicholas Yonge brought out his *Musica Transalpina*, a collection of Italian madrigals by Ferrabosco,

Palestrina, Luca Marenzio, Filippo di Monte, Orlando di Lasso and others, with two also by Byrd. In his preface Yonge refers to Byrd's book, and he says that the growth of interest in singing madrigals is quite recent. These translations were made about five years earlier, 'and albeit there be some English songs lately set forth by a great master of music, which for skill and sweetness may content the most curious ; yet because they are not many in number men delighted in variety have wished more of the same sort'. Yonge had been in the custom of having musical parties at his house at which gentlemen and merchants, both English and foreign, used to come to sing together ; for their use he imported music from Italy and the Low Countries, and so it seemed appropriate to publish an English selection of these madrigals. Many other publications followed in the next twenty years, but the singing of madrigals was not new in 1588 : at Winchester College is a manuscript collection of about ninety Italian and French four-part madrigals, dated 1564 ; in Lord Lumley's library most of the music books were Italian or Flemish, and in other households there are many records of the purchase of Italian music books, most of which were probably sets of madrigals. Many of the songs which Byrd published in 1588 are included in a manuscript at Christ Church dated 1581, and there must have been manuscript collections in numerous houses at this time.

The publication in the same year of these two collections, Byrd's and Yonge's, suggests the whole history of the madrigal in England. The stimulus, as in all the other arts, came from Italy but, as in literature and in the miniature painting of Hilliard and in the sculpture of the tomb-makers, the English genius transformed the Italian source, and the English madrigalists produced compositions which are as independent and as good as the contemporary poetry. But whereas in Italy the madrigalists had set poetry by the greatest of their poets, Petrarch, Ariosto, Bembo, Tasso, Guarini, in England the musicians preferred lighter verses, specially written for them to set. They used very little by the great poets of the age, Sidney, Spenser, Daniel, Drayton, Marlowe, Shakespeare, and were therefore less dominated by literary tradition than the Italians. The poems were less serious, more popular, and gayer, and the music to which they were set was intended not for professional singers but for amateur performance in private houses. Thus the English madrigal, for all the charm of the verses, is more purely musical than the Italian, and though it coincided with the best work of the poets it was in no way subservient to literature.

During the next few years further collections of Italian madrigals were published in England by Watson, Yonge, and Morley. These too illustrate the English preference for the lighter kind of madrigal, and Thomas Morley, who was the true founder of the English school of madrigalists, was both the most Italian in style and the best liked of them all. Modern taste prefers the work of John Wilbye and Thomas Weelkes, but whereas neither of Wilbye's sets was reprinted, and only one of Weelkes's ran to a second edition, Morley's *Canzonets* of 1593 went to four editions, and three other of his sets were reprinted. Morley's comments on the madrigal, which he regarded as the best kind of light music, help to show what especially appealed to contemporary taste in his work. 'As for the music,' he says, 'it is next unto the Motet [1] the most artificial, and, to men of understanding, most delightful. If therefore you will compose in this kind you must possess yourself with an amorous humour (for in no composition shall you prove admirable except you put on and possess yourself wholly with that vein wherein you compose), so that you must in your music be wavering like the wind, sometime wanton, sometime drooping, sometime grave and staid, otherwhile effeminate . . . and the more variety you show the better shall you please. In this kind our age excelleth, so that if you would imitate any I would appoint you these for

[1] 'under which I comprehend all grave and sober music'.

guides: Alfonso Ferrabosco for deep skill, Luca Marenzio for good air and fine invention, Horatio Vecchi, Stephano Venturi, Ruggiero Giovanelli, and John Croce with divers others who are very good but not so generally good as these.' The presence in England for most of the '60s and '70s of an Italian madrigalist of the distinction of Ferrabosco must have done much to make Englishmen familiar with the Italian madrigal, and Yonge's choice of more work by him than by any other composer for *Musica Transalpina* shows that it was much admired.

Morley's choice of Ferrabosco as one of his guides to madrigal composition was inescapable: his work must have been more widely known here than that of any other. But his choice of Marenzio shows more clearly the contemporary English taste, which Morley so well understood. Marenzio had been one of the largest contributors to *Musica Transalpina*, and in the second of these collections, Watson's *Italian Madrigals Englished*, 1590, all but five of the twenty-eight pieces are his. Morley included his work in his collection of 1598, and long afterwards John Milton, during his stay in Venice in 1639, sought especially for Marenzio's compositions, together with those of Vecchi, Gesualdo, and Monteverde.

Both Marenzio and Giovanelli made many settings from Sannazaro's *Arcadia*, and their liking for pastoral would commend them to English taste at a time when, from *The Shepheardes Calender* to *England's Helicon*, pastoral poetry was much in favour, and when Sir Philip Sidney's *Arcadia* was at the beginning of its unequalled career as a best-seller. Orazio Vecchi and Giovanni Croce, in spite of their priestly calling, had the Venetian gaiety and love of colour and incident which has always delighted the English above everything else that Italy can offer. Vecchi's madrigals were on sale in London at the end of the century, and madrigals by Croce (at that time *vice maestro di cappella* of St Mark's) had been included in collections edited by Yonge and by Morley, whose own compositions are said to resemble his very closely. But above all else, these composers whom Morley names were writing for private entertainment not for public performance, and when they did otherwise, as did Luca Marenzio in his last works, which demand experienced professional singers, they made no appeal to English taste.

The Triumphs of Oriana[1] which Morley edited in 1601, a collection of madrigals in honour of Queen Elizabeth by twenty-three English composers, also had an Italian precedent. *Il Trionfo di Dori*, published at Venice in 1592, contained madrigals by Marenzio, Giovanelli, Vecchi, and Croce, and by Palestrina, di Monte, and Gastoldi. Some of Morley's *Ballets* of 1595 were settings of texts which Gastoldi had already set, are indeed little more than transcriptions. In the *Triumphs*, *Hard by a crystal fountain* is in some respects a lengthened parody of a madrigal by Croce. Morley could not have known him personally, but John Dowland had met Croce in Venice about 1595, and had discussed music with him, and he seems to have been especially well known in England.

In the last twenty years of the sixteenth century new Italian music and Italian literature very quickly became known in England. Earlier in the century this had not been so: Boiardo, Ariosto, and Castiglione were not translated into English for many years, but Tasso, Guarini, and della Casa waited only ten years or less. Similarly, compositions by Luca Marenzio and Croce and their contemporaries were published in England almost immediately after they had appeared in Italy, with translations of the words which were rough, perhaps, but at least ready. An Italian edition of *Il Pastor Fido* was published in London the year after its first printing in Venice, and Dymock's translation came out eleven years later. Croce's

[1] Local patriotism must excuse me for here recounting a story which Anthony Wood tells. 'There was some time an ancient custom belonging to New College Fellows' by which, on Holy Thursday, some of them 'going up to a well or spring in the grove, which was strewed with flowers round about for them, they sung a song of five parts', which was Morley's *Hard by a crystal fountain*. (This is in fact in six parts.) *Tempora mutantur: nos et mutamur in illis.*

setting of the Seven Penitential Psalms was published in London, with English text, five years after the Venetian edition. The English passion for all things Italian, which led the Queen to boast that she was half Italian and Shakespeare to lay the scene of half his plays in Italy, could be even more quickly satisfied by the importation of Italian music than by the translation of Italian poetry, though for most translation would not be necessary. There was much criticism of this tardy apish nation for limping after the Italians in base imitation: Morley himself, with less justification than Shakespeare, joined the chorus of those who objected to 'the new-fangled opinions of our countrymen who will highly esteem whatsoever cometh from beyond the seas (and specially from Italy)' but he continued to publish Italian music, and to write in the Italian manner. Richard Carleton was more candid: in the preface to his *Madrigals* in 1601 he admits that he has 'laboured somewhat to imitate the Italian, they being in these days (with the most) in high request'. The composers were, after all, trying to write the kind of madrigals their countrymen wished to sing.

The madrigal remained extremely popular until about 1612, and the great majority of printed sets were published in the quarter of a century that followed Byrd's *Psalms, Sonnets and Songs* and Yonge's *Musica Transalpina.* Thus the madrigal remained in fashion rather longer than the exactly contemporary sonnet, and (although comparisons between music and poetry are fatuous rather than odious) the work of Byrd, Morley, Weelkes, Wilbye, Kirbye, Bateson, and Gibbons in the madrigal is probably even more notable than the sonneteering of Sidney, Spenser, Constable, Daniel, Drayton, Shakespeare, and Donne. There may have been more madrigalists than sonneteers in those few years, when anyone who could not sing his part in a madrigal, or who lacked skill of a sonnet, would need to hang his head in company.

So long as the madrigal was regarded, as it always was in England, as music for the entertainment of the performers, not of the listeners, the intelligibility of the words was unimportant. The singers themselves knew what they were singing, and the words of the English madrigal were sometimes trivial, or even nonsensical. In Italy, where the madrigalists set works by famous poets for professional performance, the listeners would often know by heart the sonnet of Petrarch, or the stanza from the *Orlando Furioso* or the *Gerusalemme Liberata*, and, once given the cue, would not need to hear words which they could repeat to themselves. But both in England and in Italy men began to demand that the music should not obscure the words, whether sacred or profane, familiar or new, but rather that it should reveal and illustrate them. In Italy Orazio Vecchi had even attempted to use the madrigal dramatically, a task for which it was naturally unsuited : the origins of opera must be sought elsewhere, in the classical experiments of the Florentine Camerata in imitation of the Greeks, and the development of the new *stilo recitativo*.

In England the success of the popular drama delayed the appearance of true opera for half a century, till the improbable production in Commonwealth London by that incorrigible Cavalier, Sir William Davenant, of *The Siege of Rhodes*. (This production was the first in which a woman took a part on the English stage : it was such a success, in those dowdy times, that Davenant rewrote the opera with a part for a second woman.) Masques by Ben Jonson were set in *stilo recitativo* as early as 1617 and 1621, by Nicholas Lanier, but these were isolated occasions, and neither *Lovers Made Men* nor *The Gypsies Metamorphosed* begot any operatic progeny. Instead of musical drama the English musicians invented the ayre, a solo song with lute accompaniment which had no Continental ancestry. The old polyphonic tradition was dying, and the assumption that unaccompanied vocal music was the proper medium for serious composers could no longer remain unquestioned. Both stringed and keyboard instruments were much improved during the sixteenth century, and indeed

Vincenzo Galilei considered lutes of English workmanship better than any others. Few would yet dispute Byrd's insistence that 'there is not any music of instruments whatsoever comparable to that which is made of the voices of men'; but in saying so his own voice is raised a little, as if, for the first time, someone might be prepared to contradict. And indeed Richard Mulcaster, whose views on many things were far ahead of his time, clearly regarded learning to play an instrument as not less important than singing in the education of the young.

John Dowland's *First Book of Songs or Ayres*, published in 1597 began the series of books of lute-songs. Long before this such songs as Wyatt's *My lute awake* had indicated the existence of the ayre, or something very like it, and no one is required to believe that before Dowland's time the only singing was in the unaccompanied polyphonic style. In the *Arcadia* Sidney names the lute more often than any other instrument for the accompaniment of the songs, and Thomas Whythorne had sung songs to the lute in the 1550s: his *Songs*, published in 1571, include compositions which foreshadow the later ayre, and which are no longer, as in the eighteenth century, considered barbarous. However these precursors no more set the fashion for writing ayres than the sonnets of Wyatt and Surrey established the fashion for sonneteering. That dated from the posthumous publication of Sidney's *Astrophel and Stella*; and Dowland's book set the ayre on its brief but brilliant course only nine years after *Musica Transalpina* had proclaimed the fashion for singing madrigals. Within a very few years the ayre surpassed the madrigal in popularity.

John Dowland was a virtuoso with an international reputation when his book came out. Born in 1563 he was in the service of successive English Ambassadors in Paris from 1580 to 1584, and at that time was converted to Roman Catholicism. On his return to England he must very soon have enjoyed the patronage of Robert Sidney, who stood godfather to his son Robert Dowland about 1587. A few years later Dowland sought a position in the Queen's service, which he was refused : he obtained leave from Essex and Sir Robert Cecil to travel abroad again, and during 1594 and 1595 he went about the Continent, winning golden opinions for his playing all over Germany and Italy, where his fame seems to have preceded him. In Italy he wished especially to study under Marenzio, one of whose letters to him he proudly printed in his first book (which thus presupposes English appreciation of Marenzio) ; in Ferrara he may have met, and must certainly have heard the music of, Gesualdo ; in Venice he had, he says, 'familiar conference' with Giovanni Croce ; in Florence he 'played before the Duke and got great favours'. Everywhere he was welcome for the brilliance of his playing, and though we may believe that he played some of his own compositions — the most popular of all his songs, *Lachrimae*, had been composed at least as early as 1594 — he had as yet published nothing. Even after the appearance of his first book Barnfield praised him not as a composer but as a virtuoso,

> whose heavenly touch
> Upon the lute doth ravish human sense.

Dowland returned to England disillusioned with the treacherous plotting of the Jesuits, and restored to his Anglican faith. He prepared to publish some of his songs, and dedicated the *First Book* to Sir George Carey : so he still addresses him, though Carey had succeeded his father as Lord Hunsdon in the previous year. (Lady Hunsdon was Elizabeth Spencer, the poet's kinswoman, to whom he addressed one of the dedicatory sonnets of *The Faerie Queene*, and whose beauty he celebrated in the person of Phyllis the faire in *Colin Clouts Come Home Againe*.[1]) In 1597 also Morley dedicated his *Canzonets* to Carey, fifteen

[1] There Spenser named the three sisters, Lady Carey, Anne Lady Compton and Monteagle, and Alice Lady Strange, Phyllis, Charillis, and sweet Amaryllis. In 1598, in a poem which Dowland contributed to Giles Farnaby's *Canzonets*, he named Phyllis and Amaryllis : was he thinking of the Spencer sisters ? All these were patrons of musicians, as befitted granddaughters of Sir Thomas Kytson.

of them set to the lute 'for one to sing and play alone when your Lordship would retire yourself and be more private: howbeit I wot well your Lordship is never disfurnished of great choice of good voices, such indeed as are able to grace any man's songs'. In 1598, still apparently unable to obtain a post in England, Dowland entered the service of King Christian IV of Denmark, at a salary equivalent to that of high officers of state. In spite of this he was always in financial trouble, and his improvidence at last led to his dismissal in February 1606. He returned to England where for a time he was lutenist to Lord Walden, and eventually from 1612 to his death in 1626 in the King's service. He is said to have been a cheerful person, 'passing his days in lawful merriment', which is what we might deduce from his songs: feckless and unpractical, but with an engaging charm, which, together with his brilliant playing, made him welcome wherever he went.

During the years when he was in the service of the King of Denmark Dowland published two more books of songs, with dedications to the Countess of Bedford and to Sir John Zouche. In the latter he says, 'My first two books of ayres speed so well that they have produced a third', and though no second edition of the book printed in 1600 is known the *First Book* was reprinted at least four times. In 1604 Dowland published his only collection of instrumental music 'set forth for the Lute, Viols, or Violons, in five parts'; and in 1612 he published his last book of songs entitled *A Pilgrim's Solace*. In this he claims that compositions of his had been published in 'eight most famous cities beyond the seas', in France, Germany, and the Netherlands; but by now he had to complain of the comparative neglect of his talents in England — a different story from that he had to tell in 1603 — and in the same year Henry Peacham confirmed this opinion.

So since (old friend) thy years have made thee white,
And thou for others hast consumed thy spring,
How few regard thee, whom thou didst delight,

And far and near came once to hear thee sing
Ingrateful times and worthless age of ours
That lets us pine, when it hath cropped our flowers

But it was in this year that at last he achieved his old ambition of entering the royal service, where he remained for the rest of his days.

As a writer of songs Dowland had no equal, and his fastidious choice of poems was matched by the sensibility of his settings. For these solo songs the literary excellence, which was often obscured, at least to the listener, in the madrigal, was essential. English madrigals were designed to give pleasure to the performers ; the ayres were intended for the listener as much as for the performer. To Dowland's contemporaries, who came from far and near to hear him play and sing, the virtuoso was especially delightful, but his fame endures as the first among the select company of song-writers which includes Schubert, Schumann, Brahms, and Wolf.

As with the madrigal so with the ayre : once the way had been shown English composers were quick to enter it. Michael Cavendish was the first to follow Dowland, in 1598 ; in 1600 Dowland published his *Second Book of Ayres*, and in the same year Thomas Morley published his *First Book of Ayres, or little short Songs*, which contains the enchanting *It was a lover and his lass* — the only setting of a song by Shakespeare to be published while he lived — and a setting of the eleventh song of *Astrophel and Stella.* In 1600 also Robert Jones published the first of his five books of ayres, with a dedication to Sir Robert Sidney ; ten years later he dedicated the last of a delightful series to Sidney's daughter Mary, Lady Wroth, who as a child had shown marked aptitude for playing the virginals, and whose full-length portrait, with her arch-lute resting against her arm, still hangs at Penshurst.

Another book of ayres Jones dedicated to the Prince of Wales in 1608 with a distinction of style which invites quotation. 'Almost all our knowledge is drawn through the senses :

they are the soul's intelligencers whereby she passeth into the world and the world into her, and amongst all of them, there is none so learned as the ear, none hath obtained so excellent an art, so delicate, so abstruse, so spiritual, that it catcheth up wild sounds in the air and brings them under a government not to be expressed but done, and done by no skill but its own. There is music in all things, but every man cannot find it out, because of his own jarring ; he must have a harmony in himself that should go about it, and then he is in a good way, as he that hath a good ear is in a good forwardness to our faculty.' He was at his best in setting light or humorous songs : Peter Warlock called him the Sullivan of his day.

Not all the books of ayres that were published during the twenty years while they were in fashion came out under such distinguished patronage as Robert Jones dared to invite. John Daniel, whose father had been a musician, in 1606 dedicated his *Songs for the Lute, Viol, and Voice*, which contained settings of some of his brother's poems, to Mistress Anne Grene the worthy daughter of Sir William Grene of Milton, that is, of Milton Clevedon in Daniel's native county of Somerset. In the verses in which he addresses her, John Daniel apologizes for publishing songs which had really belonged only to the two of them 'or but few besides' until now ; and he asks

> why had it not been enow
> That Milton only heard our melody ?

But this book of songs, composed for the private pleasure of a Somerset squire's family, does indeed contain several of the finest compositions of the age, and Thomas Tomkins, in coupling his name with Dowland's, may have intended to place Daniel as a writer of serious songs second only to him. How many more songs of such quality were left in manuscript, to be thrown away when the copy became tattered with much use ?

Daniel's songs, like so many in these books of ayres, had a literary quality to match the music ; but of them all those which today are best known as lyrics apart from the music, are Thomas Campion's. This is something of a paradox, since Campion is the only one of these song-writers who constantly wrote both words and music himself, so that we should expect the two elements to be more perfectly integrated than in those songs where poet and musician were different. Sometimes the composer would make his own choice of lyrics; at others he would be asked by a patron to set a favourite song, 'apparelling ditties for gentlemen', as Robert Jones called it. Campion knew John Dowland at least as early as 1595 when he addressed a Latin epigram to him in compliment of his playing; two years later he contributed another Latin epigram to Dowland's *First Book*. In 1601 he emulated Dowland, and, in collaboration with Philip Rosseter, published *A Book of Ayres*. To this he wrote a preface in the extremely terse, abrupt style which characterizes all his prose. 'What epigrams are in Poetry, the same are Ayres in Music, then in their chief perfection when they are short and well seasoned.' So he begins, this physician whose only previous publication had been a book of Latin verses, but who, in the remaining twenty years of his life, was to write a series of lyrics of a matchless, cool elegance to his own settings, as well as masques and prose treatises. He concludes this first preface with a passage which may derive from Vincenzo Galilei's *Dialogo*, 1581, but which so vigorously expresses Campion's own opinions and practice that it must be quoted. 'There are some who, to appear the more deep and singular in their judgment, will admit no music but that which is long, intricate, bated with fugue, chained with syncopation, and where the nature of every word is precisely expressed in the note; like the old exploded [1] action in comedies when, if they did pronounce *Memini*, they would point to the hinder part of their heads, if *Video*, put their finger in their eye. But such childish observing of words is altogether ridiculous, and we ought to

[1] *I.e.* the opposite of applauded, hissed off the stage.

maintain as well in notes as in action a manly carriage, gracing no word but that which is eminent and emphatical.' Amateur Campion might be, but he had thought as seriously about the technical problems involved in setting his songs as in writing his words : before long he was to express his opinions on both matters in two treatises, the one against the use of rhyme in English, which provoked Samuel Daniel's effective reply, the other on Counterpoint, which was several times reprinted by Playford so late as the time of Charles II.

About 1613 Campion published *Two Books of Ayres*, again with a brief but illuminating preface. 'These Ayres', he says, 'were for the most part framed at first for one voice with the lute or viol, but upon occasion they have since been filled with more parts, which who so please may use, who like not may leave.' (This brusque manner of his prose must have been alarming at the bedside of his patients.) 'Yet do we daily observe', he goes on, 'that when any shall sing a treble to an instrument, the standers by will be offering at an inward part out of their own nature ; and, true or false, out it must, though to the perverting of the whole harmony.' Thomas Ford, more accommodating than Campion, composed songs which might be sung by four voices without accompaniment, or by one voice to the lute with such others as might be there 'offering at an inward part'. The habits induced by taking part in a madrigal died hard, it seems, and the company in a gentleman's house might irritatingly insist on joining in a song, instead of being content to listen. To these people music was an active pleasure, not a passive ; something to share in oneself, not to be entertained with by others.

If we look back over the history of music during the past five centuries we can see why it was that the ayre came to its sudden perfection at this time. The old dominance of unaccompanied voices would eventually give place to the dominance of the modern orchestra, of instrumental music ; parallel with this great change was another, from polyphony to homophony ; and though the two did not progress at the same speed, as it were, yet during the lifetime of Dowland and Campion the two revolutions reached their crises. In these great changes of taste (for that is what they were) English composers played the leading part, and in the creation of the ayre, or art-song, and in the composition of instrumental music, especially for the virginals, they did not learn from but taught the rest of Europe.

From the polyphonic singing of madrigals to the ayre sung by one voice to the accompaniment of the lute and thence to instrumental music without voice was the progress or decline of music in the life of this one generation. *Musica Transalpina* was published in 1588, Dowland's *First Book of Ayres* in 1597, and in 1613 or thereabouts came *Parthenia, or the Maidenhead of the first Music for the Virginals* by Byrd, Bull, and Gibbons. The lateness of this first book of keyboard music is in part due to the technical difficulty of printing it : certainly much music for the virginals had been in circulation long before, and several manuscript collections still survive. Of these the most famous are the *Fitzwilliam Virginal Book* and *My Lady Nevill's Book*. Lady Nevill was most probably the Rachel Lennard who married Sir Edward Nevill, afterwards Lord Bergavenny : the forty-two pieces in her book, all by Byrd, were transcribed in 1591. Thus, as with all other forms of music, sacred or secular, motet, madrigal, ayre, in the composition of keyboard music Byrd was to the fore ; his versatility was unrivalled, he was as quick to accept the latest forms as were the younger men, and he could surpass most of them. No wonder that John Baldwin was moved, in the midst of his task of transcribing Lady Nevill's book, to the marginal exclamation : 'Mr W. Byrd, homo memorabilis'.

Far more virginal music by English composers than by those of any other country survives, doubtless because far more was written. Much has certainly been lost : *The Earl of Leicester's Virginal Book*, which is likely to have been a distinguished collection, vanished less than a century ago ; John Bull, a virtuoso of the keyboard with an international reputation comparable to John Dowland's, published nothing apart from his contributions to *Parthenia*, but almost one hundred and fifty compositions by him for the virginals survive in manuscript ; Giles Farnaby published none of his instrumental music, but there are more than fifty pieces of his in the Fitzwilliam Book, which entitle him (in modern judgment) to rank second only to Byrd as a composer for the virginals. Few other manuscripts contain work by Farnaby, which may suggest that in his own day he was not so well known as Bull and others whose work is found in many manuscripts ; or it may be that, since he alone was not an organist, he had fewer facilities for having his music copied ; but the absence of his work from surviving collections may be as fortuitous as their survival.

As the lute was the favourite instrument with men so was the virginals with women, though the name of the instrument may have less to do with *virgo* than with *virgula*. Spenser, imagining his love 'whersoever she be' thinks of her in bed, at board, or else at her virginals ; Shakespeare turns the Dark Lady's playing on the virginals to an elaborate punning compliment to her, in envy of the saucy Jacks

> O'er whom thy fingers walk with gentle gait,
> Making dead wood more blest than living lips.

Queen Elizabeth and Queen Mary were both skilled players, but so was their father Henry VIII. Already by 1526 he was employing John Heywood as a virginals player, and probably Heywood taught the Princesses, as he also taught Thomas Whythorne. (The earliest reference to virginals in England is in an inscription of 1518 on the wall of a house in Yorkshire ; in January 1525 the first Earl of Rutland paid the balance due for a pair of virginals to Lord Mountjoy, the friend and patron of Erasmus.) We hear of many families possessing virginals and also employing players, probably for special occasions, or to teach their children. Sir William Petre paid such a player in addition to supplementing his house-keeper's wages for this same purpose. Francis Willoughby, the builder of Wollaton Hall, learnt to play the virginals from the same master, Mr Horseley,[1] who taught his sister Margaret : there was never any suggestion that it was effeminate for a man to play the virginals, or improperly masculine in a woman to play the lute. Constable complimented Lady Rich on her lute-playing, and in *The Taming of the Shrew* Bianca's lessons from Petruchio's man Litio, born in Mantua, are on the lute : the occasion was not intended to detract from Bianca's femininity.

The English composers of music for the virginals were almost all, except Giles Farnaby, organists, but they differentiated better than the Italians between the resources of the two instruments. Although this Italian music must have been known in England as were Italian madrigals, the English musicians again made something new and original out of it, especially, as they did in the ayre, by drawing on a native tradition of folk-music. For the virginals they wrote variations on traditional dance tunes, though the elaborate Pavans and Galliards which make the finest of this music were far removed from the original dances. They also wrote some charming and delicate 'programme music' such as Peerson's *Fall of the Leaf* and Byrd's *The Bells*.

Other instrumental music of the time is less distinguished. Compositions for the solo lute, again usually dance music, remain mostly unpublished, but are said to lack the fine quality of the lute accompaniments to the ayre. Chamber music — the term was first used by Martin Peerson in 1630 in the title of a book of settings of Fulke Greville's poems — written for groups of instruments had been known since Henry VIII's time, and was classified as a 'whole consort' where all the instruments were of one family (strings), or 'broken consort'

[1] Mr Horseley also taught Francis Willoughby arithmetic.

where instruments of different families (strings and wind) were used. Such consorts were almost always composed of professional players who would be hired, as now, to provide the music for a dance or a wedding or a garden party or other entertainment (pl. 15). Some families maintained players in their households. Thus Philip Rosseter, in dedicating his *Lessons for Consort*, 1609, to Sir William Gascoyne of Sidbury, asks, 'To whom may I better recommend these my labours than to you, who maintain in your house such as can lively express them', that is to say, among Sir William's servants were those who could play treble lute, treble viol, bass viol, bandora, cithern, and flute, the instruments for which Rosseter was writing. No doubt, like Mary Percy at Ingatestone and Symons at Haddon, these six servants had other duties to perform: they would not be a privately supported professional sestet. In the library at Hengrave Hall in 1602 were compositions of every kind, including works for instrumental consort; but the Kytsons were probably exceptional, even in that musical age. Yet Lorenzo can assume that Portia has 'music of the house' which can be called upon at once to welcome her home.

The Queen and her courtiers would play lute and virginals and they would sing madrigals and ayres, but they would not be likely to take part in an instrumental ensemble. Morley's patron, who paid for the publication of his *First Book of Consort Lessons . . . for six instruments* in 1599 in order to have the parts 'for his private pleasure and for divers of his friends which delight in music' must have been, like the Kytsons, unusually enthusiastic. Morley dedicated his book to the Lord Mayor and Aldermen of the City of London, and recommended the compositions it contained to the skilful handling of the waits. But the Queen's courtiers would not wish to spend time in the rehearsal which would be necessary — the Kytsons, being papists, would have more time on their hands — and they would certainly not demean themselves by playing a wind instrument. Such things were not for gentlemen, because they distorted the face: had not the young Alcibiades, according to Plutarch, refused to learn to play the flute (the least disfiguring of all) for this very reason? 'To play on the viol with a stick, doth not alter man's favour, nor disgraceth any gentleman: but otherwise, to play on the flute, his countenance altereth and changeth so oft, that his familiar friends can scant know him. Moreover, the harp or viol doth not let him that playeth on them from speaking or singing as he playeth: where he that playeth on the flute, holdeth his mouth so hard to it, that it taketh not only his words from him, but his voice.' So Hamlet taunts Guildenstern with a recorder which the players have brought in, and invites him to play it. Guildenstern's ignorance, unlike Philomathes' ignorance of singing, was proper to a courtier: Hamlet is showing him up as one who always insists on the right breed of courtesy but who has nothing else to him. No one in *Hamlet*'s audience would have expected Guildenstern to play the recorder.

Music for the theatre was provided, as here, or in the final scene of *The Merchant of Venice*, by the players, or by musicians whom they employed; and there was much more of it than the accompaniment of an occasional song. In 1562 there was a dumb-show before the first act of *Gorboduc*, and 'first the music of violins began to play'. Perhaps Lord Buckhurst, who wrote the last two acts of the play, had some influence here; in that same year he brought over William Daman, the composer, from the Low Countries, and all his life he was a patron of musicians. Forty years later a German visitor to the Blackfriars noted in his diary, 'For a whole hour preceding the play one listens to a delightful musical entertainment on organs, lutes, pandoras, mandoras, viols and pipes, as on the present occasion' — he regarded it as the normal practice in London: Orsino would have made his first entry in *Twelfth Night* during the last bars of such an overture. Another foreign visitor, Hentzner, noted that a postlude of excellent music, lasting about half an hour, followed a play that he saw in 1598. There were also musical interludes between acts, as may be seen in many of the plays, where the actor who enters at the beginning of a new act will say, 'Fiddler, forbear', or 'Save thee, friend, and thy music', or something of the sort. The absence of English comment on the practice is due to our taking it for granted: the foreigners, who did not expect music in the theatre, noted it in their diaries.

Shakespeare's own interest in music and knowledge of musical terms has often been commented on as part of the myriad-minded man's extraordinary and universal expertise. His own musical education was, as we should expect, in the older polyphonic tradition, and his personal tastes may well have been conservative also in music. These are not discoverable, but the remarkable fact is not that one Elizabethan dramatist should have such knowledge, but that he could assume it in his audience — an audience that consisted mostly of London shopkeepers and working men and apprentices. This is in striking contrast with his knowledge, or theirs, of painting: Shakespeare mentions but one painter in his plays, Giulio Romano, and he thought he was a sculptor. The contrast is typical of the age: Englishmen generally had little appreciation of painting or sculpture, had destroyed quite recently much of the best mediaeval sculpture and had smeared whitewash over mediaeval wall-paintings in their churches; and they had no picture galleries to visit. Westminster Abbey and other churches contained fine collections of sepulchral monuments, but the Elizabethans were more inclined to regard these as warnings of mortality or records of worldly success than as works of art. But there were excellent opportunities of hearing music, and the audience who sat through an hour's overture before the play started must have wished to do so: if they had been as indifferent to music as to painting there would have been no music as there was no scenery.

From 1571 there had been regular public concerts on the

turret of Gresham's newly opened Royal Exchange every Sunday and holiday from Lady Day to Michaelmas. The London waits played there from seven to eight in the evening until Whitsuntide, and from eight to nine for the rest of the summer. These concerts, which continued till 1642, were free and no doubt well attended ; and the London waits were in Thomas Morley's opinion 'excellent and expert musicians' for whom he was proud to write music. From the beginning of the Queen's reign they were constantly acquiring new instruments, but they probably did not use the virginals, and not until 1613 was a singer and lutenist of their number. They could be hired for private occasions such as weddings, and proof of their ability may be seen in Sir Francis Drake's taking five Norwich waits with him on his Portuguese voyage of 1589, and in Sir Nicholas Bacon's employment of them at Gorhambury in 1587, when the Queen was there on progress.

Many other towns besides London had their waits, but perhaps only in Norwich, then the second city of the realm, were they required to give public concerts. As early as 3rd May 1553 it was decided that 'the waits of the city shall have liberty and licence, every Sunday at night and other holidays at night betwixt this and Michaelmas next coming, to come to the Guildhall, and upon the nether leads of the same hall next the council house shall betwixt the hours of seven and eight of the clock at night blow and play upon their instruments the space of half an hour, to the rejoicing and comfort of the hearers thereof'. These concerts seem to have continued annually, for orders forbidding them were issued in 1626 and again in 1629. By more than a century the concerts in Norwich and London preceded those which John Banister organized in the 1670s ; and even those were some twenty or thirty years earlier than the first public concerts on the Continent. By such means were the men and women who crowded to the theatres educated in the appreciation of good modern music ; and the composers who wrote for them made use of the traditional melodies of song and dance with which they were familiar. For as Byrd says, 'a song that is well and artificially made cannot be well perceived nor understood at the first hearing, but the oftener you shall hear it, the better cause of liking you will discover: and commonly that song is best esteemed with which our ears are most acquainted'; what is true of song is true also of instrumental music.

Everyone can enjoy a good song or a good dance-tune, and in the time of Elizabeth, when only a minority could read, some sort of appreciation of music was far more widespread than an appreciation of poetry, or even of the drama. There was music everywhere. The shyest or most unmusical, finding himself in a crowd at Paul's Cross, would join heartily in singing Psalms. In taverns and alehouses, with diffidence laughed away or otherwise liquidated, anyone would join in singing a song, which might be, 'Farewell, dear heart, since I must needs be gone', which Sir Toby sings at Malvolio, or 'a catch that will draw three souls out of one weaver'. Did not his master's singing of catches cause concern to that conscientious servant Humphrey Waspe? 'I dare not let him walk alone for fear of learning of vile tunes which he will sing at supper and in the sermon-times! if he meet but a carman in the street and I find him not talk to keep him off on him, he will whistle him and all his tunes over at night in his sleep.' This was the other end of the scale of musical appreciation from Sir Christopher Hatton's or the Kytsons', but yet Sir Toby's song was from a book of Robert Jones, and Orlando Gibbons and Thomas Weelkes set as rounds the traditional street cries of London.

The most famous of all rounds, *Three Blind Mice*, was first printed by Thomas Ravenscroft in 1609. It would be absurd to suggest that everyone who has sung it these three hundred and fifty years has appreciated that it is in canon, since there is always a number of persons ignorant of this most ingenious and difficult species of composition; but it is very characteristic of that age so to combine the intellectual and the popular, as they did in the theatre. Morley's dictum, 'In music both the ear is to be pleased and art shewed', applies with equal force to a madrigal by Wilbye or to *Three Blind Mice*, to a setting by Weelkes of the cry of a London hawker or of the Anglican service.

The twentieth-century historian is disposed to find two different, and irreconcilable, views of music in the sixteenth century, the intellectual view of music as representing more faithfully than any other art the divine harmony, and the sensual view of music as a form of pleasure. This dichotomy was unknown to Morley ; or to Campion, for whom 'the world is made by symmetry and proportion, and is in that respect compared to music', but whose ayres 'have both their art and pleasure' ; or to Gibbons, for whom 'it is proportion that beautifies every thing, the whole universe consists of it, and Music is measured by it', but whose songs 'were taught to sing only to delight' his patron ; or to John Case, who said of music, 'time cannot say that he was before her, or nature that she wrought without her', yet acknowledged that her chief end was to delight. The pleasure which music offered would vary as the auditor was skilful or unskilful, learned or ignorant, but in no other way. The unskilful would stop short at singing a round or a psalm or strumming on the cithern that he would find hanging up (in default of newspapers or transistor radios) in the barber's shop. The skilful would take his part in a madrigal or sing an ayre to the lute or play on the virginals ; and he might also speculate with much learning on the divine harmony or the music of the spheres, as Plato and Aristotle and Kepler speculated. By a paradox of the kind which always pleased them, music was at once the most intellectual and the most sensual of the arts, and could provide both forms of pleasure, which they always looked for, at their most integrated and most intense. It was like love, but it was also like the love of God ; the art most closely allied to the arithmetical basis of a reasonable Creation, yet the only one which unreasoning animals, especially the birds, could invent or enjoy. Pythagorean and clown could here meet on common ground in their enjoyment of music; both would have known enough (for both were there, in the audience) to listen, rapt, to Lorenzo's magical phrasing, yet not so rapt as to lack a detached understanding of his argument.

> Here will we sit, and let the sounds of music
> Creep in our ears—soft stillness and the night
> Become the touches of sweet harmony:
> Sit Jessica, look how the floor of heaven
> Is thick inlaid with patens of bright gold,
> There's not the smallest orb which thou beholdest
> But in his motion like an angel sings,
> Still quiring to the young-eyed cherubins;
> Such harmony is in immortal souls,
> But whilst this muddy vesture of decay
> Doth grossly close it in, we cannot hear it.

VI

LITERATURE

VI. LITERATURE

THE ELIZABETHAN APPRECIATION OF CHAUCER

If we wish to understand the taste of a past generation of men, we may learn most from observing their pleasure in the poetry or music that was written for them, in looking at the houses which they built, the pictures they commissioned, and the monuments they erected. But we may add to our understanding by examining their response to the poetry or music or architecture of an earlier age, and by comparing this with our own response to the same things. Elizabethan criticism of Chaucer is especially illuminating, for, in a sense, they were even more remote from him than we are, since scholarship had not then provided a reliable text or canon of his works, and had not recovered knowledge of his language and metre. They supposed that the reigns of Edward III and Richard II were a misty and barbarous age, and they were perpetually astonished that Chaucer could write great poetry in such a Court; yet they acknowledged that he did so, and seldom fell into the presumptuous error of saying that he wrote very well considering the difficulties he endured. They knew that a great poet is a great poet whether he writes for a heroic age or for Periclean Athens, for Viking farmers or for Elizabethan gentlemen.

Now it so happens that the Elizabethans appreciated Chaucer as no one in England had appreciated him for a hundred years before them, and as scarcely anyone was to do again for another century, until Dryden established the foundations of his modern fame. Their predecessors had been so occupied with the religious controversies of the time that they had seen in Chaucer not the poet but the Reformer, and had importunately enlisted him against the Church of Rome. To Foxe he seemed to be a right Wycliffian, and therefore a sure guide to the true knowledge of religion. They had more reason for this than we should allow, because they believed Chaucer had written several anti-Popish poems which he had not written. Foxe's view of him certainly persisted among the Elizabethans, to whom the *Book of Martyrs* was second only to the Bible in popular authority ; but it is with their appreciation of him as a poet, not with their estimation of him as a teacher that I am here concerned. The seventeenth century did not discover in Chaucer a premature Puritan — that was beyond even their controversial assertiveness ; but they ignored him as obsolete and too difficult to read in the original, and found him acceptable only in a Latin translation or in a modernized version. Indeed they regarded the obsolete language of Chaucer as a warning : they must seek a supposed perfection in their own use of English, to prevent a similar obsolescence. The fate of so great a poet who

> his sense can only boast,
> The glory of his numbers lost,

drove Waller to seek in English the envied stability of Latin ; and the Augustan movement derived, at least in part, from the cautionary tale of Chaucer's fall. Chaucer's repute was then at its lowest, and even the few who mention him with respect seem to do so out of deference to tradition rather than from any first-hand knowledge of his works. His poetry was as obscure as *Beowulf* is to the majority of readers today : a monument whose greatness they preferred to take on trust rather than to investigate.

Between the Reformers and the Ignorants[1] came the Elizabethan poets and critics who loved Chaucer and sought to

[1] Our good old Chaucer some despise : and why ?
Because say they he writeth barbarously.
Blame him not (Ignorants) but your selves, that do
Not at these years your native language know.
SIR ASTON COKAYNE : *A Chain of Golden Poems*, 1658.

understand him more thoroughly: among them the chief of all his admirers, Spenser. But before Spenser another poet, George Gascoigne, had shown something of a poet's insight into Chaucer's technique, and had realized that the roughness of his metre was only apparent.

'Whosoever do peruse and well consider his works, he shall find that although his lines are not always of one self-same number of syllables, yet, being read by one that hath understanding, the longest verse and that which hath most syllables in it, will fall (to the ear) correspondent unto that which hath fewest syllables in it: and likewise that which hath in it fewest syllables shall be found yet to consist of words that have such natural sound, as may seem equal in length to a verse which hath many more syllables of lighter accents.'

With the same humility Chaucer's Elizabethan editor said that those who could not scan Chaucer failed either because the text was faulty (as it very often was) or because they did not use their intelligence. Spenser himself at first seems not to have understood Chaucer's metre, and to have copied what he thought were its irregularities, as in *The Shepheardes Calender*, *Mother Hubberds Tale*, and elsewhere. But later reminiscences of Chaucer suggest that he had discovered the secret of his scansion, or else had assumed a regularity hidden by the garbled text before him. So, when he writes

> There many Minstrales maken melody,

he must surely have had in his head not the words alone but also the rhythm of

> And smale fowles maken melodye.

Spenser could not have read Chaucer's line with 'small' and 'fowls' as monosyllables, though whether he understood that the final e's were to be pronounced I do not know. Yet some at least of Chaucer's readers, in spite of ignorance of his language and inadequacy of texts, were willing to recognize in him a fine craftsman whose verses must have been regular and melodious, and were prepared to account for apparent harshnesses by some defect in their own understanding rather than in his skill.

They praised Chaucer also for keeping decorum, the final, objective test (to an Elizabethan) of a poem's excellence. By this Chaucer was defended against the charges of obscenity and flat scurrility. So Sir John Harington, in defending Ariosto against similar charges, refers to Chaucer and observes that in *The Miller's Tale* and *The Wife of Bath's Tale* 'only the decorum he keeps, is that that excuseth it, and maketh it more tolerable'. Francis Beaumont, in his letter to Thomas Speght, makes the same point: 'How much had he swerved from decorum, if he had made his Miller, his Cook, and his Carpenter, to have told such honest and good tales, as he made his Knight, his Squire, his Lawyer, and Scholar tell'. They had a sane comprehension of these matters, notably lacking today, for they saw that it is the context of an expression, not the expression itself, that makes for obscenity. Decorum meant, among other things, fitting a speech to the character of the speaker, as Chaucer always does with such lively insight: the Miller and the Wife of Bath were acceptable, and not obscene, because they spoke in character, whereas their words in the mouth of the Knight or the Prioress would have been intolerable. This is the fact which Watch Committees and Magistrates forget, though every schoolboy knows that almost any remark, however innocuous, can be made obscene by setting it in the context of a *tête-à-tête* between an actress and a bishop.

Chaucer kept decorum, and he did so because his observation of human character was so accurate. 'He must have been a man of a most wonderful comprehensive nature', said Dryden, 'because . . . he has taken into the compass of his *Canterbury Tales*, the various manners and humours of the whole English nation, in his age.' But though there is no doubt that the Elizabethans enjoyed this gift of Chaucer, to them his greatest work was always *Troilus and Criseyde*. There are many reasons for this preference. They relished it, as they relished *Hero and Leander* or *Venus and Adonis* or *Romeo and Juliet*, because it was a love-story, and for its sensuous description. They found the supposedly classical theme very much to their taste : it is a story they never tired of re-telling themselves. They preferred rhyme royal — 'Troilus verse', as they sometimes called it — to the riding rhyme of the *Tales* : this stanza was, said Puttenham, 'very grave and stately' and in keeping with the greater dignity of the whole poem. Also, *Troilus and Criseyde* was complete, whereas *The Canterbury Tales* were a shapeless, untidy fragment. They disliked torsos or fragments, and preferred to have their works of art unified and whole : for this reason two poets, Chapman and Petowe, wrote continuations of Marlowe's *Hero and Leander*, and Sir William Alexander and Richard Beling supplemented the *Arcadia*. They recognized that *Troilus and Criseyde* was more derivative, less original than *The Canterbury Tales*, but were unperturbed by this discovery : indeed they must have thought it an advantage, for they knew that Chaucer's pre-eminence was due to his having learnt so much from the French and Italians. They did not suppose that great poetry could be insular and provincial : it must partake of the traditions of Europe that derived from classical antiquity. This was more obvious in *Troilus and Criseyde* than in *The Canterbury Tales* which are, at least on the surface, so very English. The poets of these last hundred and fifty years have been much more English than European (except Byron, whose poetry we neglect), and our taste has become correspondingly restricted. No Italian poet could have written Wordsworth's or Tennyson's or Hardy's poetry ; but an Italian might well have written *Troilus and Criseyde* or *Venus and Adonis* or the *Arcadia*. Indeed, Italians had written these works ; and if Chaucer's debt to Boccaccio is greater than Shakespeare's to Ovid, or Sidney's to Sannazaro, that is neither here nor there. They were all indebted in the same way, if not for the same amount, to the European tradition, whereas Wordsworth, Tennyson, and Hardy were not indebted at all, and would have written as they did if they had never read a word of any other literature than English.

I do not wish to imply that these nineteenth-century writers were inferior to their predecessors, but only to explain how it is that where we habitually think of *The Canterbury Tales* as Chaucer's greatest work, the Elizabethans still more confidently preferred *Troilus and Criseyde*. For the difference in taste is not absurd, but comprehensible; and might have been deduced if there had not been ample evidence in proof. The Elizabethans sought to establish English poetry among the chief literatures of Europe, and they achieved this so well that by the time of the Romantics it was no longer in question. The nineteenth-century poets could rely on the English tradition alone, as the Elizabethan poets could not, though whether this was to their advantage I take leave to doubt.

Professor Lewis has informed us that Chaucer took from Boccaccio 'only what is still medieval, or what can be medievalized', and that 'the effect of all his alterations is to turn a Renaissance story into a medieval story'. As a statement of Chaucer's intention this may well be true, but it by no means accounts for the popularity of the poem with Elizabethan readers. They enjoyed it, or thought they enjoyed it, in spite of its mediaevalism; because they could still detect, behind the older fashion of Chaucer's apparelling, the new Renaissance spirit of Boccaccio. Very probably they enjoyed *Troilus and Criseyde* more imperfectly than we do, and made the same sort of mistakes in judging it that we make in judging *Venus and Adonis* or the *Arcadia*. To Sidney Pandarus is quintessential pimp, and little more. In Shakespeare's version of the story the characters are degraded, and the pathos is gone. Not many Elizabethan readers can have appreciated the depth of piety in the conclusion of Chaucer's poem: they expected some such palinode to end a love-poem, and were not disposed to treat it very seriously. Spenser would have understood, but then he had included in his sonnet sequence, the *Amoretti*, a sonnet on Easter.

Spenser indeed had an intimate, intuitive understanding of Chaucer which is unique. From first to last he paid homage to him with a generosity that has never been surpassed. He felt, as he said, that Chaucer's spirit survived in him, and was thereby encouraged to write an ending to *The Squire's Tale* in his *Faerie Queene*. Above all else he recognized in Chaucer the most accomplished master of English style who had yet lived, and rightly went to him as to the 'well of English undefyled' instead of to classical precedent. But I do not wish to write of Chaucer's influence on Spenser: the theme is too well-thumbed already. I mean only to suggest that though Spenser appreciated Chaucer better than anyone else of his time, he appreciated him in the same way, and for the same qualities. He considered him a learned poet — learned, that is, in the craft of poetry — and for that reason the best of English poets, from whom he could learn more than from any other writer of any age or nation. Such understanding was very remarkable when knowledge of Chaucer's language and pronunciation and metre was so imperfect, and when the texts of Pynson or Thynne were all that Spenser had to read. It is remarkable too in a time when most men were looking for inspiration either to Virgil, Ovid, and Lucan or else to the new Italian and French writers, that the greatest poet of the English Renaissance should have included in his studies what was mere English, and should have turned back towards the despised Middle Ages.

The Elizabethans, unlike later generations from Dryden to Professor Coghill, never modernized Chaucer. This may seem surprising when we remember their many and noble translations from Greek and Latin, Italian, French, and Spanish. But though they understood Chaucer's language less well than they understood Latin or Italian they did not admit any need for translation. They admired Chaucer as an English writer, as the greatest we had had before Spenser, and they admired him not principally as a story-teller, not as the sympathetic portrayer of the human comedy, but as the poet who had used this language whose resources they were once again exploring more skilfully and more copiously than any other. Modernization would therefore have denied to Chaucer the very qualities in which they thought him supreme : they asked for no reproduction but for the original, to study there the master's technique at first hand. Their judgment of Chaucer was, for a brief time, purely aesthetic, uncontaminated by morality, and undefeated by ignorance. They wrote no critical studies of his work ; they recorded no formal appreciation of this or that poem. They did better. For out of their study of Chaucer they learnt to avoid a spurious classicism, and taught the Muses again to speak English.

SPENSER: *THE SHEPHEARDES CALENDER*

THE New Poetry of the Elizabethans began with the publication, late in 1579, of *The Shepheardes Calender*. Anonymous, and accompanied by a preface and commentary signed only with the initials E. K., the book was dedicated by the poet to Philip Sidney 'most worthy of all titles both of learning and chivalry', and by the commentator to Gabriel Harvey. Spenser never claimed it for his own in any of the five editions published in his lifetime, though the author's name must have been known from the start to the group of friends about Philip Sidney, and was conjectured by many before *The Faerie Queene* made it famous. The endeavour of Sidney and his friends was to remedy the want of desert which they acknowledged in contemporary English poetry. *The Shepheardes Calender* was the first bold, public attempt to put their ideas into practice, a manifesto as well as a poem, which announced and illustrated a change of taste as certainly as did the publication of *Lyrical Ballads* in 1798, a change that was instantly recognized by those who were capable of it.

Not many of us nowadays would read *The Shepheardes Calender* if it were still anonymous. But Dryden admired it, and thought it not inferior to Theocritus or Virgil, and Spenser's contemporaries found it full of exciting promise that a great new poet had come to use the English language. It is all very well for us, knowing how nobly this promise was fulfilled, to detect, here and there in Spenser's pastorals, suggestions of the poet of *The Faerie Queene*; but how should we have responded in the 1580s?

Spenser showed characteristic foresight in allowing E. K. (whoever he was) to comment upon his poems, and so to guide, even haltingly, the understanding and appreciation of his readers. E. K. was no profound scholar, but he knew something of the classics, something of Italian and French and the older English poetry. He recognized Spenser's poetic ambition to rise above his contemporaries and to be the first English poet of the Renaissance. He understood (for Spenser no doubt had instructed him) that much was to be learnt from Chaucer, the one great English poet of the past, whose works were still read and admired. He understood, as everyone then understood, that even a revolutionary poet must work in a tradition, and that if English poetry was to take its place among the principal literatures of Europe it must do so by showing that the English language could sustain the same themes, and the same modes, as Greek and Latin and Italian.

Spenser's genius was one of the most daring and original that has ever existed. He learnt from everyone, but copied none. Sonnet, canzone, and heroic stanza he adapted with exquisite skill to meet his own needs. In language his experiments were too bold for such purists as Sidney and Daniel and Jonson, but served a mind more subtle and complex than theirs. In his Christian heroic poem he had the unique courage to deride Wrath and to assert Love as the dominant theme. He had the compulsive honesty of a distinguished mind, and the charity of a sensitive one. Loyal and generous, positive and forthright, he never shirked the expression of an unpopular opinion, or sought favour by lip-service : he was a man born

> To set down boldly, bravely to invent,
> In all high knowledge surely excellent.

Immediately before these lines on Spenser Michael Drayton had referred to the two best known poets of the 1560s and 1570s, Gascoigne and Churchyard, the poets with whose work the first readers of *The Shepheardes Calender* would inevitably make comparison. Drayton, writing more than forty years later, was looking back over the years of greatest achievement in English poetry, and could see that even Gascoigne, for all his fluency and intelligence, fell far short of Spenser, Marlowe, Shakespeare, and the rest. In his poem to Henry Reynolds he was thinking chiefly of *The Faerie Queene*, but he had already said that, in his opinion, Spenser 'had done enough for the immortality of his name had he only given us his *Shepheardes Calender*, a masterpiece if any'.

It is more remarkable to find E. K. in 1579, only eighteen months after Gascoigne's death, when the renaissance of English poetry was no more than the hope and purpose of a few young men, criticizing Gascoigne's work in these terms. 'Master George Gascoigne' (he says) 'a witty gentleman, and the very chief of our late rhymers, who and if some parts of learning wanted not (albe it is well known he altogether wanted not learning) no doubt would have attained to the excellency of those famous poets. For gifts of wit and natural promptness appear in him abundantly.' And William Webbe, in his *Discourse of English Poetry* of 1586, so much agreed with E. K.'s opinions that he preferred to quote them rather than to invent his own criticism of Gascoigne.

Four years before E. K. made his comment Gascoigne had shown his interest in the technique of English verse in *Certain Notes of Instruction* prefixed to his *Posies*. Gabriel Harvey, the Cambridge don who was a friend of Spenser and of E. K., bought a copy of this book on 1st September 1577 — it is now in the Bodleian Library — and as was his custom, made in it many marginal notes. He considered that Gascoigne's deficiencies were not so much intellectual as moral: 'Want of resolution and constancy marred his wit and undid himself'. And again, 'some vanity, and more levity, his special fault, and the continual causes of his misfortunes'. Perhaps Harvey's and E. K.'s opinions of Gascoigne may be reconciled by saying that both believed that he had not taken sufficient pains to develop a natural talent, for though poetry may be 'a divine gift and heavenly instinct not to be gotten by labour and learning' yet it must be 'adorned with both'. It is a fair judgment. This perception of Gascoigne's inadequacies was a good beginning for the new poet: for Gascoigne was recognized as 'the very chief of our late rhymers', and if the anonymous author of *The Shepheardes Calender* could be shown to be his superior, then he was well on the way to recognition.

E. K. certainly agreed with some of Gascoigne's precepts. He accepted the primacy of Invention, the discovery of new and striking ways of saying what had, very probably, often been thought, for, as his friend Harvey noted, 'Invention must guide and rule the Elocution: non contra'. Both E. K. and Gascoigne were at pains to describe the elements of good style but here they differed from each other. They derided the use of excessive alliteration, 'hunting the letter'; but E. K., justifying Spenser's use of dialect words and archaisms, was prepared to go much further than Gascoigne who advised the English poet to 'eschew strange words' in general, though he admitted that the theme might give just occasion, which was indeed the substance of E. K.'s defence. Sidney recognized the quality of *The Shepheardes Calender*, yet 'dared not allow . . . that same framing of his style to an old rustic language', because (he supposed) there was no pastoral precedent for it. But, as Dryden pointed out, by this means Spenser had admirably imitated the Doric of Theocritus.

Gascoigne did not approve the use of polysyllables, which Harvey rightly considered 'a great grace and majesty . . . so they be current English': Spenser was clearly of Harvey's opinion, and even disregarded the proviso. Gascoigne was prepared to admit the poetical licence frequently used by Spenser whereby a word might be scanned as of two syllables instead of one, or of one instead of two: *tane* for *taken*, *heaven* for *heavn* are two of his examples. On the whole, Harvey thought, Spenser used this licence with discretion.

They would have agreed with Milton that decorum was

the grand masterpiece to observe, and E. K. in his glosses draws the reader's attention to particular instances of Spenser's observation of it. In addressing the preface to Harvey he had remarked on Spenser's 'due observing of decorum everywhere, in personages, in seasons, in matter, in speech, and generally in all seemly simplicity of handling his matter and framing his words'. The New Poet must be shown to have regard for the standards of good taste then universally accepted. Shepherds must not only speak like shepherds, in rustic language, and retaining words long grown obsolete in politer company, but they must refer to Queen Elizabeth as Elisa, 'it being very unfit, that a shepherd's boy brought up in the sheepfold, should know, or ever seem to have heard of a Queen's royalty'; or they must be unable to recall Aaron's name which 'for more decorum, the shepherd saith he hath forgot, lest his remembrance and skill in antiquities of holy writ should seem to exceed the meanness of the person'. But if such skill was improbable in shepherds, skill in stars was 'convenient for shepherds to know, as Theocritus and the rest use'. (Oddly enough, Spenser himself was weak on astronomy, and made a mistake in the *November* eclogue over a zodiacal sign. Gabriel Harvey in a marginal note said that Spenser ought to be ashamed of his ignorance in such matters.) The pastoral world of Spenser's invention might, and did, refer to the actual contemporary world, but its integrity must be retained: the reader must, all the time, be able to enjoy the talk of shepherds for itself.

This is E. K.'s purpose in his preface and commentary: to show the reader how consistently Spenser has imagined the world of Colin and Hobbinol, of Cuddie and Thenot, and by glossing such words as he knew were strange, to make the speech of shepherds comprehensible. Sometimes he thinks it necessary to point out to sophisticated townsmen Spenser's felicitous observation of the countryside:

> The grieslie Todestoole growne there mought I see
> And loathed Paddocks lording on the same.

'Lording' (E. K. informs us) is 'spoken after the manner of paddocks and frogs sitting, which is indeed lordly, not removing nor looking once aside, unless they be stirred.' When E. K. is moved to praise Spenser's poetry, he does so almost always in rhetorical terms. Again, as in praising his observation of decorum, or his use of the pastoral, he is relating Spenser to the poets of the European tradition which had passed from Greece through the poets of Rome to the poets of modern Italy.

The importance of E. K. for us is in suggesting how a cultivated reader of the time might be reconciled to this New Poetry, in his justification of what was new by reference to accepted standards at the same time that he was insisting on its novelty. He must show that Spenser was better than Gascoigne or Churchyard or Turberville, and he could only do so by comparing him to Theocritus and Virgil, to Marot and Sannazaro and (not least) to Chaucer. Therefore Sidney, in rejecting Spenser's old rustic language, rejected it because he believed neither Theocritus nor Virgil nor Sannazaro provided precedents for it. What the Elizabethan reader wished to be assured was that a poet writing in English could do the sort of thing Greek and Latin and Italian poets had done, and do it equally well. This is precisely what Dryden thought Spenser had achieved in *The Shepheardes Calender* : 'Our own nation has produced a third poet in this kind, not inferior to the two former [Theocritus and Virgil]. For the *Shepheardes Calender* of Spenser is not to be matched in any modern language'. E. K. knew that its readers would compare it in this way, and so he points out the comparisons. His own favourite among the eclogues is *November* which, he says, 'is made in imitation of Marot his song, which he made upon the death of Loys the French Queen. But far passing his reach, and in mine opinion all other the eclogues of this book.' Of *October*, which 'is made in imitation of Theocritus his XVI Idillion', he notes that 'the style hereof as also that in Theocritus, is more lofty than the rest, and applied to the height of poetical wit'. The *August* eclogue is again 'made in imitation of that in Theocritus [I or VII or VIII] : whereto also Virgil fashioned his third and his seventh eclogue'. He draws more close comparisons, not always accurately, by quotation. In *February* his note on 'The blocke oft groned' is 'A lively figure, which giveth sense and feeling to unsensible creatures, as Virgil also saith : *Saxa gemunt gravido etc.*' — which Virgil doth not say. In his notes to *October* he realizes, though in a muddled way, that Plato's poetic theory lies behind Spenser's.

He commends Spenser's use of the rhetorical figures : 'A pretty Epanorthosis in these two verses, and withal a Paronomasia or playing with the word' ; 'A figure called Fictio, which useth to attribute reasonable actions and speeches to unreasonable creatures' — the pathetic fallacy of our terminology ; 'An Ironical Sarcasmus, spoken in derision of those rude wits, which make more account of a rhyming ribald than of skill grounded upon learning and judgment', and who were clearly not wanted as readers of *The Shepheardes Calender* ; 'A very poetical πάθος'. Very seldom he ventures a judgment of his own, without reference to authority, whether in the person of a poet or in the collected instances from which were derived the rules of rhetoric : 'A gallant exclamation moralized with great wisdom and passionate with great affection', or 'a fine description of the change of his life and liking ; for all things now seemed to him to have altered their kindly course'. Once or twice, to show his impartiality, he makes an adverse criticism on the use of alliteration, or corrects a statement of Spenser's, as when he points out that the story of the Oak and the Briar is not, as Spenser says, from Chaucer, 'but it is clean in another kind, and rather like to Aesop's fables', which is true. And his condemnation of the Arthurian Romances would not, we may suppose, have been endorsed by Spenser.

What E. K. does not attempt is to interpret the contemporary references in the satirical, 'moral' eclogues, *May*, *July*, and *September*. He may have thought it more tactful to leave these in obscurity, or he may have thought that they were sufficiently obvious to contemporaries to need no gloss. Spenser was quite outspoken enough, as he believed it a poet's duty to be, and E. K. may have thought it wiser not to call any closer attention to Spenser's support of the defiantly Puritan Archbishop of Canterbury, who was at the time suspended from his functions.

Spenser's own opinions about poetry appear in the *October* eclogue, which indeed E. K. compares to Spenser's lost critical treatise *The English Poet*. In Cuddie, E. K. tells us, 'is set out the perfect pattern of a poet, which finding no maintenence of his state and studies, complaineth of the contempt of poetry, and the causes thereof'. It has generally been supposed that Sidney's *Apology for Poetry* represents much of Spenser's own views, and this is most likely. Sidney also undertook to answer the contempt of poetry which was due, he said, to want of merit, and he intended to revive poetry in England both by writing it himself and by encouraging others, Spenser the chief among them, to write it too. In his essay he, like Spenser, set out the perfect pattern of 'the right poet', who is neither the divine poet nor the philosophical poet, 'but it is that feigning notable images of virtues, vices, or what else, with that delightful teaching, which must be the right describing note to know a poet by'. The right poet is the imaginative poet, who 'ranges, only reined with learned discretion, into the divine consideration of what may be and should be'; he is the poet of an imagined ideal, more serious and philosophical (as Aristotle had said) than the historian, who is confined to what has been. Such a poet must necessarily be didactic: he will (again in Sidney's words) 'delight to move men to take that goodness in hand, which without delight they would fly as from a stranger; and teach, to make them know that goodness whereunto they are moved'. Or, as Spenser wrote in the letter to Sir Walter Ralegh which he prefixed to *The Faerie Queene* in 1590 : 'some . . . had rather have good discipline delivered plainly in way of precepts, or sermoned at large, as they use, than thus cloudily enwrapped in allegorical devices. But such, me seems, should be satisfied with the use of these days, seeing all things accounted by their shows, and nothing esteemed of, that is not delightful and pleasing to common sense.'

Already, when he was writing the *October* eclogue, Spenser was ambitious to go on, as Virgil had done, to loftier poetry than these pastorals. So Piers challenges the despondent Cuddie :

> Abandon then the base and viler clowne,
> Lyft up thy selfe out of the lowly dust :
> And sing of bloody Mars, of wars, of giusts.
> Turne thee to those, that weld the awful crowne,
> To doubted Knights, whose woundlesse armour rusts,
> And helmes unbruzed wexen dayly browne.

Virgil, says Cuddie in reply, was encouraged and helped by Maecenas, but in these degenerate times neither at Court nor anywhere in England is poetry valued as once in Augustan Rome. There is no Maecenas now to set him writing a patriotic, heroic poem.

This *October* eclogue, in stating so clearly the ambition of a great poet, and in comparing the English poet to Virgil, points the moral of the whole *Calender*. Virgil was looked upon as the supreme poet of all time, and the *Aeneid* as the greatest of human achievements, 'the faultless model of didactic poetry'. A century and more after Spenser Dryden would begin the dedication of his translation with the uncompromising assertion, 'A heroic poem, truly such, is undoubtedly the greatest work which the soul of man is capable to perform'. 'Undoubtedly', and 'the greatest work', not 'in the opinion of many', and 'the highest form of literature', but absolutely the summit of all human endeavour ; and he could assume general agreement that this was so. Of these heroic poems the *Aeneid* was accepted as the best model for a poet of the Renaissance for the very good reason that Virgil had written for a sophisticated audience, and with a patriotic motive, as they did, and as Homer did not. In the circumstances it is not surprising that the poets of the Renaissance studied Virgil's career with the closest attention, and modelled their own in conformity with his. So Vida in his *Ars Poetica* advised the aspiring poet to begin his public career as Virgil had begun his, with Pastoral :

> But in no Iliad let the youth engage
> His tender years and unexperienced age ;
> Let him by just degrees and steps proceed,
> Sing with the swains and tune the tender reed.

E. K. had laboured the point in his address to Harvey, in explaining the new poet's reasons for writing pastoral, 'doubting perhaps his ability, which he little needed, or minding to furnish our tongue with this kind, wherein it faulteth, or following the example of the best and most ancient poets, which devised this kind of writing, being both so base for the matter, and homely for the manner, at the first to try their abilities', and so forth. And he names for precedents Theocritus, Virgil, Mantuan, Petrarch, Boccaccio, Marot, and Sannazaro.

To the sixteenth-century reader the publication of a volume of pastorals by a young poet inevitably challenged comparison with Virgil. Here, the reader would have thought, is a man who intends to follow the most famous of all poetical careers ; who will, in time, go on to write a heroic poem : let us see if these pastorals have in them the promise that he will be able to undertake this supreme task. Spenser's readers apparently judged that *The Shepheardes Calender* gave such an assurance : the new poet had poetical sinews in him, said Philip Sidney. William Webbe thought *The Shepheardes Calender* the equal of Theocritus and Virgil, and added 'I never heard as yet any that hath read it, which hath not with much admiration commended it'.

With patient tact Spenser refrained from publishing any more poetry until, eleven years later, he was ready with the first three books of the heroic poem to which he had alluded in *October*, and which was implicitly promised by his pastorals. When he did publish *The Faerie Queene* he prefaced it with a stanza which refers back to *The Shepheardes Calender* and which is a paraphrase of those prefatory lines to the *Aeneid* which had similarly referred to Virgil's eclogues.

Ille ego, qui quondam gracili modulatus avena
carmen, et egressus silvis vicina coegi
ut quamvis avido parerent arva colono,
gratum opus agricolis : at nunc horrentia Martis
arma virumque cano.

Lo I the man, whose Muse whilome did maske,
As time her taught, in lowly Shepheards weeds,
Am now enforst a far unfitter taske,
For trumpets sterne to chaunge mine Oaten reeds,
And sing of Knights and Ladies gentle deeds ;
Whose prayses having slept in silence long,
Me, all too meane, the sacred Muse areeds
To blazon broad emongst her learned throng :
Fierce warres and faithfull loves shall moralize my song.

Spenser knew, when he published *The Shepheardes Calender*, that he was inviting comparison with Virgil, and he emphasized this in the *October* eclogue. He was ambitious, as he told Harvey not long afterwards, to overgo Ariosto, that is, to do for English literature what Ariosto had done for Italian ; to make it comparable in dignity with the literatures of Greece and Rome. He knew that he was creating an expectation in his readers that he would advance from pastoral to heroic poetry, and, knowing that, he knew also that they would read these poems with the closest attention. They would wish to find in them the promise of an English *Aeneid*, but they would be therefore all the more critical. No doubt for that reason, and because of the experimental nature of his diction and metre, he invited, or allowed, E. K. to provide a commentary.

In addition to this constant and expected comparison with Virgil was Spenser's less obvious and more daring linking of himself with Chaucer as pupil and master. He constantly uses Virgil's pastoral name for himself, Tityrus, to refer to Chaucer, and E. K. as constantly draws the reader's attention to this. From him Spenser had learnt to compose his homely poems, but

> Now dead he is, and lyeth wrapt in lead,
> (O why should death on hym such outrage showe ?)
> And all hys passing skil with him is fledde,
> The fame whereof doth dayly greater growe.
> But if on me some little drops would flowe,
> Of that the spring was in his learned hedde,
> I soone would learne these woods, to wayle my woe
> And teach the trees, their trickling teares to shedde.

Spenser exaggerated his debt to Chaucer, but of set purpose ; he wished to associate his poetry, in his reader's mind, with the greatest of English poets as well as with the greatest of Latin. The native English strain which he emphasized in the names of his shepherds and in the un-Arcadian descriptions of scenery, as well as in his rustic diction, he ennobled by this deference to Chaucer. He was taking sides in one of the main literary controversies of the Renaissance, and was declaring his allegiance to a master who, though mediaeval, was English. Here he was on the other side from Sidney, who admitted his perplexity before the genius of Chaucer : 'truly I know not whether to marvel more, either that he in that misty time could see so clearly, or that we in this clear age walk so stumblingly after him'. Spenser was opposed to the classicists, who were more aware of the differences than of the resemblances between Chaucer's language and their own ; and while he wished to be the English Virgil he wished also to be the poetical son of Chaucer.

In Latin and in Italian there were established models for good writing, Cicero and Virgil, Boccaccio and Petrarch. In English there could be no such model, for the language had changed too much since Chaucer's time, and there was no contemporary worthy to be a model for Spenser. But in his use of language Spenser does not attempt to imitate Chaucer: he does no more than to remind his readers that English had once been capable of the greatest poetry, and might be so again. He uses a Chaucerian word or a Chaucerian cadence here and there, and with the utmost tact, merely to emphasize the English tradition which might otherwise be obscured by the Virgilian pastoral. Spenser and his contemporaries might be aware of the *patrii sermonis egestas*: their proof that this poverty was only a temporary affliction of the language was to be found in the poems of Chaucer. As Richard Mulcaster said: 'it is our accident which restrains our tongue, and not the tongue itself', a view which the famous headmaster had no doubt impressed upon Spenser when he was his pupil at Merchant Taylors' and writing his earliest English verses.

Spenser sought what E. K. in one of his more felicitous phrases calls 'the brightness of brave and glorious words', but the words must be English words, even rustic words of North country use, or words that were going out of fashion; his extraordinary sensibility to language enabled him to invent compound epithets or new forms that were acceptably delightful. Always Spenser's purpose was to enlarge the scope of the English tongue so that it might become an instrument fit for the heroic poem, to which *The Shepheardes Calender* was a prelude. This was his workshop, where he experimented with language and metre; to many of his contemporaries these experiments seemed very bold, and indeed too bold. He rejected the classicism of the Cambridge humanists such as Cheke, Ascham, and Wilson, who wished, like Bembo in

Italy, to impose a Ciceronianism on the vernacular. But where Bembo might insist on Petrarch and Boccaccio as classical models with some plausibility, there could be no such insistence in English, since the work which was acknowledged to be the best in our language was written in a form of the language which was obsolete. Spenser resisted the influence of the Cambridge where 'Petrarch and Boccace was in every man's mouth', and skilfully went one better than the theorists by the Chaucerian suggestions in his poetry. It is as if he accepted their argument for the purity of English and carried it to its logical conclusion, as Bembo had done with Italian, by setting up as his model the greatest English poet of the past. Thus he gives just enough Chaucerian flavour to his language to make plausible his repeated claim to be drawing on the well of English undefiled, while the delicacy of his taste prevents him from taking more than an occasional sip. The subtle and ironic humour of this is of the same kind that pervades *The Faerie Queene*. If it seems obscure to us that is no reason for supposing that it eluded Spenser's first readers, many of whom were well grounded in the literary controversies of the Renaissance.

For those who were less concerned with literary technique Spenser provided matter to seize their attention by writing in some of the eclogues on topics of the deepest contemporary concern, as Virgil had done. Indeed his hardihood in supporting the Puritan cause may have been too much for E. K. who (as I have said) shirked the task of interpreting the satire in the moral eclogues. Certainly Spenser took his courage in both hands from the start, when he entrusted the publication of his poem to Hugh Singleton, who only a year before had published a Puritan pamphlet, *The Discovery of a Gaping Gulf*, for which the author John Stubbs had had his right hand cut off, and the printer was still in prison. Spenser's own Puritanism, even if cloaked in fable and allegory, was uncompromising enough, and not every young poet would have risked so outspoken a defence of the suspended Archbishop of Canterbury as Spenser undertook in *May*, nor attacked High Church practices as he does in *September*. There Hobbinol gives a warning against too plain speech, as his timid original, Gabriel Harvey, may well have done. Characteristically, the warning is ignored.

'Bold' was a word applied by their contemporaries to both Spenser and Milton: both deserved it. In 1579 everything about *The Shepheardes Calender* must have seemed bold in the extreme: the choice of subject in several of the eclogues, and the forthright vigour of the poet's opinions; the innovations in metre; the defiant eclecticism of diction; the claim to have had the greatest of English poets as his master; the comparison with Virgil, implicit in the choice of pastoral, and with it the promise of a heroic poem to follow. Here at last was the New Poet whom they so eagerly awaited; one who, whether his political views or his literary theories were acceptable or not, could certainly not be ignored. Here was the English Virgil, the great patriotic poet who would glorify England, and the Queen of England, and who would show that the English language, no less than the Italian of Ariosto or the French of the Pléiade, was capable of the dignity of Latin or the subtlety of Greek. For us, nearly four centuries of achievement hinder an understanding of *The Shepheardes Calender* as anything more than an experiment, but to its first readers it came as an exciting revelation of what that achievement might be. We have been too concerned lately with its roots in the past: they saw in it the first energetic growth of the New Poetry. It may be that, in the perspective of history, the Renaissance was a Renaissance myth; but it was a myth in which men passionately believed.

SIDNEY:
THE COUNTESS OF PEMBROKE'S ARCADIA

FOR a century and a half, from the time of the Armada to the time of the '45, *The Countess of Pembroke's Arcadia* remained the best-loved book in the English language. Only then did Samuel Richardson's Pamela supplant Sir Philip Sidney's, and in accepting the inheritance she accepted the famous name. Translations into Italian and French, into Dutch and German disseminated its pleasures among readers on the Continent; continuations, excerpts, stage adaptations, and operas enlarged its audience in other ways. It was taken as a model for English prose style even from before publication down to the austere and inelegant days of the Commonwealth. Shakespeare quarried its rich vein of episode. Milton acknowledged it a work of worth and wit. Pope treasured his copy of it. Sir Walter Scott hoarded it in his capacious memory.

Yet this book, which achieved a fame scarcely equalled by any other English novel, was but a patched-up fragment which the dying Sidney (no doubt remembering Virgil) had asked his friends to destroy. They (likewise remembering Virgil) had not obeyed his wishes, and within a month of his death at Arnhem enterprising London booksellers were attempting to secure the rights of publication. One of them, William Ponsonby, went to see Fulke Greville, one of the two friends to whom Sidney had left his books, and told him that a bookseller, whose name he does not mention, was preparing to publish the old *Arcadia* which in many manuscript copies had already, passing from hand to eager hand, obtained the opening to fame. Ponsonby with ingratiating deference asked Greville if the consent of Sidney's friends, or of his father-in-law Sir Francis Walsingham, had been obtained. Fulke Greville thought not, and Ponsonby advised him to take steps to prevent publication either with the Archbishop or with Dr Cosin who (so Ponsonby said) had a copy to peruse before granting the licence to print. Ponsonby must have gone into the whole matter very thoroughly, and he was to have his reward when, in 1590, he published the first, quarto, edition of the *Arcadia*.

The book which he published was not the old *Arcadia* which his unnamed competitor had hoped to publish, but was, in Greville's words, 'a correction of that old one, done 4 or 5 years since, which he left in trust with me, whereof there is no more copies, and fitter to be printed than the first, which is so common'. Ten copies of this first *Arcadia* still survive to show us what was the 'toyful book' which Sir Philip promised to send his brother Robert, and to which he refers, in that charming dedication of it to his sister, as 'but a trifle, and that triflingly handled'. That book, he there reminds her, had been 'done in loose sheets of paper, most of it in her presence, the rest, by sheets, sent unto her, as fast as they were done'. The revised version, of which Greville believed he had the only copy, was a very much more serious and careful work, and the printing of it, Greville considered, was 'to be done with more deliberation'. And indeed it did not appear until more than three years after he had told Walsingham of his conversation with Ponsonby.

When it was published it broke off in Book III in the middle of a fight, and in the middle of a sentence. The task of editing had been done with care and honesty, and with consideration for the reader. The books, which were Sidney's only divisions, had been subdivided into chapters, with summaries at the head of each ; but a prefatory note acknowledged that 'the division and summing of the chapters was not of Sir Philip Sidney's doing, but adventured by the over-seer of the print, for the more ease of the readers'. The editor also acknowledged responsibility for choosing and placing the verse eclogues which, he says, 'were left till the work had been finished, that then choice should have been made, which should have been taken, and in what manner brought in'. The over-seer of the print, whom we may suppose to have been appointed by Greville, was very probably the translator and lexicographer, John Florio, who may have had some assistance from his friend Matthew Gwinne.

To many of the readers of this first edition the abrupt ending must have seemed disturbing and unnecessary, and it must have been quite widely known that in the original version the *Arcadia* was complete. Accordingly in 1593 a new edition was published, again by Ponsonby, in which there had been tacked on to the 1590 version the ending of Book III and Books IV and V from the old, unrevised *Arcadia*. No attempt was made to effect a neat join, but after the broken sentence with which the revised text published in 1590 had ended, an editorial note was inserted: 'How this combat ended, how the Ladies by the coming of the discovered forces were delivered, and restored to Basilius, and how Dorus again returned to his old master Dametas is altogether unknown. What afterward chanced, out of the author's own writings and conceits hath been supplied, as followeth.' The chapter divisions and summaries had now been removed, and all the verse eclogues restored.

The new editor was Hugh Sanford, secretary to the Earl of Pembroke, and there is no doubt that he worked under the supervision of Lady Pembroke, 'most by her doing, all by her directing' as he says, when she had decided 'to take in hand the wiping away those spots wherewith the beauties thereof were unworthily blemished'. By these aspersions John Florio, who was by nature irascible and petulant, was infuriated, and he poured streams of turgid abuse upon H. S. whose initials he interpreted in Latin, Italian, and English: Haeres Stultitiae,

Hostis Studiosorum, Hipocrito Simulatore, Huffe Snuffe, Horse Stealer, Hob Sowter, Hugh Sot, Humfrey Swineshead, Hodge Sowgelder, and so on and so forth. But apart from calling the new editor names, Florio had a pertinent criticism to make of his work. 'This end we see of it now', he says, 'is not answerable to the precedents: and though it were much easier to mend out of an original and well corrected copy, than to make up so much out of a most corrupt, yet see we more marring that was well, than mending what was amiss.' This criticism Sanford had modestly answered by anticipation, for though the readers 'find not here what might be expected, they may find nevertheless as much as was intended, the conclusion, not the perfection of *Arcadia*'.[1]

We need not now take sides in this controversy, but if we are to understand the extraordinary popularity of the *Arcadia*, we must know what *Arcadia* is meant. And, in spite of John Florio, the *Arcadia* which was read and re-read for a century and more was in essentials the edition prepared by Hugh Sanford. For the edition of 1613 Sir William Alexander of Menstrie, later Earl of Stirling, attempted to make more smooth the transition from the revised to the unrevised text by filling in the lacuna in Book III; but for all that, Florio's criticism, that the end was not answerable to the preceding parts, remains just. However the seventeenth-century reader

[1] In the edition of 1613 an additional note was inserted at the join in Book III: 'Thus far the worthy author had revised or enlarged that first written Arcadia of his, which only passed from hand to hand, and was never printed: having a purpose likewise to have new ordered, augmented, and concluded the rest, had he not been prevented by untimely death. So that all which followeth here of this work, remained as it was done and sent away in several loose sheets (being never after reviewed, nor so much as seen all together by himself) without any certain disposition or perfect order. Yet for that it was his, howsoever deprived of the just grace it should have had, was held too good to be lost: and therefore with much labour were the best coherencies, that could be gathered out of those scattered papers, made, and afterwards printed as now it is, only by her noble care to whose dear hand they were first committed, and for whose delight and entertainment only undertaken.

'What conclusion it should have had, or how far the work have been extended (had it had his last hand thereunto) was only known to his own spirit, where only those admirable images were (and no where else) to be cast.'

apparently preferred a book with a broken back to a fragment, or at least had been persuaded by Lady Pembroke to accept this.

For her the old *Arcadia* had been written, as her brother had said in dedicating it to her ; by her noble care the revised *Arcadia* had been completed in 1593 out of those scattered papers which had first been committed to her ; and her name stood at the head of the title in edition after edition of *The Countess of Pembroke's Arcadia.* It would then be natural for her to value her book, the original version that had passed from hand to hand, more highly than Fulke Greville, to whom Sidney had left the unique copy of his unfinished revision. In her eagerness to preserve everything of her brother's writing, 'held too good to be lost', she would be likely to prefer to see the book completed from the first draft rather than left incomplete. No doubt she, like Hugh Sanford, recognized that her edition could not provide the perfection of *Arcadia*, but in the circumstances, this was the best that could be done.

To her the book remained what it had been when her brother first wrote it, often in her presence at Wilton, or as he was hunting on the pleasant plains of Wiltshire, a romance, written for a young bride of eighteen awaiting the birth of her first child. She did not believe in Fulke Greville's editorial moralizing of the version in his possession, which seemed to transform her romance into something of more serious purpose. She knew, better than anyone, the origins of the delightful book which her dearly loved brother had written for her ; she knew what value he had set on it, and though she might discount his courtly modesty she was not persuaded that his revision, however elaborate, had made a romance into a heroical poem. For her and (we may suppose) for most of the ladies who read the book in the next century and more, the *Arcadia* remained a romance, even if the best of all romances. And the fair ladies whom in the old *Arcadia* Sidney had so often paused to address, were perhaps always its most numerous readers.

Lady Mary Wroth, the daughter of his brother Robert

Sidney, was inspired by it to write a huge romance herself. Anne Weamys wrote a *Continuation*. Marie de Médicis sent Jean Baudoin to England with the express purpose of translating the *Arcadia* into French, and in the same year in which his translation appeared another French version, by Mlle Geneviève Chappelain, was also published in Paris. Another French lady, Mlle de la Roche Guilhem, imitated it with a romance called *Almanzor and Almanzaida*. Mrs Stanley modernized it in 1725, and the novelist Jane Porter used it as a mine of aphorisms which she extracted and refined 'with Remarks' in two volumes published in 1807. More recently Virginia Woolf has paid her tribute to the *Arcadia*, both by imitation, in *Orlando*, and by an essay which shows that to her too it was a romance, though one where 'as in some luminous globe, all the seeds of English fiction lie latent'.

Ladies who have been writing novels during these three hundred and fifty years or so and a Queen of France are among the admirers of the *Arcadia*. So too was the formidable Lady Anne Clifford, who was portrayed at thirteen with, among severer reading such as Eusebius and Josephus, a copy of the *Arcadia* beside her. That she read and remembered the book long afterwards, when she had married the younger of Lady Pembroke's sons, may be known by her choosing words from it to describe her intimate feelings: 'the marble pillars of Knole in Kent and Wilton in Wiltshire were to me oftentimes but the gay arbours of anguish'. Probably the splendid phrase rose unsought to her troubled mind.

To Lady Dorothy Sidney, his Sacharissa, Edmund Waller inevitably offered compliments from her great-uncle's book.

> All the rich flowers through his Arcadia found,
> Amazed we see in this one garland bound.
> Had but this copy (which the artist took
> From the fair picture of that noble book)
> Stood at Calander's, the brave friends had jarred,
> And, rivals made, the ensuing story marred.

But with such exquisite compliments to hand how should a poet not have the wit to offer them?

Pope lent his copy of the *Arcadia* to Lady Mary Wortley Montagu who claimed credit for returning it carefully 'without damage', but long before their time the poets had been discovering ladies of much less eminence romantically engaged with the famous love-story.

> Pray Ladies breathe, a while lay by
> Celestial Sidney's Arcady,

Lovelace begs; and his friend Charles Cotton coming by surprise upon his nymph 'on a clear river's flowery side' (as Charles Cotton would) finds her, too, reading the *Arcadia.*

> The happy object of her eye
> Was Sidney's living Arcadie
> Whose amorous tale had so betray'd
> Desire in this all-lovely maid,
> That whilst her cheek a blush did warm,
> I read Love's story in her form;
> And of the sisters the united grace,
> Pamela's vigour in Philoclea's face.

This idle preoccupation of young ladies with a romance shocked the Puritans, whose feminine ideal was the *hausfrau.* 'And instead of reading Sir Philip Sidney's *Arcadia*', says Thomas Powell with frowning severity, 'let them read the grounds of good huswifery.' Milton also, though not so consistent as he might have been, was moved by his detestation of King Charles, whose delight in the *Arcadia* was well known, to refer to it as 'a vain amatorious poem'. But the ladies were undeterred, and a century later Joseph Warton took the *Arcadia* to typify the romances which were still such favourites with them.

> Shall Sidney's fables be preferred
> To my sagacious Hoyle?

he enquires, and obligingly explains his reference as 'alluding to those Ladies who have left their novels and romances for the profound study of Mr Hoyle's book on Whist'. Whatever second thoughts Philip Sidney may have had he had written the *Arcadia*, in the first place, as a romance to please the ladies ; and the ladies, who are seldom given to welcome the revision of a compliment in the cause of morality, have ever since, from Lady Pembroke to Virginia Woolf, insisted that it is indeed a romance.

Perhaps for this very reason Sidney left the incomplete revision to the ironical Greville, who remained a bachelor the better to hold his fortune together (as he said), and who was not predisposed to think his friend capable of the triviality of a romance. Besides he would be more aware than Lady Pembroke could wish to be of the transformation that Sidney had wrought upon the *Arcadia*. When, years later, Greville wrote Sidney's *Life* he gave his view of the *Arcadia*, and of what he believed Sidney's purpose had been. 'His end was not vanishing pleasure alone, but moral Images, and Examples, (as directing threads) to guide every man through the confused Labyrinth of his own desires, and life.' He points to Sidney's sagacity in the description of Basilius's withdrawal from public affairs and appointment of a subject to rule in his place, which must have seemed like a foreshadowing of James's elevation of Buckingham. He draws the obvious moral from Euarchus's election to temporary sovereignty, and from other incidents, and sums up in these words : 'To be short the like, and finer moralities offer themselves throughout that various, and dainty work of his, for sounder judgments to exercise their spirits in'. And he invites the reader to imagine how much more there would have been to instruct him 'if this excellent Image-maker had lived to finish, and bring to perfection this extraordinary frame of his own Commonwealth . . . especially if he please to take knowledge, that in all these creatures of his making, his intent, and scope was, to turn the barren Philosophy precepts into pregnant Images of life ; and in them, first on the Monarch's part, lively to represent the growth, state, and declination of Princes, change of Government, and laws: vicissitudes of sedition, faction, succession, confederacies, plantations, with all other errors, or alterations in public affairs. Then again in the subject's case; the state of favour, disfavour, prosperity, adversity, emulation, quarrel, undertaking, retiring, hospitality, travail, and all other moods of private fortunes, or misfortunes. In which traverses (I know) his purpose was to limn out such exact pictures, of every posture in the mind, that any man being forced, in the strains of this life, to pass through any straights, or latitudes of good, or ill fortune, might (as in a glass) see how to set a good countenance upon all the discountenances of adversity, and a stay upon the exorbitant smiling of chance.' Such support King Charles cannot have been alone in discovering in the *Arcadia*.

Now that modest, parenthetical '(I know)' must be respected: Greville, if anyone, must have known Sidney's purpose in the revision. When the manuscript which had been left to him was prepared for publication therefore, he insisted unobtrusively, by brief chapter headings, on this interpretation of the *Arcadia*, not as a romance, but as a heroic poem. That this was his understanding of Sidney's work is evident from a comparison of his description of it with Spenser's account of *The Faerie Queene* in his letter to Sir Walter Ralegh. The general end of his poem was 'to fashion a gentleman or noble person in vertuous and gentle discipline', but while he acknowledged that some 'had rather have good discipline delivered plainly in way of precepts, or sermoned at large' he preferred to colour them with an historical fiction, or (as Greville puts it) 'to turn the barren Philosophy precepts into pregnant Images of Life'. Ben Jonson also thought of the *Arcadia* in the context of the heroic poem for which, he told William Drummond, 'there was no such Ground as King Arthur's fiction' and (so he asserted) 'Sir P. Sidney had an intention to have transformed all his Arcadia to the stories of

King Arthur'. Whatever the truth of that statement, there is every reason for believing that Greville was not alone in regarding the *Arcadia* as a heroic poem.

Sidney's own references to his 'toyful book', 'this idle work', do not necessarily conflict with such an interpretation. For these phrases refer to the old *Arcadia* which first established the idea of the book in Lady Pembroke's mind. Besides, it was part of the courtly tradition that an author of high rank should disparage his own work in this way, using (to quote Fulke Greville once more) 'that hypocritical figure *Ironia*, wherein men commonly (to keep above their works) seem to make toys of the utmost they can do'.

We must also beware of arguing that a prose romance and a heroic poem are entirely distinct forms. They may seem so to us : we may find it absurd to set the *Arcadia* alongside the *Aeneid*, but to Sidney and his contemporaries these works were all of a kind. Fortunately Sidney himself, in his *Apology for Poetry*, discloses very clearly his opinions of this matter. To him Xenophon's *Cyropaedia* and the *Aethiopica* of Heliodorus were both 'absolute heroical poems'. In this he was following the best received opinion of his time. Sir William Alexander who understood Sidney's work well enough to attempt a transition in Book III, praised both the 'methodical intricateness' of the *Aethiopica* and the hero of it who did 'nothing that was not worthy to be imitated'. The revised *Arcadia*, not the old *Arcadia*, shows how thoroughly Sidney had understood the methods of Heliodorus, so that it is possible to describe the *Arcadia* as 'a conscious attempt to domesticate the Greek romances in English'. This is true, but the purpose of such domestication was undoubtedly as a means towards a species of heroic poem. To Sidney the interest of the *Aethiopica* was as an example of the highest kind of literature, not as a more sophisticated romance, so that when, in revising the book which he had written for his sister's pleasure, he converted (as we should say) a simple tale into an intricate romance on the pattern of the *Aethiopica*, in his own view he was doing something much more radical, for he was converting a modest and unpretentious work into something that must invite comparison with the *Aeneid* and *The Faerie Queene*. For him, as for Spenser, as for Milton, as for Dryden, the heroic poem was a poem with a moral purpose. 'For as the image of each action stirreth and instructeth the mind, so the lofty image of such Worthies most inflameth the mind with desire to be worthy, and informs with counsel how to be worthy.'

Thus the question, whether the *Arcadia* is a romance or a heroic poem is a false one, since the one kind does not exclude the other. The Countess of Pembroke was as justified in reading her brother's book as a romance as was Fulke Greville in interpreting it as a heroic poem ; but this does not mean that Greville was blind to its qualities as a story and as a portrayal of human character, or that Lady Pembroke was insensitive to the moral qualities of Pyrocles and Musidorus, of Pamela and Philoclea and Gynecia. These different elements in the work are no more to be separated in the *Arcadia* than in *The Faerie Queene*. Gabriel Harvey's comments on the book best reconcile the points of view of both editors : it was to be commended (he said) 'for three things especially . . . for amorous courting, (he was young in years ;) for sage counselling, (he was ripe in judgment ;) and for valorous fighting, (his sovereign profession was arms ;) and delightful pastime by way of pastoral exercises, may pass for a fourth'. This is judicious and sensible, with its unusual relating of the book to the personality of the author ; and if Fulke Greville chose to emphasize the 'sage counselling', he was a statesman of long experience, who found in his friend's work a political sagacity much wanting at the time when he was writing. Also his own austere temperament inclined him to recall especially Sidney's youthful gravity, 'his talk ever of knowledge, and his very play tending to enrich his mind'.

The recollection of so subtle and so versatile a personality as Sidney's was not likely to be precisely the same in the aloof Calvinist statesman and in the elegant lady who was the subject of all verse. Both were devoted to his memory, but there was inevitably a difference of emphasis ; for what man, however ordinary and undistinguished, presents the same aspects of his personality to his sister and to his closest friend ? And so far as the *Arcadia* was concerned, the careless romance, sent on loose sheets of paper as fast as they were done, stood in the forefront of the sister's memory ; but in the friend's was the careful revision, entrusted to him by the author's dying wish. In Lady Pembroke's references to the revised *Arcadia* we may discover a hint of asperity : to this Greville, who loved her as did all who knew her, made no reply but quietly to insist, long after the Countess's text had gained currency, that there was more to the *Arcadia* than vanishing pleasure alone, that it was more than a vain, amatorious poem. With this she would have agreed.

Two years before the first publication of the *Arcadia* Abraham Fraunce dedicated to Lady Pembroke his *Arcadian Rhetoric*, an anthology selected to illustrate the figures of rhetoric. His purpose (as his recent editor says) was to dignify modern poetry 'especially the fashionable heroic and pastoral . . . by relating it to rule and precept'. Fraunce had been sent to St John's College, Cambridge, under Sidney's patronage, and he remained in close touch with Lady Pembroke and her circle, dedicating a number of books to her, to her husband, and to her younger brother Robert. Fraunce knew the *Arcadia* and *Astrophel and Stella* while still in manuscript, and he also knew the unpublished *Faerie Queene* which no doubt was circulated among Sidney's friends. From all these he quotes in the *Arcadian Rhetoric*, but he gives pride of place, as his title suggests, to the *Arcadia*.

Fraunce takes examples under each heading from Homer and Virgil, and from those whom he considers the most eminent poets of Italy, Spain, France, and England — Tasso,

Boscan, Garcilasso, du Bartas, Sidney, and Spenser. But he unobtrusively emphasizes the excellence of the English poets, and especially of Sidney, by placing his English quotations immediately after those from Homer and Virgil, thereby giving them precedence over the modern Continental poets. Since he knew something of *The Faerie Queene* we may suppose that personal loyalty alone would not have led him to choose so many quotations from the *Arcadia* had he considered it to be merely a romance. Fraunce must have thought of it as a work of greater dignity, something to be set beside the heroic poems of antiquity, and beside the *Gerusalemme Liberata* of Tasso, the *Judith* and *Les Semaines* of du Bartas. (Du Bartas had referred to Sidney in his poem, and Sidney had translated *La Première Semaine*, though the translation is now lost.) The manuscript used by Fraunce was in the main, apparently, the old, unrevised, *Arcadia*, as we should expect, since there was no reason why Fulke Greville should lend him his unique revised manuscript. But there are indications of some revision also in his quotations, as there are in some of the surviving manuscripts : Sidney from time to time made minor revisions in his romance before he undertook the drastic rewriting which he bequeathed to Greville. Clearly Fraunce in 1588, two years before the publication of the revised *Arcadia*, regarded the work, in whatever form he saw it, as of far greater dignity than a romance, and chose it as a means of establishing the excellence of English poetry. The *Arcadia* is claimed as a model of good English writing, in the highest, heroic, style, and as proof that the English language is as capable as Italian, Spanish, or French of taking its place alongside Greek and Latin to be the medium of the noblest literature.

Some ten or a dozen years later the distinguished lawyer and wit, John Hoskyns, gave a copy of the 1590 *Arcadia* to a young friend of his, with passages marked for his attention, and with a commentary *Directions for Speech and Style*. Hoskyns' purpose was quite different from Fraunce's. His

Monument to Sir William Cordell, ob. 1580, Long Melford Church, Suffolk (see p. 150)

(*a*) Monument to Richard Harford, ob. 1578, Bosbury Church, Herefordshire, by John Gildon (see p. 151)

(*b*) Monument to John Harford, Bosbury Church, Herefordshire, 1573, by John Gildon (see p. 151)

treatise was not intended for publication but for private instruction, and he had no need to claim for the *Arcadia* any higher place than it had already been accorded by its many readers. But, like Fraunce, he saw in it a model of good English style, and chose to direct his young friend's attention to it in order to perfect his own style. His *Directions* therefore shows the response of a very intelligent reader of the 1590s and enables us to understand precisely how the *Arcadia* was admired by one to whom Ben Jonson owed the refinement of his style.[1]

Hoskyns found 'the best flower growing most plentifully in all Arcadia' to be metaphor. He marked those that especially pleased him with the letter M in the margin of the copy presented to his friend, but he also quoted several examples in his *Directions*, as 'Philoclea was so environed with sweet rivers of virtue, that she could neither be battered nor undermined'. He points out the baseness of the metaphor, 'the very fritter of fraud, and seething pot of iniquity', which Dametas uses in his burlesque challenge to Clinias, which he might well have quoted also as an example of decorum and so given the lie to Ben Jonson, who hastily accused Sidney of not keeping decorum 'in making everyone speak as well as himself'.

This was much the most damaging criticism of the *Arcadia* that could have been made by a contemporary, but it can very easily be rebutted. It is absurd to say that the low-life characters, Dametas, Miso, and Mopsa, speak as Sidney spoke. Of Miso indeed we are told, 'only one good point she hath, that she observes decorum, having a froward mind in a wretched body'. And if Musidorus and Pyrocles and Amphialus speak like Sidney, so they should. In fact, Sidney makes his persons speak in character all through, and his observance of decorum extends far beyond this. There is an elaborate conceit where Pamela is embroidering a purse with roses and lilies ; 'and if at any time she put her mouth to bite

[1] Jonson had read Hoskyns' treatise, and he transcribed from it several pages into his commonplace book, known as *Discoveries*.

off the silk, it seemed, that where she had been long in making of a rose with her hand, she would in an instant make roses with her lips', and much more of this sort. Philoclea apostrophizes Love, and asks 'Why dost thou in thy beautiful sampler set such a work for my desire to take out?' When Philoclea replies to Amphialus, whose prisoner she is, she matches the paradoxical situation in which she finds herself with a speech full of rhetorical antithesis which is perfectly appropriate and decorous.

'Alas, cousin, she said, what shall my tongue be able to do which is informed by the ears one way, and by the eyes another? You call for pity, and use cruelty; you say you love me, and yet do the effects of enmity. You affirm your death is in my hands, but you have brought me to so near a degree to death, as when you will, you may lay death upon me: so that while you say, I am mistress of your life, I am not mistress of mine own.'

In the pastoral parts too Sidney follows his own precept,

> A shepherd's tale no height of style desires,

and so keeps perfect decorum.

Hoskyns notices Sidney's avoidance of alliteration, the 'dictionary method' which he had derided in *Astrophel and Stella*, and the infrequency of his use of *epanalepsis*, of which he notes only one example, 'overthrow of my desires, recompense of my overthrow'. This figure he thought mild and sweet and of much use, and he also recommended the use of *polyptoton*, 'a good figure, and may be used with or without passion'. Of this Hoskyns quotes several examples from the *Arcadia*, among them the burlesque 'exceedingly exceeding that exceedingness' which he does not seem to have thought excessive.

Towards the end of his treatise Hoskyns gives a list of what in a later age would have been called *The Beauties of the Arcadia*. 'Men are described most excellently in *Arcadia*', he says, and he thinks that Sidney 'had much help out of Theophrasti Imagines', that is, from the popular *Characters* of Theophrastus which were soon to give rise to a whole series of books of Characters. If he had, then he must have read them in the Greek, for there was no vernacular translation in his lifetime, nor even a Latin one. A similar opinion is expressed by the unknown compiler of an elaborate index to the *Arcadia* some time early in the seventeenth century, who after a Table of Contents remarks, 'These few collections may readily lead to the most remarkable passages in the Book ; and were the choice pieces gathered out and sorted severally by themselves, would make as good a book of Characters as is yet extant'. Hoskyns also comments on Sidney's excellence in portraying feminine character, without suggesting (as would most modern critics) that Sidney is better here than in his portrayal of men. He notes many actions which are rarely described, the mutiny and fire in a ship, the causes of a rebellion, an armed skirmish, and so forth. To these may be added Sidney's professional expertise in describing the tournament (in which he was a famous performer), horsemanship (which he had studied in the riding schools of Vienna), swordsmanship, and hunting. His accurate and loving observation of the natural scene was the beginning of a tradition that has greatly enriched English fiction.

Hoskyns and other readers of the time might perhaps have taken for granted the extraordinary skill with which Sidney controls his intricate story without once faltering or losing the thread. 'For the web (as it were) of the story', says Hoskyns, 'he followed three, Heliodorus in Greek, Sannazaro's *Arcadia* in Italian, and *Diana* of Montemayor in Spanish.' Modern scholarship does not contest this judgment. But Sidney considered the *Aethiopica* of Heliodorus as a heroic poem, and as a model for the writing of one. With this Hoskyns, and most men of his time, would have agreed. A complex and elaborate design firmly held in the author's mind and adorned with every contrivance of rhetoric and diction, might seem to Hazlitt 'one of the greatest monuments of the abuse of intellectual power upon record', but to contemporary readers was exactly in accord with the highest standards of taste. Added to the technical virtuosity was an imaginative insight into human character and personality comparable to that with which, by the time of its publication though not when it was written, the dramatists were making men familiar, and a sententious wisdom which pointed the moral and policy of the story in many a memorable phrase. Hoskyns drew his pupil's attention to examples of political wisdom by noting 'Policy' in the margins of his copy. He must already have been familiar with the various typographical devices used to draw the reader's attention to *sententiae*, italics, the word 'sentence' or 'a hand in the margin of a book' from which Sidney himself derived a witty metaphor. Hoskyns lists some such *sententiae* in his treatise : 'Man's experience is woman's best eyesight' ; 'Who stands only upon defence stands upon no defence' ; 'There is nothing more terrible to a guilty mind than the eye of a respected friend' ; 'Love to a yielding heart is a King, but to a resisting is a Tyrant'. He also comments on the rhetorical means by which Sidney has composed these proverbial sentences, in order to guide his pupil towards a similar accomplishment, and he warns him against an excessive use of them for 'a sentence is a pearl in a discourse, but is it a good discourse that is all pearl ?'

The success of the *Arcadia*, all the more remarkable because in the form in which it was read it was a highly sophisticated work cobbled up with a more crude, immature first draft, was doubtless due to its capacity for providing some enjoyment for almost every reader. It gave the ladies the sort of pleasure they derived from those romances of which Don Quixote had so rich a collection, and which delighted Dorothy Osborne ; but it gave more pleasure than most because it was so much more than an involved adventure story, and because its sensitive portrayal of Pamela and Philoclea in love had no equal in other romances. To the more serious of its readers Sidney's political sagacity and moral authority were rewarding, providing ample quotation for the adornment of their letters or their conversation. Those who were learned in the critical theory of the time recognized in the *Arcadia* a true heroic poem on the model of Heliodorus, one moreover where matters Heroical and Pastoral were mingled, the two most admired of literary kinds which (as Sidney himself said) 'if severed they be good, the conjunction cannot be hurtful'. They are most strikingly conjoined in the very opening of the first book where the mistress of the shepherds Strephon and Claius is named Urania, the Heavenly Muse whom du Bartas had lately converted to Christianity, and whom Milton would not disdain to invoke.

Not least among the *Arcadia's* merits was the carefully elaborate prose, with its rhetorical ornament and subtle rhythms. Men contrasted it with other prose of the time, especially with Lyly's, whose *Euphues* had set a fashion soon to be mocked by Shakespeare and others. So Michael Drayton observes that Sidney

> throughly paced our language as to show
> The plenteous English hand in hand might go
> With Greek and Latin, and did first reduce
> Our tongue from Lyly's writing then in use.

Long afterwards, when the novelists of the eighteenth century had begun to oust the *Arcadia* from its supremacy, Dr Johnson, in compiling his Dictionary, 'fixed Sidney's work for the boundary, beyond which I make few excursions', and considered that Spenser and Sidney between them provided the whole English vocabulary of poetry and fiction.

In the second book, when Gynecia has been injured by the oversetting of her coach, she sends Philoclea to her sister Pamela to be out of the way. Pamela lodges with the clownish Dametas and Miso, who go to look for Philoclea. She is lying on the ground under a tree, where they fail to notice her, but they grumble to one another as they search, 'Dametas saying, that he would not deal in other bodies' matters ; but for his part, he did not like, that maids should once stir out of their fathers' houses, but if it were to milk a cow, or save a chicken from a kite's foot, or some such other matter of importance. And Miso swearing that if it were her daughter Mopsa, she would give her a lesson for walking so late, that should make her keep within doors for one fortnight. But their jangling made Philoclea rise, and pretending as though she had done it but to sport with them, went with them, after she had willed Miso to wait upon her mother, to the lodge ; where, being now accustomed by her parents' discipline, as well as her sister, to serve herself, she went alone up to Pamela's chamber, where, meaning to delight her eyes, and joy her thoughts with the sweet conversation of her beloved sister, she found her, though it were in the time that the wings of night do blow sleep most willingly into mortal creatures, sitting in a chair, lying backward, with her head almost over the back of it, and looking upon a wax-candle which burnt before her ; in one hand holding a letter, in the other her handkerchief, which had lately drunk up the tears of her eyes, leaving instead of them crimson circles, like red flakes in the element, when the weather is hottest ; which Philoclea finding, for her eyes had learned to know the badges of sorrow, she earnestly entreated to know the cause thereof, that either she might comfort or accompany her doleful humour. But Pamela, rather seeming sorry that she had perceived so much, than willing to open any farther ; O my Pamela, said Philoclea, who are to me a sister in nature, a mother in counsel, a princess by the law of our country, and which name, methinks, of all other is the dearest, a friend by my choice and your favour, what means this banishing me from your counsels ? do you love your sorrow so well as to grudge me part of it ? or do you think I shall not love a sad Pamela, so well as a joyful ?

or be my ears unworthy, or my tongue suspected? what is it, my sister, that you should conceal from your sister, yea and servant Philoclea? These words won no further of Pamela, but that telling her they might talk better as they lay together, they impoverished their clothes to enrich their bed, which for that night might well scorn the shrine of Venus: and there cherishing one another with dear, though chaste embracements; with sweet, though cold kisses; it might seem that love was come to play him there without dart; or that weary of his own fires, he was there to refresh himself between their sweet-breathing lips. But Philoclea earnestly again entreated Pamela to open her grief; who, drawing the curtain, that the candle might not complain of her blushing, was ready to speak: but the breath, almost formed into words, was again stopped by her, and turned into sighs. But at last, I pray you, said she, sweet Philoclea, let us talk of some other thing: and tell me whether you did ever see anything so amended as our pastoral sports be, since that Dorus came hither? O love, how far thou seest with blind eyes! Philoclea had straight found her, and therefore to draw out more, Indeed, said she, I have often wondered to myself how such excellencies could be in so mean a person; but belike fortune was afraid to lay her treasures where they should be stained with so many perfections: only I marvel how he can frame himself to hide so rare gifts under such a block as Dametas. Ah, said Pamela, if you knew the cause, but no more do I neither; and to say the truth — but Lord, how are we fallen to talk of this fellow? and yet indeed if you were sometimes with me to mark him, while Dametas reads his rustic lecture unto him, how to feed his beasts before noon, where to shade them in the extreme heat, how to make the manger handsome for his oxen, when to use the goad, and when the voice; giving him rules of a herdman, though he pretend to make him a shepherd; to see all the while with what a grace, which seems to set a crown upon his base estate, he can descend to those poor matters, certainly you would : but to what serves this ? no doubt we were better sleep than talk of these idle matters. Ah my Pamela, said Philoclea, I have caught you ; the constancy of your wit was not wont to bring forth such disjointed speeches : you love, dissemble no further. It is true, said Pamela, now you have it ; and with less ado should, if my heart could have thought those words suitable for my mouth. But indeed, my Philoclea, take heed : for I think virtue itself is no armour of proof against affection.' Here we see how easily and smoothly, as in his sonnets, Sidney can pass from a light conversational tone to the stately and ornate, the assurance with which, like an Elizabethan architect, he dares to set the beautiful by the grotesque, the noble by the base. He can juxtapose sentiment and humour without making either seem false ; we laugh at Dametas, we sorrow with Pamela, we smile with Philoclea. Here are the rhetorical figures, the antitheses, the metaphors, the personifications ; delicate observation of behaviour and vivid, pictorial presentation of it. Hitherto there had been no English prose of this flexibility and ease, nothing to promise that English might endure comparison with Greek and Latin. But the readers who opened the *Arcadia* in the 1590s, and who then read with a care and attention uncustomary now, were surprised into delighted recognition that here at last was prose neither Ciceronian nor workaday but mere English. In this prose was conveyed an intricate story of their favourite kind, of the adventures of two heroic young princes, and of their loves for two charming princesses, for 'even to the heroical Cupid hath ambitiously climbed'. These princes and princesses were not pasteboard figures, but living human beings, characters subtly understood by a poet, whose imagination, tender, compassionate, and humorous, inhabited there.

The sentiment and the idealism are not ours ; but they were theirs. Miss Beale and Miss Buss would not have thought Pamela and Philoclea satisfactory pupils. Dr Arnold and others have seen to it that young men do not shed tears on each others' shoulders, or kiss to comfort one another. But 'Musidorus falling down by Pyrocles and kissing the weeping eyes of his friend, besought him not to make account of his speech ; which if it had been over vehement, yet was it to be borne withal, because it came out of a love much more vehement. . . . But even this kindness made Pyrocles the more melt in the former unkindness, which his manlike tears well showed.' To the gallant and dashing Sidney, to the bold navigators of unknown seas, Pyrocles' tears were manlike. Our withdrawal of friendship into less emotional regions of experience is not necessarily all gain, and in any event we have no right to criticize an expression of sentiment which was so obviously sincere. There is no reason why they should have behaved like us, and none why we should behave like them ; but we ought to recognize that this was in fact how they did behave.

So also in love their conduct differed from ours, but we are not to accuse them of affectation on that account. Kenelm Digby composed his private memoirs of his famous love for Lady Venetia Stanley on the pattern of a romance, taking for himself the name of Heliodorus' hero Theagenes, and calling Venetia Stelliana, not (we may suppose) without some suggestion of Sidney's Stella. And if Sir Kenelm Digby was something of a fantastic whose infirmity it was, according to Lady Fanshawe, to tell tall stories, what of that austere Roundhead Colonel Hutchinson who (so Lucy herself tells us) after falling in love with the idea of Lucy before he had even seen her, and then being teased with a false report of her marriage, 'immediately turned pale as ashes, and felt a fainting to seize his spirits in that extraordinary manner, that finding himself ready to sink at table, he was fain to pretend something had offended his stomach, and to retire into the garden', and eventually to bed ?

This is not our behaviour, and the *Arcadia* may not be to

our taste ; but if it is not then it is very certain that our enjoyment of Elizabethan drama is a pretence. For the *Arcadia*, being the most successful work of fiction of the English Renaissance, reveals the taste of the age more vividly than any other. It is not, like *The Faerie Queene* or *Hamlet*, one of the supreme achievements of man's imagination : for that very reason it transcends its time less than these, and illuminates it more brilliantly. But it was written for those who, when *The Faerie Queene* was published, acclaimed in Spenser the English Virgil, and whose immediate and enthusiastic response to *Hamlet* showed how well Shakespeare too could satisfy their taste. To them the constant revival of *Hamlet* for a generation which neglects the *Arcadia* would have been incomprehensible, and they would have inferred that those who applaud *Hamlet* but have never read the *Arcadia*, neither understand nor appreciate the genius of Shakespeare.

SIDNEY: *ASTROPHEL AND STELLA*

FIVE years after the death of Sir Philip Sidney, in 1591, a London publisher, Thomas Newman, obtained a manuscript of his *Astrophel and Stella* and printed it under the title 'Syr P.S. His Astrophel and Stella. Wherein the excellence of Sweete Poesie is concluded.' He got Tom Nashe to write a lively and impudent preface, and he added a number of poems by Daniel, Campion, the Earl of Oxford, and others. 'I have been very careful in the printing of it,' Newman said, 'and whereas being spread abroad in written copies, it had gathered much corruption by ill writers: I have used their help and advice in correcting and restoring it to his first dignity, that I know were of skill and experience in those matters.' Newman's intentions may have been scholarly, but the text which he printed is a garbled and incomplete hotch-potch, to which Sidney's friends, who had not authorized the publication, reasonably objected. This edition was suppressed at the instance of Lord Burghley. Later in the same year Newman brought out a new edition with some three hundred and fifty corrections, without Nashe's puff, and without the additional poems. Matthew Lownes about 1597 published another, derived from Newman's first quarto, which is no better. Not until 1598 did a satisfactory text appear, when Lady Pembroke included the poems in her edition of the *Arcadia*.

We cannot now tell where Newman got his copies of the poems. Daniel, twenty-eight of whose sonnets had been printed in the first edition, complained in dedicating the authorized text to Lady Pembroke the following year, that he 'was betrayed by the indiscretion of a greedy Printer. . . .

But this wrong was not only done to me, but to him whose unmatchable lines have indured the like misfortune ; Ignorance sparing not to commit sacrilege upon so holy relics.' Perhaps Daniel himself had somehow shared in Newman's indiscretion, for why else should he refer to it as he does ? He would have had access to Sidney's poems at Wilton, where he was tutor to the two young Herberts, Sidney's nephews ; but if he had been somehow implicated with Newman in the first publication of *Astrophel and Stella* we should expect him to conceal this, if he could, from Sidney's friends and sister, on whose patronage he then depended.

Certainly Newman obtained a manuscript of some of Daniel's sonnets, 'uncorrected' (as Daniel complains), and it is difficult to see how he could have done so without the author's connivance, which indeed his accusations of treachery and indiscretion seem to imply. Perhaps Daniel had discussed with Newman a publication of Sidney's sonnets and had at the same time shown him this manuscript of his own. (He had so far published only a prose translation from the Italian.) Newman may have had a manuscript copy of *Astrophel and Stella* already, or may have borrowed a copy from Daniel and then, to Daniel's embarrassment, published his unrevised sonnets together with Sidney's and others. Much of this is conjecture, as it must be ; but if there is any truth in it, Daniel was almost certainly acting in good faith, if without much worldly caution, which is what we should expect of him, and had reason to resent Newman's behaviour.

The manuscript of *Astrophel and Stella* used by Newman for his first edition must have been, as he hints, a very poor one. But there are two points to be noted. First, all the songs are lumped together at the end, after the sonnets. (This may have been a clumsy piece of editing by Newman.) And, second, two poems (sonnet 37 and the eleventh song), and parts of two others (stanzas 18 to 25 of the eighth song, and stanzas 5, 6, and 7 of the tenth) are omitted. Now these poems and stanzas share one thing in common, their intimacy, so that their omission is hardly likely to be due to the unscrupulous Newman. The thirty-seventh sonnet has the bitter, scurrilous punning on the name of Stella's husband, which would at once identify her with Lady Rich. (The same pun is used again in the twenty-fourth and thirty-fifth sonnets, but in neither of these is the allusion so brutally frank, and might, I think, have been missed by those who did not already know who sat for the portrait of Stella.) In the three songs the passages omitted are those where the most passionate moments of the whole sequence are reached. We can well understand that Sidney might not wish anyone outside his immediate circle to read the exquisitely tender verses of Stella's reply to Astrophel in the eighth song, or the duet with her in the eleventh, if they were to confuse Stella with Lady Rich. This suggests that there were two versions of *Astrophel and Stella* in circulation : one for Sidney's intimate friends who knew precisely how far Stella was to be identified with Penelope, and another for those who might read the poems purely for the aesthetic pleasure they gave, but who were not to be permitted to discover (or to think they had discovered) any secret passion which might compromise her. In the poems themselves Sidney shows that he had two audiences in mind : Stella, whom Astrophel addresses ; and the 'best wits' who are pleased by Sidney's poetry but are not, we may suppose, concerned with any autobiography it may contain.

Here then is the principal question to be decided if we are truly to appreciate *Astrophel and Stella* : is it, or is it not, autobiography ? Not that a poem is better or worse because it describes what actually happened — of course not ; but we miss the subtlety of Sidney's art if we cannot see the continual shift between the two, between the fact and fiction, Philip and Astrophel, Penelope and Stella. And we must beware of yielding to Romantic prejudice by using the poems as evidence of fact. They are not. *Astrophel and Stella* can tell us nothing about Philip and Penelope that we did not know already; but conversely there is much to be learned about these poems from the known facts of their lives.

There is no need again to quote the various contemporary allusions which show that Penelope Devereux was the model for Stella. The 'Rich' puns in the poems themselves prove this beyond a doubt, and if Sidney had wished to keep it secret for a time, by 1598 (when the thirty-seventh sonnet was first printed) it must have been well known. But if Lady Rich enjoyed the compliment of being portrayed in the most splendid love-poetry then written in English, neither she, nor Sidney's widow — by then married to Penelope's brother, the Earl of Essex — nor the poets who addressed her or her lover, were inclined to emphasize the biographical element in the poems. She had been Sidney's model, just as other women had sat to great artists, to Michelangelo or Raphael or Titian or Veronese. What the painters had made of the beauty of other women, Philip Sidney the poet had made of hers. He was not content with a portrait, and he was not attempting an allegory: he was inventing a tale of love, 'the argument cruel chastity, the Prologue hope, the Epilogue despair', as Nashe describes it. Cruel Chastity had been the argument of every other Petrarchan sequence, and Sidney is so far in the tradition. Here and there he takes an incident from his own life to invigorate the story: he remembers his first meeting with Penelope when she was a child; he describes a tournament in which he took part, probably in 1581; he refers to men's high hopes of him after his embassy to the Emperor Rudolph; he tells of seeing her pass by on the Thames, the wind ruffling her golden hair. Nor need we disbelieve this simply because Petrarch also saw Laura pass by in a boat on the Rhône: it is after all possible that both women did sometimes go by river, and that their poets saw them. But beyond a few poems we cannot claim with Charles Lamb, literally, that 'time and place appropriates every one of them'.

For what are the facts? In September 1576 Philip Sidney was in Ireland with his father, when he was summoned to the death-bed of Penelope Devereux' father, the Earl of Essex, in Dublin. Essex died before Sidney could reach him, but he left this message: 'Tell him I send him nothing, but I wish him well, and so well, that if God do move both their hearts, I wish that he might match with my daughter'. When her father died Penelope, whom Sidney must already have known, was about fourteen — Juliet's age; Sidney was twenty-one. The sophisticated and elegant youth, whose gifts and charm had already won him a Continental reputation, was unmoved by Penelope's childish beauty. In a sonnet he later regretted this arrogance, when he

> could not by rising Morn foresee
> How fair a day was near.

The recollection was actual, but the regret, surely, may be imaginary; for the imaginative response of a poet to an incident in his life is not necessarily immediate. The incident may be recollected in tranquillity and then invested with an emotional significance that is not autobiographical but dramatic.

As for Penelope herself, there is nothing to suggest that she was ever much moved towards Philip Sidney. She knew him well and must have delighted in his company and in the poems he wrote for her. She was hardly likely to be so naïve as to take them literally, as a declaration of Sidney's passion for her. A beautiful woman might pose for an artist who wished to paint a grand decorative design without being his mistress, and without any suggestion that he so desired her. Besides, already in her teens, before Sidney wrote these sonnets, she had pledged herself to the handsome and gallant Charles Blount, and to him, throughout the rest of her life, she remained passionately, defiantly faithful. She was married in 1581 to Lord Rich, but at the instance of her guardians and against her will. She even made her protest at the wedding ceremony itself. Her marriage lasted, nominally, until 1605 when Lord Rich divorced her, but in these years she had borne at least five children to Charles Blount. After her divorce, to the scandal of all who had so long condoned her adultery, she married him, by then created by James I Earl of Devonshire. She was of great and memorable beauty, with her golden hair and her black eyes; she was a headstrong, passionate, wilful woman, tender, loyal, and indiscreet. Doubtless it is not beyond the utmost of feminine caprice for the reluctant wife of one man, and the devoted mistress of another, to contemplate adultery with a third: but, as her conduct towards Charles Blount shows, Penelope was anything but capricious.

Too many readers of *Astrophel and Stella* have ignored the opening lines of the first sonnet in their haste to acclaim the Romantic enthusiasm of its last: 'Look in thy heart, and write'. Surely, they say, this is all we need to know: Sidney here proclaims that he is turning from literary tradition and precedent to that spontaneous overflow of powerful feelings which Wordsworth assures us is the spring of all poetry. But Sidney would have mocked at so crude a recipe for poetry: is a man then a poet if he knock his foot against a step, and curse? His feelings surely are powerful, and in that cursing and swearing that ensueth he alloweth them freely to overflow. For to Sidney a sonnet, like any other poem, was something constructed with skill and artifice. At the end of his *Apology for Poetry* he says to the Philistine, 'thus much curse I must send you in the behalf of all Poets, that while you live, you live in love, and never get favour for lacking skill of a Sonnet'. And as Professor Lewis has wisely observed: 'when a poet looks in his heart he finds many things there besides the actual. That is why, and how, he is a poet.'

What else then does Sidney say in this sonnet?

George Clifford, 3rd Earl of Cumberland, Queen's Champion, *c.* 1590, by Nicholas Hilliard (see p. 31)

15

Courtiers of Queen Elizabeth, attributed to Marcus Gheeraerts the Elder

Loving in truth, and fain in verse my love to show,
That she (dear she) might take some pleasure of my pain :
Pleasure might cause her read, reading might make her know,
Knowledge might pity win, and pity grace obtain,
I sought fit words to paint the blackest face of woe,
Studying inventions fine, her wits to entertain.

This is logical enough. Astrophel (not Sidney, but the lover whom he is imagining as the hero of his poems) proclaims his love, and says that he wishes to write verses about it in order that his lady might take pleasure in his melancholy, the mood then considered proper to lovers. She will read his verses for the pleasure they give, and so will learn of his suffering and come to pity him. This is the Horatian recipe for poetry, commonly accepted in the Renaissance, the combination of instruction with delight. Sidney, in a famous passage of the *Apology*, had emphasized the prime importance of delight, 'for who will be taught, if he be not moved with desire to be taught ?' If Stella is to be taught the truth of Astrophel's love she must be moved with pleasure in his verses. This is the argument, which is seemingly rejected in favour of a speaking from the heart : Stella, for all her literary tastes, is to love Astrophel for himself, not for his verses, as he loves her for herself alone.

Sidney is being far more subtle than at first appears. He is presenting Astrophel to us as the direct, manly lover, 'a fellow of plain and uncoined constancy'. He is none of your 'fellows of infinite tongue, that can rhyme themselves into ladies' favours', not one who seeks fame by his verses, nor who cares about their artistry except as a means to winning her. So does Sidney criticize contemporary love-poetry in the *Apology* :

'But truly many of such writings as come under the banner of unresistable love, if I were a Mistress, would never persuade me they were in love : so coldly they apply fiery speeches, as men that had rather read Lovers' writings, and so caught up certain swelling phrases, which hang together, like a man which once told me, the wind was at North West, and by South, because he would be sure to name winds enow, — than that in truth they feel those passions: which easily (as I think) may be bewrayed by that same forcibleness or *Energia* (as the Greeks call it) of the writer.'

In his own sonnets he achieves this forcibleness (it is perhaps their most outstanding quality) by portraying Astrophel and Stella enclosed within their own private world of passion, concerned only with their feelings for one another. But, simultaneously, throughout the sequence, we are aware of the sophisticated and learned poet, with his rhetoric and puns and metrical ingenuity — the poet whom Astrophel the lover deprecates. He is conscious of another audience than Stella, the Stella who must be assured that her lover cares nothing for Petrarch or for the fame of a poet. For him Stella is a cultivated lady of literary tastes, whose wits he must try to entertain, who is more moved by poetry than by life, who is so far from reserving his poems to herself that she sings and recites them to others.[1] She is part and representative of that audience of 'best wits' who delight in the poetry, and the skill of it, and who are not at all interested in its efficacy, in the success of Astrophel's wooing:

> Then think my dear, that you in me do read
> Of Lovers' ruin some sad Tragedy:
> I am not I, pity the tale of me.

This Stella is much closer to Penelope, who may well have sung Sidney's songs to their friends.

There are thus four characters in the poems, Astrophel and Philip, Stella and Penelope; and the elaborate counterpoint thereby effected provides the most intense enjoyment in their

[1] Byrd set the sixth song, which was published in *Psalms, Sonnets and Songs*, 1588, where he also includes two funeral songs for Sidney. He refers to Lady Rich in *Songs of Sundry Natures*, 1589. A setting of the eighth song by Charles Tessier was published in Robert Dowland's *A Musical Banquet*, 1610. This may well have been written long before, for in 1597 Tessier dedicated to Lady Rich *Le premier livre de Chansons et Airs de Court*, which, he said, were composed in England.

reading. Now and again the imaginary character and the actual meet and coincide and coalesce, but only to part once more. We cannot say, here, or here, Sidney is telling us of himself or of Lady Rich. No : the delight is in detecting the two themes running together, now divergent, now convergent. We may suppose that there was an especial pleasure for Penelope and the rest of Sidney's circle in noting those moments where Stella was recognizably Penelope, or where Astrophel did what Philip had lately done.

The Romantic insistence on 'Look in thy heart, and write' turns Sidney's poetry upside down. For this is the Muse's advice to Astrophel, not to Sidney : it is the poet Sidney addressing the character created out of his own vital imagination, recognizing that if his imagined lover is to be convincing to the poet's audience he must first be convincing to his own audience within the poem, to Stella. This he cannot be if he is for ever reminding her of poor Petrarch's long-deceased woes, of dictionaries' method, of an ambition to be known as a poet. The lover's ardour, not the poet's adornment of it, is what will move the lady (or so she believes) ; and she is more likely to be persuaded by his wooing if he is not all the time reminding her of his excellence as a poet, or of his hope to be remembered as one. So Astrophel never, like Daniel or Spenser or Shakespeare or the rest of the sonneteers, boasts that he will eternize the lady : he introduces no such irrelevance, knowing that if he is to win her he must convince her of the truth in the first song :

> To you, to you, all song of praise is due,
> Only in you my song begins and endeth.

She will not be complimented if she suspects that she is nothing more than the means to the fame of a poet. That was Penelope Rich's service to Philip Sidney when he took her as the model for Stella : but Stella, the character created from this model, is a child not of the brazen world of nature, but of the golden world of poetry.

There is a passage in the *Apology for Poetry* which has often been quoted in support of the Romantic interpretation of *Astrophel and Stella* as a poem about Sidney's love for Lady Rich and her response to him. Sidney has just been referring to his own unexpected reputation as a poet, and then says: 'Only, over-mastered by some thoughts, I yielded an inky tribute unto them'. But it is odd to take this not very serious statement as proof that Astrophel is a self-portrait. For one thing we cannot be certain that he is referring to the sonnet-sequence at all: he wrote the *Apology* before he wrote most of these poems, perhaps before he wrote any of them, so that the reference is much more likely to be to the poems inserted in the *Arcadia*. Then 'an inky tribute' is not quite the language that, say, Wordsworth would have used of the Lucy poems, or of *The Prelude*. And Sidney does not refer to feelings, or sensations, overmastering him, but to thoughts. If we look at the context of his remark we shall discover what these thoughts were: they were not about any woman, but about the state of English poetry at the time, and its disrepute. He had been thinking of this, and had very justly concluded that 'the very true cause of our wanting estimation is want of desert: taking upon us to be Poets in despite of Pallas'. The thoughts which had overmastered him and led him to write poetry were how to improve English poetry, how to make English poetry comparable to the Italian and French poetry that he had lately discovered during his Continental tour. He found contemporary English poetry feeble; he considered that this was due not so much to lack of talent as to lack of study, to the poets' writing 'in despite of Pallas'; and he determined to initiate, if he could, a revival of English poetry. But he rightly attempted this not by precept only, but by example, not merely by saying how poetry should be written, but by writing it.

Astrophel and Stella is his finest and most sustained poem, for it is a unity, not a collection of poems. In it, by his invention of Astrophel, he overcame that difficulty of the cold application of fiery speeches which he had derided ; but at the same time he exerted all the literary skill and ingenuity and learning which he, and every other poet of the Renaissance, thought essential to a work of art. Astrophel must eschew such things if Stella is not to suspect his sincerity. Sidney must use them if he is to delight his readers. In other words the poet, while using the Petrarchan tradition must pretend that he is not doing so.

Thus the scholars who have identified sources of Sidney's sonnets in Petrarch and Serafino and Pontano and the rest are proving only what every reasonable person already understood, that Sidney was literate, and that he wished to derive his own poetry from the great European tradition. Petrarch had set the fashion for writing poetry about individual human personality : truly he was both 'the first modern man', and the first modern poet. Inevitably, in bringing the New Poetry to England, Sidney followed Petrarch. But if it was Petrarchan for the poet to exploit his own personality in his poems, it was no less Petrarchan to adorn these poems with every rhetorical device, and conceit, and pun, and with a metrical variety that was refreshingly new. So we miss half the enjoyment of these poems if we fail to notice such things : if we scorn the eighty-ninth sonnet because the rhymes throughout are confined to the words 'night' and 'day' ; if we find the quadruple pun on 'touch' in the ninth sonnet tiresome, or the variations on the theme of a kiss in sonnets 73 to 83 tedious. The Elizabethan reader, who so much admired these poems, was both educated and alert, and he expected from poetry intellectual as well as emotional pleasures. He enjoyed being moved, but he also and at the same time enjoyed observing the skill that moved him. Sidney was 'the English Petrarch' : this implied the recognition in Sidney's poems not of the Petrarchan theme alone, but of the Petrarchan style and manner, even of conceits and phrases used by Petrarch. For just as the eighteenth-century man of taste liked to recognize in a country house both plan and detail derived from Palladio, so the sixteenth-century courtier enjoyed rediscovering in English a felicitous line which he too remembered from Petrarch. 'Petrarchan' or 'Palladian' are words that denote an instructed taste: if we take pleasure in a Palladian building or a Petrarchan sonnet we do so not for their intrinsic merit only, but because we have enjoyed the models from which they derive and are aware of these at the moment of looking or reading. It is therefore the business of a Burlington or a Sidney to remind us of Petrarch or Palladio.

Sidney's skill in the presentation of character, so elaborate in the *Arcadia*, is here in *Astrophel and Stella* exercised *in petto*. We are shown Astrophel in many moods, jealously scornful of Stella's husband; impatient at her coyness; laughing at her prim concern that he should take a virtuous course; resigned to humour her; irritated by her apparent preference for a lap-dog or a pet sparrow;[1] triumphant at length, and in imagination anticipating, as he rides down to her country house, the delights of her embraces; then finally rejected, and forced to be content with but an occasional glimpse of her; at the last, dismissed, and despairing. He is ardent or gentle, gay or despondent, reckless or remorseful as the situation changes. He laughs and weeps, grumbles, teases, cajoles, pleads, insists, threatens. He is vigorous and varied, skilled in the accomplishments of a courtier, humorous, witty, able (sometimes) to laugh at himself, of great charm. In a word, he is such a man as Mercutio would have approved, or as Sidney was.

Stella shares Penelope's unusual beauty. She is not unlike Petrarch's Laura, but then it is within the bounds of possibility that two women might, after the passage of time, and making

[1] Serafino's mistress also had a lap-dog, and Catullus' Lesbia a sparrow, which died. But I cannot see that this is a reason for saying that no other ladies, real or imaginary, could keep pets without plagiarism. Perhaps Serafino and Catullus merely suggested to Sidney that they were worth writing about.

allowance for poetic imagination, be of similar stature and complexion. She is, or to Astrophel seems to be, more concerned with his good name than her own ; she is angry when he steals a kiss as she lies sleeping ; she gives him, all through, very little encouragement, and in the end rejects him, but with such exquisite tenderness that we know she too is heart-broken. She is, except in appearance, not very much like Penelope, being closer to Philoclea than to Pamela ; closer, perhaps, to Frances Walsingham, whom Sidney married.

Spenser, in his elegy *Astrophel*, which he dedicated to her, made this equation : he would hardly have done so had he identified Stella with Penelope. But we need not deduce that Spenser in Ireland was ignorant of the facts. He did not confuse fact with fiction : that is all. He recognized Stella as the name of the woman whom Astrophel loved, but so far as Sidney's poem was concerned, did not trouble about any identification. When he came to write his pastoral elegy he used the name Astrophel, naturally enough, and here he was equating Astrophel with Sidney. Therefore, if he referred to Sidney's widow, he must refer to her as Stella. It is clear that in Sidney's sonnet sequence Spenser took Astrophel and Stella to be imaginary characters. So it is with the other poets who wrote of Sidney, or who addressed poems to Lady Rich or Charles Blount : not one of them read Sidney's poems as mere self-revelation.

They would not have expected such a motive in a poet. They would have thought that Sidney, as they, intended to write good poems, to shape each sonnet and modulate each song with the greatest skill he had. They were led, by the publication of *Astrophel and Stella*, to try to emulate him, and Newman's inadequate editions let loose the flood of sonnets in the last years of the century. Its example was in one respect unfortunate, for, because Newman had placed all the songs at the end of the sonnets instead of interspersed among them, the English poets took a sonnet sequence to be a sequence of sonnets alone. But one of the chief delights of Petrarch's two sequences had been the metrical variety introduced in *ballata*, *sestina*, *canzone*, and madrigal. When, in 1598, Sidney's poems were correctly arranged it was easy to see how much the sequence gained by the insertion of the songs. *Hamlet* would not be improved by extracting the songs from their contexts and printing them at the end: but Sidney uses the songs in his sequence as Shakespeare uses his songs, briefly to interrupt the development of the plot and so to precipitate, in crystalline clarity, the mood, the emotional tone of that moment. In three of the songs (the third, eighth, and eleventh) he also continues the narrative; and in the eighth song is reached the dramatic climax of the whole sequence.

The story of Astrophel and Stella moves slowly at first, and in the opening section, which comprises the first thirty-two sonnets, there is much of Virtue and Love and Reason. For Love, no less than poetry, must be approved on rational grounds as something natural, in accordance with the divine order. These poems are full of conceits, of classical reference and allusion, even if these things are used only to be rejected by Astrophel. But Astrophel's rejection of these irrelevances does not mean that Sidney disparages them, or that his audience should pass them over. There is the formal, logical pattern of sonnet 5 to be enjoyed: 'It is most true . . .', 'It is most true . . .', 'True . . .', 'true . . .', 'True, and yet true . . .'. In the seventh sonnet the paradox of black beauty (a favourite theme for centuries before Sidney, and for long after) is adapted in praise of Stella's black eyes. The puns on 'touch' in the ninth sonnet seemed 'horrible' to Sidney's best editor, but to the contemporaries of Shakespeare, for whom 'a quibble was the fatal Cleopatra for which he lost the world, and was content to lose it', their ingenuity would have provoked applause. Heraldic blazoning is imposed upon classical myth (13), metaphor is drawn from architecture (9), accountancy (18), astrology (26), or campaigning (29); Sidney is as much at home in conceits about Cupid's bow (19) or his dislike of cold North climes (8), as he is in references to the contemporary political situation (30), to his own disappointing career (21), or to the poetry of the time (6). Sidney would not have thought any one of these methods preferable to another : he was using all the literary techniques of which he was a master, but using them to show Astrophel, the lover, rejecting them in his addresses to Stella. To say that they were irrelevant to Astrophel was another way of saying that autobiography was irrelevant to the poetry : for Astrophel's audience was Stella. If Sidney, in the character of Astrophel, had actually been addressing Penelope, as Stella, then, presumably, he would have eschewed all this elaboration, and would have written directly, as Astrophel speaks.

The last sonnet in this first section recurs to the 'Look in thy heart, and write' of the first. Astrophel addresses Morpheus 'the lively son of deadly sleep', whose reply recalls, as it must be intended to recall, the Muses' earlier advice :

> Fool, answers he, no *Indes* such treasures hold,
> But from thy heart, while my sire charmeth thee,
> Sweet *Stella's* image I do steal to me.

By now the character of Astrophel is firmly established in the reader's mind, and the tale of his love for Stella can be told.

The second section of the sequence now begins, with the thirty-third sonnet, and ends with the sixty-third. In it we see the progress of Astrophel's love from the first despairing cry of self-rebuke, when he remembers his blindness to Stella's childish beauty, through the discovery of some kindness in her, to the first signs of a real response to his courtship.

In the thirty-third sonnet Astrophel speaks out as he has not done till now, and recalls his first meeting with Stella in terms which (as I have said) clearly enough suggest Sidney's recollection of first meeting Penelope Devereux when she was a child. The vivid, colloquial directness of this sonnet is achieved by the means which, in the earlier sonnets, Astrophel had said were unnecessary :

> I might, unhappy word, O me, I might.

We, vaguely, commend the colloquial impression which the line makes. An Elizabethan critic would have been more precise : he would have noted here both *epanalepsis* and *aposiopesis*, as in the sixth to eighth lines he would have delighted in the figure *expeditio*, and so on. Even before *Astrophel and Stella* was published Abraham Fraunce had used passages from it to illustrate the rhetorical figures, among them the two which I have noted in the first line of this sonnet. Now the fact that Elizabethan critics commented on the poetry of the time in this way, by reference to the rules of rhetoric, does not mean that we must do so. We, as they, remark the effect, but are content with this : their rationalism made them also note the cause. Their enjoyment of the poetry was not necessarily more intense than ours, only more intelligent. In the same way a highly trained musician will get a more sophisticated enjoyment out of listening to a fugue than will the ordinary, untrained listener. He may not be more moved by it, but he will have in addition an intellectual appreciation of the means to that end, of the skill that moves him.

I know that it is in vain to try to persuade a twentieth-century reader that there is more than pedantry in Elizabethan rhetoric. Yet, look again at the thirty-ninth sonnet which is, I suppose, one of the best known and most often quoted : deservedly so. But how many of those who read it in anthologies notice the craftsmanship that has gone to its making — the balancing pairs of similes in the second and third lines, that are rounded off by filling the whole of the fourth line with one simile ; the unemphatic alliteration ; the suspense created at the eighth line, where the tribute to be paid is suggested, only to be disclosed in the final line? Then 'sweetest bed' I have heard criticized as a weak phrase : but surely the reference is to lavendered sheets. And some readers resent Grosart's observation that 'a rosy garland' owes something to the proverbial *sub rosa* — as if prettiness alone were enough. Or the casual, off-hand rhythm of the eighth line may be regarded as a blemish, as if Sidney had not contrived and intended it to contrast with the regular beat of the stately opening. This device, of suddenly moving from the formal to the colloquial is very characteristic of *Astrophel and Stella*: it had already appeared in the first sonnet where, as here, it suggests the vigorous, forthright Astrophel who speaks to Stella plain soldier.

So again in the virile, grumbling first line of the next sonnet:

> As good to write as for to lie and groan,

— and then the proud yet humble appeal to Stella not to destroy one who is none of the basest. After this comes the magnificent sonnet on the tournament, very probably that which took place before the French Ambassadors in 1581. Sidney himself certainly took part in that Whitsun tournament as one of the four Foster Children of Desire who were to lay siege to the Fortress of Beauty where Queen Elizabeth was enthroned. Sidney, we are told, 'proceeded in very sumptuous manner, with armour part blue, and the rest gilt and ingraven, with four spare horses, having caparisons and furniture very rich and costly, as some of cloth of gold embroidered with pearl, and some embroidered with gold and silver feathers, very richly and cunningly wrought: he had four pages that rode on his four spare horses, who had cassock coats, and Venetian hose of all cloth of silver, laid with gold lace, and hats of the same with gold bands and white feathers, and each one a pair of white buskins. Then had he a thirty gentlemen and yeomen, and four trumpeters, who were all in cassock coats and Venetian hose of yellow velvet, laid with silver lace, yellow velvet caps with silver bands and white feathers, and every one a pair of white buskins; and they had upon their coats, a scroll or band of silver, which came scarf-wise over the shoulder, and so down under the arm, with this poesy, or sentence, written upon it, both before and behind, *Sic nos non nobis.*'

This glimpse of Sidney, resplendent on a ceremonial occasion, is suggestive of Elizabethan taste ; for it would not be more crude to suppose that Sidney's presence at this tournament was evidence of his passion for Elizabeth, than it is to take his sonnet as proof that he was in love with Penelope. Also the language of compliment, whether to a Queen or to a mistress, must always be ceremonious, within an accepted convention which is as well known to the lady who receives the compliment as to her courtier or her lover. All this gives no reason for refusing to allow the imaginary Astrophel to take part in a tournament : it is very much in character, for him as for Sidney. This was one of Charles Lamb's favourite sonnets, and no wonder ; for Sidney has given such immediacy to his description of the tournament, and the chatter among the spectators, that he truly persuades us that he is talking about himself. So, no doubt, he is, but only in order to tell us more about Astrophel.

He can achieve this same illusion that we are actually present at the moment he describes when we have no reason to suppose that he is reporting personal experience. It is a quality of his imagination, this vivid clarity and power. So, when Astrophel begins to resent his slavery to Stella, in the forty-seventh sonnet, he is ready to dismiss her from his mind, until, suddenly, she herself appears, and his resolution hardly survives the uttering of a brief denial.

> Let her go : soft, but here she comes. 'Go to,
> Unkind, I love you not.' O me, that eye
> Doth make my heart give to my tongue the lie.

Yet it is characteristic of the Elizabethan appreciation of poetry that these very lines are chosen by Abraham Fraunce along with precedents from Homer and Virgil as an example of the figure *aposiopesis*. He might also have taken the preceding lines,

> I may, I must, I can, I will, I do
> Leave following that which it is gain to miss,

as an equally good example of *auxesis*, for such they are. The point is simply this: that Sidney's most lively colloquial effects are as much the result of his training in rhetoric as are the most formal and apparent conceits. For he had observed that English poets had failed because they had been so presumptuous as to attempt to write poetry 'in despite of Pallas', without studying the great poets of other literatures, and he therefore made no such mistake himself. (E. K. in his introduction to Spenser's *Shepheardes Calender* had already made a similar criticism of Gascoigne. Men who thought of poetry as an intellectual pleasure rather than as a glandular secretion were certain to emphasize the need for learning.) Energy, forcibleness, was the quality that Sidney missed in the love-poetry of his contemporaries, and that he sought in his own. But, whatever Astrophel may have told Stella, this was not achieved through some unconsidered inspiration, without taking thought. Or are we to accept whatever any character in a poem or a play may say about poetry as the author's opinion? Is the poet bound to speak in his own person whenever he refers to his art, and only then inevitably to fail in dramatic presentation of character?

When I attribute Sidney's most memorable effects to his training in rhetoric I mean nothing recondite or perplexing, but only that he was drawing on his knowledge of good writers of the past to improve his own writing. For the rules of rhetoric were derived from observed instances: if you were moved to pleasure by a passage in Virgil or Cicero you very sensibly inquired how it was done. The rhetoricians classified these literary effects by a study of the means, and though the names may smack of pedantry the study itself was of inestimable profit to the New Poets. Therefore when Sidney criticizes his contemporaries for coldly applying fiery speeches he is criticizing not their lack of inspiration, but their lack of learning. They were merely imitating effects noticed in Petrarch without a true understanding of their causes, as if an architect were to attempt to build a house by observation of the outside, and without any knowledge of stress and thrust. To the men of the Renaissance the world was harmonious and ordered, the creation of a rational intelligence, and therefore comprehensible to reason. Even in poetry, though some initial divine gift was prerequisite, it could and must be developed by a rational process, by thinking how to write well, and by noting how others had done so. There is no mystery in rhetoric : it is no more than a code of rules for intelligent reading, especially designed for those who wish to write well. It is as important, and as dull, as grammar, and, as with grammar, its rules are only truly known when they have already been forgotten. Sidney no more said to himself when composing a sonnet : 'Now for an *epanalepsis*', or 'This is the moment for a *prosopopoeia*', than we say 'Here I must use the possessive pronoun', or 'At last, the chance for a conditional clause'.

To the rules of grammar which we all still learn as children Sidney appeals with a gay flippancy in the sonnet that ends the second section of his sequence. Stella had refused his advances with 'No, no !' which he takes to mean 'Yes',

> For Grammar says (to Grammar who says nay)
> That in one speech two Negatives affirm.

There follows a pause marked by the first song, with its assurance that Stella alone is Astrophel's concern, although in two recent sonnets he had referred to her singing his poems, or reading them to him. In this song then he is once again promising her that he is intent on winning her, not on the pleasures of poetry : that she is to treat Astrophel's addresses to her as serious, not as the expected accomplishment of a courtier. He had even dared to recount the Courtly nymphs' disparagement of him as a lover because he did not behave with the fashionable sentimentality. He is to convince Stella by the candour of his passion, not by its conventional refinement.

When the final section of the sequence begins, at the sixty-fourth sonnet, immediately this seriousness is emphasized; and so the mood remains as the story of Astrophel's love passes now from hope to the verge of fulfilment only to end in despair. For five sonnets Astrophel hopes that Stella's new, tentative kindness may lead to her yielding; and then in the sixty-ninth sonnet she seems at last to yield, even if on conditions. The poetry conveys most movingly the immediate response of one who has at last been released from his bonds:

> Gone is the winter of my misery,
> My spring appears, O see what here doth grow.

His triumphant joy brings forth the trumpet-call of

> I, I, O I, may say that she is mine.

And then, with that ironical self-observation which is so frequent in Renaissance poetry, he ends the poem with a reference to Stella's prim insistence that Astrophel must still take a virtuous course, so that we can almost see him shrug his shoulders:

> No kings be crowned, but they some covenants make.

The urbanity of that line lightens the tension of the whole sonnet, turning what might have seemed bombast into the eloquence of a joyful heart.

Astrophel has not yet received the reward for his constancy, and for three sonnets his mood is one of impatience, with typically frank admissions of desire for the woman whom he loves. This passage is interrupted by the second song, where Astrophel finds Stella sleeping and wonders whether he dare kiss her. He does; she awakes and scolds him (as he expected) but her anger only delights him. The kiss, so long wished for, is celebrated in seven of the next ten sonnets, now in Sidney's most elaborate style, now in his most colloquial ; now with a cool savouring of his delight, now with ardent longing for its renewal. In the seventy-ninth sonnet he parodies the sugared style affected by some of the French sonneteers :

> Sweet kiss, thy sweets I fain would sweetly endite
> Which even of sweetness sweetest sweetener art.

In the eighty-third Astrophel pretends jealousy of Stella's pet sparrow, which she owned (no doubt) because Catullus' Lesbia had, but also because the familiar 'Philip Sparrow' gave Astrophel an opportunity to refer to his 'good brother Philip'. And we are not sure whether Astrophel was thinking more of Stella's sparrow or of Philip Sidney, whether he was threatening pet or poet, for either might well stand between him and Stella. This gay, delightful poem very well illustrates the complexity of them all : the more we think about it the more we are aware of the interplay between Astrophel and Philip, Stella and Penelope.

The third song follows, to make another interlude ; and then come two sonnets describing a visit to Stella in the country, a visit on which Astrophel clearly hoped to remedy the defect which he had just observed in Stella's husband, that he 'wanted horns'.[1] But it was not to be ; and in the fourth song which follows Sidney shapes one of his most perfect lyrics about the very words of Stella's refusal :

> No, no, no, no, my dear, let be.

Again, the immediacy of this is derived not from mere reporting of what Penelope said one evening in 1582, but from literary skill and observation. There was 'a Neapolitan song, which beginneth : *No, no, no, no*' to whose tune Sidney wrote

[1] It is to be noted that in this sonnet (78) there is no pun on the name Rich ; for the more vividly Stella is presented to the reader the less is she to be identified with Lady Rich.

another song, and that, surely, for this occasion also, prompted his Muse.

One lamenting sonnet,

> Alas, whence came this change of looks ?

is followed by a group of five songs ; and it is in the eighth song that the climax of the whole story is told, with such snail-horn delicacy of feeling, such imaginative perception of Stella's own tenderness, that you must indeed be of an earth-creeping mind if you do not recognize in it one of the supreme achievements of English lyric. In its context especially it gains by contrast with the crude jealousy of the seventy-eighth sonnet, and the impatient lasciviousness of the eighty-fourth and eighty-fifth. It blends, as Sidney at his best always blends, the colloquial and the ornate, wit and feeling. The song seems at once an idyllic conversation and the record of natural talk, combining the polished wit of

> Their eyes by love directed
> Interchangeably reflected,

with the dramatic vividness of these broken lines :

> Grant, O grant, but speech alas,
> Fails me, fearing on to pass,
> Grant, O me, what am I saying ?
> But no fault there is in praying.

An Elizabethan reader, while being not less moved than ourselves by such lines, would also have rejoiced in the skill which had contrived them so to move him. He would have noted the metre of this poem, alternating couplets in masculine and feminine rhyme, and he would probably have recognized that this too, like the compound epithet, was a new device introduced by Sir Philip from France. He would have remarked the pathos achieved by this metre, as in the last stanza, where it is not at all obscured, but rather enhanced, by the wit of the final line, when the poet suddenly stands aside and observes his work.

Therewithal away she went,
Leaving him so passion-rent
With what she had done and spoken,
That therewith my song is broken.

But latterly no one seems to have noticed the deliberate contrast of pronouns in this stanza : Stella has left Astrophel so passion-rent that therewith Philip Sidney's song is broken.

The last song of this lyrical interlude is a pastoral lament,

Stella hath refused me,

by which the tension is slackened, and the personal grief thrust off in a more impersonal portraying of it. This impersonal art is nowhere better shown than in the eighty-ninth sonnet, the third in a group of six on his absence from Stella. This is the sonnet in which there are only the two rhyme-words, 'night' and 'day'. Sidney uses this device, which nowadays might seem as irrelevant as an acrostic, to convey the tedium of Astrophel's life without Stella. Mere monotony is avoided by changing the pattern of rhyme from night-day-day-night in the octave to night-day-night-day in the sestet.

Immediately after this very formal poem Astrophel again disclaims any poetic ambition, and reverts to the more colloquial and direct. The tenth song, with its reference to Astrophel's 'greedy licorous senses' continues, and concludes, this temper.

For twelve sonnets Astrophel laments his absence from Stella, and instead of kisses the theme now is tears and sighs and sleepless nights. A lady seeks to comfort him ; he hears that Stella is ill ; he sees her passing by on the Thames ; he overhears gossip about himself. Then, in the eleventh and last song, a sad and melancholy serenade is fashioned, as so often by Sidney, out of the tones of conversation. This brief, forlorn appeal to Stella at her window fixes the final mood of despair. Contrast this poem with the fourth song : in both Stella refuses Astrophel. There, Astrophel was at first full of joy and confidence, close to Stella in the moonlit night, whispering his invitation to her, gaily assuring her that they will not be disturbed, and then, quite suddenly, brought to the blackest despair by her persistent refusal of him, which he had not at all expected. Here Stella is the first to speak, and she is dominant and abrupt in her dismissal of her dispirited lover, who no longer expects from her any other answer than 'No'. To this theme the last four sonnets are given, the Epilogue (as Nashe had said) Despair.

Such then is Sir Philip Sidney's *Astrophel and Stella*, whose publication led to the sonneteering of the 1590s. The fame of these poems derived principally not from the fame of their author but from their own varied excellence, which I have tried to denote. They very well suited, and indeed helped to shape, Elizabethan taste. For the sonnet can be defined only by its form, and it therefore provided, like fugue or sonata, an accepted mould in which the poet could exhibit his technical mastery. It was a challenge, or an invitation, to every aspiring poet, and there is nothing more absurd than to complain that many Elizabethan sonnets are mere literary exercises : a man is not to be reprehended for exercising literary skill if he is a poet. In the best of the sonnets, as in Sidney's, there is far more than that, certainly : the skill should be exercised to some purpose. But this element of virtuosity is always present, and sometimes it is present alone. We should hesitate to reject any work of art, whether a poem, or a sonata, or a jewel, or a palace, because there is nothing to it but the skill that went to its making. This is what the Elizabethan sonneteer was trying to do : to make an object of a particular kind, and make it well. To fall in love, to be led towards hope, and to be rejected is a not uncommon sequence of misfortune which has been described by very many poets. Those whom we still read are those who, like Petrarch or Sidney, have matched their insight with a perfection of form. For it is not so much what a poet says but rather how he says it that makes him to be remembered.

The question of sincerity, once much bandied about, is therefore beside the mark, as Giles Fletcher pointed out in the dedication of his sonnet sequence, *Licia* : 'A man may write of Love and not be in love ; as well as of husbandry and not go to the plough ; or of witches and be none ; or of holiness and be flat profane'. The Elizabethan reader did not consider every poem with a naïve literalness : he allowed for the creative power of imagination. Besides, he was sensible enough to understand that when we read love-poems we read them to illuminate our own experience of love, not to pry into someone else's. We are all of us, I trust, far more interested in our own lives than in Philip Sidney's or Penelope Rich's — even supposing that had been Sidney's subject. It does not matter in the least whether we can identify Stella, or Licia, or Delia, or Cynthia : what does matter is that we should be able to transfer the lines to ourselves, thereby to enlarge our imaginative understanding ; and that we should appreciate elegant phrasing or recondite wit, subtlety of metre, and vitality of metaphor. The poet — we have it on the best authority — the poet gives to airy nothing a local habitation and a name : to airy *nothing*, not to solid self.

'Shakespeare', said Dr Johnson, 'seems to write without any moral purpose.' The sonnet was a means, perhaps the principal means, to this emancipation. For the Elizabethans quickly forsook the older insistence on didacticism and developed a highly sophisticated taste for the refined pleasures of poetry. Astrophel's persuasiveness is not severely moral : he is impatient of Stella's demure restraint. Sidney ensures that while in imagination we share the emotional experience of the lovers our intelligence is diverted and delighted by the skill of the poet. *Astrophel and Stella* is thus the strongest assertion of the claims of the New Poetry. It set a fashion for the poets, and largely determined the taste of the generation of Shakespeare.

SHAKESPEARE: *VENUS AND ADONIS*

SHAKESPEARE'S first published work, *Venus and Adonis*, was more popular with contemporary readers than anything else that he wrote. However much his plays were enjoyed on the stage men preferred until long afterwards to see them rather than to read them in private; but his poems were read and re-read. By the time of Shakespeare's death *Venus and Adonis* had gone through some ten editions, and another half-dozen followed in the next twenty years. Marlowe's *Hero and Leander* was scarcely less popular, and the two poems were not seldom named together, as they are by Harebrain in Middleton's play *A Mad World My Masters*: they were 'two luscious marrow-bone pies for a young married wife' and therefore (thought Harebrain) to be conveyed away from her.

But if an Ovidian sensuality attracted readers to these poems, there was certainly something more, just as there is more, far more, to Ovid himself. There is sophisticated wit and brilliant craftsmanship, vivid metaphor and polished metre —'the elegancy, facility, and golden cadence of poetry'— all things very much to the taste of the more serious readers of the time, who would not have been much stirred by mere sensuality. (That, if they wished, they could find in many other poems which never attained the popularity of *Venus and Adonis*.) Clearly it is not enough to explain the success of Shakespeare's poem in the sixteenth century as we might account for the sales of a Sunday newspaper in the twentieth.

Nearly thirty years had passed since Arthur Golding produced his translation of Ovid's *Metamorphoses*. Here, like the mediaeval writers, Golding tried to make Ovid respectable by interpreting his stories allegorically. In 1589 Thomas Lodge had for the first time, in his *Scilla's Metamorphosis*, treated a story of this kind (at least in part) other than allegorically, by concentrating on the pleasurable elements, and by writing without any moral tendentiousness. As on other occasions, Lodge had shown the way to poets greater than himself, and both Marlowe and Shakespeare followed with their Ovidian poems in 1593, poems which were as emancipated as the sonnets from any concern with instruction, and which had as their only purpose to delight the reader.

For us there can be no question which is the better poem. Hero and Leander are creatures from a mythical world in whom we can believe without hesitation : magnificent nude figures painted with all the decorative richness of a Veronese. By comparison Shakespeare's poem is coarse and provincial. Venus, the Goddess of Beauty, has grown buxom, and blowzy. Adonis is a gauche young bumpkin embarrassed to find himself alone with an amorous lady of the Court. They are made too human, without being wholly human, so that the reader is uncomfortably stranded between two worlds, the human world of the plays, and the world of myth. We are told that Adonis is transformed into a flower, and we refuse to believe it ; we are not envious, as we should be, when he lies in the arms of the Queen of Love. Venus' lust is offensive and stifling. She threatens to smother the boy with kisses, plucks him from his horse, and marches off with him under her arm. This suggests not the dalliance of the gods, but the copulation of spiders. Venus sweats, her face doth reek and smoke, her blood doth boil ; Adonis is entangled in her arms like a bird in a net ; when she kisses him her action is like that of an eagle tearing its food. No wonder Adonis was discouraged. And the only excuse he can think of to escape from her is to say that he is getting sunburnt.

This unpleasing picture of mature female lechery preying on youthful male coyness is contrasted with the normal relation of the sexes in the episode of the stallion and the breeding jennet. Adonis springs from Venus' twining arms, and similarly his courser breaks the reins that tie him to a tree: but the stallion breaks away to go to the jennet, whereas Adonis breaks loose to escape from Venus. The stallion's

> eye which scornfully glisters like fire
> Shows his hot courage and his high desire;

but Adonis' scorn of Venus shows just the opposite. The stallion, nervous, excited, and boisterous, offers his love to the coy, reluctant jennet, who at first 'being proud, as females are' spurns him. Then she grows kinder, and 'unto the wood they hie them'. The rôle of the two sexes is here natural, in accordance with the divine order on which Shakespeare so often and so devotedly insists: it is very different from the abnormal, unnatural, and disgusting passion of Venus for Adonis, who is more feminine, both in appearance and in behaviour than she. Adonis is a 'stain to all nymphs'; Venus' tears must quench 'the maiden burning of his cheeks' which are tenderer than her tender hand that feels them. His ear is pretty, his hand lily-white, his bosom soft, his complexion white and red, like a girl's, so that when Nature made him she was with herself at strife. An anonymous satirist in 1620 made a revealing comment on the reversal of the rôle of the sexes in the poem: 'Goodness leave me, if I have not heard a man court his mistress with the same words that Venus did Adonis, or as near as the book could instruct him'. Adonis' horse, on the other hand, is a superb male animal which

> as he should,
> Welcomes the warm approach of sweet desire.

For Shakespeare this Greek tale of the love of a goddess for a mortal could not remain in the world of myth to which it belongs. Shakespeare's imagination, unlimited in its human understanding, intruded into the supernatural only among witches, ghosts, and fairies, creatures beneath, not above, the dignity of human beings. Whatever his private beliefs may have been, for the dramatist, necessarily, 'our little life is rounded with a sleep'. *Venus and Adonis* suffers therefore from the defects of Shakespeare's supreme qualities as a dramatist. For the story he has to tell he makes his characters too human, and too dramatic: he thinks of Venus only as more powerful than Adonis, when he should describe her as more divine; they are not enough idealized; and they talk too much.

But when all this has been said, the poem remains unsurpassed among its kind except by Marlowe's, and for twenty or thirty years it continued to please the cultivated audience for which it was written. Already, within a few years of its publication, Gabriel Harvey tells us that 'the younger sort takes much delight in *Venus and Adonis*', and both the regularity with which it was reprinted, and the paucity of copies that survive, show how much it was read. For the thumbed and dog-eared octavos, not the tall clean folios indicate a book's success. The book that a man carries with him and thrusts away into his pocket is the book that he takes pleasure in, not the handsome volume left on the seat in a window's bay for guests to glance through.

The 'younger sort', the Earl of Southampton and his friends, would have been interested in the abnormal love-story simply because it was abnormal, in reaction against the popular taste which, about the same time, was acclaiming *Romeo and Juliet*.[1] It is characteristic of an intelligentsia to show its contempt for usual contemporary taste by preferring the opposite. So Donne's flouting of decorum would have been pointless if decorum had not been the principle governing accepted good taste in his day. (Max Beerbohm took the process one stage further, mocking the sophisticated self-consciousness of Bloomsbury by associating himself with those

[1] In other verse tales of the time the rôle of the sexes is reversed: Drayton's *Endimion and Phoebe*, 1595; Thomas Edwards' *Cephalus and Procris*, 1595, which also contained his version of the story of *Narcissus*; Thomas Heywood's *Oenone and Paris*, 1595.

whom the highbrows contemned: going out to buy an Old Carthusian tie, and wearing it defiantly.) Shakespeare was trying to satisfy the taste of his new and powerful friends before he was quite mature enough to do so: he was sensitive to their preferences, but had not altogether suppressed his own. His detachment, 'the utter *aloofness* of the poet's own feelings from those of which he is at once the painter and the analyst', is, as Coleridge saw, certain promise that here was a poet of rare gifts; and Shakespeare's first readers also would have noted this. Yet I doubt whether the natural description in the poem, which especially delights us nowadays because it seems so personal to Shakespeare, much interested them. They would be more likely to observe that the violets on which Venus leant were described with an epithet customarily given to a woman's breasts, blue-veined, than to delight in the vivid picture of the dive-dapper. They might compare the divine lightness of Venus' footstep,

> The grass stoops not, she treads on it so light,

to a similar lightness of Flora's step in Botticelli's *Primavera*. For, unlike Hazlitt, they would have welcomed Shakespeare's 'strange attempt to substitute the language of painting for that of poetry', since the Plutarchan tag about poetry being a speaking picture was ever ready on their lips as they paraded through the gorgeous galleries of decorative poetry which they so much enjoyed. Shakespeare may have read Lodovico Dolce's letter on Titian's *Venus and Adonis*, which had been sent to Philip II of Spain in London in September 1554. It was one of the paintings which Titian called a *poesia*.

Spenser himself had treated the story of Venus and Adonis, as a tapestry, hung in his Castle Joyeous:

> The wals were round about apparelled
> With costly clothes of Arras and of Toure,
> In which with cunning hand was pourtrahed
> The love of Venus and her Paramoure
> The fayre Adonis, turned to a flowre.

Nor do we for a moment hesitate to accept this metamorphosis in Spenser's telling of the story. For here Venus is tender of heart, Adonis not actively reluctant, but merely heedless. She is not predatory as in Shakespeare, but infinitely gentle : not a muscular woman pinning down the unlucky Adonis by the strength of her arms, or heaving up his hat, but quietly crowning him with flowery garlands, bathing his eyes with ambrosial kisses, sprinkling him with nectar, and finally, by her own divine gift, changing him into a flower. She is a goddess still and he an inhabitant of a mythical world where transformation into a flower after death is appropriate and credible. For this, not only is Shakespeare's Adonis too human, but his flowers are too flower-like. Adonis is a lad from a Warwickshire village, and the flowers on which Venus lies were but lately flowering in a woodland near his home, so that we do not believe that the one can be changed into the other. But Southampton and his like, valuing natural description much less than we do, may not have been troubled at this, and would perhaps more easily have accepted the metamorphosis, because they knew that this was the end of the story.

Shakespeare does not, like Spenser, tell us that Venus brought about the transformation : it merely happened, 'and in his blood . . . a purple flower sprung up'. He does not show us the process, the gradual development, as Ovid does : he has no wish to emphasize the grotesque, though the grotesque was very much to the taste of his age. This element in his story did not much interest him, as it interested Pollaiuolo and Giulio Romano and Bernini. His realization of human personality and his descriptions of flowers and foliage were too vivid and precise for him to be able to merge the one into the other. His language is pictorial, adjectival, static, not verbal and rapid as in Greek poetry or in Shelley's. It is inept to the making of myth.

Marlowe suitably decorates his poem with reminiscence of

classical legend: in describing Hero and Leander in the opening lines he refers to Apollo, to this story of Venus and Adonis, to Cupid, to the Voyage of the Argonauts, to Endymion and Phoebe, to Circe, Jupiter and Ganymede, Pelops, Hippolytus. His ornament is learned and decorous. Shakespeare's romantic observation of the country scene delights us, but it is out of keeping with his theme, rustic and irrelevant. As Hazlitt says, 'his images do not blend with the poem, but seem stuck upon it', so that, however delightful in themselves, they neither enlarge his characters nor advance his story. To admire these passages beyond all else in the poem, as we do, would have seemed to Shakespeare's contemporaries like botanizing in Giorgione's *La Tempesta.* We may take pleasure in identifying Giorgione's vegetation, or we may remember the dabchick, and poor Wat, and the mounting lark, and the snail in his shelly cave; but, if this is all, we have by no means appreciated either picture or poem.

When Shakespeare attempts to be learned like Marlowe, he is not very clever. His treatment of the traditional set-piece of the Banquet of Sense is perfunctory: it was expected of him, but he did not take much trouble over it. Ficino, in his commentary on Plato's *Banquet* (*Symposium*) had arranged the five senses in order, below the power of reason: sight, hearing, smell, taste, touch. Touch was the most earthly of the five, because it depended most on physical contact. Sight was the most spiritual, because no physical contact was necessary. The senses were regarded by Ficino as steps on the ladder to rational apprehension. Two years after the publication of *Venus and Adonis* Chapman brought out his *Ovid's Banquet of Sense*, a poem which can be read as an adverse commentary on Shakespeare's poem.[1] It is notoriously obscure and difficult, even

[1] In his *Hymnus in Cynthiam* (1594) there is already a derogatory reference to *Venus and Adonis*:

> Presume not then ye flesh-confounded souls,
> That cannot bear the full Castalian bowls,
> Which sever mounting spirits from the senses,
> To look in this deep fount for thy pretences.

among Chapman's works, but it is capable of interpretation. Chapman at least provides an Argument, in which he informs the reader that Ovid, newly enamoured of (Augustus' daughter) Julia, whom he calls Corinna, is led on from hearing her singing to the lute, through the senses of smell, sight, and taste, 'to entreaty for the fifth sense and there is interrupted'. This scheme, which is the Ficinian scheme used by Shakespeare, is mixed up in Chapman's poem with another, that of the Five Lines of Love, and there is a counterpoint between the two motifs. This second scheme derives from Donatus' commentary on a passage in Terence's *Eunuchus*: 'Quinque lineae perfectae sunt ad amorem: prima visus; secunda loqui; tertia tactus; quarta osculari; quinta coitus'; sight, conversation, touching, kissing, coition. In the poem Ovid sophistically defends the banquet of the senses (which is implicitly opposed to the Platonic, or Ficinian, scheme) for its own sake. He uses much learning to prove that the progress of love is, so to say, down the ladder. But surely Chapman is being ironical: his poem is as much a rejection of erotic poetry, whether or not he was especially thinking of *Venus and Adonis*, as his continuation of *Hero and Leander* is a rejection of Marlowe's sensuous opening, 'taking up that magical poem and putting it into a bodice and skirt', as Katherine Mansfield said.[1] This interpretation of the poem is confirmed by the group of ten sonnets called *A Coronet for his Mistress Philosophy* which follows immediately after *Ovid's Banquet of Sense*. It is absurd to consider the poem, as most have done, as of similar intention to *Venus and Adonis*: the irony is obscure, but it should

[1] As Professor Lewis has said in his Warton lecture on *Hero and Leander*: 'Ceremonie, for Chapman, is what distinguishes a fully human action from an action merely necessary or natural'. This is very characteristic of an age in which ceremony — doing something in a seemly and civilized manner — was regarded as of equal importance with doing anything at all. Sexual passion is necessary perhaps, and natural certainly; but for human beings it can only be made tolerable by being surrounded with proper ceremony, made dignified and imaginative. Chapman compares it with our appetite for food and drink, and he prefers the civilized accompaniments of a good dinner to the mere animal satisfaction of hunger and thirst.

be detected. Naturally, the sensuous delights of Marlowe and Shakespeare appealed, and appeal, to far more than Chapman's involved intellectualism ; but Chapman's poems are worth struggling with for themselves and as commentaries on two more famous, and better, poems.

Ficino and the Florentine neo-Platonists meant little to Shakespeare and mean less to most of us, though a cursory allusion to fashionable psychology was as much in place in Shakespeare's poem as it would be in a poem written for a similar audience today. But the qualities for which Shakespeare was most praised were neither his learning, nor his sensuality, nor his observation of nature, but the smoothness of his verses and the elegance of his rhetoric. 'The sweet witty soul of Ovid lives in mellifluous and honey-tongued Shakespeare', said Meres and (most perspicaciously) 'the Muses would speak with Shakespeare's fine-filed phrase if they would speak English'. Jonson echoed Meres when he wrote of Shakespeare's 'well turned and true filed lines' : pedantic schoolmaster and great classical poet alike admired Shakespeare for his exquisite craftsmanship.

These are the very qualities which we least notice or even find tiresome.

> Speak, fair, but speak fair words, or else be mute,

is as likely to irritate as to please a modern reader. Neither is he often to be heard commending the *traductio* in

> She's Love, she loves, and yet she is not lov'd ;

and, like Adonis, he will probably be observed to smile disdainfully at the puns in Venus'

> I'll be a park and thou shalt be my dear.

But Bowdler (in Heywood's *The Fair Maid of the Exchange*) thought to win Mall Berry by quoting the line.

Again, the elaborate interlacing in

> Her eyes petitioners to his eyes suing,
> His eyes saw her eyes, as they had not seen them,
> Her eyes woo'd still, his eyes disdain'd the wooing,

will strike a modern reader as artificial and therefore displeasing, whereas to Meres or Jonson it would have seemed artificial and therefore pleasing. For some of the rhetorical devices we miss, because we are not trained to observe them; others, such as puns, we have come by various ways to think of as comic; and others again we take exactly as the Elizabethans took them, yet, where they approved, we disapprove. Three hundred and fifty years ago *Venus and Adonis* was praised because it was artificial: now it is praised where it is 'natural'. We prefer the passages which convince us that Shakespeare had watched a dabchick diving in the Avon, or a hunted hare on the downs above Stratford. They enjoyed the poem because it showed that a new poet had learnt to speak with the Muses' tongues in English: because his poem seemed as refined and elegant and witty and artificial as Ovid. They appreciated it as a work of art and were not concerned at all with glimpses into the early life of a great poet. Very probably they missed certain things in the poem that we delight in, but they judged the poem as a whole, and judged it as a poem. They were not deflected by what Tovey called 'sentimental excuses for inattention': they did not value poems as 'human documents' or as clinical data for the psychoanalyst, but as poems. They were more accustomed to appreciating the great works of art with which they enriched their lives, and had a trained understanding of literary technique. This was part of the education of a gentleman, and was to be attained by writing both verse and prose, for (as Castiglione says) 'it happeneth very seldom, that a man not exercised in writing, how learned soever he be, can at any time know perfectly the labour and toil of writers, or taste of the sweetness and excellency of styles'. Castiglione does not fall into the personal heresy of saying that none but a poet can truly understand poetry: he says only that a man who has attempted, however unsuccessfully, to write will have a better understanding of those who have succeeded. For such men, who could truly savour his poetry, Shakespeare wrote.

They also welcomed the smoothness of his verse, 'the first and most obvious excellence of the poem' in Coleridge's opinion, but a quality which is sometimes fatuously criticized now. We may with some justice object to Tottell's editing of Wyatt, in which he smoothes away the roughnesses of the metre, though no doubt Tottell had good reasons for what he did. But it is absurd to ask for the reverse: to wish Shakespeare's smooth lines rougher. To do so is wholly to misunderstand the effect of metre. Shakespeare was not writing songs, like Wyatt, and had no need to leave something to the musical accompaniment to achieve: in his melodious stanza he was writing his own accompaniment. Also he was writing the kind of metre in which, because of its very regularity, any least shift of accent will be all the more apparent. He gains his emphasis subtly therefore, not in the crude manner of contemporary satirists who supposed rough metre was suited to their matter.

Shakespeare wishes to concentrate his reader's vision on Venus' stealthy approach to Adonis, and throws the accent out of place, on to the adverb that suggests that concentration:

> O what a sight it was, wistly to view
> How she came stealing to the wayward boy.

The shifted accent catches our attention so sharply because it is so unusual in this regular verse. Similarly, Shakespeare shows us the trembling anxiety of Venus when she is looking for Adonis, fearing he is dead, by a slight irregularity in the line:

> Variable passions throng her constant woe.

Here the metre perfectly matches the contrast between 'variable' and 'constant'. The metre would have been regular, the meaning would have been the same, had Shakespeare written,

> Her changeful passions throng her constant woe;

but the effect would have been altogether lost. These slight variations from a very regular norm are fully as effective as the crude and frequent irregularities in Donne's satires, or in Browning; but they require a more sensitive, and more educated, reader. Shakespeare can make a line sombre and heavy by a collocation of accents:

> And homeward through the dark laund runs apace;

or he can give it speed and lightness by inserting an extra unaccented syllable:

> The many musits through the which he goes
> Are like a labyrinth to amaze his foes.

He is already, in this his first published work, a master of metrical subtlety. It was one of the reasons for the immediate success of his poem.

We cannot hope to share Elizabethan taste exactly: we are more naïve, we are less well educated, we read too fast, we live in a more complex age, we haven't time. . . . But something may be gained by considering how the men and women for whom Shakespeare wrote his poem appreciated *Venus and Adonis*, for he gauged their taste so well as to satisfy it at once. That is the primary fact, that Shakespeare was writing for a known taste which he was sensitive enough to judge. From that followed recognition by his readers. They expected their artists to please their taste, not to compel it; and desired not new-fangledness, but excellence. They did not wish to be stimulated by something never done before, but to be delighted by something done better. Would we so promptly and so generously have recognized Shakespeare's genius, and enjoyed his poetry? But would a poet of our day be as shrewd, and as modest, as Shakespeare?

SHAKESPEARE: *HAMLET*

FROM the beginning, even before there was a published text to refer to, *Hamlet* provoked discussion. Spenser's friend, Gabriel Harvey, jotting down a note in his copy of the new edition of Chaucer, contrasted the play with Shakespeare's popular poem of *Venus and Adonis*: that, he had noticed, delighted the young men, whereas *Hamlet* and *Lucrece* 'have it in them to please the wiser sort'. They were more serious works, with an appeal not to the jaded taste of cynical men of fashion but to those who looked for profounder moral purpose in poetry, who expected it to instruct as well as to delight; who respected the memory of Sir Philip Sidney, and admired in Spenser the arch-poet of England. Spenser died about the time when Shakespeare was writing *Hamlet*, leaving half-finished the noble poem in which he set forth the pattern of the ideal courtier, the perfectly balanced man; and Sidney's successor, who in all things had modelled himself on that heroic example, the Earl of Essex, now paid the charges for the burial of Spenser's body in Westminster Abbey.

The theme of *Hamlet* is the primitive but then still potent theme of revenge, which surges up from

> the dark backward and abysm of time

to confront a polished Renaissance courtier with its insufferable challenge. The courtier of Castiglione's and Spenser's imagining, of Sidney's or Essex's presentation, was not simply the accomplished attendant upon Majesty or the loyal executant of commands; he was both, and more than both, for he must be ready with advice to his Prince, and willing to submit to the over-ruling of that advice ; he must be capable of undertaking a ceremonious embassage, or of leading his men in battle. He must adorn his Prince's Court with the grace of his manners and the elegance of his learning ; he must support it by political sagacity and martial courage. In the twentieth century he would be called upon (as many have been) to play the part of the intellectual as man of action ; but for us this has been one of the coarse necessities of a brutal century, not the fulfilment of a civilized ideal. Hamlet's problem was not that he was called upon to act (for the highest end of knowledge was of well doing and not of well knowing only, as Sidney had said) but that he was to act in circumstances of primaeval bloodiness for which his courtly training had not prepared him. In the end he must die, because his nature has been destroyed by his terrible task ; but Hamlet dies not through any necessity of the plot, but by accident. The necessity lies within him. So it was that the wiser sort, seeing the play, would have pondered on Essex's situation in Ireland where he was sent on a task for which Spenser, the senior civil servant with long experience of the country and some knowledge of the man, had advised his appointment.

That is not to suggest that when Shakespeare wrote his play he was thinking especially of Essex : he may have been — we shall never know. But he was imagining the sort of man Essex was in a situation of anachronistic ferocity such as Essex encountered and failed to endure. Mountjoy, who after a quarrel which led to a duel, had been reconciled in friendship with Essex, met and overcame the things that defeated Essex in Ireland ; but it is hardly enough to say that he was a better soldier (as no doubt he was) with some implication that he was more coarse-grained and more the man of action, Laertes to Essex's Hamlet. The evidence is all the other way. Mountjoy's love of private retiredness, we are told, 'did alienate his mind from all action, yet his desire of honour and hope of reward and advancement by the wars . . . made him hotly embrace the forced course of the war'. He was a man of considerable learning, with a fine library in which he took great pride; an aristocrat of more ancient lineage than Essex, one whose ancestor had been the friend of Erasmus; the life-long lover of Essex's sister, whom in her youth Sidney had celebrated as Stella; sensitive but not touchy, resolute but not aggressive, 'a gentle enemy, easily pardoning, and calmly pursuing revenge'. Daniel's portrayal of him in the most perceptive literary portrait we have of any Elizabethan suggests a man of action comparable to Shakespeare's Henry V, but also a man of learning, one who (like Essex) presented books to Sir Thomas Bodley's new library, and carefully annotated his own. He had the perspicacity to appoint William Laud to be his chaplain, as Essex picked out John Donne to be his secretary. And when he had to defend himself for marrying the divorced Lady Rich, he had recourse to a solid array of patristic learning which would hardly have been endurable to the impatient Essex. But though he delighted in study, he also (according to his secretary, Fynes Moryson) enjoyed 'reading play-books for recreation'. (Among these was there, perhaps, a copy of *Hamlet*?) Nashe long before recorded a discussion of the qualities required in the true courtier, in which it had been concluded that Sir Philip Sidney best fulfilled the ideal; but among the living there was 'nothing so generally applauded in every man's comparisons' as Mountjoy's 'most absolute perfections'. Nashe, it is true, was addressing Mountjoy, Sir Charles Blount as he still was, but his compliment cannot have been absurd, for though compliment flourishes in hyperbole it wilts in ineptitude.

Hamlet was no Mountjoy, for the desire of honour could not overcome his distaste for action, nor could he pursue revenge calmly. Had he existed he might have been brought into Nashe's discussion of Castiglione's ideal as fitly as were Sidney or Mountjoy, but he was called upon to show a resolute temper, of which occasion, as for Essex, discovered his lack.

He saw too many sides of the question to be capable of easy decision. But the courtier, like the modern civil servant, was normally called upon not to decide, but to provide the knowledge necessary to decision, which was then to be made by the Prince as now by the Ministers of the Crown. Sometimes, when the courtier had to serve his Prince in the wars, decision would be his, and then, in an Essex or a Hamlet, the native hue of resolution might well be sicklied o'er with the pale cast of thought.

Hamlet must have been associated in the minds of the better-educated members of the play's first audience with the well-known ideal courtier of Castiglione's description, or with Spenser's Sir Calidore. For the others, the working-class majority, more actual examples of the courtier would come to mind. Polonius' reference to 'falling out at tennis' must have recalled to many the famous quarrel of Sidney and the Earl of Oxford over the right to a game of tennis. Hamlet's 'Dost know this water-fly ?' would momentarily bring into ludicrous juxtaposition with the affected Osric Essex's enemy Sir Walter Ralegh.[1] Hamlet's disdain of the Italian calligraphy is more likely to have had a particular reference than a general, for Sidney, Southampton, Mountjoy, and many another courtier did not despise it : but the audience would know that some man of fashion wrote a scurvy hand, just as today they would know that a certain field-marshal affected two cap-badges. Polonius' precepts to Laertes parody Lord Burghley's well-known letter of worldly advice to his son Robert, another, and most successful, enemy of Essex. Rosenkrantz and Guildenstern were the names of two Danish courtiers who came to England on a diplomatic mission in 1593 : both, like Hamlet, were graduates of Wittenberg. In such ways, as so often, Shakespeare brought the play home to the less sophisticated majority by inviting their recollection of recent history, of things and persons they knew at first hand. They would

[1] The Queen's nickname for him was Water.

enjoy the play all the more if he could involve them in it by this means, just as the ballad-singers not long before would involve their audience by a similar refusal to allow the events described to seem remote in time.

There were more general references which could be variously applied by the audience. Hamlet is a sonneteer in the fashion of the time ; he looks at Ophelia 'as a' would draw her face' ; he has an especial interest in the theatre, can compose a speech for insertion in *The Murder of Gonzago*, and by his comments on acting shows himself a frequenter of plays. In his behaviour to inferiors he reveals the graceful courtesy of a gentleman : both Essex and Mountjoy were renowned for this. Polonius and Laertes at first assume that Hamlet's affection for Ophelia is mere frivolous gallantry, as if Hamlet were Sir Calidore and Paridell in one. Polonius' misunderstanding of Hamlet's character in this way leads him to treat Ophelia as so much bait :

> I'll loose my daughter to him.

Very properly Hamlet calls the old pander a fishmonger, and thereafter, perhaps unjustly doubting Ophelia's innocence, treats her with obscene contumely.

This and much else persuades other characters in the play that Hamlet is mad ; but we, in our detachment, are not to think of him as Polonius and Ophelia, Gertrude and the King think of him. They are deluded through

> the artful balance whereby
> Shakespeare so gingerly put his sanity in doubt
> without the while confounding his Reason ;

but we, of the audience, are reasonable beings who recognize in Hamlet a man conforming to the courtly ideal of the time of the first Elizabeth who is suddenly confronted with a primitive and loathsome task.

This could happen. Spenser was present 'at the execution of a notable traitor at Limerick, called Morrogh O'Brien. I saw an old woman which was his foster-mother take up his head whilst he was quartered, and sucked up all the blood running thereout, saying that the earth was not worthy to drink it ; and therewith also steeped her face and breast and torn hair, crying and shrieking out most terribly'. It is difficult to think of Essex watching a scene of such savage horror with the equanimity which Spenser implies in his record of it ; and in recommending Essex as a fit person to bring peace to the savage island, Spenser misjudged the man, not the task. But it is surely no less difficult to think of Hamlet contemplating murder on the assurance of a ghost. He has to be quite certain of his duty, to be sure that he is not led to murderous revenge through hallucination or the disgust which he feels at his mother's hasty and, to him, incestuous remarriage. He has a sane distaste for the task that has been laid upon him, as had Orestes : revenge in him is dull, and he must be spurred to it by the honourable example of Fortinbras and his men. And yet, to him, such an example is gross as earth : he has no more enthusiasm for the code of honour,

greatly to find quarrel in a straw,

than had Musidorus in *Arcadia*, or the shepherds in the pastoral world of *Aminta*. Hamlet was not mad : he was merely too reasonable to accept the word of a ghost, or a principle of honour which could seem an impediment, a tyrant of the mind.

Yet we must remember that whatever the proportion of the wiser sort in *Hamlet*'s first audience, it was very small. To the majority the theme of revenge was probably the most satisfactory basis for a dramatic plot, one that would fix their attention as would no other, and to them the play was one in a series which they knew well and enjoyed. They were not predisposed to admire a man who sought revenge : 'Vengeance is mine, saith the Lord', and man must not interfere with the divine justice. They would hardly have known the specious arguments in favour of revenge put forth by Continental writers such as Romei and Gentillet, which were the province of courtiers: and Hamlet, who was one of these, clearly found them difficult to accept, and so would win the audience's sympathy. Even the duel was never legal in England, nor accepted as part of the English code of behaviour. It was foreign, Italian, suspect, and Hamlet was no Italianized Englishman.

The many habitual theatre-goers in the audience would compare Shakespeare's play with Kyd's *Spanish Tragedy*, with his lost *Hamlet*, perhaps with Marston's *Antonio's Revenge*. The cruder among them would find excitement in Hamlet's long-drawn-out agony of indecision, by whose means the act of revenge is always about to happen, and as often postponed. Others, more aware of the subtler characters and finer ideals of their betters, would recognize in Hamlet something more than a means of dramatic tantalization, and would think, very likely, of Essex, their popular hero — the man who, in the absurd rebellion which he was soon to lead, supposed that he could count on the London multitude. Or some might think of Southampton, of Rutland, of Bedford, young noblemen who were each about as unfitted to take part in armed revolt against the Queen as in an act of murderous revenge.

I am not concerned to explain Shakespeare's conception of Hamlet's character — too many have foundered in so impossible an adventure — but rather I would try to imagine some of the suggestions this portrayal may have had for its first audience, for men and women who had followed the inconsistent, irresolute career of the Earl of Essex in these last years. No other courtier of the time lived so much in the eye of the many as Essex; to none since they had followed Sidney to his grave in St Paul's did they give such affection. In *Henry V*, written after Essex's appointment as Lord Deputy, Shakespeare had imagined the citizens of London going out to welcome him home, victorious from Ireland. But Essex failed, and Shakespeare and these Londoners knew the story of his melodramatic return to the Queen at Nonsuch, and of his subsequent disgrace. Their admiration was suspended, and they were puzzled at their hero's behaviour : they would not now condemn him, nor would they, in a few months' time, turn their affection into loyalty to him against the Queen. The less intelligent would shrug off his conduct as mad ; the more thoughtful, the wiser sort, would ponder upon it and remain perplexed as, ever since, they have been perplexed by the character of Hamlet.

At so many points do these two characters, Essex's and Hamlet's, coincide, even for us who never followed Essex's personal fortunes through that incomparable decade of England's history, who never heard his quick and brilliant speech, never saw his handsome, melancholy face. We have to reconstruct Essex's character from the fragmentary descriptions, the incompetent portraits, the 'old mouse-eaten records' of the historians which Sidney spurned : but when Hamlet was first acted Essex was the most vivid personality in the mind of every man in London, and all were as subject to his charm as we are to Hamlet's. For that is perhaps the most remarkable quality of all in Hamlet, his charm ; a quality which Rosalind has, and Viola, and Elizabeth Bennet, and Peer Gynt, and how few others in all literature. We are apt to see only the insufficiency of Essex's character for the part he was called upon to play, and so to diminish him that we wonder how he could have been so universally admired. But Hamlet, who is no historical portrait of Essex but rather an ideal presentation of the sort of man Essex then seemed to be, can make us briefly rediscover what it felt like, in the winter of 1600, to be a spectator of that high tragedy of his fall.

Thus it was that the play of *Hamlet* not only pleased the wiser sort, it pleased all : from the very first it drew the crowds to the theatre as well as delighting those who bought the quarto text and took it home to read at their leisure. These would not be many : plays were to be seen on the stage, not read in the library, and those who collected plays, like Sir John Harington, were very exceptional. But it was worth while to offer for sale a pirated edition soon after the play had been acted, and again, within a few months, to publish an enlarged text 'according to the true and perfect copy' of Shakespeare's manuscript.

The members of that first audience would respond to the drama of *Hamlet* and to the character of the Prince in various ways according to their experience and sophistication. But to the poetry of it, especially in Hamlet's own speaking, how could they respond ? It is all very well for J. M. Synge to say that when Shakespeare 'sat down to his work he used many phrases that he had just heard, as he sat at dinner, from his mother or his children'. But even he cannot have heard many men speaking like Hamlet, and the majority of his audience can have had yet fewer opportunities. For Hamlet talks not only like a man of a certain class in society, he talks like a very clever man, with a swift intricacy of language which bewilders Polonius and Osric, Ophelia and Gertrude, but also Horatio and Guildenstern. Must it not then also have bewildered the groundlings, and even the exalted twopennies and threepennies in the galleries ? Some of the things that puzzle us would not have puzzled them : they, like the King, associated pleurisy and plus, as we do not ; would be quicker than we are to catch Hamlet's obscene *doubles-entendres* ; would probably know more than a modern Londoner about the fermentation of barley. (The countryside was still within walking distance, and many had but lately come in to London.) But elsewhere,

What's Hecuba to him, or he to Hecuba ?

Yet we have no more reason to doubt that an audience of working men and shopkeepers in Elizabethan London, or of English sailors who acted *Hamlet* on board Captain William Keeling's *Dragon* off Sierra Leone a few years later, responded to Shakespeare's language than to question the record of the awarding of the first prize to Aeschylus's *Oresteia* by a not very dissimilar audience in Athens two thousand years before. And certainly the more refined audiences who paid their sixpences and shillings in the private theatres a few years later were not rewarded with plays of equal vigour, or with poetry of comparable elegance.

The truth is that whatever contemptuous gibes Shakespeare and his fellows flung at the groundlings (often, perhaps, to provoke an enraged howl from them and simultaneous laughter from the galleries), they were encouraged to their finest work by these rough plebeians who would

> clap their brawny hands
> To applaud what their charmed soul scarce understands.

In return, by some strange power of language, Shakespeare could detain his audience, take them out of, and above, themselves, because they in their naïvety would respond by submitting their souls to be charmed, where the more self-conscious man of fashion would affect to disparage, and stay aloof. So in *Hamlet* the play which had pleased not the million, was caviare to the general, but which the courtiers had thought excellent, proved in excerpt, to be drivelling bombast. This, surely, is Shakespeare's oblique comment on the taste of the two or three thousand men and women to whom, one afternoon near the end of the Queen's reign, the Lord Chamberlain's men at the Globe Theatre first presented his *Tragical History of Hamlet*.

THE DONNE FASHION

When in 1612 Michael Drayton published the first part of *Poly-Olbion*, the work which he hoped would assure him a high place among the poets of England, he rather sourly admitted to the general reader, 'there is this great disadvantage against me; that it cometh out at this time, when verses are wholly deduced to Chambers, and nothing esteemed in this lunatic age but what is kept in cabinets, and must only pass by transcription'. This is the complaint of the professional against the amateur, of the man who has dedicated his whole life to poetry and to the study of poetry against the man for whom poetry was merely the means of giving evaporations to his wit. Michael Drayton, publishing a noble folio, with its dedication to the Prince of Wales, its annotations by John Selden, its maps after Christopher Saxton, is suddenly hesitant with doubt, wondering whether the poem to which he has devoted so much care and labour will be to the taste of the new Jacobean age, the iron age that had too quickly succeeded the golden age of Elizabeth. Yet *Poly-Olbion* must be printed, and could not pass by transcription: it was a public, not a private poem, to be thought of as a book, not as a sheaf of manuscript or a series of entries in a commonplace album; something to lie on a table in a tall bay-window for reading at leisure, not a paper to be pulled from the folds of a man's doublet and read to a gay, convivial company.

Ironically, at this very time, John Donne was regretting the only publication of his verses which he allowed in his lifetime. 'Of my Anniversaries,' he wrote to a friend, 'the fault that I acknowledge in myself is to have descended to print anything in verse, which, though it have excuse, even in our times, by example of men which one would think should have little have done it as I; yet I confess I wonder how I declined to it, and do not pardon myself.' He had been prevailed upon for the first time to print his verses by Sir Robert Drury, father of the girl whom Donne, though he had never seen her, so extravagantly celebrated in these poems. They had been ill received by his friends — Ben Jonson told him, in his brusque way, 'if it had been written of the Virgin Mary it had been something' — and while he was abroad, travelling on the Continent with Sir Robert and Lady Drury, he heard from England many censures of the book.

Donne's judgment, that the poems on Elizabeth Drury ought not to have been printed, was certainly right. They were as private as the verse-letters which he now wrote to appease the ladies whom he had offended by these hyperboles, the Countess of Bedford, and two of the daughters of Penelope Rich. They should have remained private, as did his other obsequies, or as his elegies and verse-letters and love-poems. All these were written for the personal pleasure of a sophisticated company of Donne's friends and of those to whom his wit and learning had gained him introduction. Hitherto he had kept his poems in manuscript, had denied them to the anthologists, and, somehow, had protected them against the piracy of unscrupulous printers. He was persuaded to an error of judgment when he allowed the *Anniversaries* to be published: he wrote verses not for the general reader but for his friends.

Michael Drayton would have been as scornful of Donne's exiguous octavo, if he had seen it, as of Donne's habit of passing his poems round in manuscript. It was, I suppose, especially galling for him, since some at least of Donne's friends were also Drayton's: the two poets must have met through Christopher Brooke, or Ben Jonson, or (most likely of all) at Sir Henry Goodere's house at Polesworth in Warwickshire. Donne's most intimate friend for many years, with whom he exchanged weekly letters, the younger Sir Henry Goodere married his cousin Frances, daughter to the elder Sir Henry in whose house Drayton had been brought up. Her sister Anne, who married Sir Henry Rainsford, was Drayton's devoted friend throughout life, the Idea of his youthful sonnets, his hostess every summer at Clifford Chambers, the recipient of his last, moving verses. The younger Sir Henry Goodere was himself something of a versifier : like both Donne and Drayton, and nearly everyone else, he contributed to Coryate's *Crudities* ; and he wrote his elegy on Prince Henry. (This appeared in the same collection, *Lachrymae Lachrymarum*, with poems by Donne and other friends of his, Sir Edward Herbert, Sir William Cornwallis, George Gerrard, and Joseph Hall.) Goodere also, like Donne, wrote an epithalamium for the Princess Elizabeth. These were public occasions on which any poet might try his skill : it was not to such poems that Drayton had so irritably referred. But there exists in manuscript in the British Museum a copy of verses headed *A letter written by Sr H. G. and J. D. alternis vicibus* which (as an epigram by Thomas Pestell confirms) was written triplet by triplet, on some private occasion, by Sir Henry Goodere and John Donne. Michael Drayton would not have objected to such frivolity : he did much the same thing on convivial evenings in the Apollo room at the Devil and St Dunstan where Ben Jonson's club used to meet. What he did resent was that these private poetical entertainments should be more fashionable than the serious patriotic poetry which he was attempting. Drayton too wrote poems for his friends, for Anne Goodere and William Browne and Henry Reynolds and George Sandys, but he did not expect them, or anyone, to value such poems above *The Barons Wars* or *England's Heroical Epistles* or *Poly-Olbion*. He published his verse-letters eventually, with collections of his other poems, because he was a craftsman who delighted in the products of his own skill, and because it would have seemed affected to keep them still private.

Indeed, in the poem to Henry Reynolds, where he recalls their talks together about the poets and gives his brief, vivid summaries of the merits of each, he returns, at the end, to the old grumble of 1612, and dismisses unnamed those

> whose poems, be they ne'er so rare,
> In private chambers that encloistered are,
> And by transcription daintily must go,
> As though the world unworthy were to know
> Their rich composures.

Not Donne's poetry but the fashion for it annoyed him ; most of all perhaps the silly habit of keeping it in manuscript for thirty years, with all the suggestion of a superior literary clique that this implied. Drayton rightly considered himself one of the chief poets of his time, and he found it tiresome that men like Goodere should pride themselves on the possession of a body of poetry which was not accessible, as was his own and Ben Jonson's and Samuel Daniel's and William Browne's, to the world's censure or approbation. Jonson, who admired Donne's poetry for some things, took much the same view of this coterie poetry as Drayton. 'Poetry in this latter age', he wrote, 'hath proved but a mean mistress to such as have wholly addicted themselves to her, or given their names up to her family. They who have but saluted her on the by, and now and then tendered their visits, she hath done much for, and advanced in the way of their own professions.'

Poetry to Donne was a less serious study than to these others : he had no theories of diction or prosody to expound ; he did not write about poetry, as they did ; even in his letters he very seldom discusses literary topics, and when he does it is nearly always in a spirit of banter or disparagement. His library contained little poetry, and he confessed that he was 'no great voyager in other men's works'. He hardly ever refers to the poets who were his contemporaries. Donne used verse to compliment, or amuse, or rival his friends, and would not, except on one regretted occasion, publish these poems, as

Drayton, Daniel, and Jonson published their epistles. He was carefree and light-hearted in the use of an exceptional talent: as one of the Oxford men who contributed an elegy to Donne's poems wrote,

> thy careless hours brought forth
> Fancies beyond our studies, and thy play
> Was happier than our serious time of day.
> So learned was thy chance; thy haste had wit,
> And matter from thy pen flowed rashly fit.

He wrote, like his friends Sir Henry Wotton, Sir Edward Herbert, Sir Henry Goodere, Sir William Cornwallis, Sir John Roe, Christopher Brooke, Rowland Woodward, with never a thought of the printed page, and never, therefore, a thought of his poems as in competition with the professionals'. They deplored the affectation of fashionable persons who 'esteem of verses upon which the vulgar in a stationer's shop hath once breathed as of a piece of infection, in whose fine fingers no papers are wholesome but such as pass by private manuscription'. Donne, for his part, deplored the growing custom of publishing such private poetry, and thought it unpardonable in himself to have published the *Anniversaries*, in spite of the example set by such as Sir Henry Wotton, Sir Walter Ralegh, and Sir John Davies in contributing to Francis Davison's *Poetical Rhapsody*. He had refused to do so, for Davison had tried to get 'Satires, Elegies, Epigrams etc.' by Donne, but without success. Even *The Bait* never joined Marlowe's and Ralegh's poems, to which it is a pendant, in *England's Helicon*. Donne's friends were less strict than he in keeping their poems private, and he was contemptuous of their profligacy.

The *Satires*, which were among the earliest of Donne's poems, had attained some notoriety before the turn of the century, and perhaps Donne would have published these but for the ban which was laid upon satires and epigrams by the Archbishop of Canterbury and the Bishop of London in June 1599. Satires and sonnets were in the air of the 1590s and there is nothing unusual in Donne writing satire at the same time as Lodge, Marston, Hall, and Guilpin: many young men were doing so. Probably Donne already knew Joseph Hall in the 1590s; he knew him well later, may have owed his introduction to the Drurys to him, and gave him one of the bloodstone seals which were dying gifts to a few special friends. Everard Guilpin had read Donne's first satire before writing his own fifth, which was published in 1598, and must therefore have had access to a manuscript; he was, very likely, the Mr E. G. to whom Donne addressed a verse-letter, about 1593. Later, when Donne returned from the Cadiz and Islands Voyages, Guilpin mocked at his affected airs. Another early reader of the *Satires* was Donne's chamber-fellow from 1592 at Lincoln's Inn, Christopher Brooke, who owned copies of the first and fourth of them, and was perhaps addressed in the second. To him Donne wrote a number of verse-letters, including the two which are still the most famous, *The Storm*, written when he was weather-bound in Falmouth at the outset of the Islands Voyage in 1597, and *The Calm*, written when they were lying off the Azores. Brooke was a minor poet who contributed to *England's Helicon* and, according to Anthony Wood, was well known to and admired by other poets of his time, Jonson, Drayton, William Browne, George Wither, and John Davies of Hereford as well as Donne. He was a most loyal friend to Donne and both he and his younger brother Samuel suffered imprisonment for their part in Donne's clandestine marriage: Christopher Brooke gave away the bride, and Samuel performed the marriage ceremony.

At Oxford Donne had got to know Henry Wotton and Edward Herbert, both of them destined to serve their country with distinction, both of them poets of more than courtly elegance. He must have met Magdalen Herbert who was keeping house for her son while he was up at the University, but his friendship with her, which was to produce some memorable poems and a famous funeral sermon, seems not to have begun till somewhat later : the eight or nine years difference in their ages would have seemed more discouraging to Donne at twenty-six than when he was ten years older. Her fifth son, George, Donne came to know well, and gave him, but not Edward, one of his bloodstone seals together with a copy of verses. George Herbert, precociously aware of his great gifts as a poet, dedicated them to the service of God, and rejected the tortuous wit that marked the verse of his elder brother and Donne and their friends :

> Must all be veiled, while he that reads, divines,
> Catching the sense at two removes ?

George Herbert did not live long enough to publish his poems, but his dying message to Nicholas Ferrar with his manuscript, 'desire him to read it : and then, if he can think it may turn to the advantage of any dejected poor soul, let it be made public', shows, however humbly, his hope that his poems might be published. Like Donne and the others of his circle, George Herbert knew the ways of Learning, of Honour, and of Pleasure, but when he was sixteen years old he had already determined that the gift of poetry which he knew he had in him, a gift greater, perhaps, than any of these others, must not be dissipated in the frivolous way in which he saw them using theirs. His brother, not he, might set Donne to rival his obscurity for the sake of unseasonable laughter. For him poetry was too valuable a talent to be wasted so, on fictions and false hair, on the propositions of hot blood and brains.

Henry Wotton was poet and wit, connoisseur of architecture and painting, and served as English Ambassador three times in Venice and once at The Hague. His famous *bon mot*, that an Ambassador is an honest man sent to lie abroad for the good of his country left King James not amused : it is easy to suppose that it delighted Donne. His company, said Izaak Walton, was 'one of the delights of mankind'. In spite of Wotton's frequent and lengthy absences abroad his friendship with Donne lasted, and he too was among the chosen friends to whom Donne sent his bloodstone seal shortly before his death. In 1605, during Wotton's first embassy to Venice, he had with him another friend of Donne's, Rowland Woodward, who had perhaps accompanied him to Venice in the previous year. He had asked Donne for copies of his poems to take with him, but in a verse-letter to him Donne, reluctant as ever to circulate his poems, alleges that his Muse is affecting a chaste fallowness, and that

> she to few, yet to too many hath shown
> How love-song weeds and satiric thorns are grown
> Where seeds of better arts were early sown.

But he may have relented and sent Woodward some copies now, for many years later, when he was in Holy Orders and inclined to be ashamed of his early unregenerate verses, Woodward possessed a handsome manuscript containing a large selection of his poems ; and at this time he was prepared to exchange complimentary verses both with Rowland Woodward and with his brother Thomas. It is pleasing to think of Sir Henry Wotton, the versatile and observant English Ambassador, picking his way through Donne's weeds and thorns in Woodward's company ; probably he too had copies of some of Donne's poems besides the letter addressed to him at his going to Venice in 1604.

Certainly he kept among his papers till his death a copy of Francis Bacon's poem *The World*,

> The world's a bubble, and the life of man
> Less than a span,

which had initiated a poetical debate in 1597. The question proposed was, 'Which kind of life is best, that of Court, Country, or City ?' which had been the subject of an ancient debate whose record is preserved in the Greek Anthology. Probably it was well known to the Elizabethans. In 1574 the Dutch painter Cornelis Ketel, then in England, had painted, on the back of a portrait of an unknown man, a *putto* blowing soap-bubbles, with an allusion similar to Bacon's. Now prompted by Bacon's poem Thomas Bastard, a Wykehamical epigrammatist whom Wotton would have known at New College, entered the debate with a poem addressed to Wotton; Donne did likewise with the poem that begins,

> Sir, more than kisses, letters mingle souls;

and Wotton replied with a poem to Donne.

This kind of poetical interchange, which had the authority of the antique world to recommend it, was natural to a group of friends with a gift of poetry. Fifteen or twenty years earlier Philip Sidney, Edward Dyer, and Fulke Greville had indulged in similar pastimes; and the pair of poems written by Christopher Marlowe and Sir Walter Ralegh (to which Donne later added a third) are known to everyone. Even Romantic poets did not disdain such things: in February 1818 Keats informed his brothers that 'the Wednesday before last Shelley, Hunt and I wrote each a sonnet on the River Nile'; and Mary Shelley's *Frankenstein* is the grisly survivor of a competition in ghost-stories suggested by Byron to the Shelleys, Claire Clairmont, and the egregious Dr Polidori, when they were together at Geneva some eighteen months before. Francis Bacon provoked a more serious literary debate than any of these, about the time when he wrote *The World*, for there can be no doubt that his *Advancement of Learning*, Fulke Greville's *Treatie of Human Learning*, and Samuel Daniel's *Musophilus* are closely linked together. That is another, and larger, question: here only the occasion of one of Donne's poems is to be noticed, in a contest of wits among the associates of Essex in whose house Bacon was living and Greville was a constant visitor, with whom Wotton and Donne sailed both on the expedition to Cadiz and on the Islands Voyage.

Essex, the self-appointed but acknowledged successor to Sir Philip Sidney as — among other qualities of the perfect courtier — patron of poets, numbered among his clients Spenser and Daniel, William Warner and Sir John Harington. After his fall Fulke Greville destroyed the play which he had written on Antony and Cleopatra, to avoid implication in the disaster; the less worldly-wise Daniel found himself in trouble because his play *Philotas* was interpreted as a plea for support of Essex; and Shakespeare's *Richard II* had been revived in order to arouse public sympathy for Essex's cause. In Essex's circle, as in Sidney's, the poets devoted to him were of various abilities or diverse tastes: he and his friends admired Spenser as England's arch-poet, the English Virgil, and when he died Essex arranged that he should be buried near his master Chaucer, in Westminster Abbey; they enjoyed the mellifluous, honey-tongued Shakespeare of the poems and sonnets; but they were not thereby precluded from an enjoyment of the purity of Daniel, of the asperity of Fulke Greville, of the gaiety of Harington, or of the fantastic wit of Donne. They would have thought it very absurd if anyone had said that Donne's poems were written in reaction against Spenser's or Shakespeare's or the sonnets. They were being written at the same time, and the private friends among whom Shakespeare circulated his sonnets included many of those into whose tingling hands Donne thrust his love-song weeds.

Throughout the twenty-five years when he was writing his secular poems Donne was constantly in the company of the courtly admirers of the great public poets, of Essex, and Ralegh, who also was on the famous voyages of 1596 and 1597; of Sir Thomas Egerton and his wife Alice Spencer, whom Spenser and Milton both honoured; of her daughters, the Countesses of Bridgwater and of Huntingdon; of the Countess of Bedford. This familiarity with the men and women who encouraged and admired the greatest poets of their time was essential to Donne's own achievement. For the evaporations of so learned a wit could be caught only by those who were well read in the poetry of Spenser and Sidney, of Marlowe and Shakespeare, of Jonson and Daniel and Drayton, and therefore so well trained to the standards of decorum, that they could enjoy Donne's reversals of it. The fashion for Donne's poetry presupposes an enjoyment of the great public poetry of the age; of his age, for if (as Ben Jonson said) he wrote all his best poetry before he was twenty-five, then he was at his best when Spenser and Shakespeare and Daniel were at their best, and somewhat before Drayton and Jonson and Campion.[1] In his poems he was not deriding the good taste of the time as old-fashioned; he was exploiting it for the sake of wit, and of a recondite wit that was likely to be enjoyed most by a circle of like-minded friends. He supposed, rightly or wrongly, that his poetry would be understood only by those friends for whom he wrote it, and even when in 1614 he was thinking of publishing a collection of his poems this was to be 'not for much public view, but at my own cost, a few copies'. These friends, whose names we know from his correspondence with them in verse and prose, were not many — 'but a short roll of friends writ in my heart', he said. He could not have expected that his poems would be widely read, or that they would long survive the company for whom he meant them. Jonson, one of these friends, advised the young to read Sidney before Donne: indeed they must, for otherwise they cannot understand Donne.

When Donne intends satire he leaves us in no doubt of his intention. In the second satire he mocks at bad poetry, at the excessive use of legal metaphor which his fellow-lawyer Sir John Davies derided even more pungently; at the fulsomeness of some sonneteers, which Shakespeare also laughed at. Donne may even have been making an attack especially on

[1] The young Milton, seeking for informed and judicious criticism of his *Mask*, chose to send it to Sir Henry Wotton. But Milton, who admired our sage and serious Spenser, not our late fantastics, knew that Donne's oldest friend must be deeply read in the best English poetry.

Shakespeare, as dramatist and actor — he was, we know, a great frequenter of plays — as sonneteer, as one of those 'who write to Lords, rewards to get'. (Did he, in his later obsequiousness to Lady Bedford, Sir Robert Drury, and the despicable Earl of Somerset, ever recall those lines ?) But he would have been the first to laugh at those who see in his *Elegies* (which derive from Ovid's *Amores*) poems of a vital originality that they find entirely lacking in *Venus and Adonis* or *Endimion and Phoebe* (which derive from 'the silenced tales of the *Metamorphoses*'). The sweet witty soul of Ovid lives again in Shakespeare, but it has a parallel life in Donne.

To argue that Donne's love poetry is more original, more personal than that of his contemporaries reveals ignorance of the nature of his, or their, poetry and not much comprehension of the nature of love itself. It is not more original to prefer the earlier work of a Latin poet to the later work of the same poet ; to write satire when several other poets are writing satire, rather than to write sonnets when others are writing sonnets ; to imitate Tasso's *Sopra la Bellezza* rather than to plunder *Gerusalemme Liberata* or to translate from the *Aminta*. As for being personal, when in 1625 Sir Robert Ker invited him to write an obsequy on the Marquess of Hamilton, Donne protested : 'You know my uttermost when it was best, and even then I did best when I had least truth for my subjects'. Spenser in *Colin Clouts Come Home Againe*, in the *Amoretti*, in the *Epithalamion* deliberately revealed far more of his own life and personality than ever Donne would have wished to do. Or are we to search in the annals of London for reference to a fat cripple who spent his time in a basket-chair ? to someone who employed an eight-foot-high iron-bound serving-man ? Queen Elizabeth's porter was such a man.

Donne's poetry is not personal, it is dramatic ; concerned with an imagined, not with an experienced, situation. It is witty, not spontaneous, and the wit derives, as learned wit so often derives, from a reversal of the familiar and accepted.

When Byron irreverently referred to some new recruit to the House of Lords as 'created not begotten' he was relying on his hearer's recollection of the words of the Creed. When Max Beerbohm observes that 'to do justice to such a subject would require a pen far less brilliant than mine', much of our pleasure comes from our surprise : he has said 'less' when we expected him, from long familiarity with a phrase, to say 'more'. But we do not rush to the conclusion that he is attacking modesty, nor even that his main purpose was to disparage a cliché. He is being witty in the tradition of wit ; in the tradition of Ovid (and of how many since ?) who detected Nature imitating Art.

Thus it adds nothing to our enjoyment of Donne's poem *The Sun Rising* when we are told that the line

> Go tell Court-huntsmen that the King will ride,

refers to King James I's well-known passion for hunting. Perhaps it does ; perhaps it was written in ink, not in pencil ; in a room full of people after a good dinner, not in bed, late in the morning ; but none of this matters. We must not be asked to know everything about a poem, but only what is relevant to our enjoyment of it. That is what it is for. It is relevant to refer, as Grierson does, to Ovid's *Amores* : Donne and Ovid had much in common. But it is still more relevant to recall a passage in Spenser's *Epithalamion.*

> Who is the same, which at my window peepes ?
> Or whose is that faire face, that shines so bright ?
> Is it not Cinthia, she that never sleepes,
> But walkes about high heaven al the night ?
> O fayrest goddesse, do thou not envy
> My love with me to spy :
> For thou likewise didst love, though now unthought,
> And for a fleece of woll, which privily
> The Latmian shephard once unto thee brought,
> His pleasures with thee wrought.

Spenser appeals to the moon, Donne to the sun, not to intrude upon his love-making. Spenser is writing a passionately serious poem, and keeps decorum ; Donne is writing for the sake of witty effect, and breaks it. In the 1590s, when both were writing, men were educated enough to detect this : the principle of decorum was so much a part of their response to the arts that they could at once recognize its reversal, and take pleasure in the wit with which this was done. For Spenser on his wedding-night the moon is a fair goddess who must be gently reminded of her love for Endymion — with a characteristic smile he suggests that it was not a very serious affair, 'for a fleece of woll' — and so she is to be cajoled into respecting the privacy of the poet and his bride ; for Donne prolonging in imagination some illicit affair, the sun is a busy old fool, a saucy pedantic wretch, whose Puritanical reminder to Donne and his doxy that it is time to get up (and anyhow they had no business to be in bed together) provokes an improper violence of language. Thus the reversal of decorum is in itself decorous : Spenser's language would be as unsuited to the context of Donne's poem, as Donne's to the *Epithalamion.* Tasso objected to Dante's reference to the sun as *lucerna del mondo* — 'you can almost smell the lamp-oil', he says — but he was not dogmatically asserting that it can never be permissible to refer to the sun in such terms, he was objecting to a particular instance. Neither Tasso nor Spenser would have objected to Donne's poem.

Tasso indeed, as William Drummond realized at the time, provided the model for the most extravagant of Donne's poems in this kind, *The Anagram* : 'one shall hardly know who hath the best', Tasso or Donne, says Drummond. And Tasso's 'Stanzas against Beauty' had a long tradition behind them. The poets of the Renaissance could rely on the educated sensibility of their audience, and knew that those for whom they wrote might be amused by a reversal of the expected, because this is an ingredient in wit. *The Anagram* was not written in derision of poems that praise woman's beauty, for Donne, as many poems show, was by no means reluctant to such praise. When he came to write an Epithalamium for the marriage of the exquisite Princess Elizabeth he wrote easily in the tradition which Spenser had used twenty years before, however much his poem may fall short of Spenser's in imagination or in execution. Sir Henry Wotton wrote for the Princess his most famous poem,

> You meaner beauties of the night,

and both he and Donne tempered their wit to praise her with a charm and elegance that were appropriate.

Not long before when Prince Henry died Donne's good sense (which was never very certain) had left him : he wrote, he said, 'to match Sir Edward Herbert in obscureness'. Perhaps he had already repented and sought to make amends to the Prince's beloved sister ; he had soon grown ashamed of the frigid and tortuous poem which he had written when Lord Harington, Lady Bedford's brother, died ; and Lady Bedford herself seems to have rebuked him for making the death of her cousin Cecilia Boulstred the occasion for an exhibition of ingenuity. Grierson is surely right to accept the manuscript attribution to her of the poem

> Death be not proud,

which is clearly a reply to Donne's

> Death I recant.

We know, from Donne himself, that she wrote poems, and that once at least she addressed some lines to him. She might well have been offended by the tasteless insincerity of the poem which he sent her on the cousin who had just died in her house at Twickenham, and it is in keeping with her gentle and pious character to have rebuked him thus by a poem written in deliberate contrast with his. But even if the attribution to Lady Bedford is rejected, the point remains, that some member of her entourage saw fit to reply to Donne's poem on Miss

Boulstred, and that the two poems make a pair of which Donne's must have been composed first, and of which it is the inferior in feeling. Ben Jonson, who had written a coarse epigram on Cecilia Boulstred while she was alive, now dashed off a complimentary epitaph while George Gerrard's man waited at the door. Her death was mourned with a similar lack of sincerity by others of Lady Bedford's poets.

Lucy Harington had married the third Earl of Bedford on 12th December 1594, a few weeks before her fourteenth birthday, and she very soon attained a place second only to that of her older cousin, the Countess of Pembroke, in the esteem of men of letters. To her the elder Sir Henry Goodere had introduced Drayton a little before this, and he asked her to offer Drayton whatever help he might need. 'That excellent and matchless gentleman,' says Drayton, 'was the first cherisher of my Muse, which had been by his death left a poor orphan to the world, had he not before bequeathed it to that lady whom he so dearly loved.' Sir Henry died a few months after Lucy's marriage, but already Drayton had dedicated *Matilda* to her, and his *Endimion and Phoebe* was probably a gift on her marriage. In the next year or two he addressed a number of poems to

> Renowned Lucy, virtue's truest friend,
> Which dost a spirit into my spirit infuse.

After 1597 Drayton fell out with Lady Bedford : not only did he no longer dedicate poems to her, but in a poem printed in 1606 he was unchivalrous enough to make a pointed attack upon her, though afterwards he had second thoughts and suppressed the offensive lines. The cause of the quarrel was probably jealousy of some rival for Lucy's patronage. A few years later Ben Jonson, too, was complaining that Lucy had

> a better verser got,
> (Or Poet, in the Court account) than I,
> And who doth me (though I not him) envy.

Jealousy of one another among Lady Bedford's poets (and not only hers) seems to have been endemic. Jonson's rival was almost certainly Samuel Daniel.

Jonson was notoriously quarrelsome, and though he made friendly references to Daniel in the first edition of *Every Man in his Humour*, and again in *Cynthia's Revels*, both in 1601, by 1616 he had altered the first of these to a cruel parody, and he told William Drummond, when he visited him at Hawthornden, that 'Daniel was at jealousies with him'. The shy and retiring Daniel can be exonerated from blame, but Jonson, who was neither shy nor retiring, may well have thought that he, not Daniel, should have been invited to write the first masque for Queen Anne, and also the play which was presented for her at Christ Church when she visited Oxford in 1605. Lady Bedford was certainly responsible for the first of these two commissions, and Daniel dedicated to her *The Vision of Twelve Goddesses* which was performed on 8th January 1604. In that month Jonson and his friend Sir John Roe (another poetical member of Lady Bedford's circle) were thrust out of Court by the Lord Chamberlain himself for some unmannerly behaviour, which was very possibly at the performance of Daniel's masque. Daniel, needless to say, never stooped to such pettiness or ill manners : he was too modest, and too much of a gentleman. Neither does he, like Drayton, complain of the circulation of private poems by Donne and his friends, though his brother John, the musician, in dedicating his *Songs* to Mistress Anne Grene, has some comments to make. He apologizes to her for publishing what had been 'but yours and mine before', which is, in a sense, taking from her again a gift he had made her. By so doing he fears he may detract from the value of the work,

> For oft we see how things of slender rate,
> Being undivulged, are choicely held in store,
> And rarer compositions once exposed
> Are (as unworthy of the world) condemned.

Samuel Daniel, who contributed some, if not all, of the songs to this delightful book, would have agreed. A far less arrogant or vociferous man than Jonson or Donne or Drayton, he preferred to keep his own counsel, and to write, indifferent to fashion or acclamation, to please himself. His best gifts were for reflection and argument, as we see them in the epistles which he addressed to some of his friends among the great, including Lady Bedford. The unemphatic ease of his verse misled many of his contemporaries into thinking (as Arnold thought of Pope) that 'his manner better fitted prose'. But we need not assume that so sensitive and discriminating a judge of poetry as Lady Bedford failed to enjoy his poems. There is every reason to believe that she did enjoy them : she helped him before she helped Ben Jonson or Donne, and more than she helped either.

Before she knew Donne she asked Jonson to borrow a copy of the *Satires* for her : he did so, and sent them to her with a copy of his own verses. Donne said that his acquaintance with Lady Bedford 'was in the beginning of a graver course than of a poet', and there is no certain proof that he met her until 1608. By the autumn of that year he was reconciled to his father-in-law, and could resume his life among the eminent from which he had had to withdraw after his marriage. In that year Lady Bedford gave her consent to Donne's naming his infant daughter, who was baptized on 8th August, Lucy, and before long Donne was telling Sir Henry Goodere, through whom he was probably first introduced to her company, that she 'only hath the power to cast the fetters of verse upon my free meditations'. She must have known of his reputation as a poet for some years, but could not accept him into her circle so long as he was out of favour : now he was no longer the most daring and impudent member of a group of gifted and irreverent young men, but the middle-aged father of a family, and set upon a graver course than when he sailed to Cadiz and the Azores with Essex. Or perhaps it would be nearer the truth to say, that was the impression he preferred to give. Hoskyns' *Convivium philosophicum*, which must have been written between September 1608 and November 1612, records the meeting of a not excessively grave company at the Mitre, of Donne and his old friends Sir Henry Goodere and Christopher Brooke, with others such as Hugh Holland and Inigo Jones, and John Hoskyns himself who was no sobersides. But perhaps such occasions were becoming more infrequent.

Now, as in the nineties, Donne was accepted into the company of those who enjoyed the published works of the chief poets of the time. Spenser was dead, and Jonson had taken his place as the leading man of letters of the age. (For Shakespeare, who had by now confined himself to the theatre, was *hors concours*. Yet the Phoenix of his *The Phoenix and the Turtle* was very probably Lady Bedford.) Daniel was employed at Court, and so was John Florio who, as early as 1598 had dedicated to Lady Bedford his Italian dictionary, *A World of Words*, where he complimented her on her knowledge of Italian, Spanish, and French. She gave him room in her house while he worked on his translation of Montaigne, in which she encouraged him : 'You often cried Coraggio, and called çà çà, and applauded as I passed', he remembered. There could hardly be a greater contrast between the prose of Florio and the prose of Daniel, unless it were between the poetry of Donne and the poetry of Daniel ; but Lady Bedford's taste rejected none of these. The poets themselves might quarrel and disparage each other's writings ; they might be at jealousies because Lucy the bright seemed now to shine more favourably on one, now on another ; she might not have quite Lady Pembroke's authority in restraining their factious tempers. But she would not have expected to dispute the old Horatian saying that the race of poets is an irritable race. For herself she could, and did, enjoy Daniel's epistle, Jonson's epigrams, and Donne's verse-letters that were addressed to her ; she obtained for Daniel the commission to write a masque, and took part in several of Jonson's ; she would patronize Drayton's English heroic narratives, and Chapman's translation of Homer. Her gay and frivolous kinsman, Sir John Harington, sent her for Christmas 1600 a copy of Philip and Mary Sidney's translation of the Psalms (which Donne also admired) and accompanied the gift with some of his own epigrams. Probably about the same time Jonson obtained the copy of Donne's *Satires* for her, and in 1601 he sent her the copy of *Cynthia's Revels* with a specially printed leaf of verses addressed to her. If Donne's poetry has been more to the taste of these last thirty or forty years than Jonson's or Daniel's that is no reason for supposing that it was more to the taste of Lady Bedford. Indeed her rebuke to him for his poem on Cecilia Boulstred, and his own admission that his elegy on her brother and his fantastic *Anniversaries* offended her, suggest that she may have found his elaborate exhibitionism sometimes tedious.

But she exchanged verse-letters with him, and must, like others of her circle, have delighted in his wit and learning. All her poets except Drayton (who soon left her) were men of learning ; Jonson, Chapman, Daniel, no less than Donne. His especial gift was his wit. This she would appreciate because in it she saw the familiar rules of decorum reflected in reverse ; because in private chambers it was gay and amusing to contemplate the established standards of good taste turned upside down. Donne's poetry is the poetry of those who were the arbiters of taste in the 1590s and 1600s when they were talking together in private ; when they found it entertaining not to concur with the opinion of the common reader. About the time when Donne entered Lucy's orbit he made a very revealing admission to Sir Henry Goodere : 'Sometimes' (he wrote) 'when I find myself transported with jollity and love of company, I hang leads at my heels, and reduce to my thoughts my fortune, my years, the duties of a man, of a friend, of a husband, of a father, and all the incumbencies of a family ; when sadness dejects me, either I countermine it with another sadness, or I kindle squibs about me again, and fly into sportfulness and company'. Whether it had always been so, who now shall say? Probably before he was a husband and a father he found it less obligatory to hang leads at his heels: but his secular poetry derives from his love of company, and from his awareness that in the company of his friends he would be at his best. They would sharpen his wits, would challenge him to rival their own efforts, in a formal debate about Court, Country, and City, in a contest for obscurity of expression, in an exchange of compliments, or of insults. Daniel used to withdraw to his garden-house for months at a time 'the more retiredly to enjoy the company of the Muses'. Donne's Muses frequented the houses of the great, where the rooms were crowded with the gallant and the gay, where learning must serve lively conversation, where wit would invite and expect riposte.

Spenser built poems with the amplitude of design and the richness of ornament of the mansions where his patrons lived. But the lives of those who lived in these houses were not always solemn and unrelaxed, any more than Spenser's poetry is: they did not spend all their time in the Long Galleries. Donne caught the tone of voice of the best company of his time in their hours of relaxation, in their private chambers: the ready learning and the instant wit, the generosity of praise and the cruelty of ridicule, the impudence and the flattery. The monarchy of wit was, as Carew said, universal then: Donne ruled it alone partly because the friends who might have shared in a triumvirate, Edward Herbert and Henry Wotton, had other things to do, and partly because he had the poetic gift to carry his wit beyond his immediate company. He was reluctant to allow the permanence of print to something that was by nature extemporary and fleeting. He even hesitated to send copies of poems to friends who already knew them, for the delight that first greets a sally of wit can be spontaneous only once, and the smile that assents to its repetition is likely to pause at the corners of the mouth. Later, though becomingly ashamed of his youthful audacities, Donne was more willing to part with copies of his poems: emulation of his manner had become (as he might have said) the done thing, but the brilliant company of his younger times, which had brought it into being, was now, through death or ambition, dispersed.

NOTES AND REFERENCES

MY purpose has been to provide a list of sources for those statements which do not derive from my own personal observation, e.g. of monuments in churches. Before the detailed references to Chapters II to V I have listed works of modern scholarship which have been especially valuable, and I have not usually repeated the sources therein indicated. These lists are very far from complete: e.g. in Chapters II and IV the earlier County Histories, compiled by the distinguished antiquaries of the eighteenth and nineteenth centuries, have been invaluable, but the volumes of the Victoria County Histories or of the Royal Commission on Historical Monuments often summarize these at the same time as they supersede them. Dr Pevsner's *Buildings of England* series has been most helpful in pointing out the locality of Elizabethan monuments which I might otherwise have missed. But it so happens that, owing to a personal history which is irrelevant here, most of the counties which I myself know best are not yet described, for this period at least, either in V.C.H., or R.C.H.M., or Pevsner. For these therefore my own judgment must at present suffice.

Four books which I have not listed were published too late for me to benefit from their authors' learning: Eric Mercer's *English Art 1553–1625*, Edward Croft Murray's *Decorative Painting in England, 1537–1837*, Roy Strong's *Portraits of Queen Elizabeth I*, and W. B. Ringler's authoritative edition of the *Poems* of Sir Philip Sidney.

CHAPTER I

P. 4. Morley: *A Plaine and Easie Introduction to Practicall Musicke*, 1597.

5. Aristotle: *Politics*, VIII. 3.
Gower's self-portrait: J. W. Goodison, *George Gower Serjeant Painter to Queen Elizabeth, Burlington Mag.*, XC, pp. 261-4, 1948; E. K. Waterhouse: *A Note on George Gower's Self-Portrait at Milton Park, ib.* p. 267.
Charter granted to the company of Painter-Stainers: E. Auerbach, *Tudor Artists*, 1954, pp. 110, 114.

6. Sir William Segar: E. K. Waterhouse, *Painting in Britain, 1530–1790*, 1953, p. 20.
Margaret, daughter of Sir John King: MS. by William Burton quoted in J. Nichols, *History and Antiquities of Leicestershire*, 1800, III, p. I, pp. 489-90.

P. 6. Hilliard: *A Treatise concerning the Arte of Limning*, ed. P. Norman, *Walpole Soc.*, I, 1912.
Leonardo da Vinci: *Paragone*, tr. I. A. Richter, 1949, ch. IV.
Evesham: *v.* ref. to p. 161.

7. Drayton's coat of arms: B. H. Newdigate, *Michael Drayton and his Circle*, 1941, pp. 150-1.
a sauce to everything: Castiglione, *The Courtyer*, tr. Sir Thomas Hoby, 1561.
'I will not see your man': F. Chamberlin, *Sayings of Queen Elizabeth*, 1923, p. 291.

8. *Metamorphoses*, tr. George Sandys, 1632.

9. 'one upon happy hope conceived': W. Camden, *Remaines concerning Britaine*, 1604. (*Impresses.*)
Astraea: F. A. Yates, *Queen Elizabeth as Astraea, J. Warburg and Courtauld Inst.*, X, pp. 27-82, 1947.

11. Stone's statue is now in the Guildhall: M. Whinney and O. Millar, *English Art 1625–1714*, 1957, p. 108.

12. The combustions and tumults: Sir Henry Wotton, *The Elements of Architecture*, 1624.
Yonk: C. Hussey, *Longleat, Country Life*, 15 Apr. 1949.

13. Meres: *Palladis Tamia*, 1598.
Mulcaster: *The First Part of the Elementarie*, 1582.
Daniel: *A Defence of Ryme*, 1603.
Bacon: *Novum Organum*, I. lxxxiv.

14. Milton: *The Reason of Church Government*, II, 1641.
eternize: Spenser, *Amoretti* LXXV; cf. Shakespeare, *Sonnets*, 55, 81.

15. Daniel: *Musophilus*, 1599, ll. 954-5.
they 'sang and said *Te Deum laudamus*': *The Diary of Henry Machyn*, ed. J. G. Nichols, *Camden Soc.* XLII, p. 178, 1848.

16. The Law of Reason: R. Hooker, *Of the Lawes of Ecclesiasticall Politie*, 1593, I. viii. 9.

17. Marvell: *The Rehearsal Transpros'd*, 1672.

18. Spenser: *A letter to Sir Walter Raleigh*, prefixed to *F.Q.*
Milton: *op. cit.*
King James's speech: *The Political Works*, ed. C. H. McIlwaine, 1918, p. 344.
King Charles's proclamation: cf. Sir Richard Fanshawe's poem in *Il Pastor Fido* 1648.
Nonsuch was granted: J. Dent, *The Quest for Nonsuch*, 1962, pp. 207-16.

19. Hooker: *op. cit.*, IV. i. 3.

21. For 'tis the evening crowns the day: Daniel, *A Funerall Poeme upon the death of the late noble Earle of Devonshyre*, 1606, ll. 380-2.

P. 23. to beare themselves aright: *F.Q.* VI. ii. 1.
Jonson accused Sidney: *Conversations with Drummond.*
Dr Johnson: *Preface to Shakespeare*, 1765.

24. Berenson: *Italian Painters of the Renaissance*, 1930, p. 244.
O! when degree is shak'd: *T. & C.* I. iii. 101-10.

25. fine-filed phrase: Meres, *op. cit.*
for not blotting his lines: Jonson, *Discoveries.*

26. in the art of persuasion: Wotton, *op. cit.*

27. reason is, and ought only to be: D. Hume, *A Treatise of Human Nature*, 1739, II. iii. 3.

28. Tresham's Triangular Lodge: J. A. Gotch, *The Buildings by Sir Thomas Tresham*, 1883.
Hawsted: Sir J. Cullum, *The History and Antiquities of Hawsted*, 1784, pp. 131-2. (An illustration in ed. 2, 1813, proves that the figure was really a wodehouse.)
Wotton: *op. cit.*
In all inventions of capricious ornament: quoted in J. Lees-Milne, *The Age of Inigo Jones*, 1953, p. 53.

29. Lumley Inventories: ed. L. Cust, *Walpole Soc.*, VI, 1918.
Platter: *Travels in England*, 1599, ed. C. Williams, 1937, pp. 195-6.
Harington: *The Metamorphosis of Ajax*, 1596.
Orlando Furioso, 1591, XLII. 71-5.

30. an excellent water work: Platter, *op. cit.*, pp. 199, 197.
they imitate a castle: J. Nichols, *Progresses of Queen Elizabeth*, 1788.

31. Sir Henry Lee: E. K. Chambers, *Sir Henry Lee*, 1936; H. A. Dillon, *An Almain Armourer's Album*, 1905.
Edward VI abolished St George: Sir H. Nicolas, *History of the Orders of Knighthood of the British Empire*, 1842, I, pp. 179-80.
that misty time: Sidney, *Apologie for Poetrie.*
In those days: J. Nichols, *op. cit.*

32. live like the old Robin Hood: *A.Y.L.*, I. i. 110-13.
Sidney: *op. cit.*
Oberon: this ancestry is confirmed in *Duke Huon of Bordeaux.*
Bess of Hardwick: E. C. Williams, *Bess of Hardwick*, 1959, p. 72.

33. more likely to emulate a historical hero: Tasso, *Discorsi del Poema Eroico*, II.
the foundation of a whole philosophy: Sir K. Clark, *The Nude*, 1956, p. 13.
Shute: *The First and Chief Groundes of Architecture*, 1563.
Campion: *Observations in the Art of English Poesie*, 1602.

34. Wotton: *op. cit.*
Pope: *An Essay on Criticism*, 1711, ll. 68-9.
a model of universal nature: Bacon, *Gesta Grayorum*, 1594. (J. Spedding, *Letters and Life*, 1861, I, p. 335.)

P. 35. there is no land unhabitable: R. Thorne, 1527, in R. Hakluyt, *The Principall Navigations, Voiages, and Discoveries of the English Nation*, 1589.
You must therefore: Morley, *op. cit.*
Chaucer keeps decorum: Harington, preface to *Orlando Furioso*, 1591.

36. Milton: *Of Education*, 1644.
error of intermixing: preface to *Samson Agonistes*, 1671.

37. always a man by sundry ways: Castiglione, *op. cit.*
the wiser sort: *Gabriel Harvey's Marginalia*, ed. G. C. Moore Smith, 1913, p. 232.

38. nature's world is brazen: Sidney, *op. cit.*

Chapter II

General

The Victoria County History of England.
The Royal Commission on Historical Monuments.
N. Pevsner's *The Buildings of England.*

P. 43. the gatehouse has become a gateway: H. A. Tipping, *The Story of Montacute and its House*, 1933, p. 10.

44. Leland: *Itinerary*, ed. L. Toulmin-Smith, 1907–8. I, p. 7, II, p. 56.
Bacon: *Of Nobility*.

45. Raglan Castle: A. J. Taylor, *Raglan Castle*, 1950. (*M.O.W. Guide.*) *v.* also *A Description of Raglan Castle* in Hist. MSS. Commission 12th Report, Pt. IX, pp. 1–3, 1891, from which my quotations are taken.

46. Chamberlain: *Letters*, ed. N. E. McClure, 1939, I, p. 376.
a stiff Papist: D. Lloyd, *State Worthies*, 1670, p. 582.

47. Queen Elizabeth at Kenilworth: J. Nichols, *Progresses of Queen Elizabeth*, 1788.
Dudley Castle: W. D. Simpson, *Dudley Castle, the Renaissance Buildings, Archaeological J.*, CI, pp. 119–25, 1946.
Shute: *The First and Chief Groundes of Architecture*, 1563.
Laneham: *A letter*, etc., 1575, in Nichols, *op. cit.*

49. Burghley to Hatton: letter dated 10 Aug. 1578; Hatton to Heneage: letter dated Sept. 1580, both quoted in E. St J. Brooks, *Sir Christopher Hatton*, 1946, pp. 158, 159.

50. I know I have the body: F. Chamberlin, *The Sayings of Queen Elizabeth*, 1923, p. 15.

51. an engraving: F. A. Yates, *Queen Elizabeth as Astraea, J. Warburg and Courtauld Inst.*, X, pp. 27–82, 1947.

P. 51. Willoughby employed musicians: W. L. Woodfill, *Musicians in English Society from Elizabeth to Charles I*, 1953, p. 275.
commissioned Gower: J. W. Goodison, *George Gower Serjeant Painter to Queen Elizabeth, Burlington Mag.*, XC, pp. 261–4, 1948.

52. Bacon: *Of Building*.

53. Wollaton derives from Serlio: Summerson, *Architecture in Britain, 1530 to 1830*, 1955, p. 31.
of pompous show: *F.Q.*, V. ix. 21.

54. Hatton to Burghley: T. Wright (ed.), *Queen Elizabeth and her Times*, 1838, II, p. 98.
Kirby Hall: G. H. Chettle, *Kirby Hall*, 1947. (*M.O.W. Guide.*)
Summerson: *John Thorpe and the Thorpes of Kingscliffe, Architectural Rev.*, Nov. 1949, pp. 291–300.
Longleat: C. Hussey, *Longleat, Country Life*, 8, 15, 22, 29 April 1949; M. Girouard, *The Development of Longleat House between 1546 and 1572, Archaeological J.*, CXVI, pp. 200–22, 1961.

55. Sharington: W. G. Clark-Maxwell, *Sir William Sharington's work at Lacock, Sudeley and Dudley, Archaeological J.*, LXX, pp. 175–82, 1913.
Wotton: *The Elements of Architecture*, 1624.

56. Camden: *Britain* (tr. P. Holland), 1610, p. 245.

57. Burghley to Smith: Summerson, *op. cit.*, p. 22.

58. Sadler to Cecil: *C.S.P. Scottish*, 1547–63, p. 248.
Spenser: *Mother Hubberds Tale*, ll. 1172–9.

59. for the mansion of his barony: F. Peck, *Desiderata Curiosa*, 1732, I, p. 33.
Tresham: J. A. Gotch, *The Buildings by Sir Thomas Tresham*, 1883.

60. Longford Castle: Summerson, *op. cit.*, p. 38; MS. History by H. Pelate, 1678.

61. the nobility live commonly close together: T. Sprat, *The History of the Royal Society of London*, 1667, I. xx.

66. Bacon: *Of Building*.

71. Burghley to Hatton: *v.* ref. to p. 49.
many gentlemen and strangers: Barnaby Rich, *Fare-Well to the Militarie Profession*, 1581.

72. Wotton: *op. cit.*

74. Morley: *A Plaine and Easie Introduction to Practicall Musicke*, 1597.

75. Heneage to Hatton: Brooks, *op. cit.*, p. 160.

76. Smith: Summerson, *op. cit.*, p. 334.

77. From Harmony: Dryden, *A Song for St Cecilia's Day*, 1687.

78. King James's cynical observation: quoted in *Audley End*, 1958. (*M.O.W. Guide.*)

80. Lord Howard of Bindon to Lord Salisbury: D. Piper, *Some portraits by Marcus Gheeraerts II and John de Critz reconsidered, Proc. Huguenot Soc. London*, XX. 2, p. 212.

P. 81. Lady Anne Clifford: *Diary*, ed. V. Sackville-West, 1923, pp. xxxix, xlv.
Cavendish to Thynne: E. C. Williams, *Bess of Hardwick*, 1959, p. 33.

84. Cotton: *The Wonders of the Peake*, 1681, ll. 1389-92, 1405-14.
Chatsworth, Hardwick: B. Stallybrass, *Bess of Hardwick's Buildings and Building Accounts, Archaeologia*, LXIV, pp. 347-98, 1913.

85. Countess of Shrewsbury visited Willoughby: Williams, *op. cit.*, pp. 205-6.
Bacon's aphorism: *Gesta Grayorum*, 1594. (J. Spedding, *Letters and Life*, 1861, I, p. 336.)
Camden: *op. cit.*, p. 508.

Chapter III

General

C. H. Collins Baker and W. G. Constable, *English Painting of the 16th and 17th Centuries*, 1930.

F. W. Reader, *Tudor Domestic Wall Paintings, Archaeological J.*, XCII, pp. 243-86, 1935: XCIII, pp. 220-62, 1936.

G. Reynolds, *Nicholas Hilliard and Isaac Oliver. Monograph and Catalogue*, 1947.

E. K. Waterhouse, *Painting in Britain, 1530-1790*, 1953.

E. Auerbach, *Tudor Artists*, 1954; *Nicholas Hilliard*, 1961.

P. 93. Hill Hall: F. W. Reader, *A Classification of Tudor Domestic Wall-Paintings, Archaeological J.*, XCVIII, pp. 181-211, 1941.

94. Queen Hoo: art. by J. Cornforth, *Country Life*, 15 Mar. 1962.
Harvington Hall: H. R. Hodgkinson, *Recent Discoveries at Harvington Hall, Trans. Birmingham Archaeological Soc.*, LXII, pp. 1-26, 1943.
Oft cruel fights: Sidney, *Astrophel and Stella*, sonnet 34.
Eastbury Manor House: *London Survey Cttee.*, Monograph 11, 1917.
Rothamsted House: F. W. Reader, *op. cit.*, 1941.
Peacham: *The Art of Drawing*, 1606.

95. the moral of preventing discord: Dryden, *A Parallel of Poetry and Painting*, 1695.
Wotton: L. Pearsall Smith, *Life and Letters of Sir Henry Wotton*, 1907, for letters and will. *v.* also Wotton, *The Elements of Architecture*, 1624.

96. Lambeth: *Copy of the Inventory of Archbishop Parker's Goods at the time of his Death*, ed. W. Sandys, *Archaeologia*, XXX, pp. 1-30, 1844.

P. 96. Leicester House: W. J. Thoms, *Pictures of the great Earl of Leicester*, *N. & Q.*, 13 Sept. 1862. *v.* also appendix to C. L. Kingsford, *Essex House, formerly Leicester House and Exeter Inn*, *Archaeologia*, LXXIII, pp. 1–54, 1923. (Inventory for probate of the goods of Robert, Earl of Leicester.)
Hardwick Hall: D. Piper, article on *Painting* in *The Tudor Period, 1500–1603* (*The Connoisseur Period Guides*), 1956.
Lord Lumley: L. Cust, *The Lumley Inventories*, *Walpole Soc.*, VI, pp. 15–35, 1918.

98. Lord Arundel: M. F. S. Hervey, *The Life, Correspondence and Collections of Thomas Howard Earl of Arundel*, 1921.

99. series of effigies: *v. inf.* p. 144.
Earl of Leicester: in addition to Thoms, *op. cit.*, and Kingsford, *op. cit.*, *v. Inventory of Household Furniture etc. at Kenilworth Castle, belonging to Robert Dudley, Earl of Leicester An. Dom. 1583*, *De L'Isle and Dudley MSS.* I, pp. 278–98.

102. Zuccari's drawing is in the British Museum, with another of the Queen.

103. Donne's will: E. Gosse, *Life and Letters of John Donne*, 1899, II, pp. 359–63.

104. a desire for ancient masterpieces: A. Cecil, *A Life of Robert Cecil, first Earl of Salisbury*, 1915, p. 383.
Hatfield House inventory: transcript in N. P. G. by Mrs Pamela Tudor-Craig, Nov. 1959.
Pieter van der Heyden's engraving; F. A. Yates, *Queen Elizabeth as Astraea*, *J. of Warburg and Courtauld Inst.*, X, pp. 27–82, 1947.

106. Sidney sat to Veronese: *v.* my *Sir Philip Sidney and the English Renaissance*, 1954, pp. 69–71.

108. discussed perspective with Hilliard: N. Hilliard, *Treatise concerning the Arte of Limning*, ed. P. Norman, *Walpole Soc.*, I, 1912.
Titian's Venus and Adonis: H. Tietze, *Tizian*, 1936, I, p. 217.
Paul Hentzner: *A Journey into England in the Year MDXCVIII*, 1757.

109. Harington: note to canto XXXIII of *Orlando Furioso*, 1591.
Ascham: *The Scholemaster*, 1570.
William Burton: J. Nichols, *History and Antiquities of Leicestershire*, 1800, III, pt. i, pp. 489–90.

110. Castiglione brought Raphael's *St George*: J. Cartwright, *Baldassare Castiglione*, 1908, I, pp. 169 *sqq.*
Girolamo da Treviso: P. Pouncey, *Girolamo da Treviso in the Service of Henry VIII*, *Burlington Mag.*, XCV, pp. 208–11, 1953.
conversation with Hilliard: Hilliard, *op. cit.*
Richard Haydocke: *A Tracte containing the Artes of curious Paintinge Carvinge and Building*, 1598.

P. 111. the first truly informal portrait: D. Piper, *op. cit.*
Ketel: *v. Bodleian Library Record*, VI, pp. 579-81, 1960.
Wotton: *op. cit.*

112. Greville: *Treatie of Humane Learning*, st. 109.

114. Jacques le Moyne des Morgues: R. Hakluyt, *The Principall Navigations, Voiages, and Discoveries of the English Nation*, 1589.
John White: L. Binyon, *The Drawings of John White, Walpole Soc.*, XIII, pp. 19-24, 1925.

115. Charles de l'Ecluse came: *C. Clusii Atreb. Aliquot Notae in Garciae Aromatum Historiam*, 1582.
Inigo Jones: *Designs by Inigo Jones*, ed. P. Simpson and C. F. Bell, *Walpole and Malone Socs.*, 1924.

116. Ralegh: preface to *The History of the World*, 1611.
some cunning person: *C.S.P. Dom. 1547–80*, p. 232.
Judgment of Paris: J. D. Reeves, *The Judgment of Paris as a device of Tudor flattery, N. & Q.*, January 1954.
Horace Walpole: *Anecdotes of Painting in England*, 1762, ch. VII.

117. Harington: *Nugae Antiquae*, 1769.

118. eyes and ears: F. A. Yates, *Allegorical Portraits of Queen Elizabeth I at Hatfield.*
portrait at Siena: Yates, *Queen Elizabeth as Astraea*, 1947; F. Saxl and R. Wittkower, *British Art and the Mediterranean Tradition*, 1948, p. 39.
Camden: *Remaines concerning Britaine*, 1604.

119. Manilius: *Astronomicon* V. 267-8.
And ever, as the crew: *F.Q.* VI. x. 14.
the Ambassador of Mary Queen of Scots: *Memoirs of Sir James Melville*, ed. A. F. Steuart, 1929, p. 94.

120. one little flower of gold: Sir H. Nicolas, *Memoirs of Sir Christopher Hatton*, 1847, p. 157.

121. *Dat poenas laudata fides*: Lucan, *Belli Civilis lib.* VIII. 485. *v.* D. Piper, *The 1590 Lumley Inventory, Burlington Mag.*, XCIX, pp. 224-31, 299-302, 1957.

122. Now I perceive every fool: W. B. Devereux, *Lives and Letters of the Devereux Earls of Essex*, 1853, I, p. 194.

123. as they themselves recognized: e.g. Haydocke, *op. cit.* (*To the Reader*), and Hilliard, *op. cit.*
Donne: *The Storme*, ll. 3-5.

124. Harington: note to canto XXXIII of *Orlando Furioso.*
contemporary Italian theory: J. Pope Hennessy, *N. Hilliard and Mannerist Art Theory. J. Warburg and Courtauld Inst.*, VI, pp. 89-100, 1943.

128. as Sir Philip Sidney wrote: letter of 18 Oct. 1580.
Lady Rich to Jean Hotman: quoted in *The Poems of Henry Constable*, ed. Joan Grundy, 1960, p. 28.

P. 129. A sweet attractive kind of grace: Matthew Roydon, *An Elegie or Friends Passion for his Astrophill*, printed with Spenser's *Astrophel*, 1595.
Puttenham: *The Arte of English Poesie*, 1589.

131. Drayton: *To . . . Mr Robert Dover*, ll. 2-3, in *Annalia Dubrensia*, 1636; cf. *Upon the Death of the Lady Olive Stanhope*, l. 28.

Chapter IV

General

To references for Chapter II add:

J. Weever, *Ancient Funerall Monuments*, 1631.

A. C. Fryer, *Wooden Monumental Effigies in England and Wales*, *Archaeologia*, LXI, pp. 487-552, 1909.

J. G. Mann, *English Church Monuments, 1536–1625*, *Walpole Soc.*, XXI, pp. 1-22, 1933.

K. A. Esdaile, *English Monumental Sculpture since the Renaissance*, 1927; *English Church Monuments 1510–1840*, 1946.

P. 135. Terri: brass to Alice, wife of Sir John Cassey, Deerhurst, Glos.

136. a fond thing: Article XXII.
funeral effigies: W. H. St J. Hope, *On the Funeral Effigies of the Kings and Queens of England*, *Archaeologia*, LX, pp. 517-70, 1907.

137. contract: E. P. Shirley, *Original Documents. Extracts from the Fermor Accounts*, A.D. *1580*, *Archaeological J.*, VIII, pp. 179-86, 1851.

138. Lumley inventories: ed. L. Cust, *Walpole Soc.*, VI, 1918.

139. brought my Lord Salisbury: H. A. Tipping, *Hatfield House*, *Country Life*, 26 Mar. 1927.

140. Cornwall triptych: *v.* C. Hussey in *Country Life*, 26 Dec. 1947.

141. For soul is form: Spenser, *Hymn in Honour of Beauty*, l. 133.

142. house of ancient fame: *Prothalamion*, l. 131; cf. *Colin Clouts Come Home Againe*, ll. 537-41.
the Despencers: in 1595 Clarencieux King of Arms Lee granted to Sir John Spencer a pedigree which connected the family with the Despencers. J. H. Round, *Studies in Peerage and Family History*, 1901, pp. 279-329.
Sitsyllt: A. L. Rowse, *Alltyrynys and the Cecils*, *E.H.R.*, Jan. 1960, pp. 54-76.
nothing else but ancient riches: F. Peck, *Desiderata Curiosa*, 1732, I, p. 64; cf. Spenser, *Mother Hubberds Tale*, l. 1183.
Wriothesley: A. R. Wagner, *English Genealogy*, 1960, p. 312.

143. Willoughby: E. C. Williams, *Bess of Hardwick*, 1959, p. 205.
Hughenden: E. J. Payne, *The Montforts, the Wellesbournes, and the*

Hughenden Effigies, Records of Buckinghamshire, VII, pp. 362-412, 1892; cf. G. Lipscomb, *The History and Antiquities of Buckingham*, 1847, III, pp. 588-90.

P. 144. Camden: *Britain* (tr. P. Holland), 1610, p. 742.
Sir John de Hauteville: this is Pevsner's suggestion; cf. J. Collinson, *The History of Somersetshire*, 1791, II, p. 92 (100), and A. C. Fryer, *op. cit.*

145. Queen Elizabeth's proclamations: in Weever, *op. cit.*

147. a step of marble stone: R. F. Scott, *On the Contracts for the Tomb of the Lady Margaret Beaufort, Archaeologia*, LXVI, pp. 365-76, 1915.

148. Cobham: R. H. d'Elboux, *The Brooke Tomb, Cobham, Archaeologia Cantiana*, LXII, pp. 48-56, 1950.

149. Dugdale: *Visitation of Shropshire*, quoted and illustrated in Esdaile, 1946; cf. R. W. Eyton, *Antiquities of Shropshire*, 1855, II, p. 253.

151. Gildon: *v.* F. C. Morgan, 1935, ref. under Evesham, p. 161.

154. Philip and Francis: J. Stow, *The Survey of London*, 1598.
Fuller: *Holy State*, 1648, p. 174.

159. Hollemans: K. A. Esdaile, *The Inter-action of English and Low Country Sculpture in the 16th Century, J. Warburg and Courtauld Inst.*, VI, pp. 80-8, 1943.

161. Evesham: Mrs A. Esdaile, *Mr Epiphanius Evesham, The Times*, 30 January 1932; cf. A. Vallance, *The Ropers and their Monuments in Lynsted Church, Archaeologia Cantiana*, XLIV, pp. 147-64, 1932; K. H. Jones, *The Hawkins Monument by Epiphanius Evesham at Boughton-under-Blean, Arch. Cant.*, XLV, pp. 205-8, 1933; F. C. Morgan, *Two Hereford 16th Century Sculptors, John Gildon and Epiphanius Evesham, Trans. Woolhope Nats. Field Club*, 1935, III, p. 18, 1938; id. *Further Notes on Monuments by Epiphanius Evesham, Trans. Woolhope N. F. C.*, 1938, pt. III, pp. 201-3.
Lord Rich's tomb: K. A. Esdaile, *The Monument of the first Lord Rich at Felsted, Trans. Essex Archaeological Soc.*, New Ser. XXII, pp. 59-67, 1940.

164. the man that keeps the Abbey tombs: Donne, *Satire* IV, ll. 75-7.
Gawdy: *Letters*, ed. I. H. Jeaves, 1906, p. 160.

165. Lady Margaret Hoby: *Diary, 1599-1605*, ed. D. M. Meads, 1930.
Morison: *Itinerary*, III, ii. 2.

Chapter V

General

Grove's Dictionary of Music and Musicians, 5th ed., ed. E. Blom, 1954, Supplementary volume, 1961.

G. Reese, *Music in the Renaissance*, revised ed. 1954.

P. Warlock, *The English Ayre*, 1926.

E. H. Fellowes, *William Byrd*, 1936; *English Cathedral Music*, 1941; *English Madrigal Composers*, 1948; *Orlando Gibbons and his Family*, ed. 2, 1951.

M. C. Boyd, *Elizabethan Music and Musical Criticism*, 1940.

W. L. Woodfill, *Musicians in English Society from Elizabeth to Charles I*, 1953.

A. Einstein, *The Italian Madrigal*, 1949.

P. 171. as Daniel foresaw: *Musophilus*, ll. 947-52.
Guarini: *v*. Daniel's sonnet prefixed to Dymock's translation of *Il Pastor Fido*, 1602.
Morley's work in Germany: *v. Grove*, arts. Daniel *Friderici*, and Valentin *Haussman*.
pavan from the Landgrave of Hessen: published by Robert Dowland in *Varietie of Lute Lessons*, 1610.

172. Mulcaster: translation from *Biographica Britannica*, 1746–66, p. 1007.
composed ballets and music: F. Chamberlin, *Sayings of Queen Elizabeth*, 1923, p. 306.

173. Sir James Melville: *Memoirs*, ed. S. F. Steuart, 1929, p. 95.
lists of the musicians: Woodfill, *op. cit.*, Appendix E.

175. Chapel Royal: Woodfill, *op. cit.*, ch. VII.

176. England one God: Samuel Rowley, *When You See Me You Know Me*, 1605.
Thomas Fuller: *The Worthies of England*, 1662 (*Westminster*).

178. Cranmer's letter: quoted by Fellowes, *English Cathedral Music*, pp. 25-6.

179. Royal Injunction: Fellowes, *op. cit.*, p. 37; Reese, *op. cit.*, p. 796.
Bishop Jewel: Boyd, *op. cit.*, p. 5.
during the singing service: B.M. Royal MS. 18 B XIX, quoted by D. Stevens, *Tudor Church Music*, 1961, p. 65.
Hooker: *Of the Lawes of Ecclesiasticall Politie*, V. xxxvii. 1.

180. by means whereof the laudable science: Fellowes, *op. cit.*, p. 53.

181. Hooker: *op. cit.*, V. xxxviii. 3.

182. Morley: *A Plaine and Easie Introduction to Practicall Musicke*, 1957.
Byrd: *Psalmes, Sonets and Songs*, 1588.
Father of English Music: poem by G. Ga. in *Gradualia*, II. 1607.
one never without reverence: Morley, *op. cit.*

183. did shine as the sun: T. Ravenscroft, *A Briefe Discourse of . . . Musicke*, 1614.
had a virtuous contention: Morley, *op. cit.*
Waterhouse: Morley, *op. cit.* MS. in University Library Cambridge.
Whythorne: *Autobiography*, ed. J. M. Osborn, 1961, p. 247.

P. 184. Peacham: *The Compleat Gentleman*, 1622.
Byrd: *Psalmes, Sonets and Songs*, 1588.
he called William Hewes: W. B. Devereux, *Lives and Letters of the Devereux Earls of Essex*, 1853, I, p. 145.
Whythorne: *op. cit.*, p. 51.
especially that song: F. Greville, *The Life of Sir Philip Sidney*, 1652.
Sidney accounts: Woodfill, *op. cit.*, Appendix B. (Same ref. for other such accounts.)

185. a well-known letter: 18 Oct. 1580.
Basciami mia vita: B. Pattison; *Music and Poetry of the English Renaissance*, 1948, p. 179.
di Monte and de l'Ecluse: P. Bergmans, *Quatorze Lettres Inédites du Compositeur Philippe de Monte. Acad. R. de Belgique. Classe des Beaux-Arts. Mémoires*, 1921. T. I, fasc. ii.
Sir A. Basset: *Sidneiana*, ed. S. Butler, 1837.
Sidney to Earl of Sussex: 16 Dec. 1577.

186. Byrd's setting of the sixth song is in *Psalmes, Sonets and Songs*, 1588, and of the tenth song in *Songs of sundrie Natures*, 1589.

187. Farmer: *Set of English Madrigals*, 1599.
Petre family: F. G. Emmison, *Tudor Secretary*, 1961, esp. ch. X.

188. Gawdy: *Letters*, ed. I. H. Jeaves, 1906, pp. 4, 123.

190. the daughter of the Earl of Northumberland: letter quoted by M. H. Glyn, *About Elizabethan Virginal Music and its Composers*, 1934, p. 63.
Arthur Throckmorton: A. L. Rowse, *Ralegh and the Throckmortons*, 1962, p. 92.

191. Music by the instrument: Mulcaster, *Positions*, 1581.
Thus when this Courtly Gentleman: *Mother Hubberds Tale*, ll. 753-756.

192. Whitlocke: *Liber Famelicus, Camden Soc.*, 1868, p. 12.
Mulcaster made his pupils write exercises: *First Part of the Elementarie*, 1582.

193. Bess of Hardwick: *v.* E. C. Williams, *Bess of Hardwick*, 1959.

194. Puttenham: *The Arte of English Poesie*, 1589.
Laneham: *A letter*, etc., 1585, in J. Nichols, *The Progresses of Queen Elizabeth*, 1788.

195. Sieur de Champagny: Sir W. Segar, *Honour Military and Civil*, 1602.
On another occasion: Sir J. Harington, *Nugae Antiquae*, 1769.
in the following year: *Songs of sundrie Natures*.

196. consumed vainly the greatest part: dedication to Edward VI of the *Concordance*, 1550.

199. Morley's comments: *op. cit.*

200. Milton sought: E. Allodoli, *Giovanni Milton e l' Italia*, 1907.

P. 201. A. Wood: *Life and Times*, 1891, I, p. 289.
Dowland met Croce, address to the Reader in *The First Booke of Songs or Ayres*, 1597.
Croce's setting of the Psalms, *Musica sacra*, 1608.

202. Morley: *op. cit.*

204. Galilei: *Dialogo della Musica*, 1581.
Byrd: *Psalmes, Sonets and Songs.*

205. he obtained leave: his letter to Sir R. Cecil, 10 Nov. 1595, is printed in full by Warlock, *op. cit.*
Barnfield: Sonnet I, in *Poems in divers humors*, 1598.

206. lutenist to Lord Walden: *A Pilgrimes Solace*, 1612, title-page.
passing his days: Fuller, *op. cit.*
Peacham, *Minerva Britannica.*

207. aptitude for playing the virginals, Rowland Whyte to Sir Robert Sidney, 23 Oct. 1595, quoted by Woodfill, *op. cit.*, Appendix B.

208. Tomkins, in *Songs of 3, 4, 5, and 6 parts*, 1622.

209. apparelling ditties: To the Reader in *The First Booke of Songes and Ayres*, 1600.

210. Ford: *Musicke of Sundrie Kindes*, 1607.

212. Spenser: *Iambicum Trimetrum* in *Two other very commendable Letters*, 1580.
Shakespeare: *Sonnet* 128.

213. Constable: *Poems*, ed. Joan Grundy, 1960, p. 125.

215. Plutarch: Life of Alcibiades in *The Lives of the Noble Grecians and Romans*, tr. T. North, 1579.
Gorboduc: G. H. Cowling, *Music on the Shakespearean Stage*, 1913, p. 17.
a German visitor: Frederic Gershow, *Diary, Trans. R. Hist. Soc.*, 1892.
Hentzner: *A Journey into England*, 1757.

216. Fiddler, forbear: *T.Sh.*, III. i.
Save thee, friend: *T.N.*, III. i; cf. *L.L.L.*, III. i; *M.M.*, IV. i etc.
Giulio Romano: *W.T.*, V. ii. 108.
public concerts: Woodfill, *op. cit.*, chs. II and IV.

217. Morley: *First Book of Consort Lessons*, 1599.

218. Byrd: *Psalmes, Songs and Sonnets*, 1611.
Humphrey Waspe: Ben Jonson, *Bartholomew Fair*, I. iv. 77.
Robert Jones: *First Booke of Songes and Ayres*, 1600.

219. Morley: *A Plaine and Easie Introduction to Practicall Musicke.*
Campion: *Observations in the Art of English Poesie*, 1602; *A Booke of Ayres*, 1601. (To the Reader.)
Gibbons: *The First Set of Madrigals and Mottets*, 1612.
Case: *The Praise of Musicke*, 1586.

Chapter VI

The Elizabethan Appreciation of Chaucer

P. 224. Foxe: *Ecclesiastical History*, etc., ed. 2, 1570, II, p. 965.
Latin translation: Sir Francis Kynaston, *Amorum Troili et Cressidae Libri duo priores*, 1635.
Waller: *Of English Verse* in *Poems*, 1668.
225. Gascoigne: *Certayne Notes of Instruction*, in *Posies*, 1575.
There many Minstrales: *F.Q.*, I. v. 3; cf. *Prologue* to *Canterbury Tales*, l. 9.
226. Harington: *Preface* to his translation of *Orlando Furioso*, 1591.
Beaumont: letter prefixed to Speght's edition.
Dryden: *Preface* to *Fables Ancient and Modern*, 1700.
227. Puttenham: *The Arte of English Poesie*, 1589.
228. Lewis: *The Allegory of Love*, 1936, p. 177.
Sidney: *Apologie for Poetrie*. 'The Terentian Gnatho and our Chaucer's Pandar so exprest that we now use their names to signify their trades.'
229. Spenser: *F.Q.*, IV. ii. 32 *sqq*.

Spenser: *The Shepheardes Calender*

P. 231. want of desert: Sidney, *Apologie for Poetrie*; so other references.
Dryden: dedication of *Virgil's Pastorals*, 1697.
232. Daniel: *Delia*, sonnet LII (first published 1592).
Jonson: *Discoveries*.
To set down boldly: Drayton, *Elegie to Henry Reynolds*, ll. 83-4.
233. Spenser had done enough: Drayton, *To the Reader*, in *Pastorals*, 1619.
Harvey: *Marginalia*, ed. G. C. Moore Smith, 1913, p. 166.
234. Milton: *Treatise of Education*, 1644.
239. the faultless model: M. Akenside, *The Pleasures of Imagination*, 1744. (*The Design*.)
240. But in no Iliad: Vida's *Art of Poetry*, tr. by Christopher Pitt, 1725.
241. to overgo Ariosto: Harvey to Spenser in *Three Proper and Wittie Familiar Letters*, 1580.
243. Mulcaster: *The First Part of the Elementarie*, 1582.
244. Petrarch and Boccace: Harvey in *Three . . . Letters*.

Sidney: *The Countess of Pembroke's Arcadia*

To save space I have not here reprinted references to the history of the *Arcadia* which will be found in my *Sir Philip Sidney and the English*

Renaissance, 1954. Quotations from Sidney (other than those from the *Arcadia*) are from the *Apologie for Poetrie*.

P. 248. Florio: F. A. Yates, *John Florio*, 1934, pp. 195-206.

249. Sir William Alexander: *v.* his own comments in *Anacrisis*, in *The Works of William Drummond*, 1711, p. 161.

250. the pleasant plains of Wiltshire: Aubrey, *Brief Lives.* (*Sir Philip Sydney.*)

251. Lady Anne Clifford: *Diary*, ed. V. Sackville-West, 1923, p. xxxix; cf. Hartley Coleridge's essay in *Lives of Illustrious Worthies of Yorkshire*, 1835, p. 271.

252. Pope lent his copy: *Correspondence*, ed. G. Sherburn, 1956, II, p. 194. Warton: *Odes on Various Subjects*, 1746. (*To a Lady who hates the Country.*)

253. the better to hold his fortune together: Sir Robert Naunton: *Fragmenta Regalia*, 1641.

255. to domesticate the Greek romances: S. L. Wolff, *The Greek Romances in Elizabethan Prose Fiction*, 1912.

256. Harvey: *Pierces Supererogation*, 1593.

259. Jonson owed: Aubrey, *op. cit.* (*John Hoskyns.*)
Jonson accused Sidney: *Conversations with Drummond.*

261. an elaborate index: MS. in my possession.

262. Hazlitt: *Lectures on the Dramatic Literature of the Age of Elizabeth*, 1820, VI.

263. du Bartas: *L'Uranie*, 1574, tr. by King James VI in *The Essayes of a Prentise*, 1584.
Drayton: *Elegie to Henry Reynolds*, ll. 87-90.

267. Lady Fanshawe: *Memoirs*, 1829, p. 73.

Sidney: *Astrophel and Stella*

P. 269. This edition was suppressed: *Accounts of the Wardens of the Stationers' Company*, 1591, Arber i, p. 555.
Matthew Lownes published another: J. Buxton, *On the date of Syr P. S. his Astrophel and Stella . . . printed for Matthew Lownes, Bodleian Library Record*, VI. 5, pp. 614-16, 1960.
Daniel complained: *Delia*, 1592.

270. a prose translation: *The Worthy Tract of Paulus Jovius*, 1585.

272. Charles Lamb: *Some Sonnets of Sir Philip Sidney*, in *Last Essays of Elia*, 1833.

273. Tell him I send him nothing: W. B. Devereux, *Lives and Letters of the Devereux Earls of Essex*, 1853, I, p. 139.

274. Professor Lewis: *English Literature in the Sixteenth Century*, 1954, p. 328.

P. 275. a fellow of plain and uncoined constancy: *Henry V*, V. ii. 155.

282. a quibble was the fatal Cleopatra: Johnson, *Preface to Shakespeare*, 1765.

285. Sidney proceeded in very sumptuous manner: J. Nichols, *Progresses of Queen Elizabeth*, 1788.

Shakespeare: *Venus and Adonis*

P. 295. The elegancy, facility, and golden cadence of poetry: *L.L.L.*, IV. ii. 126. Ben Jonson said of Shakespeare: 'he flowed with that facility, that sometime it was necessary he should be stopped'.—*Discoveries*.

297. Goodness leave me: *Haec Vir, or The Womanish Man*. In Sharpe's *The Noble Stranger*, 1640, Pupillus wishes for 'the book of Venus and Adonis to court his mistress by'.

298. Harvey: *Marginalia*, ed. G. C. Moore Smith, 1913, p. 232.

299. Coleridge: *Biographia Literaria*, 1817, ch. XV.
blue-vein'd: cf. *The Rape of Lucrece*, ll. 407, 440; Sidney, *Arcadia*: 'A naked Venus of white marble, wherein the graver had used such cunning, that the natural blue veins of the marble were framed in fit places, to set forth the beautiful veins of her body.'
Hazlitt: *Characters of Shakespeare's Plays*, 1817 (*Poems and Sonnets*).
Titian's *Venus and Adonis*: H. Tietze, *Tizian*, 1936, I, p. 217.
Spenser: *F.Q.*, III. i. 34-8.

301. Hazlitt: *loc. cit.*

302. Terence: *Eunuchus*, IV. ii. 12, *v.* H. T. Karsten, *Commenti Donatiani ad Terenti fabulas Scholia*, 1912–13, I, p. 186.
Katherine Mansfield: *Letters*, ed. J. M. Murry, 1928, II, p. 106.

303. The sweet witty soul of Ovid: F. Meres, *Palladis Tamia*, 1598.
Jonson: *To the Memory of my beloved, the Author Mr William Shakespeare*, l. 68. (Prefixed to the First Folio, 1623.)

305. Coleridge: *loc. cit.*

Shakespeare: *Hamlet*

My principal debt is to Professor Dover Wilson's edition (1936).

P. 307. Harvey: *Marginalia*, ed. G. C. Moore Smith, 1913, p. 232.

308. Sidney: *Apologie for Poetrie*.
Spenser: *A View of the Present State of Ireland*.
Mountjoy's quarrel with Essex, *v. sup.* pp. 121-2.
Mountjoy's love of private retiredness: Fynes Morison, *An Itinerary*, 1617, II. i. 1.

P. 309. Daniel: *A Funerall Poeme uppon the death of the . . . Earle of Devonshyre*, 1606.
Nashe: dedication of *The Anatomy of Absurditie*, 1589.

310. quarrel of Sidney and the Earl of Oxford: F. Greville, *Life of Sir Philip Sidney*, 1652.

311. the artful balance: R. Bridges, *The Testament of Beauty*, 1929, I. 578–80.
Spenser: *op. cit.*

312. *Aminta*: cf. Daniel, *A Pastoral*, translated from the final chorus of Act I.

313. Romei: *The Courtiers Academie*, 1598 (tr. J. Kepers).
Gentillet: *A Discourse upon the Meanes of Wel Governing*, 1602 (tr. S. Patericke).
Antonio's Revenge: traditionally dated 1599, but it may be later than *Hamlet*.

314. old mouse-eaten records: Sidney, *op. cit.*
Hamlet pleased all: A. Scoloker, *Epistle to the Reader* in *Daiphantus*, 1604.

315. Harington: F. J. Furnivall, *Sir John Harington's Shakspeare Quartos*, *N. & Q.*, 17 May 1890.
Synge: *Preface* to *The Playboy of the Western World*, 1907.

316. clap their brawny hands: Dekker, *Prologue* to *If it be not good the Devil is in it.*

The Donne Fashion

General

The Poems of John Donne, ed. H. J. C. Grierson, 1912.
E. Gosse: *The Life and Letters of John Donne*, 1899.
John Donne, Complete Poetry and Selected Prose, ed. J. Hayward, 1929.

P. 317. evaporations to his wit: Donne, letter to Sir Henry Goodere, c. 1608.

318. Jonson: *Conversations with Drummond.*
denied them to the anthologists, *v.* n. to p. 321.

319. Pestell: *Poems*, ed. H. Buchan, 1940, p. 28.

320. Poetry in this latter age: *Discoveries.*
Donne's library: G. Keynes, *A Bibliography of John Donne*, 1958, Appendix IV.

321. esteem of verses: Richard Niccols, *The Furies, With Vertues Encomium*, 1614.
Davison had tried to get: B.M. MS. Harl. 298 lists these among 'Manuscripts to get', but nothing of Donne's was included in any edition of *A Poetical Rhapsody*.

P. 322. probably Donne already knew Hall: R. C. Bald, *Donne and the Drurys*, 1959, p. 83.
Guilpin: R. E. Bennett, *John Donne and Everard Guilpin, R.E.S.*, XV, pp. 66-72, 1939.

323. Herbert's message to Ferrar and letter to his mother are in Izaak Walton's *Life*, 1670.

325. Ketel's painting: C. H. Collins Baker and W. G. Constable, *English Painting in the 16th and 17th Centuries*, 1930, p. 37.

326. Greville destroyed the play: *Life of Sir Philip Sidney*, 1652.
Daniel found himself in trouble: letter printed by H. Sellers, *A Bibliography of the Works of Samuel Daniel, Oxford Bibliographical Soc., Proc. and Papers*, II, pt. I, pp. 51-2, 1928.
Richard II revived: Bacon, *A Declaration of the Practises and Treasons attempted and committed by Robert late Earl of Essex*, 1601.

327. as Ben Jonson said: *Conversations with Drummond.*
Sidney before Donne, *Discoveries*.

328. the silenced tales of the *Metamorphoses*: T. Carew, *An Elegie upon the death of . . . Dr John Donne.*
The sweet witty soul of Ovid: F. Meres, *Palladis Tamia*, 1598.

330. Tasso objected: *Discorsi del Poema Eroico*, IV.
as Drummond realized: Drummond, *Character of Several Authors*, in *Works*, 1711.

331. to match Sir Edward Herbert: Jonson, *Conversations with Drummond.*

332. Drayton: dedication of *Englands Heroicall Epistles*, V, 1597.
Renowned Lucy: *Mortimeriados*, 1596, ll. 261-2.
pointed attack: *Eighth Eglog* of *Poemes Lyrick and Pastorall*, 1606.
a better verser: *Epistle to Elizabeth Countess of Rutland*, ll. 68-70.

333. *Every Man in his Humour*, V. iii. 284-9, 1601; V. v. 23-7, 1616.
Cynthia's Revels, IV. i. 32-4.
Jonson and Roe thrust out: *Ben Jonson*, ed. C. H. Herford and P. Simpson, 1925, I, p. 39.

334. his manner better fitted prose: Drayton, *Elegie to Henry Reynolds*, l. 128.

335. *Convivium philosophicum*: L. B. Osborn, *The Life, Letters and Writings of John Hoskyns*, 1937, pp. 196-9, 288-91.
You often cried Coraggio: dedication of his translation of the *Essayes* of Montaigne, 1603.

336. Harington sent her: *Letters and Epigrams*, ed. N. E. McClure, 1930, p. 87.

337. Daniel used to withdraw: T. Fuller, *The History of the Worthies of England*, 1662. (*Somersetshire.*)

INDEX OF PERSONS

For the forms of foreign names of musicians I have relied on *Grove* and for those of artists on *Thieme-Becker*. q.=quoted.

INDEX OF PLACES

THE END

PRINTED BY R. & R. CLARK, LTD., EDINBURGH